An Introduction To Child Development

G C Davenport

Collins Educational
An imprint of HarperCollins*Publishers*

Published 1991 by Collins Educational
An imprint of HarperCollins*Publishers*
77-85 Fulham Palace Road
Hammersmith
London W6 8JB

Reprinted by Collins Educational 1992, 1993

© G C Davenport and CollinsEducational Limited 1988
First published 1988 by Unwin Hyman Limited
Reprinted 1989 (twice), 1990

British Library Cataloguing in Publication Data

Davenport, G C
An introduction to child development
1. Children, Development
I. Title
155.4

ISBN 0 00 322258-6

Artwork by Vesna Pivcevic
Cover Artwork by Ian Hands
Typeset by Nene Phototypesetters Ltd, Northampton
Printed and bound by Scotprint Ltd, Musselburgh

Contents

Author's Acknowledgements

To Jane, for all her encouragement, support, and proof reading, and for letting me off my share of the household chores during the writing of this book.

To my parents, Rosa and Denis, for their love and help in everything I've ever attempted.

To Alison Wadeley, for her patience and diligence in reading and reviewing this book, and for making many suggestions for improvements.

To Vesna Pivcevic for all her hard work, creativity and skill in producing the artwork.

To everyone at Augusta Place Playgroup, who didn't object to having their photographs taken, and to Kaley and Penny, Stacey and Steve, for letting me take theirs.

Finally to countless students who have, over the years, inspired me in so many ways.

The author and publisher would like to thank the following for providing photographs for this book: Dr John Bowlby (page 41); Mary Evans Picture Library (pages 103 and 131); B F Skinner (page 135); Albert Bandura (page 141); Colorific Photo Library Ltd (page 158); Martyn Chillmaid (pages 207 and 254); David Linton (page 245); William Vandivert (page 243).

Preface – Notes to the student

The layout of the book

This book follows the syllabus laid down for the Southern Examining Group's GCSE Psychology: Child Development course. Here is a brief summary of the way the syllabus is broken down into topic areas.

Chapter One gives a brief introduction to child psychology and its links with biology. Then we will look at the main methods used by psychologists for conducting their research. You need to know about scientific and other methods of collecting information, and you must understand something about the advantages and disadvantages of each. You may have to do some research project yourself as part of your course, and you may be using some of the methods described in Chapter Two. Otherwise your teacher may think it's better to leave Chapter Two until later.

In the next three chapters we examine some of the child's early experiences, particularly the development of the child's emotions, from soon after birth, and through the early years of life. There have always been differences of opinion about important issues in psychology. In these chapters we will contrast the view that babies and their mothers have a special bond that shouldn't be broken, with the idea that babies are capable of developing a variety of satisfying relationships with a number of different people.

Two other aspects of individual development which we study next include one of the earliest, most influential, and most controversial of views on the origins and development of personality, that of Sigmund Freud. The other looks at the work conducted on explaining how children learn, and how some aspects of their behaviour can be conditioned. We will study some applications of these theories to "real life" in the next chapter. We will also examine an alternative view of how children come to know things. This sees "how children learn" being the result of how mature the child's thinking is. This view challenges the old idea that children are simply "little adults", claiming that they actually use completely different rules of logic from those used by adults. It also challenges the traditional idea that we are all born with a certain amount of intelligence which can be measured using standard intelligence tests.

The next chapter describes some of the attempts which have been made to understand children's moral development. We note some of the ways in which school affects the child's life, and examine some of the ideas psychologists have had of "intelligence" and "intelligence testing". We also look at the contribution made to our intelligence and perception by both our genes and our environment.

We will then look at what psychologists have found out about how children's language develops, and how children's ideas develop about what sex they are, and what this means. The last chapter concerns children's aggression.

The main features of the book are:

The text, which contains the essential information.
A number of exercises designed to see whether you are understanding the work.
Occasional "summary boxes".
Occasional background readings which illustrate some of the points being made. (You do not have to know what is in these readings for the purposes of the exam.)
Occasional suggested activities which may help you to apply your knowledge.
Occasional comments and questions.
Reviews at the end of each topic.

Finally – I hope you enjoy your study of child psychology. It is a fairly new area for psychological enquiry, yet we have still learned quite a lot about the fascinating world of children.

What the course and exam require from you

The GCSE is different from the old style exam. It is designed so that you will achieve certain aims and objectives. Here is a summary of what the examiners expect you will achieve during your studies:
1 You'll learn about some of the main ways that psychologists have looked at child development. Not all psychologists have agreed and several have suggested quite different theories to explain various aspects of development. You'll know some of the limitations and

strengths of the main theories. Some early ideas have now been changed or rejected. You need to know about a few of them, and about some of the new approaches.

2 You need to understand how psychologists apply their knowledge of how children develop emotionally, intellectually, socially, and behaviourally, at home, in school, in other forms of care etc. You'll need to know about some of the research on children's development, and whether the research findings are scientifically acceptable.

3 You need to know about the various ways in which psychologists have investigated children's development. They use observations, experiments, interviews, case studies etc. Each method has its own uses, advantages, and drawbacks. You will discover what these are.

4 You'll need to show that you can use one or two of these techniques of gathering data yourself later on. You may be conducting a piece of original research on some aspect of child development in your own area.

5 You'll learn how to understand and interpret the conclusions from psychological research, how to read graphs, bar charts, pie charts, histograms, and tables, as well as understand written descriptions of research. You'll also be able to present psychological data in the ways described above.

Exercise – Terms

This first exercise may be one of the most valuable. Here is a list of the kind of words you will see in your exam questions. Look each one up in a dictionary and write down what each one means on a sheet of paper, and refer to it each time the word appears in a question or exercise.

analyse	argue	cite	compare
contrast	describe	differentiate	discuss
distinguish	evaluate	examine	explain
illustrate	interpret	outline	state
summarise			

Note to the teacher

Most of the exercises and questions in this text have been used usefully in the classroom. Some may provide opportunities for classroom discussion out of which ideas for coursework may develop. It was never my intention that a teacher would use all (or necessarily any) of the exercises. I hope that some may prove useful.

Some teachers may prefer not to tackle the methods chapter, Chapter Two, so early in the course. For example, those who will leave the coursework component until the second year of a two year course may need to steer their students away from those parts of the exercises which refer to aspects of methodology.

G C Davenport, July 1988

1 An Introduction to Developmental Psychology

Developmental psychology is a fairly new branch of psychology. It is the scientific study of *how we grow and develop*, from birth until death. It includes trying to understand topics such as emotional development, personality development, the development of intelligence, thinking, communication, and of living with others.

Man – The evolved animal

Developmental psychology studies the various skills and abilities humans have, including how we acquire them. Human beings are fairly complicated animals, so the first influences that we can mention are biological. As mankind has evolved biology has affected our behaviour in a number of ways.

Other influences on our development

Great discoveries were being made in biology in Europe during the last century, and some biologists and psychologists argued that many of our skills, such as intelligence and personality, are genetically inherited in the same way as our sex or the colour of our eyes. (This became known as the "**nature**" view.) Others disagreed. They argued that we are the product of all the experiences that we have had as we

Exercise – Adaptation

1 What might a "caveman" do under the following conditions:
   When it gets cold at night?
   When he is being chased through the forest by a wild pig?
   When he is chased to the edge of a lake by a mountain lion?
   When he is hungry?

2 What would a deer do under the same circumstances?

3 Imagine you are in a "caveman's cave". What do you see around you?

4 From your previous answers, what does man have that other animals do not have?

Background reading – Introduction to developmental psychology

Many people used to believe that children were simply "little adults" who were useful for doing chores, learning their father's trade and looking after the family's animals etc. Their idea of childcare was simply "looking after" the children until they were a few years old. The 20th century has been called "the century of the child". This description reflects the amount of scientific and psychological interest there has been in studying how children develop during the last 100 years or so, and particularly since the Second World War.

REVIEW – Adaptation

Human beings are not biologically well adapted to conditions on the earth. Instead they use their intellect to allow them to dominate it.

grew, we have free will and can change, and be changed by, our environment. (This is the "**nurture**" view.)

A Caveman's Cave

The nature/nurture debate

"Normal" humans inherit 23 pairs of chromosomes, each probably containing something like 10 000 to 20 000 genes. Our genetic inheritance is a mixture of our parents' genes and is called a **genotype**. A

Background reading – Man and evolution

There are about 30 million species of living things on this planet, human beings are one of them. We are not a particularly attractive creature compared to some of the other species. We shout and argue and moan. We're quite aggressive, and we're almost the only species that actually makes war on itself. We walk on what should be our hind legs (and suffer frequent back pain in later life as a result!). There are nearly five billion of us, and we seem to be one of the worst adapted species of living thing on the planet! We can't fly like birds, or even jump very high. We're not very good in water. We can't run as fast or far as many animals, we can't hear as well as a bat, can't smell as well as a dog, nor see as well as a bird of prey. We have lost most of our body's protective hair covering and have to wear clothes to protect us from the weather. Nature hasn't provided us with any "tools" like claws or sharp teeth for digging holes, climbing trees, or killing our food. We are not even well equipped to defend ourselves.

The earth has existed for several thousand million years. There have been some forms of life on the earth for about two and a half thousand million years. "Man" has been around for only about two million, yet despite all the limitations human beings have come to dominate the earth and all its other animals.

During our evolution our brains have grown in size and complexity. The human brain is one of the most complex structures in the world. (In fact we have the most complex nervous system of any animal.) This has given us one major advantage over the other animals. We have the ability to *think*, to *look ahead* and to *foresee the consequences of our actions*. Thinking allows us to *organise our actions and behaviour*, and to *invent machines and tools* that do things for us. Man can *organise* himself and *adapt* his behaviour. He can *change* his environment to suit him, whilst the other animals can only live in theirs. During childhood we acquire the basic ideas and skills which we will need later in life.

genotype is a sort of "blueprint" or "plan" of what we will be like as we grow. Many early psychologists believed that most of our personality, intellect, sex role behaviour etc was the result of our genes and couldn't be interfered with. This is quite a frightening thought. It means we have no "free will" and needn't be responsible for our actions.

Nowadays we know that this early view is quite wrong. We don't always achieve the prediction of our genotype anyway. If our mother had certain diseases, smoked heavily, or had an accident whilst pregnant, or if we are close to starvation, then we may remain undersize, underweight, or have some mental problems. What we actually become is called the **phenotype**.

We are born with many abilities, for example, certain aspects of our visual system are there right from birth. But much of what we become is a result of the experiences we have and the people we mix with. Whether our family are strict or easy going, what our friends were like, the culture we live in, how much money we have etc, all combine to make each of us what we are. The argument between these two views is called the **nature–nurture debate**.

The "nature" side of the "nature/nurture debate" says that our skills are innate, the "nurture" side says they are socially learned. Do you think that intelligence, personality, and how aggressive people are, is the result of (a) nature, (b) nurture, or (c) both?

Maturation

Another biological influence upon us is the rate at which we mature. **Maturation** is the process of physical growth. Maturation starts with conception. All normal foetuses develop at about the same rate. We learn to use our hands, to move our heads, to crawl and walk, etc according to a particular scale which is more or less the same for most children. It is **genetically determined**. We can only learn to adapt our behaviour when we are **maturationally ready**, for example most babies can stand alone, holding onto furniture, at around six months. They can't walk unaided for another six months. You can try hard to teach a six month old to walk, but you won't succeed. They're simply not maturationally ready.

Human beings do not mature very quickly. For the first few years of life human beings are the most helpless of any species. By a few weeks of age many animals and birds can fend for themselves. In the West we seem to need 15 years or more! Almost 25% of our entire lives is spent as an immature child. No other animal spends such a long time learning about and preparing for, adulthood.

Maturation is the process of physical growth. When does it start and finish?

Background reading – Maturation

All people pass through the same stages of maturation in the same order. For example crawling comes before walking, and we must be fairly experienced at walking before we are able to run very well. However we don't all mature at *exactly* the same rate. Some children might stand at five months, others not until ten months. If all children mature at *roughly* the same rate, and we all pass through the same stages of development, why aren't all children the same? The answer is that at conception each person's combination of genes is unique. For example some people have genes that contribute to very early motor skills (moving around), whilst others do not.

Is development continuous, or does it happen in stages?

We have seen that there was some disagreement about whether our genes or our environment contributed most to our development. There was also a disagreement about whether certain of our skills, such as acquiring language, personality, a sense of right and wrong, intelligence etc are developed through fixed and identifiable stages, or whether they develop continuously, just expanding a little more each day.

Continuous or Staged Development?

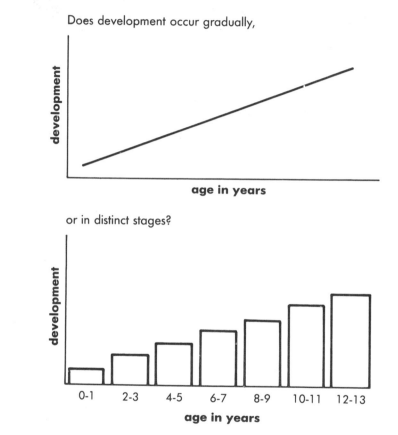

Does development occur gradually,

y-axis: development
x-axis: **age in years**

or in distinct stages?

y-axis: development
x-axis: 0-1　2-3　4-5　6-7　8-9　10-11　12-13
age in years

Early Maturation

If certain skills do develop in stages (and there is plenty of evidence that certain skills do) then the following rules must apply. (We'll take developing language as our example.)

1 Each stage must have a particular kind of behaviour that is not found in previous stages, for example, the first stage in acquiring language is "babbling". This does not generally occur before four months, and ceases as the next stage (learning first words) is mastered.

2 The kind of behaviour (and thinking) that goes with each stage must be different. For example, as children acquire words they can communicate with those around them. They can ask questions and state their preferences. They could not do this earlier.

3 All children must go through the stages in the same order and at approximately the same age, for example babbling (four months to one year), using words (one year to 18 months), using simple

sentences (18 months onwards). This must be true of children all over the world. It is this combination of mental events (like thought, memory, intelligence, perception etc), and actual behaviour (such as speaking, being aggressive, solving problems etc) that is the subject matter of developmental psychology.

Exercise – Stages or continuous development?

It was suggested earlier that those skills which are linked to maturation could appear in stages, those which are learned need not. Using this argument, which of the following do you imagine might occur in stages?

Becoming sociable, behaving aggressively, behaving appropriately to one's sex, intelligence, language, vision, showing affection, being generous.

Exercise – Who do you support?

Give your answers to these questions. The conclusions may not mean anything to you now, but they will later!

1 Which do you think makes the greatest contribution to what we are like, our genetic inheritance, or the environment we grow up in?
(a) 70%+ genetic inheritance,
(b) 60%–70% genetics, 30%–40% environment,
(c) half each,
(d) 60%–70% environment, 30%–40% genetics,
(e) 70%+ environment.
Answer **1** (a), (b), (c), (d) or (e)?

2 Are any personality characteristics which are formed in childhood more or less fixed for life?
(a) yes
(b) no
Answer **2** (a) or (b)?

3 Does mental development
(a) unfold continuously throughout life, or
(b) go through distinct stages?
Answer **3** (a) or (b)?

4 Are children
(a) basically naughty little creatures who need to be kept under control?
(b) neither good nor bad?
(c) basically good?
Answer **4** (a), (b) or (c)?

5 Do children
(a) actively shape their own future personalities?
(b) develop as a result of the way they are brought up?
Answer **5** (a) or (b)?

Pick out the pattern that comes closest to yours

Question No	**1**	**2**	**3**	**4**	**5**	
	c	a	b	a	b	You have similar ideas to Sigmund Freud.
	d	b	a	c	a	
	d	b	b	b	b	You favour the American behaviourist view.
	e	b	a	b	b	

REVIEW – Biological inheritance

We are born with the genetic potential to develop in certain ways. If our environment is stable we will fulfill this potential. Early psychologists were concerned with seeing which skills were genetically inspired and appeared with maturation, and which were socially learned. Those skills which are linked to maturation should appear in stages, those which are learned need not.

Exercise

Have you any ideas about the answers to these questions? You should, by the end of your course.

1 What do you think the world looks like to a baby?

2 What is the first thing babies recognise?

3 How do babies learn to talk?

4 Why do most children think that things which move are alive?

5 Does one's home life determine one's behaviour?

6 Does watching violence on TV make us more violent?

7 Why are children from the same family often so different?

8 Why are some children friendly and cheerful, whilst others are moody and timid?

9 Will severe punishment teach a child not to be "naughty"?

10 Will children from deprived homes be more likely to become delinquent?

11 Why are we born with some reflexes, such as sucking and grasping?

12 Do dreams mean anything important?

13 Why might some people forget their dentist's appointment?

14 When do children learn about ideas like "longer" and "shorter", "faster" and "slower" etc?

15 Do animals have language?

16 Are males "the stronger sex"?

17 Will giving children lots of educational toys make them more intelligent?

18 Are childminders good or bad for children?

19 Why might a two year old call all four legged animals a "doggie"?

20 Do babies need mothers?

2 How Psychologists Study Children

Before looking at some of the explanations psychologists have offered for children's development, you need to know something about the methods they use to gather the information on which they base their claims. The most obvious ways are **informal methods** which include talking to parents and children, watching children's behaviour, reading what people have written about children, and what children have written about themselves. These informal methods are useful for gathering some basic ideas about childhood. They may be a starting point from which researchers can do further research. **Formal methods** are more scientific; they include making detailed observations of specific aspects of children's behaviour, conducting experiments, preparing case studies etc. Each method has its advantages and disadvantages. Each method will be introduced here, with some comment on its uses and limitations. As you go through the course you'll see actual examples of their use, and further discussion of them.

Activity Find an account of some research on children in a newspaper or magazine. If you can't find one, choose one from a psychology book.

Studying Children

Some types of research will try to produce findings which are true of all members of a particular group. For example, studies of children's attitudes towards aggression, "right" and "wrong", the "opposite sex" etc, require psychologists to find groups of children, at various ages, whose attitudes and behaviour are *representative* of all children at each age. Any conclusions which can be drawn from these **cross sectional** studies may be applied to all other children. The problem here is whether we can be quite sure that those children who were studied actually were representative of all children. Studying the attitudes towards various activities at school of fifty children between the ages of five and six may not provide conclusions that are true of all five to six year olds. One way around this is to take quite a large number of representatives then the more that are studied, the higher the probability that they will be representative. If psychologists can be sure that the people studied are typical of all the people in their group, then it is possible just to study a fairly small number of them, and still have acceptable results.

Cross sectional studies take representatives from the whole group, and study them, using whatever methods are most appropriate. Conclusions from cross sectional studies may then be applied to all other members of the group.

Cross Sectional Studies

Alternatively psychologists may be interested in how people change as they grow older, or if they change when they move to different environments. For this they use **longitudinal studies**. These usually take a smaller group of people to study than do cross sectional studies. For example we could take a group of two and three year olds who have spent all their lives in an orphanage. They are all studied at one time, then they are studied again later, and possibly again, later still, for example when they are 7, 14, 21, and 28 years old. This sort of study is useful for seeing how ideas and behaviour change as people grow, or as their environment changes.

A Longitudinal Study

One of the problems in psychology is that we tend to concentrate on studies which were conducted in Europe and America, since these are easier to acquire and understand. Many are written in English and researchers can visit and talk to each other. Funds for such research may be more available in the West, but this is a problem because we may be finding things which are actually only "true" of American, British, or European children. We must also study children in other cultures. For this we do **cross cultural studies**. Cross cultural studies are studies of some aspect of development, such as how males and females are expected to behave, in different cultures. They show up any similarities and differences in development. For example psychologists could find that children everywhere start to talk at about the same age, yet the age at which they learn to read varies.

Here is an example of one cross cultural study which might show some of the difficulties.

Cross cultural studies of the peer group

Urie Bronfenbrenner devised a "dilemmas test" for 11 and 12 year olds from America, Russia, England, and Germany which consisted of 30 imaginary situations to which the child had to respond. In each case the child could do what an adult would want him to, or what a group of imaginary friends would want him to. Here is an example:

"You and some classmates find a sheet of paper on the floor which has the answers of a test that you're going to have in class tomorrow. The teacher must have dropped it. Your friends decide to say nothing about it, and want you to keep quiet too. Then you'll all get better marks".

Each child was asked "Would you go along with them, or would you refuse?" Other stories gave children the choice of wearing fashionable clothes not approved of by adults, not doing homework so that they could be with friends etc. In each case the choice was:

(a) Refuse to go along with my friends
    absolutely certainly, fairly certainly, probably.
(b) Go along with my friends
    absolutely certainly, fairly certainly, probably.

In all four cultures tested more boys said they would disobey adults than girls. The English were the most disobedient, followed by the Germans and Americans, and the least likely to disobey adult wishes were the Russians.

Exercise – Cross cultural studies

1 What age range is being studied here?

2 What do you think Bronfenbrenner means by "a dilemmas test"?

3 Why did Bronfenbrenner ask what the children would do? What was he trying to find out?

4 Think of another "dilemma" which Bronfenbrenner could have used.

5 Which country had the most disobedient children, and which had the least disobedient?

6 Why must psychologists be careful in generalising from studies of European and American peer groups to "all children"?

There are a number of problems with cross cultural studies. They can be expensive and time consuming. They also rely on the observer's interpretation of what they see. For example an observer may interpret how some native Indian children from a particular culture solve a puzzle. In our culture we may think that "doing things quickly" shows intelligence. If the children were very slow in solving it, the observer might conclude that the children of this culture weren't very intelligent. The culture being studied simply may *not* see speed as important. It could be that there isn't any equivalent phrase for "quickly" in the culture's language. The conclusions from studies

Longitudinal studies follow a (usually smaller) group of subjects for various periods of their lives.

Cross cultural studies show the effects of different child rearing styles on how children develop. Watch out for Margaret Mead's work later on.

Can you think of some topics that you know something about, that your parents or grand-parents could not have known about when they were your age?

conducted on some children in one country, at a particular time may not be true of all children everywhere. Also few cultures remain completely unchanged between each generation. The children of each generation know many different things compared with the children of previous generations.

Exercise – Types of research

1 Briefly explain what is meant by the following terms: cross sectional study, longitudinal study, and cross cultural study.

2 Here are some examples of research projects. Which of these three types of studies was used?
(a) Research into the age at which babies in African tribes and in British towns form their first emotional bonds with their mothers.
(b) Research into the effects of giving pre-school children lots of extra attention on their emotional stability as adults.
(c) Research into the attitudes of five, ten, and fifteen year olds today towards television.
(d) Research into the effects of children receiving various amounts of punishment for different things, and their adult personalities.
(e) Research into the different ways in which different societies rear their children.
(f) Research into British children's understanding of such social issues as "looking after people with physical and mental handicaps", "the elderly", "poverty", and "unemployment".

3 Why do psychologists conduct cross cultural studies?

4 What sort of things might psychologists learn from longitudinal studies conducted on children adopted from an orphanage?

5 Outline the main advantage of doing a cross sectional study.

Having decided whether our research is going to be cross sectional, longitudinal, or cross cultural in nature, we must now decide on which actual methods to use to gather the data.

Some of the main methods psychologists use for collecting data

Naturalistic observation

This technique was invented by scientists (called **ethologists**) who study animal behaviour in the wild. The subjects of the research are observed in their own environment, without the researcher interfering in any way. Observing children's play in school playgrounds or in a special "play room", through a one way mirror, are good ways to discover how play changes as children grow. The observer won't try to record everything that happens but will be looking for particular aspects of behaviour such as a child being helpful, or independent, or aggressive etc. With naturalistic observation it is possible to see how particular behaviour occurs in various settings, for example, aggression when alone, aggression with others, aggression at home etc.

There are a few problems with naturalistic observation as a method of gathering factual, scientific data. It isn't possible to record everything that one child does, much less if there are several children to be studied. Important things will always be missed. Secondly the presence of a "strange" observer may alter the child's behaviour. Nowadays a popular tool of naturalistic observers is the video camera, but some children become "shy" when they see a camera, whilst others want to "show off". Either way the behaviour may not be "natural". Thirdly there is a possibility of "**observer bias**". This means that the observer might already have some ideas about why children behave in certain ways, and might interpret the observation to confirm her or his own ideas. Behaviour which doesn't support their beliefs may be ignored.

Case studies and clinical interviews

Case studies are detailed studies of the background of one person, or group of people. Studying the behaviour of members of one particular family, or the behaviour of one gang of Hells Angels, or one group of children with a particular disease, could each be a case study. Case studies are often used in clinical psychology where they concern someone who has some psychological problem or disorder such as extreme aggression, severe shyness, or "childhood schizophrenia". Apart from gathering medical records, school reports, and any other information which may be helpful in understanding someone's present state of mind, the usual technique for gathering personal and sensitive information is the **clinical interview**. During their interview sessions the researcher asks the patient various questions relating to their "problem". The answers are interpreted by the interviewer to build up a picture of how the patient sees herself or himself, and other people and things in their life.

There are four main problems in using case studies for collecting data about childhood development. Firstly young children can't be given clinical interviews in the same way that adults can. Apart from any other reasons, their particular "problem" may limit their understanding of the questions or their willingness or ability to answer them. Secondly, when case studies are built around adults recalling their childhood, the clinical interview relies on their memories, which aren't always very accurate. Thirdly, case studies often try to explain someone's present state of mind by what has happened to them when they were much younger. Fourthly, even if psychologists do find out the causes of one person's problems, these tell us nothing about what causes anyone else's problems.

Surveys

Surveys consist of **questionnaires** and **interviews**. Answers may be written down or recorded for later analysis. Questions can be arranged in a strict order, or asked in the order the interviewer thinks most suitable. They can be open ended, for example, "What are your favourite pastimes?". Or they may be multiple choice, for example, "How many cooked meals do you have each day, one, two, three, or more than three?"

Surveys are not widely used by child psychologists for several reasons. Children sometimes refuse to give answers, or give answers according to how they feel about the person asking them. Also the

Naturalistic observation means studying the subjects in their own environment. It is a useful, and widely used method in child psychology. What sort of things could you study using it? What are the main advantages of using it? What are the main limitations of using it?

Naturalistic Observation

Case studies provide detailed information about one individual, or a small group of people. They may give specific insights into their subjects' behaviour, but do not give general explanations for aspects of child development.

researcher may assume that a question means one thing, the child may interpret it to mean something quite different! (What exactly is a "cooked meal" anyway?) Finally, parents can't always be relied upon to remember how they brought up their children, or to tell the whole truth if asked.

Questionnaires and interviews are sometimes useful for obtaining some "impressions", but contain too many problems to be of much use in child psychology.

Exercise – Some methods for gathering data

1 Why do psychologists collect information?

2 So far we've mentioned observations, case studies, and surveys. Which could be used to study the largest number of people at any one time, and which the least number?

3 Which method would be best for studying:
(a) how babies play?
(b) a mental patients' early childhood?
(c) what people think of radio programs for children?

Experiments

Psychologists using most of the methods previously discussed do their best to observe and record children's behaviour. They do not generally interfere with it. Experiments do interfere quite deliberately. They are carefully controlled situations, which allow psychologists to show that one thing *does* cause some change to occur in another. Anything which can change is called a **variable**. Intelligence, time of day, warmth, amount of noise etc are all common **variables**. For example a psychologist could give some pre-school children special training in language skills ("language skill" is a variable) to see if they would make better progress in primary school than they might otherwise make. Scientists try to control everything in the situation, for example, the amount of pre-school training given, and they keep careful notes of the subjects' progress. If subjects in the experiment receive different instructions, or have different things done to them, or go through the steps of the experiment in a different order, any of these things could explain some of the differences in their scores. Clearly all the subjects in the experiment must have **standardised** instructions and procedures.

Standardising the instructions and procedures of the experiment involves deciding exactly what the instructions and procedures should be for the group being studied. It wouldn't be reasonable, for example, to expect children to understand the same instructions as adults. Every subject must then have exactly the same instructions and procedures applied to them.

Experiments can allow "proof" to be gathered, but there are many problems involved in using them on humans.

The main difficulties of using experiments on children are that children don't always co-operate, they can't always understand what the experimenter asks them to do, and people do not always behave "naturally" in an experiment.

Natural experiments

There are many aspects of human development that psychologists might like to know more about, but can't investigate by controlled experiments. For example, will severe punishment (one variable), stop a child from doing very dangerous things like playing with fire (amount of "playing with fire" is another variable)? Where would we find sufficient mothers who would allow us to experiment on their children? How can we always be observing the child, in case it starts to play with fire? How could we deliberately allow children to take some matches, just so that we can punish them later? How could we ask someone to do the punishing? The problems are enormous. Here is another example:

Some researchers have been interested in the effects of very early contact between mothers and their newborn infants. Their idea was that those mothers (and fathers) who had a large amount of close contact with their babies during the first hours and days after birth would build a stronger relationship with the child than those who did not have this early contact. Ideally the researchers might have wanted to take two similar maternity wards which took women from similar backgrounds, of similar age etc. One ward could have its routine altered, so that the baby and parents spent more time together, whilst in the other the infant and its parents would not spend a lot of time together. Unfortunately hospitals are unlikely to completely change their routines, particularly in sensitive or potentially dangerous areas such as maternity or intensive care, just to suit pyschological research. However, there is a possible solution to these problems. Different hospitals have different routines and procedures (ie different variables), and it may well be possible to find one that only allows a few hours contact, and another which allows several hours contact. The researchers do not themselves control the amount of early contact. Differences in it already exist. Finding out whether differences in the amount of early contact *does* lead to any differences later under these circumstances, would be called a natural experiment.

One further example of a natural experiment could involve some orphanages which are inadequately staffed and provide very few toys and games for the children, and others which are well staffed with plenty to stimulate the orphans. It should be possible to measure the intelligence of the children in the different orphanages to see if the amount of stimulation seemed to have any effect on their intelligence.

One problem with natural experiments is that human behaviour isn't usually the result of just one or two features in a situation, but can be affected by all sorts of others too. For example the well equipped orphanages may all be in countries where there is plenty to eat and drink, and where there are good medical facilities. The children in the deprived orphanages may be in poorer countries and may not have good physical health and conditions. These differences may also effect their intelligence. In a controlled experiment such differences could be taken into account. In a natural experiment it may be impossible to do so.

Correlation

It is not possible to study all human behaviour by the methods listed so far. For example, psychologists couldn't study the statement "The more a father was abused when he was a child, the more likely he is to severely abuse his own children", or "The younger a child is when it is removed from its mother and placed in a deprived orphanage, the more disturbed its emotional development will become". Each of these statements says that two aspects of behaviour are related. The first statement claims a relationship between "the frequency with which a father was abused when he was younger" and "frequency of abuse of his own children". The second identifies "length of time spent

When it would be impossible to conduct a controlled experiment researchers may be able to do a natural experiment. They do not control the main features of different situations, differences in the features they are interested in (variables) already exist.

Can you think of some other differences in the two maternity hospitals that might upset the natural research on the effects of extra contact following birth, and the closeness of the mother/child bond later?

What are the main variables in the natural experiment on "orphanage upbringing" and "intellectual development"?

Correlation is a statistical technique for predicting the probability of things occurring together. It does not prove that one causes the other.

in a deprived orphanage" and "extent of emotional development". These variables couldn't deliberately be manipulated.

Instead psychologists might find instances where one of these things already exists; and count how many times the other occurs. For example, we could find some children who spent some time in a deprived orphanage, and we could test their development. Or we might check the medical records of people who abused their children, and see if they themselves had been abused. Statistical analysis of this information will give a measure of how likely it is that the two things occur together.

Correlation is a statistical technique for measuring *the extent to which* two or more things vary together. It cannot show that one thing causes the other. Correlational studies are widely used by developmental psychologists.

A Summary of the main methods of data collection used in psychology

Type	Advantages	Disadvantages
Cross sectional studies	Findings may be true for the whole population. They are useful for discovering "typical" or "normal" behaviour.	May be impossible to find a large enough group with all the relevant variables. If the group is too small the influences of some individuals in it may be too great.
Longitudinal studies	Show the effects of time on changes in attitudes, behaviour etc.	May "lose" some subjects. May be "out of date" before the results are published.
Cross cultural studies	Show what factors are genetic in origin, and which are environmental.	Practical difficulties of language and expense. Misinterpretation of cultural values.
Observations	No interference by researcher so behaviour should be "natural".	Things can be missed or misinterpreted. No "proof".
Case studies	Allows detailed analysis of particular problems.	No generalisatons are possible.
Surveys	Large group provides lots of data.	Limited range of questions which can be asked. Can't rely on respondents to answer or tell the truth.
Experiments	Allow control of relevant variables and offers proof of one variable causing a change in another.	Are artificial and people may not behave "normally".

Natural experiments	Allow investigation of variables which could not be tested in other experiments.	Other variables, which may also be relevant are unlikely to be controlled.
Correlational studies	Used (where experiments can't be) to show statistical relationships.	Can not show cause.

Exercise

Read this extract from an imaginary article on intellectual development. There will be questions relating to it throughout the rest of this chapter:

"Children's Intelligence"

"Scientists in Britain and Germany have been studying how children of seven to ten years of age solve problems. They have both reached much the same conclusions. The British group had noticed that between the ages of seven and ten the way children think about the appearance of things changes. A junior school in a well off part of London was used in the research. At the beginning of the summer term the parents were asked if they would mind if their children were used. Sixty-one of the children's parents agreed. One day was set aside for the tests and the children all gathered in the main hall where the tests were to be administered. The children were each shown five different objects such as plasticine, water, and rows of buttons, each of which could be changed in some way (eg the plasticine was rolled into different shapes, and the water poured into various shaped jugs). The children were then asked questions about the objects. One question was "is there more plasticine in the sausage shape than there is when it is rolled into the ball shape?" Their replies were written down by the teachers. For example, "Alan, aged eight years, two months, said that a piece of string curled up was shorter than the same piece when it was stretched out." Later the psychologists analysed these reports and tried to find any differences between the older children and younger children's replies. They concluded that younger children's ideas about objects are dominated by the way the objects look.

"In Germany ten schools were chosen, representing poor to well off areas, some in city and some in rural areas. Fifty children were picked to represent each school. They were matched for non verbal intelligence, sex, and personality. The parents were told to collect their children an hour later than normal as the research was to be conducted after classes over four days, and as it was nearly Christmas they wouldn't want to be standing around in the cold. The researchers predicted that children from better off homes will be more advanced intellectually than children from poorer backgrounds. They decided that the ways children used various toys would be a good way of assessing their intellect, so they observed children playing with various educational toys, and recorded them on video. They were rated by the psychologists for imagination, co-operation, independence, and leadership qualities. They found that children from poorer areas used little imagination, and were rather unadventurous. They played with the toys in a repetitive way, frequently making the same mistakes over and over. The better off children scored higher on all the tests, and would experiment with the toys and games to see what they could be made to do."

1 At what time of year were the British children, and German children, studied?

2 Who recorded the British children's answers, and how was the German children's behaviour noted?

3 Outline the differences in the ways the British and German children were chosen?

4 How did the German researchers assess the children's intellect?

5 What were the scientists trying to discover?

6 Summarise the conclusions of these studies in your own words.

Exercise – Advantages and disadvantages of methods used in psychology

Fill in the gaps in the table:

A Summary of the main methods of data collection used in psychology

Type	Advantages	Disadvantages
Cross sectional studies		
Longitudinal studies		
Cross cultural studies		
Observations		
Case studies		
Surveys		
Experiments		
Natural experiments		
Correlational studies		

REVIEW – Methods used in psychological research

Whilst experiments allow control of all the variables, they are not the only technique psychologists use for data collection. Psychologists use observations, case studies, natural experiments, correlations, cross sectional and longitudinal methods, and cross cultural techniques. Each has its advantages and disadvantages.

Exercise – Methods for collecting data

Ron is nine years old. He is a very anxious and nervous boy. He is very shy and hides from strangers. He sometimes complains of nightmares, and occasionally wets the bed. Medical records show that he was rather slow to develop, and was undersize as a baby. The health visitor suspected that Ron wasn't as well cared for as he should have been, although she couldn't prove anything. She suspected he was being neglected, although he never showed signs of being abused in any way.

1 What are Ron's "symptoms"?

2 What did the health visitor suspect?

3 If she was correct, would it completely explain what Ron is like now?

4 Explain your last answer.

5 Name three aspects of children's behaviour which could be studied by naturalistic observation.

Stating questions for research

If you ask parents about "the best way to bring up a child", you'll hear answers ranging from "by using strict discipline and teaching respect" to "encouraging the child to go at its own pace, doing what it wants to do". The one thing most of the parents answering your questions probably have in common is that they'll all say their way is "common sense". To find the correct answers to questions such as this scientists need to do research. Research involves looking for relationships between things such as "does having deaf parents affect a child's language development?", or "does being brought up by very strict parents make us frightened of other people?" Most psychologists try to be **objective**. This means basing one's statements only on the facts and not on opinions. To achieve this **objectivity** many psychologists use scientific methods to investigate our behaviour.

Not all of the methods we mentioned earlier will produce objective data. Science demands "proof" that one thing causes another, or leads to a reduction in another. For example we hope that medical science has proved that the tablets our doctor gives us actually will reduce the pain we are in. Some psychologists conduct experiments to gather proof about human behaviour. Unfortunately not all sources of information in our society rely on proof at all, and this can sometimes give a misleading picture of how some things may be related.

Psychologists generally prefer to gather objective data rather than rely on common sense answers that are often contradictory.

Exercise – Research

1 What's the difference between the ways in which some people explain behaviour, and the ways in which many psychologists try to?

2 What sort of things do you think research in child psychology is going to be about? HINT If you can't think of many things, look at the list of contents of this book.

In all sciences the process of "finding out" involves a particular procedure called "the scientific method". It starts with making some observations to gain an idea about what factors go together. For example if psychologists found that 18 month old boys were generally noisier and more adventurous than 18 month old girls they would have the basis for doing some research. Or in the primary school a psychologist could observe that ignoring an attention seeking child seems to reduce its disruptive behaviour. If we're interested in doing some research in this area we'll find out what other research has already been conducted (ie read up all the books and journals where this sort of research is published). We may want to do some original research, which no one has thought of before, or we may want to check on the reliability of some research that has already been conducted. We could observe several primary school classes to see how teachers treat attention seeking children.

After making their observations and doing their reading psychologists should have a clear idea about what their research is going to be about. Before starting any research this has to be stated precisely, otherwise they may stray off the point, and never know for certain if they've proved anything! Other researchers won't be able to test their claims either. This statement is called a **hypothesis**. If we are going to investigate the hypothesis experimentally we call it the **experimental hypothesis**. It is sometimes called the **alternate hypothesis**, especially where the research does not take the form of an experiment.

All research starts with observation.

REVIEW – Doing research?

Any subject that wants to be accepted as a science must deal in facts rather than opinions. These must be collected and presented objectively.

Exercise – Observation

What evidence is there in "Children's Intelligence" that the British researchers had made observations before doing their research?

Testing hypotheses

Hypotheses are statements that scientists wish to test. For example "A teacher ignoring a child when it is seeking attention will reduce the child's attention seeking behaviour" is a hypothesis. In this experiment the experimenter would control one thing, (ignoring the child), and the child is going to "control" the other, (its behaviour). So, in our example, the experimental hypothesis states that altering one of these variables ("ignoring the child when it is seeking attention"), will make the child change the other variable (reducing its attention seeking). To put it exactly, a hypothesis is *a testable statement of a relationship between two or more variables.* Any variable that the experimenter controls is called an **independent variable** (IV for short). Any variable in the subject's behaviour which alters as a result is called a **dependent variable** (DV).

When stating a hypothesis researchers must define precisely what they mean by all the terms used. For example, what exactly do we count as "attention seeking" behaviour? "Attention seeking behaviour" may be defined as any of the following: "being out of its seat for more than two minutes in every five", "shouting", "asking more than three questions in five minutes", and "pulling at the teacher's clothes". The teacher will ignore the child when it is doing any of these things. From

REVIEW – Hypotheses and variables

A hypothesis is a statement which a researcher is going to test. It states that two variables are related in some way and therefore, if the researcher can alter one of them this may cause the subject to alter the other. The researcher must control the independent variables, any changes in the subject's behaviour are called dependent variables.

another hypothesis, when we say "babies need lots of love", what exactly do we mean by "love"? And exactly how much is "lots of"? This procedure of defining all our terms is called **operationalising**.

Exercise – Operationalising variables

1 Read this hypothesis and list the six terms to be operationalised.
   "Rewarding a child when it is being good and ignoring it when it is being disruptive will make it behave better".

2 Imagine you really were going to test this hypothesis. Give your operational definition of each of the six terms in the hypothesis.

3 What operational measure of the children's intellect was taken by the German researchers in "Children's Intelligence"?

Other things in the situation can also affect a child's behaviour. For example, even though the teacher is ignoring the child, the other children are not. Their complaints may be just the kind of attention the child wants. Here the independent variable "the teacher ignoring a child's attention seeking" will have little effect. Other things in the situation, apart from the teacher, are influencing the child's behaviour. They are called **situational variables**. The time of day, the temperature, and the amount of noise, are examples of common situational variables.

The children we study will be different too, for example, there will be differences in personality, intelligence, aggressiveness, sociability etc. Each of these **subject variables** could alter the way each child behaves. If we find that a quiet, frightened child does stop seeking attention when it is ignored this doesn't prove that ignoring all children's attention seeking will reduce it. An aggressive, moody child may be more violently attention seeking than a frightened, lonely or bored child. It would be simple if every time we ignored an attention seeking child it gradually behaved more "normally". Worried parents of aggressive children would probably be delighted to know that all they need to do to stop their child's aggression is to ignore them when they are shouting and hitting. Unfortunately life isn't so simple! A

Scientists must operationalise all their variables and procedures so that they can be "held constant" and applied to all the subjects. This helps to ensure that any differences in the subjects' behaviour is a result of the IVs.

Situational variables can be anything in the situation where the research is being conducted that might influence some of the subject's behaviour.

Background reading – Some hypotheses with the IVs and DVs

Hypothesis	IV	DV
Giving babies lots of love teaches them trust.	The amount of love given by the parents	The amount of trust shown by the baby
Talking to children increases their langue skills.	Amount of talking to child	Size of child's vocabulary
Encouraging children to make decisions helps to make them independent.	Amount of encouragement in decision making	Amount of child's independent behaviour
Watching violence on TV makes a child more violent	Number of violent TV programmes seen.	Amount of violence shown by child.

The most common subject variables in psychology are age, sex, intelligence, personality, upbringing, and previous experience.

teacher can't ignore an attention seeking child who is about to pour the paint water all over another child, or one who is walking down the table through all the other children's art work. A parent can't ignore a child who is screaming at the top of its voice, or is kicking its younger sister! These wide differences in subject variables could make it difficult to predict from research on a few subjects.

Exercise – Variables

An experimenter investigates the possibility that children will apply their knowledge of the Green Cross Code better if they are taught to sing its rules to themselves as they approach the kerb. She teaches each child the song, and gives them praise and sweets when they can sing it without mistakes. Later she observes them crossing the "pretend street" she has made in the playground. They all sing the song, look right and left etc, and cross very carefully.

1 What hypothesis is being tested here?

2 What variables is the experimenter controlling in this experiment? What is the name for the variables that experimenters control?

3 What is the name of the variables which may change as a result of those the experimenter is controlling?

4 Name two situational variables which were different for the British and German children in "Children's Intelligence".

5 What subject variables did each school's children have in common, in the German study?

Exercise – Experiment on observational learning

Read about this experiment and answer the questions at the end.

A psychologist wanted to show that children of three and four could be affected by behaviour they observed around them. She selected two groups of ten children, matching them (as far as possible) for age, intelligence, and personality. Each group watched a different Punch and Judy show. Group A saw Mr Punch behaving very badly. He laughed when he saw another puppet fall over and wouldn't help it to stand up. In Group Bs performance Mr Punch was upset when the other puppet fell, and went to help straight away.

The children were observed in their playgroups for the next week and the number of times each child ignored another who was upset, or went to help was counted. The average scores for each child were:

	Offers of help	Times Ignored
Group A	7	18
Group B	21	5

1 What is the IV?
2 What is the DV?
3 What is the hypothesis in this experiment?
4 What do you think the phrase "matching them for age, intelligence, and personality" means?
5 Further analysis of the data revealed that Group A consisted of seven boys and three girls, and group B contained six girls and four boys. In view of this can you suggest any other explanations for the differences between the two groups scores?

Exercise – "Children's Intelligence" *see* page 15

1 What hypothesis is the British team testing in "Children's Intelligence"?

2 Give an example of an independent variable used by the British group.

3 What measures of the dependent variable were taken by the German team?

Exercise – An experiment on teaching rats

An experimenter noticed that some of her laboratory rats twitched their whiskers whenever their food was brought into the laboratory. She decided to test whether she could teach the rats to twitch their whiskers when she flashed a light. First she measured the exact amount of whisker twitching that went on when the food was brought in. Then she flashed a bright light on and off just before each meal. The rats soon started to twitch their whiskers when they saw the light.

1 What 2 independent variables are being controlled here?

2 What is the dependent variable and how is it measured?

3 Why did the experimenter measure the rat's movements before flashing the light?

4 Write a hypothesis for this experiment.

Refuting hypotheses

A hypothesis which states something like "ignoring an attention seeking child, except when it is behaving properly, will eliminate its attention seeking behaviour" will probably never be proved to be completely correct. There'll always be some children who refuse to stay in their seat. In fact few hypotheses in psychology (or many other areas of science) are ever proved absolutely correct. Instead we have to find a way of measuring the extent to which a hypothesis is proven.

For example, imagine that a psychologist observed that rats twitch their whiskers as they approach food. She could conduct an experiment to teach thirty rats to associate a flash of light with food, so that they would twitch their whiskers when they saw the light. Her hypothesis might be "flashing a light immediately before giving a rat its food will lead to the animal twitching its whiskers when it sees the light." However, she could find that 9 of them never learned the association, whilst 12 learned it quite quickly, and the rest sometimes twitched their whiskers, and sometimes did not. In this case has she proved her hypothesis? Has "flashing a light immediately before giving a rat its food led to the animal twitching its whiskers when it sees the light"? Not completely, only some of the rats learned the association. But the hypothesis isn't completely wrong either because some of the rats did learn.

In testing any experimental hypothesis there are only two possible explanations. Either any changes in our subjects' behaviour were caused by the experimenter manipulating the independent variable, or they were not. In our example, either those rats that twitched their whiskers when the light was flashed had learned to associate the light and the food, or they had not. Scientists state these two possibilities thus:

1 "Flashing a light before presenting food will not teach a rat to twitch its whiskers, and any such whisker twitching that does occur happens by chance". This is called the **null hypothesis**.

2 "Flashing a light before presenting food will teach a rat to twitch its whiskers". This is the **alternate hypothesis**.

What we need to decide is "what is the probability that our results did occur by chance, and that the null hypothesis is correct?" If we can reject the null hypothesis we are able to accept the alternate hypothesis. Luckily there are a number of tests which estimate how likely it is that changes in the independent variable really are causing changes in the dependent variable, ie that flashing the light really is causing rats to twitch their whiskers. These tests have to show that the probability of the two variables being related is greater than a minimum of 19 out of 20. We would accept that the rats had learned to twitch their whiskers when the light flashed if they twitched their whiskers nineteen times out of every twenty times the light was flashed. We would describe this finding as **significant**. Anything less than nineteen out of twenty doesn't allow us to reject the null hypothesis. Since we can't reject the null hypothesis we can't accept the alternate one. To summarise, a researcher must:

1 State the null hypothesis, and the alternate hypothesis.

2 Use an appropriate statistical test to work out the chances that the results could have been obtained under the null hypothesis.

3 If the tests show that the chances are better than 19 out of 20 that the results could not have been obtained by coincidence then we must reject the null hypothesis (and, since there are only two possible explanations, we must therefore accept the alternate hypothesis).

Background reading

Here are some examples of alternate and null hypotheses:

Alternate hypothesis	Null hypothesis
Picking a baby up as soon as it starts crying will cause it to cry less	Picking up a crying baby will not make it cry less, and any reduction in crying that does occur happens by chance.
Talking to young children will produce an increase in their language skills.	Talking to young children will not produce an increase in their language skills, and any increase that does occur happens by chance.
Encouraging children to make decisions helps them to become independent.	Encouraging children to make decisions will not help them to become more independent, and any increase in their independence that does occur happens by chance.
Watching violence on television makes children behave more violently.	Watching violence on television does not make children behave more violently, and any increase in their violence that does occur happens by chance.

4 If the tests show that the odds are less than 19 out of 20 that the results could have occurred by chance then we must not reject the null hypothesis (and we must therefore reject the alternate hypothesis).

Exercise – The null hypothesis

1 What was the IV in our "attention seeking child" experiment?

2 Name some DVs that we're going to be looking for from our attention seeking child.

3 State the "attention seeking child" hypothesis in its null form.

4 What do experimenters expect will happen to dependent variables when they control independent variables?

5 State the British researchers' hypothesis in "Children's Intelligence" in its null form. (*See page 15.*)

Exercise – Null hypotheses

Two psychologists noticed that older children tend to "boss" younger children around. They decided to try to use this to teach the older children about responsible behaviour. The older children joined in a role playing game in which they had to look after a younger child. The rules of the game made it difficult for them not to. They were praised by a teacher who was playing the role of "mother" for behaving so responsibly. The children's parents were asked to look for any changes in the way older children behaved towards their younger brothers and sisters, and many parents reported that their children had become more responsible.

1 What prompted these psychologists to begin this experiment?

2 Their hypothesis was "A child who is rewarded for behaving responsibly will be more likely to look after younger children." Why do scientists state experimental hypotheses?

3 Why do scientists state null hypotheses?

4 Name four of the main variables that experimenters control.

5 Why are "operational definitions" used?

6 How many children altogether were studied in "Children's Intelligence"?

7 Design a simple experiment to test the hypothesis that "giving a baby extra contact with its mother just after birth makes the bond between them even stronger". You have ten mothers who are about to give birth who will co-operate. What two groups do you need? What IVs and DVs will you use? You can have one year to conduct your experiment.

Sampling

In order to conduct any research we need some people (or animals?) to study. The **subjects** (which can be abbreviated to "**Ss**") which are to be studied are called a **sample**. If we were studying children in playgroups we could find the nearest playgroup to where we live, and study them. But this wouldn't be very satisfactory since they may not be representative of all playgroup children. There is a procedure we must go through to draw our sample.

REVIEW – Stating topics for research

Psychologists often like to collect their data in an objective way, and this often means following the scientific method, that is, doing some observation, formulating some hypothesis and stating it in its experimental and null forms. Every variable and every stage in our research must be carefully operationalised before the hypothesis can be tested.

23

A "target population" is the group the research is aimed at, and a sample is the group of subjects, drawn from the target population, which will be studied.

To obtain a **sample** researchers must first identify the **target population**. This is the group that the study is concerned with, for example, a study on "the attitudes of college students towards smoking" would have a **target population** of "all college students".

Exercise

What is the target population in the following studies:

1 An experiment to try to teach chimps to use deaf and dumb language.

2 An investigation into the moral development of pre-school children.

3 A study of the development of language skills in deaf children.

4 An experiment to investigate the effects of television on four to six year olds.

5 Research into the causes of a fear of spiders.

The next decision is about how many Ss to study. This will be determined by four main factors.

Firstly it depends on how large the target population is. The target population "three to five year olds in Britain" contains hundreds of thousands of children. Psychologists studying this target population will probably need quite a large sample if it is to be truly representative. If the target population is much smaller, for example, three to five year olds in day nurseries, the sample may be much smaller, and still be representative.

The second factor concerns how many Ss are available to be studied. If a psychologist wants to study language development in deaf children, but only knows six deaf children, and doesn't know how to find any more, then she or he doesn't have much of a sample. The few studied may not be representative of all deaf children.

Thirdly we will want enough Ss to make our sample representative of the target population. If a psychologist studied ten mothers who took heroin twice a week or more during pregnancy, found that eight of them had babies who were mentally handicapped, would you accept that heroin abuse during pregnancy causes mental handicap? A sample size of ten is too small to base such a claim on. If 80% of a sample of one thousand heroin users had handicapped children, this would be far more acceptable evidence. Unfortunately developmental psychologists rarely have the resources to have so many children in their samples.

Finally we do not want so many Ss that the study will take too long (and cost too much!).

The size of the sample used by psychologists is always a compromise between these four factors.

Deciding how many Ss to study will always depend on the number there are to study, the number that will be needed to make the study representative, and the number which the researcher has resources to study.

Having decided on the size of the sample a psychologist must then choose a method of drawing it from the target population. There are many ways of drawing a sample; for example:

1 Random sampling Here every member of the target population has the same chance of appearing in the sample. Names could be picked out of a hat, each possible subject could "draw straws", or the researcher could stick a pin in names in the phone book. One popular method is to give each member of the target population a number, then to take numbers from "random number tables" which are simply lists of numbers that have no pattern and are in no particular order. Each member of the target population whose number was chosen would be sampled. An exact definition of a **random sample** is "A sample where no member of the target population has any greater chance of being chosen than any other".

2 Systematic sampling   Here every 5th or 7th (or any other number) name is taken from a list of the target population. For example, if there are 50 families in your street, and you wanted a 20% sample of them, you could use every 5th family.

3 Quota or judgement sampling   A list is made of each variable which may have an effect on the research. For example let's say a study is being conducted on the psychology of being housebound. The main people who are housebound are some old people, some ill people, and some mothers of young children. If these three groups account for 20%, 10% and 60% respectively of all housebound people, the sample will have to contain these three groups in those proportions. Gathering such a sample would be extremely time consuming and difficult to do. This method is rarely used in psychology.

4 Self selected samples   Here subjects choose themselves, for example, they might answer an advertisement in a paper, or reply to a postal questionnaire. Most people do not answer newspaper adverts, and the "non return rate" for postal questionnaires is often around 70 per cent. Those people that do respond must be untypical, since most people do not respond. So the sample will be **biased**. ("Biased" means "not representative".)

5 Imposed sampling   This is where the Ss aren't given the choice as to whether they want to be a part of the research. Babies and children can't be consulted, although, of course, their parents can.

6 Opportunity sampling   This is where the researcher takes advantage of having some Ss available to include in the research. For example, students at colleges and universities are often used by their tutors to take part in the tutor's research.

Design of investigations

As we mentioned earlier, some researchers have hypothesised that giving newborn babies and their mothers extra time together, in the days following birth, would strengthen the mother/child relationship. An experiment could be devised which would give one group of mothers some extra contact with their babies, and another group would have the usual amount of contact. The closeness of the mother/child relationship in the two groups could be measured over the next year or so. If the researchers are correct, then the mothers who had extra contact should have a closer relationship than the mothers who had the usual amount of contact.

This experiment had a fairly simple design and uses one **experimental group**. They are the mothers who have the extra contact. It also has one **control group**. This consists of mothers who have the usual number of hours of contact with their babies. Control groups are used so that comparisons may be made between the behaviour of their members, and the members of the experimental groups. If mothers in

In any research it is useful to have a group whose behaviour hasn't been manipulated by the researchers, to compare with the experimental group, whose behaviour has been manipulated. This is the "control group".

the experimental group have closer relationships with their babies than mothers in the control group, then we could say that having extra contact does lead to closer relationships.

It's important that the Ss in each group are as similar as possible, otherwise any differences that are found to exist between them may be because the subjects in each group were different to begin with. Researchers have to decide how to divide their sample between the various experimental and control groups. There are three main choices: independent measures, repeated measures and matched subjects.

Exercise – Samples

10 four year old boys with a wide range of intelligence and different personalities were sampled. 10 four year old girls were found with abilities and personalities which were similar to the boys. They all came from three inner city playgroups. They were given a choice of toys to play with. Most of the boys preferred the more active, noisy toys, like balls and drums. Most of the girls preferred sitted quietly playing with dolls and clothes.

1 The sample used here is not likely to be representative of the target population "four year old children". What evidence is there in the passage to support this.

2 What would psychologists be saying about the target population "four year old girls" if they generalised the findings from this study?

3 Outline the main factors governing the size of the sample psychologists use.

4 Define the term "random sample". Begin "A random sample is one where no . . ."

5 How was the sample chosen by (a) the British team and (b) the German team, in "Children's Intelligence"?

6 Why aren't self selected samples ever representative?

1 Independent measures (or independent groups)

This is probably the easiest method. The sample is divided randomly into the various conditions.

Unfortunately there are two possible dangers with this research design. Firstly if the research involves some kind of testing we must make sure that each subject in each experimental group receives exactly the same treatment as every other. They must hear the same instructions about how to complete the test, and each must go through the same procedures. We mentioned this earlier, its called **standar-**

Background reading – An example of independent measures design

In an experiment to discover whether encouraging children to make decisions for themselves will help them become more independent, a psychologist randomly divides a group of five and six year olds into two experimental groups, and one control group. Experimental group One will have teachers who try to make the children think for themselves, and stick with their decisions. Experimental group Two are always told what to do by their teachers. The controls have their usual teaching which sometimes encourages independence, and sometimes wants the children to obey rules. All the children will then complete a series of tests to measure their independence.

disation. Secondly if we accidentally put some children who have already been encouraged to be independent into one experimental group, and some who are still dependent on other people in another experimental group, then whatever results we obtain won't be the result of their being in the group. They may have been like that anyway. If this occurs we say the results have been "**confounded**".

Exercise – Confounding variables

The parents of 30 seven year old children responded to an advertisement some researchers had placed in a local newspaper. The children were randomly divided into an experimental and a control group. Both groups were asked to remember all the objects in a large picture, which they saw for one minute. As soon as the picture was removed the experimental group were told an exciting story about some children, like themselves, who found some stolen property whilst playing. They told their parents and the police, and were given a day out at the zoo as a reward by the owner of the stolen valuables. The children seemed to find the story quite exciting. The control group were told a neutral story about the job of the Post Office. Few of them seemed particularly fascinated.

Half an hour after hearing the stories both groups of children were asked to recall as many of the objects in the picture as they could. The experimental group could remember half of them, the control group could remember about two thirds.

1 What kind of sampling technique was used to draw this sample? What was the final sample size?
2 Which group could remember least of the objects, and which could remember most of them?
3 Explain why "It is important that the Ss in each group are as similar as possible".
4 What explanation could you offer for the findings of the research described above?
5 Why do scientists use control groups?
6 Find as many potentially confounding variables as you can in "Children's Intelligence". Compare your list with other people's.

Background reading – An example of confounding variables

Remember: The independent variable is the one that the researcher manipulates. At the same time the researcher tries to hold all the others constant. If an independent variable creeps in, which the experimenter isn't controlling, this can confound the results. For example, do you remember the groups of children who saw Punch and Judy shows where Mr Punch behaved in different ways? Those who'd seen Mr Punch being aggressive tended to be more aggressive themselves. Those who'd seen Mr Punch being helpful became more helpful. But were these changes in the children's behaviour simply the result of having seen Mr Punch's behaviour? If Group A saw the Punch and Judy show last thing at night when they were tired (tiredness is a subject variable), whilst Group B saw it when they had just had a lesson about helping others and felt they wanted to be helpful (motivation is a subject variable), this might explain some of the differences in their scores. The experimenter isn't controlling these variables. If "tiredness" and "motivations" do have an effect on the results they are called **confounding variables**. Obviously it's important that both groups saw Mr Punch under similar conditions and circumstances.

2 Repeated measures

In repeated measures design all the Ss are put into both control and experimental groups.

There are three distinct advantages to using this design, over independent groups design.

(a) There are far more scores than with independent groups. We have 20 scores from the "easy going" playgroup described in the background reading, and 20 from the "strict" playgroup, making 40 scores in all. If we'd used independent groups and put half our sample in each nursery we would only have had 10 scores from each, making 20 in all. (b) Secondly it reduces the risk of confounding. Since each subject becomes a member of each group, we can't have any group containing different sorts of Ss. (c) Thirdly it allows us to see if any of the conditions in the research is usually accompanied by any particular behaviour by the subjects.

One possible problem with repeated measures design is that the experiences the Ss have in one condition (eg the experience of being in the easy going playgroup), might affect how they behave in the next one (eg how they behaved in the strict nursery). These are called **order effects** and could cause confounding.

There's a simple way to eliminate this problem. Put half the sample of children in the strict playgroup first, then into the easy going one, and the other half in the easy going one first, and the strict one later. This should eliminate most order effects. The technique is called **counterbalancing**.

REVIEW – Repeated Measures Design

Using repeated measures design lets us put all members of our sample through each condition in the research, thus giving us many more scores. There may be a need to counterbalance to avoid any order effects.

Exercise – Repeated measures design

Make up a hypothesis for an experiment which could use repeated measures. (NB do not use one already mentioned.)

3 Matched Subjects

In this design each experimental group of subjects must be as similar as possible. The researcher decides which subject variables are important, finds pairs of Ss who are similar, and puts one of them into one group, and their partner into the other group.

There are enormous problems with this research design. How could we possibly know all the relevant variables in any research? How could we measure every one of them accurately? Where could we find a sample who had an equal distribution of them? Consequently this technique is very rarely used.

Background reading – An example of repeated measures design

We want to discover if children prefer "strictly run" playgroups to ones where they are more free to choose what to do. We could take 20 children, put them in an easy going playgroup for a month and measure their levels of enjoyment. Then we could put them into a strictly run playgroup for a month, and see if there are any differences in their levels of enjoyment. So repeated measures means using the same subjects in each experimental condition.

Exercise – Matched subjects design

1 What variables are being controlled in the experiment described in the "Research Report" in the background reading?

2 Can you think of any other variables that could affect the levels of aggression in children?

3 What might happen if the intelligence tests and personality inventories weren't very accurate?

4 How easy do you think it would be to find 20 five year old boys and girls who would be so similar?

5 Which type of research design was used by the German team in "Children's Intelligence?

6 Which was used by the British group?

Exercise – Research design

Which of these hypotheses could be tested with (a) independent measures, (b) repeated measures, (c) matched Ss, (d) couldn't be tested at all.

1 "Seeing a film of someone behaving in a caring way makes children more caring".

2 "Encouraging boys to be soft, emotional, and caring will make them grow up to be weak and effeminate".

3 "Solvent abuse leads to brain damage".

4 "Learning ability varies with the level of noise".

5 "To discover if chimps can be taught to use (deaf and dumb) sign language".

6 "Increasing physical punishment increases aggressive behaviour in two to five year olds".

7 "Do eight week old babies think that when something is hidden from them it no longer exists?"

Data collection and interpretation

No matter which type of research we've conducted, or which methods we've used, or how we've chosen and arranged our sample, we're going to produce quite a mass of information, most of it in the form of

REVIEW – Matched subjects design

In matched Ss design all of the important variables are identified, and the same number of Ss with each of them are put into each experimental condition. It is extremely difficult to do, and this technique is not widely used.

Background reading – An example of matched Ss design
Extract from a Research Report

Hypothesis: to investigate the effects of watching violence on TV and levels of aggression in five year old children.

Sample: twenty boys and twenty girls.
Research Design used: matched Ss.
Relevant variables: age, intelligence, personality, sex.

Number of experimental groups: two.
Procedure: each five year old given personality inventories and standard intelligence tests. Each group given equal numbers of above average, average, and below average intelligence boys and girls, ensuring each group contained children with similar personality characteristics.

numbers. These numbers are called "**raw data**" because they haven't been "treated" in any way yet. Usually the first thing is to arrange them in rank order, ie from the lowest score to the highest score. If the score relates to a particular subject we may want to keep some note of who achieved that score. We call the first subject S1, the second S2 etc.

For example, here are the raw scores (in percentages) for 10 students in a class test: S1=60, S2=75, S3=75, S4=55, S5=60, S6=65, S7=55, S8=75, S9=70, S10= 60. The lowest score is 55%, so we write that down. The next score above that is 60%, so that is written below 55%. This goes on until all the scores have been listed. What we might now want to know is how many students gained each score. To do this we construct a **frequency count**. Take S1's mark (60%), and draw a vertical line next to the appropriate percentage. So we have:

55%
60%   I
65% etc

Continue doing this until all the subjects' marks have been recorded. When you find a score occurring again, put another vertical line next to the first. If you reach a fifth score you put a diagonal line through the previous four. (It looks rather like a garden gate!)

If you did a frequency count for these scores it would look like this:

Score   Number of Ss achieving it
55%   II   (ie Two S's achieved 55%)
60%   III
65%   I
70%   I
75%   III
N=10 ("N" stands for Number of Ss)

Data can be summarised and presented in either "pictures" or "numbers". We will look at each in turn.

1 Pictures

The main ways of displaying results in pictures are tables, graphs, histograms, and pie charts.

Pie charts

Pie charts are circles (which might resemble a pie!) with segments cut out. Each segment represents a percentage of the whole. They give a very vivid impression of the share of something which the various groups have. They are useful if we know what all the factors or groups involved are, and if we know what the total amount is. We could use a pie chart to display what proportion of all the families in Britain lived in the various kinds of family organisations, eg two parent families, one parent families, single people, etc. We can find the official statistics for the total number of families that there are in Britain, and we can list just about all the family arrangements that people can make. We couldn't use a pie chart if we didn't know the totals. For example we can't know the total amount of aggression between children that occurs in primary schools, so we couldn't construct a pie chart to show what proportion of it involves kicking, hitting, spitting, throwing things etc.

A Pie Chart

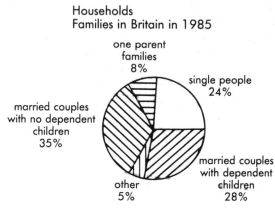

Households
Families in Britain in 1985

one parent
families
8%

single people
24%

married couples
with no dependent
children
35%

married couples
with dependent
children
28%

other
5%

Tables

Tables are the most basic way of presenting data. They can show data with great accuracy, up to many decimal places, for example:

Vocabulary use by time of day in 3 two year old children

Here are the number of words spoken by 3 two year old children during a 5 minute observation period just before lunch.

Here the same children are recorded in two conditions. Condition one was conducted before 10 am, and condition two was conducted after 7 pm.

Subject	Words
S1	37
S2	23
S3	11
N=3	

Subject	Condition 1 before 10 am	Condition 2 after 7 pm
S1	27	40
S2	35	35
S3	10	7
N=3		

Tables must always be clearly titled and labelled so that people can see the results "at a glance".

Exercise – Vocabulary

1 At what time of day does S1 talk the most?

2 Describe S2s speaking habits.

3 Which child is the most talkative?

4 Which is the least chatty child?

5 What do these tables tell you about the speaking habits of S1, S2, and S3?

Exercise – IVs and DVs

Read this description of an experiment.

An experimenter wanted to see if newborn chicks could recognise their food by its shape. He took two groups of chicks. Some were one day old, the others were one week old. He gave each group four, small, differently shaped objects which they could peck at. One resembled grain. The others were cubes, cones, and pyramids. On average the one day old chicks pecked 9 times at the cubes, 12 times at the pyramids, 6 times at the cones, and 48 times at the food shaped objects. The seven day olds pecked 4 times at the cones, 5 times at the pyramids, 7 times at the cubes, and 86 times at the food shaped objects.

1 Complete this table to show these results.

A Table to show the pecking behaviour of newborn chicks to different objects.

Age	"Food shapes"	Cubes	Cones	Pyramids
One day				
One week				

2 What were the IVs in this experiment?

3 How was the DV measured?

4 What conclusions would you draw from your table?

A Data Curve

Performance improves with study time

number of hours spent learning

Overlapping Curve

Two children's scores

four week period

Graphs and histograms

Graphs are used to show trends in how some aspects of behaviour change over time, or as the subject's experience changes. Here's a graph that shows the effect of flashing a light just before feeding some laboratory rats, and the number of them who began to twitch their whiskers.

Lines drawn on graphs are called **data curves** (even if they are straight lines). It is possible to have overlapping lines on a graph, to show comparisons, eg number of acts of helping, over a four week period before and after seeing Mr Punch behaving caringly towards other puppets.

Histograms (or "**bar charts**") are used to show the frequency (or number of times) with which a particular score occurs. For example, three groups of children saw some adults behaving aggressively towards a large doll. One group saw the adult behaving aggressively, and being congratulated for it, another group saw the aggressive adult, but there was no comment made by anyone else, and a third group saw the adult being punished for its aggression. The children were then given a large doll, and their behaviour towards it was recorded. On page 296 is a histogram showing the average number of aggressive acts performed towards the doll by each group of children.

With histograms, the scores are always placed on the horizontal axis, and the frequency, or how often each score occurs, is placed on the vertical axis.

Exercise – Histograms

Imagine that a journalist friend of yours is writing a report about a local school which is taking part in some research on intelligence testing. She asks if you'd help with the illustration, and you agree to construct a histogram to display these I.Q. test scores. ("I.Q." stands for "intelligence quotient". It has been used as a way of expressing someone's intellectual capacity.)

Here are a few hints . . . (a) count how many scores there are, (b) find the lowest score, (c) find the "interval" between the scores (what steps do they go up in?), (d) make a list of all the scores from lowest to highest, (e) find how many times each score occurs (eg how many Ss scored 120, how many scored 70 etc) by using a frequency count, (f) arrange these I.Q. scores in rank order along the bottom axis, (g) plot the frequency for each score on the vertical axis. Do all this now.

S1=140 S2=90   S3=80   S4=100 S5=110 S6=120 S7=50   S8=70
S9=90   S10=120 S11=90 S12=130 S13=100 S14=150 S15=110 S16=60
S17=130 S18=100 S19=140 S20=100 S21=120 S22=110 S23=60 S24=100
S25=130 S26=120 S27=110 S28=90 S29=80 S30=100 S31=70 S32=110
S33=80 S34=80 S35=70 S36=90

If you've constructed the histogram correctly, it should be perfectly symmetrical ("symmetrical" means equal on either side of the middle).

Which method to use?

At the end of the day which method you use to display your results will be largely your own personal choice, bearing in mind some of the points we've been making here. Tables are able to show data most accurately. If precise figures are necessary then they may best be displayed as part of a table. Graphs are useful for showing the way behaviour changes over time, or with experience, or with age, etc. They are good if some "trend" is being measured. They are also useful where two sets of scores can be overlapped. Pie charts are useful for showing percentages of the whole of something. If you happen to know what all the factors are, and what the whole is, pie charts can be very useful. Histograms are useful for showing the frequency with which certain scores occur.

2 Numbers

Apart from showing their data in the form of pictures, psychologists often want to know what a "typical", or "average" score is. There are three ways of finding a "middle" score. They are called the "**measures of central tendency**". It is also useful to know what the spread of scores is, between the lowest and highest scores. This is called the **range**.

The three "measures of central tendency"

The mean: The mean is found by adding all the scores together, and dividing by the number of scores. For example, five psychology students get the following percentages in their end of term test: 57%, 63%, 72%, 77% and 86%. Adding the scores together gives us 355, which, when divided by five (the number of scores) comes to 71. The mean average is 71%.

A Histogram

Results of 2 groups of children on an IQ test.

Group 1 (with practice)   Group 2 (no practice)

The three ways of describing the "middle" or "typical" score in a group of scores are the mean, median, and mode. Each has its uses, although the mean is probably the most widely used.

The median: All the scores are arranged in rank order, from lowest to highest, and the middle one is the median. In the scores 57, 63, 72, 77, and 86, the median is 72. If there is an odd number of scores the median is easy to find. Count the number of scores, and find the one where there are as many scores below it as there are above it. It will be the median. If there is an even number of scores the median is the mid point between the two central scores. Take the two in the centre, add them together, divide by 2, and there's the median. For example, in the scores 57, 63, 72, 77, 81, and 86, the median is the mid point between 72 and 77, that is $72 + 77 = 149 \div 2 = 74.5$.

The mode: The mode is simply the score that occurs most often. If we construct a frequency count it is the score that has most marks against it. If three people score 12/20, whilst only two people score 13/20, then the mode is 12. The mode in these scores is five, because there are more marks for five than for any of the other numbers.

1	I
2	I
3	II
4	III
5	IIII
6	II

Exercise – Central tendency

1 Here are the results of a control, and an experimental group, in an experiment on reaction time and tiredness. The experimental group's reaction time was measured by their score in three versions of a space invaders game, and they were tested just before bedtime. The controls were tested at midday.
Experimental group scores: 17, 32, 34, 58, 69, 70, 98, 142
Control group scores: 61, 62, 64, 65, 65, 66, 68, 69
(a) Find the mean average for each.
(b) Can you think of any way in which this research could be confounded.

2 Find the median of the following two sets of scores:
(a) 78, 97, 102, 109, 131, 197, 201
(b) 9, 6, 0, 1, 14, 26, 2

3 Do a frequency count, then find the mode, of the following scores:
(a) 3, 3, 9, 1, 7, 6, 1, 0, 1, 0, 9, 8, 5, 8, 6, 3, 1, 2, 7, 2, 8, 3, 5, 9, 8, 3, 1, 3
(b) 17, 12, 19, 17, 15, 13, 14, 12, 11, 10, 19, 16, 18, 17, 14, 13, 12, 11, 15, 18, 10, 18, 17, 14, 18, 13, 11, 12, 14, 17, 18, 14, 10, 19, 17

The Range

Sometimes knowing the mean, median, or mode simply isn't enough. Here are the scores for ten psychology students in their class test: 45%, 47%, 47%, 49%, 49%, 50%, 52%, 53%, 53%, and 55%. The "average score" is 50%. It seems that everyone in the group is remembering about half of the work. The mean seems to give a reasonable indication of the progress of the whole class. In another class, the ten students scored 20%, 21%, 22%, 32%, 53%, 60%, 65%, 70%, 77%, and 80%. The mean average is still 50%, but some children are obviously understanding a lot more than others. A teacher would treat these two classes quite differently. The difference between the highest and the lowest score is called the **range**. The **range** is simply found by subtracting the lowest score from the highest score. In the scores 57, 63, 72, 77, 81, 86, the range would be $86 - 57 = 29$.

Exercise – Displaying results in numbers

1 What is the range of the following scores?
27, 37, 42, 45, 51, 55, 70, 72, 83, 87, 98, 98

2 Results (by %) for a group of boys and girls on a literacy test

Boys				Girls			
S1	58	S11	13	S1	86	S11	37
S2	61	S12	45	S2	72	S12	56
S3	54	S13	64	S3	53	S13	75
S4	47	S14	52	S4	68	S14	29
S5	76	S15	86	S5	83	S15	85
S6	75	S16	75	S6	93	S16	79
S7	34	S17	35	S7	54	S17	35
S8	44	S18	43	S8	53	S18	75
S9	92	S19	37	S9	57	S19	79
S10	64	S20	42	S10	87	S20	78

(a) What is the total sample size?
(b) What is the range of scores for boys?
(c) What is the mode of all the scores?
(d) What is the mean average score for boys?
(e) What is the median score for girls?

One other type of result that we mentioned earlier comes from **correlation studies**.

Correlation Studies

As we mentioned earlier, there are some areas of human life on which it isn't possible to conduct experiments, observations, case studies, surveys or other kinds of research. Psychologists can't conduct research on things which might be dangerous, impractical, immoral, unethical, illegal etc.

Exercise – Testing hypotheses in psychology

Here are some hypotheses that couldn't be tested using the methods discussed so far.
(a) "Removing a child from its mother and bringing it up in a deprived orphanage will limit emotional development."
(b) "A father who was abused when he was a child is more likely to abuse his own children."
(c) "Severe punishment stops bad behaviour in children."

1 Think of three examples of behaviour on which you couldn't conduct an experiment.

2 Write as many reasons as you can think of for why psychologists couldn't do such experiments. (HINT. Think of as many PRACTICAL problems as you can first.)

Developmental psychologists are often interested in "things which go together". Some children suffer from high levels of anxiety, others have low levels of anxiety. Some children have more bed wetting "accidents" than others. A psychologist may want to know whether increasing levels of anxiety and the greater likelihood of bedwetting "go together". Others may want to know if growing up in environments which have less and less stimulation "goes with" lower and lower I.Q. scores.

Here is the procedure for finding the **correlation**: we will take the two variables "number of years spent in a deprived orphanage", and "level of intellectual development". First, find a group of people who spent various lengths of time in a deprived orphanage. Ideally the larger the group the better. Second, find an accurate and acceptable test for "intellectual development". Third, give each person the test. Fourth statistically analyse (correlate) each person's I.Q. score, and the number of years that person spent in the deprived orphanage. This correlation will produce a number which expresses the relationship between the two variables.

Correlation is represented by a number between -1 and $+1$. The greater the amounts of two variables tending to occur together, the nearer the number will be to $+1$. Children's weight and height are **positively correlated**, that is taller children tend to weigh more than shorter children. This is nowhere near "always true". Some tall children are quite light, and some shorter children are quite heavy. (The correlation for height and weight amongst British adult males is 0.47, and for females is 0.35, *Knight 1984*). We could test whether weight and height are positively correlated amongst children by measuring the weight and height of a large number (10 000 ought to be enough) of them. Correlating the scores for height with the scores for weight should produce a positive number. This is called a **positive correlation**.

If two variables such as "how late someone stays up every night" and "the quality of the work they produce" were correlated we'd probably find that children who didn't stay up too late too often, generally produced better work, whereas those who consistently stayed up late generally produced poorer work. If children who always went to bed very late always produced the poorest schoolwork, then the variables "time of going to bed" and "quality of schoolwork" would have a **perfect positive correlation**, represented by $+1$. This is rarely found in the real world, and certainly not in psychology. There'll always be some people who seem able to stay up late and still produce good work.

Negative correlation occurs when increasing the amount of one variable goes with a decrease in the amount of another. Increasing the amount of anxiety in children's lives may correlate with a reduction in their emotional development. A negative correlation of -1 means that when one variable is at its maximum, another one is at its minimum. The variables simply do not occur together.

A correlation of 0 means that there is no relationship between the variables. For example if someone correlated the variable "increase in size of vocabulary between three to seven year olds in Wolverhampton" with the variable "number of apples sold in Oxford each year between 1950 and 1989" they would almost certainly find a correlation of 0. Apple consumption in Oxford and children's speaking habits in Wolverhampton are unlikely to be statistically related.

Apart from expressing correlations as numbers, scientists also express them in pictures. The score each subject makes is plotted on a **scattergram**. The value of one variable is plotted in one axis (eg the number of years spent in an orphanage), and the value of another variable (eg emotional stability) on the other.

Scattergrams

Each *x* on the scattergram is the point where the pair of scores that each child made on the two dimensions named on the axes would cross. One of the children here spent three years in an orphange and scored 50% in the emotional stability test. Another child spent 11 years in the orphanage and only scored 10%.

Looking at the general spread of the marks gives an idea of the extent to which the two variables go together. This scattergram shows that the children who spent longest in an orphanage had lowest scores on the tests of emotional stability. Spending a long time in a deprived environment, and getting high scores in tests of emotional stability are negatively correlated.

Three scattergrams to show correlations

The first **scattergram** shows an example of two variables which are perfectly negatively correlated. It shows the scores for the amount of emotional disturbance that twelve children suffered during their childhood, and their I.Q. scores as adults. The children who suffered the most disruption had the lowest I.Q. scores. So the greater amount of the variable "emotional disturbance" there was, the less the amount of the variable I.Q. there was.

The second scattergram shows that the two variables "amount eaten" and "number of letters written" are not correlated at all. This is represented by a correlation of 0. Some of the subjects ate a lot, some ate a little. Some wrote many letters, some wrote few. The two variables are not statistically related.

The third scattergram shows the two variables "doing all of one's homework", and "getting good results in tests" are perfectly positively correlated. The more homework each child did, the higher marks they achieved in exams.

There is something extremely important you must remember about correlations. Correlations only show that two variables are statistically related. They do not prove that one variable causes the other. Some third variable could cause them both. For example the variable "number of violent films watched" might correlate with "amount of aggression shown by children". A third variable which explains both these things might be that the children's parents watch violent films and are aggressive. The children may be imitating their parents. Correlation can only describe a *statistical relationship* between two variables, it cannot explain how that relationship comes about.

Three Scattergrams

Emotional disturbance and IQ scores

IQ scores

perfect negative (−1)

Amount of food and number of letters written to friends

letter written

no correlation (0)

Amount of homeworks handed in and exams passed

exam mark

perfect positive (+1)

Psychologists often have to use correlational methods, so be careful that you do not confuse them with experiments. Of all the methods available to psychologists experiments are the only ones that are sometimes able to show cause.

Exercise – Correlation 2

1 Fill in five scores which might show the direction of the following scattergrams
(a) "lots of stimulation" and "enquiring mind", and
(b) "darkness", and "clarity of perception", and
(c) "speed of running", and "children's musical knowledge".

2 Complete this table by ticking the appropriate box to describe the correlation

Type of correlation	Negative correlation	No correlation	Positive correlation
(a) "lots of stimulation" and "extent of enquiring mind"			
(b) "amount of darkness", and "clarity of perception"			
(c) "speed of running", and "amount of children's musical knowledge".			

3 What two variables were the German researchers trying to correlate, in "Children's Intelligence"? (See page 15.)

(See page 15.)

REVIEW – Correlation

Correlation is a statistical technique for measuring the extent to which two variables occur together. Positive correlation (up to +1) means that the more there is of one variable, the more there will be of another one. Negative correlation (down to −1) means that the greater amount that there is of one variable, the less there will be of another.

Some cautions in interpreting psychological research

We've looked at several of the main methods that psychologists use for gathering their information, and at the main ways in which they analyse and communicate it. By now you will have realised that none of the methods psychologists use for gathering information are perfect. There are three types of problems with their methods. The first consists of problems with subjects. The second involves problems with situations (and the researchers themselves). Thirdly there are problems in drawing conclusions from the research.

Problems with subjects

These are to do with subject variables.

All children have different intellectual abilities, memory abilities, personalities, willingness to co-operate, desire to tell the truth etc. Can we be sure that their participation was honest? The very fact that someone is "in some research" may alter the way they behave.

Exercise – An extract from a fifth form girl's diary

MONDAY five o'clock: Some lecturers from the university were visiting school today. They came into our class after lunch and asked if any of us fancied being in a psychology experiment. The guy who asked was really nice. I wanted to volunteer straight away, but Jane was shaking her head. At break she said she thought the lecturers were old and ugly. Everyone calls her boyfriend "Gonzo" so what does she know? I managed to persuade her though, at least we'll be out of school for a day.

TUESDAY Just had tea: Jane said she'd changed her mind about doing the experiment. I had to promise her I'd go ice skating with her and Gonzo next week before she'd come. Ugh. I HATE ICE SKATING, and Gonzo is a drip.

WEDNESDAY 10 pm: Must get an early night tonight, I want to be fresh for the experiment in the morning. Jane's gone to the midweek disco. She's stupid 'cos she won't be home 'til midnight.

THURSDAY Lunch time: Jane was really grumpy when I met her this morning. I wasn't going to let her spoil my day though. When we got to the psychology department the same guy who'd been at school met us. He explained that it was an experiment on "perception". We had to look through a hole into this machine which would flash three letters and a big number at us. Straight away we had to count backwards from the number we'd seen until he asked us what the letters had been. I thought it would be easy, but Jane needed it explaining again. This research must be really important, so I'm going to do my best this afternoon.
Five pm: Just got home. Had a great day. I got loads of my tests right. Hardly any of the others did though. Jane couldn't even count backwards half the time. Anyway she split up with Gonzo last night so I don't have to go skating with them next week. BRILLIANT!

1 Write a paragraph which explains why this research may have been confounded. Include as many examples of confounding subject variables as you can find.

2 How was the sample of British children chosen in "Children's Intelligence"? (See page 15.)

3 Do you think this produced a representative, typical cross section of British seven to ten year olds? Explain your answer.

4 Explain why the German sampling was better than the British attempt.

Problems with situations

These are to do with situational variables.

All the members of each experimental group must be tested under the same conditions in the same situation as all the other members. If the weather is warmer, the place brighter, the other people friendlier, the time is different, the background noise is greater etc then these situational variables may affect the children's behaviour.

How Ss are used in the research can also alter their behaviour. Social psychologists have shown that people behave quite differently when they are the only person being tested than they do when they are in groups. People are more likely to agree with what the other people are doing and saying when in a group. People are less likely to say and do what they really think and feel if they know that other people are listening and watching.

One particular situational variable is the researcher himself or herself. His or her behaviour towards the children may affect the

REVIEW – Cautions

We can't always accept all of the findings from psychological research because subjects vary, situations vary, and there are problems with the way some research is designed.

children's behaviour. This is called "experimenter bias", or "experimenter effects". If the experimenter is in a bad temper, tired, or hungry, etc, and it shows in their attitude or behaviour, then this might affect how the child feels about doing the research.

Drawing conclusions from data

Before finally deciding to accept the findings of any particular research we might want to ask the following questions:

1 Was the sample representative of the population to which the results are to be generalised?

2 Were the tests reliable? Research is described as reliable if it would show the same results if we repeated the test (using the same subjects), in the future.

3 Are the tests valid? Validity means "does the research actually measure what it says it measures?" Many I.Q. tests, for example, are criticised for not actually measuring "intelligence" at all.

4 Many psychological studies can only show correlations between variables, we cannot say that one causes the other.

5 Scientists should never generalise from case studies, and it's never wise to generalise to all members of any group from a study conducted on a small sample of it.

Exercise – Problems with research

1 Write a paragraph which summarises the main problems people face when understanding the conclusions from psychological research.

2 The research described in "Children's Intelligence" is badly flawed. Outline as many of the differences between the British and German research as you can, and say why each makes the research unacceptable.

3 Write a report on the research activity that was referred to at the beginning of the chapter. Comment on as many of these things as possible.

   The type of research, the aim of the research, the methods used, the target population, the sample used, the procedures, the results, and the conclusions.

Background reading – Experimenter effects

An experiment by Rosenthal and Jacobsen in "Oak School", a Californian elementary school, showed how teachers affected the performance of some of their pupils. The teachers were told that the children were being given a new kind of intelligence test which could predict which pupils were about to improve very dramatically, in their schoolwork. They didn't know that Jacobson and Rosenthal had randomly chosen 20% of the children who would be "bloomers". After a year those 20% had developed considerably! Obviously the teachers must have behaved differently towards those children, although they were sure that they hadn't.

If you could have secretly observed this class during the year, what differences do you imagine you'd notice in the treatment of the "bloomers" and the others?

3 Early Views on Emotional Development

In the next three chapters we will be looking at the special bond that develops between an infant and the person, or people, who look after it. If you watch parents communicating with their babies you will notice a number of differences in the way they behave, compared to their usual behaviour. They talk more, their voices are lower, there's more repetition of phrases, there's more handling, and they are generally more warm and loving. The baby, in turn, soon learns to recognise the people who take special care of it, and who seem to enjoy being with it. They develop a special emotional relationship which many psychologists have seen as being extremely important to future mental health. That's not to say that everyone sees this early bond being so important. Humans seem very flexible in the way they develop, and all sorts of early disadvantages can be overcome later. In this section we'll explore the theories and findings concerning emotional development in babies.

Most newborn animals are fairly defenceless and need an adult to look after them. Most baby animals cannot catch their own food, and mammals, for example, need their mother's milk. Without an adult to feed the baby, many would die. Other animal species feed on the young and inexperienced too. Birds of prey, for example, will catch and kill young monkeys, particularly if no older monkeys are offering any protection to the young. Most infant animals are reared for the first weeks and months by one or both of their parents. Lionesses will hunt other animals, and drag their bodies back for their young to feed from. Her mate will stay with the young. One of a pair of birds will leave the nest to hunt for food for their young, leaving the other to protect them. So why do parents and babies tend to stay together? Many baby animals must be born with some kind of an urge to form some kind of a special bond with their parents, and their parents may have some urge to form a bond with them. This two way bond usually means that the newborn will try to stay close to its parent, and that the adult will feed and protect the infant. Some argue that humans too have a similar sort of bond. In humans it is called an **attachment bond**.

The first major investigation of this attachment bond was conducted by the influential British child psychiatrist Dr John Bowlby. Bowlby maintains that this bond must be successfully made between human babies and their mothers. It forms the basis for healthy mental development. However not everyone agrees with Bowlby's views.

In this chapter we will be looking at:

1 John Bowlby's influential views on attachment and childcare.
2 What evidence Bowlby's conclusions were based on, and was it scientifically acceptable?
3 What impact did his conclusions have on society?

What two reasons are given in this paragraph for why some infant animals need parents? Would the same reasons be true of humans? Can you think of any other things that human mothers provide for their babies?

Dr John Bowlby

Very many psychologists supported theories which saw our biological inheritance as having a major effect on our early behaviour. Write a brief explanation of Bowlby's view of the role of the mother in early childrearing.

4 What other evidence existed which might not support Bowlby's claims?

5 So is Dr Bowlby right?

1 The Early Research by John Bowlby

During the 1940s and 1950s, John Bowlby studied how and why babies make attachments. The main theories available at the time all maintained that the need to make a bond was something that was part of our biological inheritance. The idea of women having "maternal instincts" to have and care for babies was widely believed. Bowlby collected research findings about children's emotional development, particularly children who had been separated from their mothers. He reasoned that one good way of discovering the importance of forming and keeping a successful attachment would be to study children who hadn't been allowed to form one, or who had formed one and then had it broken.

Bowlby theorised that if children whose attachments were disrupted did not develop healthy personalities, then this might be evidence that unsuccessful attachments may lead to abnormal personality development. Bowlby also noted evidence from studies of animals who had been deliberately reared without their natural mothers. He became convinced that this early bond was very important for future mental health. The role of the mother is obviously extremely important too. Bowlby claimed that children do need their natural mothers, or at least a permanent mother substitute, with whom to form an attachment.

Bowlby thought that babies have a biological need, or **instinct**, to form an attachment. They need to get near to their mothers, or to get their mothers to come to them, particularly when they are unhappy, or unsure about something. Babies use such genetically inherited skills as smiling, crying, gazing, grasping, clinging, babbling, crawling, and anything else that will keep their mothers close. Bowlby believed that this would be a two way relationship, and that mothers also have a biological need to be near, and to protect, their young.

Bowlby thought that instincts, which are a part of our genetic makeup, must not be frustrated, otherwise normal, healthy mental development could be disrupted. He found several studies conducted

---

Background reading – Attachments

An attachment is an emotional bond which develops between an infant and an adult. When it is formed the baby will try to stay close to that adult, and will appear to want to be cared for by the adult. By the end of the first year the infant will not be afraid of that adult, whilst it will appear frightened of other adults. The infant will also become distressed if it is separated from those adults to whom it is attached.

Here's a definition. . . . Attachment is "an affectionate two way relationship that is formed between an infant and another person". A respected colleague of Bowlby's, Mary Ainsworth, defines it as "An affectional tie or bond that an individual . . . forms between himself and another specific individual."

during the 1930s and 1940s which had shown that children who had never formed an attachment, or whose attachments were threatened, suffered all kinds of emotional problems later.

Exercise – Early Ideas

Here is a quote from Bowlby's 1948 book *Maternal Care and Mental Health*.

"Among the most significant developments in psychiatry during the past quarter of a century has been the steady growth of evidence that the quality of parental care which a child received in his earliest years is of vital importance for his future mental health ... it is this complex, rich and rewarding relationship with the mother in the early years, varied in countless ways by relations with the father and with siblings, that child psychiatrists and many others believe to underline the development of character and mental health ... the evidence is now that the prolonged deprivation of the young child of maternal care may have grave and far reaching effects in his character and so on the whole of his future life."

1 How would we see "... this complex, rich and rewarding relationship with its mother ..." in action?

2 Put this sentence in your own words "... prolonged deprivation of the young child of maternal care may have grave and far reaching effects in his character and so on the whole of his future life."

3 What sort of "grave and far reaching effects" do you think maternal deprivation might have?

Exercise – Attachments

1 What is meant by the term "attachment"?

2 Outline Bowlby's main conclusion about the relationship between babies and mothers.

3 What sorts of things do parents do which might encourage the baby to attach to them? (HINT look back to your answer to Question 1 in the previous exercise.)

4 Why do you imagine mothers might want to attach to their babies?

5 Looking at your last two answers, is attachment the result of genetic factors which we are born with, or do we learn to make attachments, or both? Give reasons for your answer.

Bonding Behaviour

REVIEW – Bowlby on attachments

John Bowlby believed that humans have some biological need to have a close, loving bond with their mothers, or a permanent substitute mother. If this bond isn't allowed to form, or is broken, emotional development will be disrupted.

Background reading – Biological needs or instincts

Instincts are "unlearned patterns of behaviour that exist in all members of a particular species, and which appear under certain circumstances". We are born with certain instincts which will automatically make us behave in certain ways when particular things happen. If something suddenly frightens you, your instinct to survive prepares your body for running away, fighting etc. These instincts are said to have "survival value". Different instincts and reflexes exist in different species, for example, male monkeys have an instinct that triggers threatening behaviour towards other males who challenge them for their mate. Lionesses do the same if some danger threatens their cubs. Male sticklebacks will attack anything that is the same colour as themselves. (Any idea why?)

2 John Bowlby's evidence for claiming that babies need their mothers

In addition to his understanding and experience of psychoanalysis, Bowlby's evidence comes from his own research, some other research on children, and some animal studies. We will study each in turn.

During the 1930s and 1940s Bowlby worked at a clinic for mentally disturbed adolescents. He selected 44 of his "patients" who were thieves. A few had been convicted of theft. He studied their backgrounds and their characters, between 1936–1939. Their case notes revealed that 17 of them (39%) had been separated from their mothers for six months or more before they were five years old. This *maternal separation* would have disrupted the child's attachment. Bowlby took another 44 adolescents who had emotional problems, but who were not thieves. Only two of them had been separated from their mothers. Bowlby concluded from these observations that *maternal deprivation contributed to delinquency*.

Bowlby published his conclusions in a scientific paper entitled *44 Juvenile Thieves* in which he states: "There is a very strong case indeed for believing that prolonged separation of a child from his mother (or mother substitute) during the first five years of life stands foremost among the causes of delinquent character development."

Criticism Bowlby is saying that separating a child and its mother for some time, during the child's first five years of life, makes it more likely that the child will behave like a delinquent. His evidence in this study comes from finding almost 40% of a small sample of just 44 thieves had spent some time apart from their mothers during their early childhood. He seems to have overlooked many other variables which could equally well explain their delinquent behaviour, including the reasons for the separation in the first place, and what had happened to the children since the separation.

Exercise – Causes of delinquency

Let's take an imaginary delinquent who was maternally deprived as a child. Let's look at the reasons for his separation. Imagine that the mother was an alcoholic who wasn't able to care for the child, and that the father looked after the child most of the time. Imagine that when the child was two years old his mother had an accident and had to go into hospital for several months to recover. The father had to get a job to pay hospital fees, transport etc so the child was cared for by a neighbour.

1 Who cared for the child most of the time before it was two years old?

2 Who is the child mostly being separated from?

3 Suggest a possible explanation for any distress the child shows, apart from maternal deprivation.

4 Imagine that this child is a teenager, living in London, during the economic depression before the war. If you can't imagine, find out what it was like, and give three possible reasons for why he might become a delinquent.

5 Bowlby is using information from his case studies.
  (a) What is the main drawback of the case study method?
  (b) How reliable are generalisations made from case studies?

John Bowlby's *44 juvenile thieves* are a biased sample since they were drawn from a target population of juvenile thieves. If we wanted to study the effects of maternal deprivation, our target population should be "all those who had been separated", not "all juvenile thieves". Children get separated from their mothers for all sorts of reasons, for example, death, long term hospitalisation, divorce etc. They don't all become delinquents. Why should short term deprivation lead to delinquency, when long term deprivation may not?

John Bowlby's analysis of his case studies revealed that 14 of the 17 juvenile thieves who had been maternally deprived were particularly cold and uncaring about their crimes, their victims, or even themselves. They seemed to have no shame for what they'd done. They appeared not to have any guilt feelings. They admitted that they almost certainly would continue to steal. They seemed quite detached from "normal" standards of decency. Bowlby believed that these cold and uncaring youngsters had suffered greatly from losing their mother's love. They appeared to be incapable of normal emotion. Bowlby described their condition as "**affectionless psychopathy**". Only two of the sample of non thieves showed similar affectionless symptoms.

Exercise – 44 Juvenile Thieves

Outline the main scientific objections to Bowlby's study of juvenile thieves.

Other research on children noted by Bowlby

After the Second World War there were many thousands of orphans and refugees who needed care and attention. It wasn't possible to organise detailed and controlled psychological research on a large scale, but numerous small scale studies and observations were done, all of which seemed to point to the fact that children without parents suffer all kinds of problems. In 1950 the World Health Organisation appointed John Bowlby to write a report summarising the current knowledge about the relationship between children's mental health and being homeless. Its conclusions were to have some very far reaching effects, and was to revolutionise people's views about attachment. To find support for his ideas about attachment John Bowlby turned to research done in America on some maternally deprived children.

In the 1940s **Rene Spitz** and **Katharine Wolf** had observed 123 babies for the first year of their lives. They were being cared for by their unmarried mothers in a penal institution. When the infants were between six and eight months old their mothers were temporarily moved to another block and the infants were looked after by other people. During the three month separation "the child either did not see its mother at all, or at best, once a week." Each baby was looked after by the mother of another child, or a girl in the later stages of pregnancy. Spitz and Wolf noted that the babies cried more, they lost their

In psychology "affect" generally refers to such human mental events as emotion, mood, feelings etc. Psychopath used to be the general term which described someone who had no moral feelings, no sense of guilt or shame for anything they'd done.

REVIEW – Bowlby's own research

From his own studies of 44 juvenile thieves, Bowlby concluded that being separated from the person with whom one had formed an attachment may lead to retarded emotional development, characterised by a lack of normal feelings. Delinquency would be one sympton of this "affectionless psychopathy".

John Bowlby became well known and highly respected for his research on the early mother/child relationship. He collected findings from several other studies.

Do you think these reactions prove that each child is missing its mother? Can you think of any other possible explanation for their behaviour?

appetites, and they failed to gain weight. The researchers concluded that these reactions were the result of being separated from their mothers. When they were reunited with their mothers their conditions returned to what they had been before the separation.

Criticism Spitz and Wolf showed that there are short term physical effects of maternal deprivation, despite the high quality nursing they received. But would these effects continue if other adults continued to provide high quality loving care? We don't know what these babies were like as adults, so we don't know if their separation had any permanent effects. This study doesn't prove that babies need their mothers. It does show that they become upset and depressed when their routines are disturbed.

Bowlby also noted a longitudinal study of two groups of 15 orphans conducted by a New York psychologist, **William Goldfarb** in 1943. The children in each group were matched for sex, age, and the social class background of their parents. Almost all of one group had been fostered from an understaffed orphanage before they were nine months old, and had grown up in a normal family. The other group had all spent at least the first three years in the orphanage before they were fostered. Goldfarb visited each child four times. Firstly when they were three years old, then at six, eight, and twelve. He measured their intelligence, language skills, social maturity, ability to form relationships etc. In each case the "early adopted children" did much better than the "late adopted children". This was just the kind of evidence Bowlby was after since it showed that those who had a "mother" earliest did best.

Criticism The children may not have had the same amount of intelligence to begin with. Remember Goldfarb matched the two samples for age, sex, and social class background. He didn't match them for intelligence. It isn't possible to test the intelligence of babies. It's quite likely that the children who were adopted earliest were chosen by their new parents because they appeared more lively, more alert, and brighter as babies. If they were brighter as babies they may continue as bright children. Also the children brought up in the orphanage lacked all sorts of stimulation and contact, not just maternal stimulation. For the first nine months they were isolated in cubicles to prevent the spread of any infectious diseases, so had little human contact. This group lived in almost complete social isolation during the first year of life, and the next two years weren't much better since the nurses didn't have the time or training to spend long with any individual child. This severe lack of contact and stimulation with people may well have had an effect on future development, but may have nothing to do with being separated from one's mother.

What is a "longitudinal study"? What research design did Goldfarb use?

Evidence from many other observations, correlational studies, and case studies were reported by Bowlby throughout the 1950s and 1960s. Although he modified some of his earlier claims Bowlby still maintains that the evidence supports the view that babies need their mothers, or a permanent substitute mother, and that separation during the first five years must be avoided.

Bowlby was impressed by some observations being done by his colleagues **James** and **Joyce Robertson** in England between 1948 and 1952, and later during the 1960s. These concerned children, mostly between 18 months and three years, who went into hospital or residential nurseries, for periods of from a few days to several weeks. The Robertsons were convinced that, contrary to medical opinion, separating babies from their mothers was harmful. They obtained a cine camera and set out to make some filmed observations of children during their separation which could be shown to as many people who were involved with childcare as possible.

Exercise – One separated child

Here is a summary of the observations of one separated child.

John (aged 17 months), was put into a fairly typical residential nursery for nine days whilst his mother had a second child in hospital. His father was at work all day, and there were no relatives nearby to look after the child. Four of the five other children had been in the nursery almost all of their lives. They were aged 15 months to two years and were noisy, demanding, and aggressive. John was a quiet, loving child. He seemed troubled by the noise and fighting going on around him, and tried to get near the nurses for some attention. They had to spend most of their time with the more demanding children, and John was left out. His father visited him in the evening, and John was obviously happy to see him, and wanted to go home with him. On one occasion John fetched his "outside shoes". The child continued to try to get some attention from the nurses, and even when he succeeded they soon had to put him down to tend to one of the others. John protested at first, and became angry that he couldn't get attention. After some days John's distress worsened. He started to cry pitifully, for long periods of time.

This distress lasted for several days. The nurses gave John all the attention they could, but it was nowhere near enough. He began to refuse food, and he wouldn't sleep. He had a slight cold, and was sick. With each day that passed John's condition worsened. His cries of distress became huge sobs of despair.

As the separation neared its end, John's behaviour changed again. He stopped trying to get near to the nurses. Instead he would play with whatever toys he could, particularly a large cuddly toy. He began to ignore his father on his nightly visits. John slowly became emotionally detached. When his mother finally came he didn't seem to want to know her. He wouldn't go to her, wouldn't look at her, and resisted her attempts to comfort him. John had started by being loving, and seeking companionship. Over the nine day separation this changed to being distressed, despairing, and finally to becoming emotionally detached.

Over the next few months, it was obvious that John had changed. He cried more, had occasional tantrums, and didn't show affection as he used to. One day, when John was six years old, he looked up at his mother and said "Mummy, why am I so horrible to you?" His early experiences may have had long term effects.

1 Why was John separated from his parents?

2 How many children were in the nursery altogether?

3 What was the general level of behaviour like?

4 How did John respond in the first few days?

5 What was John's attitude towards his father's visits in the early days?

6 What changes occurred in John's behaviour after the first few days?

7 How does the passage describe the change in John's emotional state?
8 How would you describe John's behaviour, as the separation came to an end?
9 How did John's behaviour change in the months after the separation?
10 Does this study prove that maternal separation leads to emotional instability? Explain your answer.

After making several such studies, the Robertsons' concluded that children who are separated from their mothers pass through the same sequence of behaviour. It starts with **Distress**. This gives way to **Despair**, and finally becomes **Detached**. Detachment refers to how the children refuse to allow anyone to become involved with them.

How convincing is Bowlby's "evidence" so far?

These studies rely mostly on observation. Whilst James Robertson filmed, Joyce sat in her corner, watching and taking notes. Observations can still sometimes miss important events, and can be interpreted in different ways. Certainly the medical profession were very critical of the Robertson's conclusions when they were shown some of the filmed observations. Other kinds of studies may point to probable connections between variables, but they can't *prove* that one caused the other. The only way to be certain is to do experiments.

Obviously we can't do controlled experiments on the variables "maternal deprivation" and "emotional development in children". We'd never find parents willing to let us conduct such experiments. Where could we keep the isolated children? How could we feed and care for an isolated baby? Who would pay for the study? Who would publish the findings? And what about the moral and ethical implications of such research? Not to mention the legal, political, and social implications. Surely no psychologist would want to do such research anyway? The same restrictions do not apply to animals. Despite these reservations the pioneering work of James and Joyce Robertson does provide a major insight into what happens to children who are separated from their caregivers and put into residential nurseries.

Exercise – Separated children

1 What is meant by "maternal deprivation"?
2 What name did John Bowlby give to the condition which described someone who appeared to have no emotions and no guilt feelings?
3 Bowlby claimed that we would have developed a need to be near our mothers through evolution because it would have had some "survival value". What does "survival value" mean?
4 Summarise and evaluate Bowlby's evidence from these three studies on children.

Some animal studies

Many of Bowlby's early ideas on the importance of forming a relationship shortly after birth appeared to be confirmed discoveries made by an Austrian ethologist, **Konrad Lorenz**. (**Ethology** is the science which tries to explain the biological reasons for animal behaviour in their natural habitat.)

REVIEW – Other research on children

John Bowlby's collection of studies of "institutionalised" children suggested to him that the lack of a mother can have disastrous consequences for healthy mental development. However all the studies he quoted can be interpreted in other ways.

To provide conclusive "evidence" scientists need to do experiments. Since these aren't possible with humans Bowlby turned to some studies with animals. What do experiments allow us to do, that observations, correlations, case studies etc do not?

Ethology

During the 1930s Konrad Lorenz had observed that newly hatched greylag geese will follow the first thing they see after hatching. It appeared to be an *instinctive* reaction, although Lorenz did find that not all goslings had it. Presumably the "instinct" tells them that the first thing they see must be their "mother", or at least a caregiver. Lorenz noticed a group of goslings following him, just after hatching, so they couldn't have had much idea about what their caregiver looked like! They must have *learned* that he was their "mother". Lorenz called this specific behaviour "**imprinting**". Imprinting is a very rapid form of attachment. Lorenz was the first to scientifically investigate imprinting. At first he thought it only existed in goslings.

He conducted an experiment by removing some eggs from a mother goose and hatching them separately. As each hatched he showed the gosling a particular object, including a matchbox tied to a length of string! Sure enough they imprinted and followed whatever they were shown. He kept one egg on its own so that when it hatched the first thing the gosling saw was him. It followed him everywhere, even ignoring other geese when it was old enough to mate. In another experiment he mixed some goslings who were imprinted on him with some who were imprinted on their mother, putting them all under a box. When the box was lifted the goslings immediately followed the thing they were imprinted on. Lorenz concluded that imprinting would be irreversible.

Lorenz found the goslings were particularly sensitive to this "following" behaviour for just a few hours after birth. If they didn't imprint during this "**critical period**", then they wouldn't imprint at all. Similar reactions were observed in some other animals. Lorenz hatched a Jackdaw chick and it imprinted on him. When it was mature it tried to mate with him.

Some Experiments on imprinting

Many laboratory experiments and natural observations have been conducted on imprinting since Lorenz first discovered it. Most conclude that imprinting isn't a simple reflexive response to follow the first thing an animal sees, but a specific kind of learning, as Lorenz had shown.

Hess conducted several laboratory experiments to discover the kind of stimuli ducks would imprint on. These included toys, models of ducks, even flashing lights! In one experiment he found that ducklings

Imprinting

Background reading – Lorenz

Lorenz concluded that imprinting

1 is totally automatic,

2 is permanent, and irreversible,

3 occurs very briefly, just once in an animal's life, in a "critical period" during which time the animal must see some object to imprint on,

4 affects several important areas of later behaviour, for example, choice of partner for mating,

5 and doesn't always happen!

Could there be anything similar in humans? Are we born with any kind of need to imprint on our mothers? Humans can't follow their mothers because they can't crawl for the first few months, or walk for a few months after that. Bowlby believed that humans would have some instinctive needs for early bonding behaviour, even if they weren't the same as imprinting.

would imprint on a remote controlled model duck, especially if there were some obstacles in its path. In fact the more effort the animal had to put into following the object, the stronger the imprinting seemed to become. Hess proposed that imprinting could occur during a critical period between 12 and 17 hours after hatching.

Guiton, however, showed that imprinting wasn't quite so inflexible as Lorenz and Hess seem to think. He kept ducklings alone until after the critical period had ended. He then showed them a moving object, and they imprinted on it. He suggested that it's not just time that is important in deciding what an animal imprints on, but other factors in the environment. He uses the term "sensitive period" rather than "critical period". Guiton also found that imprinting was reversible. Putting some cockerels who had imprinted on some yellow rubber gloves in a pen with some hens soon changed their sexual preferences.

Exercise – Ethology

1 Give two reasons why Lorenz could not have used human subjects instead of geese in his research.

2 What is imprinting, and how can we tell if an animal has imprinted on something?

3 What is meant by the term "sensitive period"?

4 Why might the "following response" have some "survival value" for the goslings?

Some research with non-human primates

All non-human primates spend a lot of their time near to their mother. As infants they cling on to her, and as they grow they rarely stray very far away. Females are more likely to stay close to their mothers than males. Perhaps studies of their attachment bonding may provide clues to the role of attachment in humans.

"Primates" are the highest order of mammals. Human beings are amongst one of the three orders of primates.

A number of studies had been conducted on gorillas and chimpanzees, and some experiments had been done on rhesus monkeys and baboons. John Bowlby believed that some of the evidence from these studies confirmed his views on the importance of the early bond.

Background reading – The advantages of using (non-human) primates in research

1 Apes and chimps are closest to humans in the evolutionary scale. Many people believe we descended from apes. Apes tend to have similar relationships with their family and equals as we do with ours. They are even a similar shape to us.

2 They mature quickly. Rhesus monkeys reach puberty at about four years of age, and by six years they are mature and can reproduce.

This rate of maturation means that experiments which require the animals to reach maturity can be conducted over a reasonably short period of time.

3 They used to be fairly easy to get hold of, and researchers could put them in laboratory cages and conduct experiments on them! Now laws protect animals from certain types of experiments.

Harry and Margaret Harlow

conducted a number of experiments on rhesus monkeys during the 1960s and 1970s. In their earliest experiments they **privated** a group of rhesus monkeys. Privation means removing the means by which the animal can satisfy its needs, (in this case for social contact.) The infant monkeys were isolated in cages just after birth, some for three months, others for six months, some more for twelve months. When these "isolates" were released into the company of "normally reared" monkeys their behaviour was badly disturbed. "Normal" young monkeys play fairly "rough and tumble" games. The isolated monkeys couldn't join in. If a monkey approached the isolates in a playful way, the isolates would attack themselves. They buried their heads under their arms and would bite themselves and pull out lumps of their own hair.

Neglecting an Infant

After three months privation all the monkeys appeared emotionally disturbed. Those who were released avoided other monkeys and crouched in the corner. They were allowed 30 minutes a day "play period" with a normally reared, same age, playmate. Gradually their behaviour improved and, after a year or so, it resembled the behaviour of "normal monkeys".

The IVs here are the periods of time for which the monkeys were isolated: three, six and twelve months. The DVs are the animals responses to their isolation, ie inability to play, attacking themselves, being very withdrawn.

The Harlows conclude that there is a sensitive period of six months for isolation of rhesus monkeys. If isolated for any longer, they would never recover. Exactly what are these monkeys being isolated from?

After six months privation those animals kept in isolation's behaviour was even more solitary and self-destructive. Those who were released preferred to be alone and play with their own toys. They appeared to be afraid of the normally reared monkeys. Very slowly their behaviour did improve.

After twelve months privation they were totally withdrawn, bewildered, and completely indifferent to everything around them. They couldn't be left for long with the "normal" monkeys, because the rough and tumble games would probably have seriously injured, or even killed them. When they were sexually mature the females would look appealingly at a "normally reared" male but had no idea about courtship behaviour. If mated they didn't know how to behave as mothers and they neglected their first infants badly. An isolated male would grab at a female and begin mating behaviour whilst not even in genital contact.

Exercise – Harlow's early experiments

Summarise the differences in the dependent variables between each of the three experimental conditions.

In another experiment the Harlows isolated eight monkeys in cages which contained two "surrogate" mothers. A "surrogate" is anyone or anything which "stands in for", or "plays the part of" something else. One surrogate mother was a doll made of wire mesh, the other was made of wood, and covered in towelling. Four monkeys were put in cages where the wire surrogate had a feeding bottle attached, the other four had the feeding bottle in the towel covered model. All eight monkeys would cling onto the towelling model for around 15 hours a day, regardless of which had the bottle. No animal spent more than an hour or two in any 24 on the wire model. It was obvious that the infants needed the comfort they received from contact with something soft.

Harlow's 'Surrogate Mothers'

Harlow concluded ". . . contact comfort is a variable of critical importance in the development of affectional responsiveness to the surrogate mother." This "contact comfort" was more important than feeding. This was especially true when the animals were afraid. Harlow put various frightening objects in their cages, for example, a mechanical teddy bear and a wooden spider. The monkeys clung onto their surrogate mothers. When put into a "test room" containing various toys the monkeys would explore and play so long as the cloth mother was present. If it wasn't there, or if the wire model was there, the monkeys "would rush across the test room and throw themselves face downwards, clutching their heads and bodies. . . ." (Harlow). The wire mother clearly gave them no comfort at all.

From these and other early experiments Bowlby concluded that baby monkeys need their mothers for comfort and for learning how to get on with others. He believed it was a kind of imprinting, although it is quite different from what Lorenz meant.

John Bowlby seems to have taken the IV "*maternal privation*", and the DV "*emotional immaturity*" and assumed that one caused the other. However Harlow's monkeys weren't just being isolated from their mothers, but from all other monkeys. The severe problems these monkeys suffered may not simply be the result of *maternal privation* but rather a result of *social privation*.

Frightening Objects

What are the main differences in the ways imprinting occurred in Lorenz's study, and how Harlow's monkeys behave towards the surrogates?
HINT Think of time.

Write two sentences. One beginning with "Maternal privation means . . .", and the other, "Social privation means . . ." If you can't do this without too much difficulty you're not thinking enough about what you're reading! Go back to the beginning of this section and read it again before going any further.

REVIEW – Some research with animals

Bowlby found evidence for the existence of a special bond between goslings and their mothers in Konrad Lorenz's classic studies in ethology. The Harlow's rhesus monkey experiments showed that being denied the chance to mix with other members of the species leads to severe withdrawal. However we must not generalise the findings of animal behaviour studies to human behaviour.

Background reading – Generalisations from animal studies

There is always a danger if scientists try to generalise from the behaviour of animals to humans. Rhesus monkeys are not capable of the same kinds of thought, affection, understanding, or behaviour as humans. Some biologists say we shouldn't even generalise from the behaviour of experimental animals to the behaviour of wild animals. Animals who are kept in cages and fed by humans, may behave quite differently from animals that live in social groupings, who run free, and hunt their own food in the wild.

Exercise – Harlow's surrogate mother experiments

1 What is an IV, and what is a DV?

2 Outline some of the main advantages to using animals in psychological research.

3 What do psychologists mean by a "surrogate mother"?

4 What IVs are being used in Harlow's "surrogate mother" experiment?

5 What DVs were being measured in that experiment?

6 What's the difference between maternal privation and maternal deprivation?

7 Here are the main techniques used by psychologists: case studies, experiments, natural experiments, surveys, longitudinal studies, cross sectional studies, naturalistic studies, correlational studies. Which technique did each of these use?
Bowlby's research on "44 Juvenile Thieves".
Spitz and Wolf's "prison babies" study.
Goldfarb's "orphanage study".
The Robertson's work.
Lorenz's discovery that goslings will follow objects pulled by string.
The Harlow's research with rhesus monkeys.

8 What is generalisation?

9 Evaluate the evidence from the animal studies which Bowlby used to support his views on attachment.

3 The Impact of John Bowlby's theories

John Bowlby's theories were very popular in the 1950s and 1960s. The World Health Organisation (WHO) quickly supported Bowlby's claims. They described him as "the wise man of the Western World". In 1951 a WHO Expert Committee concluded that "permanent damage to the emotional health of the future generation" could be caused by putting children in day nurseries!!

Bowlby's theories also seemed to explain many of the problems that parents and doctors had noticed themselves. What he said about children and mothers seemed to "fit the facts". However there may have been political implications. Men were returning home from the war and needed jobs. Women were being encouraged to give up their jobs in favour of the men. Looking after your children would make it impossible to do a full time job.

Several professions concerned with children began to change some of their practises to avoid unnecessary separation of mothers and children. For example in the health services, many maternity wards started allowing young children to stay with their mothers for longer periods, both before and after the delivery. In some cases sleeping facilities were made available for children to have their naps and still be near their mothers when they woke up. In short and long stay

Many influential organisations began to recognise the contribution that Bowlby's theories were making to our understanding of early childhood. His conclusions did seem to "fit the facts", although some critics claimed that they were also socially "convenient".

children's wards, mothers were encouraged to spend more time with their children. Overnight accommodation was often provided in more serious cases so the mother would be nearby if the child woke up. "Ward mothers" were appointed in some areas. They were usually local women who spent time playing with the children.

Many social workers were taught to regard the separation of a child from its mother as the worst possible solution to the family's problems. Bowlby had claimed that "a bad home is better than the best institution." Whatever difficulties stood in the way of the mother and the child staying together, those difficulties must be overcome if at all possible.

Even some aspects of the law were changed to give more rights and benefits to parents. Family allowance benefits, single parent allowances, housing benefits and so on have all been used, during the last 30 years or so, to support the mother and child. These were other ways of making it possible for mothers to give up their jobs. Many feminists have resented the way that women have been encouraged to stay at home with the children, and discouraged from having a career. They also complain that the mother is automatically blamed If anything goes wrong with the children.

Exercise – Bowlby's influence

Outline some of the influences that Bowlby's work has had on childcare practises during the last 30 years.

4 Some studies which contradict Bowlby's views

Bowlby, and others, have consistently pointed to the importance of the early years for normal healthy development. Other researchers, notably **Ann** and **Alan Clarke**, have consistently challenged this view. They do not believe that the early years of life have such great influences on future mental health, and on our behaviour as Bowlby claimed. There have been some studies of baby animals and humans who have been separated from their parents which do not support John Bowlby's claims. We'll mention some of them here.

The Bulldogs Bank study

At the end of the Second World War **Anna Freud** and **Sophie Dann** began a *case study* of six war orphans who had been taken prisoner with their mothers by the Germans, and put into concentration camps during World War Two. Their mothers died within a year and the infants were looked after by many of the other prisoners in a "Ward for Motherless Children" in a transit camp. Conditions were very hard, food was scarce, and there were no toys. Forming any secure attachments with an adult would have been simply impossible since many of the prisoners were moved during their captivity. After the war they were moved to several reception centres, until they were eventually brought to a reception centre in the Lake District in England.

REVIEW – Bowlby's influence

Bowlby and his supporters produced theories and explanations that were very influential, particularly amongst those concerned with childcare, such as social workers, nurseries, and the health services. However many saw the implications of his theories being unfair to women.

Six war orphans formed the subjects of a case study by Anna Freud and Sophie Dann.

On arrival the youngest was three, and the oldest was three years 10 months. They had several things in common. For example they had all been *maternally privated* since none could really have known its mother. They had all arrived at the transit camp before they were a year old. They'd always been together. They'd been moved around a lot, and they were not pleased at being moved again. (After two months in the reception centre they were moved again, to a children's home called Bulldogs Bank.) They were very "under stimulated" since they'd never had anyone looking after them for long enough to offer them much stimulation. For example, they couldn't talk very much, and they mostly used a few German and Czechoslovakian swear words. They didn't know what to do with normal toys, and they destroyed all of the toys they could find, and most of the furniture too! They did each "adopt" one special toy, usually a cuddly toy, which they kept near them and always took to bed with them.

They were all fairly hostile and aggressive towards adults, or very cold and uninterested in them. They would only turn to an adult if they actually needed something, otherwise they wouldn't take any notice of adults at all. One last thing they had in common was that they were totally devoted to each other. They did everything together and refused to be separated for any reason. For example, if one couldn't go out, none would want to go. If one woke up at night the others would also soon be awake. When one stopped eating, the others would soon stop too. They did everything as a group. There wasn't any single child who was always the leader, each would take the lead in different activities. To put it simply, they appeared to be totally attached to each other.

Although they had different needs it was impossible to treat them as individuals since they were always together as a group. No one child was dominant all the time and they co-operated over nearly everything. Eventually they learned to speak and play like "normal children". Gradually they formed emotional relationships with some of the adult members of staff.

They slowly recovered from their early privation, but remained attached to each other. What this study shows is that children can survive without mothers, although we do not know if any of them suffered emotional problems in their later lives.

The children didn't seem to have the "normal" feelings of three to four year olds. They were hostile, aggressive, or indifferent to adults, and destructive towards toys and furniture.

Constant patient and loving care from their nurses slowly helped these children to behave more reasonably. They formed some emotional relationships, and gradually became more independent. Their early experiences had had a powerful effect but the children were recovering from them.

REVIEW – The Bulldogs Bank studies

The six war orphans studied by Freud and Dann in the late 1940s were maternally privated, but had made very strong attachments to each other. Since there were no continuous caregivers, and little else to offer stimulation, the babies provided social stimulation for each other.

Exercise – The Bulldogs Bank children

1 What kind of mothering do you think the children had during their first few years?
2 How would you describe and explain their behaviour towards each other?
3 What does John Bowlby mean by "affectionless psychopathy", and what things might cause it?
4 Would the hypothesis "ignoring the children when they were being disruptive and rewarding them when they were being good" work with these children when they first arrived at Bulldogs Bank? Give reasons for your answer.
5 Bowlby said that a child who hadn't made an attachment to its mother would suffer later. What alternative hypothesis might the Bulldogs Bank study suggest instead?

Some institutional children

Studies of children brought up in institutions show they do not automatically develop the symptoms of affectionless psychopathy. What they are like as adolescents and adults largely seems to depend on factors like whether they had ever formed an attachment, whether they had formed one which had been broken, and how long they were in the institution before being adopted. **Barbara Tizard** and **Jill Hodges** found that children who spent most of their childhood in an institution could still form loving relationships. We will return to this later.

Severe deprivation and isolation

In 1972 **Jarmila Koluchova** reported the case of identical twin boys in Czechoslovakia who had suffered severe deprivations. They were born in September 1960. Their mother had died shortly after they were born and their father couldn't really cope. At the age of eleven months they were taken into a children's home where they were found to be normal, healthy children. Their father remarried within a few months, and the twins returned to their father and stepmother when they were 18 months old. They had two older sisters, and a stepsister and stepbrother. The stepmother was a selfish, unpleasant woman who had no idea about bringing up young children. (Her mother had looked after her children when they were young.) The father was of below average intelligence, and his job on the railways took him away from home quite a lot. The family had recently moved to a city suburb where nobody knew them, or knew that the family should have contained six children.

Their stepmother treated them terribly. They were kept in a small unheated room with a sheet of polythene for a bed and very little

It is too simple to say that children must form attachments during some "sensitive period". Many factors are involved in the likelihood of successful attachments being formed.

The twins had been cared for, mainly in a nursery, until they were 18 months old, when they returned home to their father and stepmother.

Background reading – The institutionalised child

In the past some orphanages have been so understaffed and under equipped that the children in them were nearly as isolated as Harlow's monkeys. It wasn't uncommon for a deprived orphanage to have one caregiver for every ten or more children. Contact with the babies was usually little more than changing and bathing them, and propping a feeding bottle against their pillows at feeding time. The babies spent most of their time in their cribs (without many opportunities to get out and practice motor skills). They had few or no toys to play with, and nothing much to look at. Since the 1940s some studies have been done on children who spent their first year or more in these sorts of institutions. They show that for the first three to six months, the infants' behaviour is fairly normal – they smile and babble at caregivers, and they cry for attention. During the next six months these normal reactions slowly disappear. They become more rigid in the way they sit and lie. They don't respond to caregivers, and their language fails to appear at the proper time (10–12 months). They look bored by their surroundings and stop trying to get someone to play with them or give them attention. You may see there is some similarity in these children's behaviour and that of Harlow's isolated monkeys. This early behaviour has gone through the three stages described by the Robertsons, from **distress** to **despair**, to **detachment**.

If the same reactions occur in both monkeys and humans, where do you think it comes from? Is it a learned reaction, like learning to talk? Or is it genetically inherited? Or both?

Until they were taken away from their parents at seven years of age the twins received no love and little care from their parents. They were assessed to be at the same stage of development as a normal three year old. (Their stepmother was eventually sent to prison for four years for her neglect of the children.)

With constant patience, stimulation, and enormous loving care, these children did make a good recovery, physically, emotionally, socially, and intellectually.

REVIEW – Severe deprivation

Koluchova studied twin boys who were raised in a children's home for their first 18 months of life where they were found to be normal and well adjusted. Between 18 months and seven years they suffered severe deprivation and beatings whilst living with their father and stepmother. With intensive care, specialist education, and a loving foster home they were able to develop intellectually, socially, and emotionally.

furniture. They were poorly fed. Sometimes the mother would lock them in the cellar. She would beat them with a wooden kitchen spoon, covering their heads with a mattress in case anyone heard their cries. Their father was also once seen beating them with a rubber hose until they lay unmoving on the ground.

The twins suffered these conditions for five and a half years. When they were finally examined, at the age of seven, they were severely physically and mentally retarded. Their bodies were covered in scar tissue from the beatings. They had severe rickets, a disease of the bones caused by lack of vitamin D. They couldn't stand straight, walk, or run, and their co-ordination was poor. They hadn't been taught to speak, had no knowledge of eating habits, and were very frightened of people, and of the dark. It was impossible to give them a standard intelligence test since they couldn't understand the instructions, and they weren't familiar with things like "pictures" on which some tests are based. It was estimated that their IQ's would be in the 40s. Instead of giving them standard intelligence tests, their abilities were compared to normal children of their age. Their development was equivalent to that of a three year old.

The twins were put in hospital until they were well enough to go to a special school for mentally disadvantaged children. They made good progress at school. When they were sociable enough they were fostered by a particularly kind and loving woman who lived with her sister who also loved children. She seemed to know exactly what the children needed, and Jarmila Koluchova said "There is a happy atmosphere in the whole family, full of mutual understanding." By the age of 11 the twins' speech was normal for their age. They enjoyed some school subjects, such as reading and playing the piano, and were both fairly creative. By 15 the twins' I.Q. scores were normal, and their emotional state had improved greatly. The atmosphere at home was warm and friendly, and although the boys still remembered their early experiences they rarely talked about them, even to their foster mother.

Exercise – Koluchova's study

1 What is the main advantage of longitudinal studies?

2 Give some examples from the passage of the kind of things the twins were deprived of.

3 What evidence is there in the passage that these children improved socially and intellectually?

4 How do Koluchova's findings fit in with Bowlby's theory?

Another study by the Robertsons

Earlier we mentioned 17 month old John, who was studied by the **Robertsons** when he spent nine days in a residential nursery. The Robertsons studied several such children, and noticed the same sequence of behaviour in each of them. It started with distress, this gave way to despair, and finally turned into detachment. One reason why John had suffered was because no one would offer to be a substitute for his mother. Thomas was one of four children who the Robertsons offered temporary fostering to in their own home. He was 28 months, a year older than John, when his mother went into hospital to have another baby. The Robertsons visited Thomas in his own home before his mother went away and took him to visit their home, to let him get to know them. This would reduce the "strangeness" of the new place when his mother was gone. He was a friendly, outgoing child and was quite comfortable with them.

He settled in with the Robertsons well, although he obviously missed his mother. Every day during separation Thomas received constant, patient, high quality care from Joyce Robertson, supported by her husband and teenage daughter, Jean. Thomas had brought some favourite things from home, including a photograph of his mother and him. These things reminded him of his home and his mother, and comforted him. Thomas was pleased when his father visited each night, but understandably upset when his father had to leave. (Thomas wouldn't let anyone else sit in the chair his daddy had sat in, and his father left him his pen "to look after"). Thomas had a few problems with food and sleep, and as the separation went into the second week he did cry more for his mother. But Joyce Robertson's patience and reassurance always quietened him.

The Robertsons used a kind of "**play therapy**" to explain to Thomas what was happening to him, his mother, and his father. They had dolls who they pretended were the people involved. Thomas and the "Thomas" doll would see "daddy" going to see "mummy" in the hospital, and "mummy" coming out of the "hospital" where she'd been "resting" to see "Thomas" and take him home.

When Thomas' mother finally came he was a bit unsure of her and whether she would be going away again. But this reaction only lasted a few minutes, Thomas was happily and successfully reunited with his mother. In the following months it appeared he had changed a little. He was rather more aggressive and harder to control than he had been before. Separating him from his mother still had some slightly unfortunate effects, despite the care he had received.

The Robertsons wanted to show that it is important that young children should not be separated from their mother. If this was inevitable then putting them into residential nurseries or similar places would be very distressing. If they had to be separated then giving the child a temporary foster mother was essential.

The fostering of Thomas was largely successful. Joyce Robertson's constant care helped Thomas cope with his emotional problems caused by the separation from his mother.

Exercise – The Robertsons' observations

1 Briefly outline the main differences between the ways John and Thomas were treated.

2 Briefly mention the main differences in the ways John and Thomas responded?

3 What do you think was the point of a) bringing some toys and a photograph from home, and b) the "play therapy" sessions?

4 What evidence is there in the passage that Thomas' father was trying to help reduce the child's loss?

5 Explain how this study might contrast with Bowlby's theory of the role of the mother in forming attachments.

REVIEW – Temporary fostering

James and Joyce Robertson have shown that taking children into their own home and giving them constant, consistent high quality care can overcome most problems which a child might have during a short term separation from its parents.

Harlow's later studies

Over ten years after the **Harlow's** first experiments, **Harry Harlow** and **Steven Suomi** isolated four male rhesus monkeys for six months (which seemed to be the end of the sensitive period for normal emotional development.) One three-month old female monkey was then put into each isolate's cage (these were to be "therapists".) At three months of age the females were likely to cling onto the isolates for *contact comfort* and play gently. Suomi and Harlow believed that the isolates would tolerate this and that they would slowly join in with the younger animal's play.

For the first four weeks, each isolate saw its "therapist" for two hour sessions, three days a week. The amount of contact increased, and by three months each isolate saw its therapist in the company of another isolate/therapist pair, several times a week. By 12 months of age their behaviour was almost normal. By three years, and by now in the company of "normal" monkeys, they had fully recovered. (Melinda Novak used a similar therapy as Suomi and Harlow on some 12 month isolates, and eventually "rehabilitated" them.)

A 'Therapist Monkey'

Providing isolated monkeys with some social contact helps them overcome their problems. Humans mature less quickly and would need a lot more care and stimulation.

REVIEW – Therapy as a "cure" for isolation

Gradually introducing privated animals to "normally reared" ones can lead to the development of "normal" behaviour.

This experiment seems to confirm the Bulldogs Bank study. What did those children and these monkeys have in common?

Exercise – Will therapy help?

1 What was the experimental hypothesis of Harlow's early experiments? "To discover . . ."

2 What could you say about the relationship between the infant monkey and its mother, after studying Harlow's early experiments?

3 What were Harlow and Suomi trying to discover in the later experiments? Express this as their experimental hypothesis.

4 What were the conclusions of the later experiments?

5 Do Harlow's later experiments support Bowlby's views? Explain your answer.

Michael Rutter's correlational studies

Michael Rutter and his colleagues studied one group of nine to twelve year olds on the Isle of Wight. A second study was conducted on a group of children of parents who had suffered mental problems in London. He was particularly interested in the causes of anti-social behaviour, such as juvenile delinquency and theft. Rutter found no significant correlation between separation from either parent and high levels of anti social behaviour. He investigated two other possibilities. One was that the cause of the separation may be important. Children of parents who argue and are constantly in conflict will probably feel anxiety and stress. Rutter suspected that there might be a correlation between the amount of stress which children felt, and the likelihood of them becoming involved in anti social behaviour. The other possibility was that separation from both parents, rather than separation from just one parent, might also have something to do with becoming anti social, since it would mean that the child was taken away from home, and having its life disrupted.

Rutter tested the possibility that anti social behaviour could correlate with factors other than maternal deprivation.

To test the first possibility Rutter used several measures of the quality of the family relationships, including questionnaires and clinical interviews. He could divide the sample into "good" families, "fair" families, and "poor" families. "Good" families had warm, loving, and secure relationships, free from high levels of stress. Rutter found no increase in anti-social behaviour in the children from these homes, or in children from homes described as "fair". There was a positive correlation between coming from a "poor" home where there was separation from one parent. Rutter suggests that it was *not* the separation of the child from one of its parents which correlated well with anti social behaviour, but rather the *cause* of the separation. As Rutter says, "The largest differences in anti-social behaviour are associated with the marriage rating and not with separation experiences." Those separated because of stress in the home were four times more likely to become delinquent than where the separation was due to illness, ie it's not the fact of divorce but the unhappiness and stress in the home which lead to it which correlates significantly with emotional disturbance. If children from warm, loving homes are maternally deprived, they can recover. (This is true of children who are adopted by other parents.) Ideally what children need is the opportunity to form strong attachments, and a stress free home life.

Rutter found positive correlations between the amount of stress in a child's background, and the likelihood of the child becoming deviant.

Rutter's conclusions are supported by other studies which find a relationship between factors in the home and social development. One found a correlation between factors in the home and the number of times a juvenile appeared in court. Those who got into trouble once had homes where there had been an outbreak of conflict. When the conflict was settled the child did not offend again. Where the conflict continued the children continued to get into trouble.

Another challenge to one of John Bowlby's assertions was Michael Rutter's finding that separation from either of the parents did not correlate with increased anti social behaviour, but separation from both parents did lead to a small increase amongst those families which are insecure to begin with. Perhaps Bowlby's emphasis on maternal separation may have been misplaced. In Rutter's words, "This difference . . . suggests that the association may not be due to the fact of separation from both parents, but rather to the discord and disturbance which surrounded the separation."

Exercise – Michael Rutter's correlational studies

1 What does "no significant correlation" mean?

2 What methods did the researchers use to rate the families as "good", "fair", or "poor"?

3 Summarise Rutter's conclusions about the possible causes of anti-social behaviour.

4 This research takes the form of correlation studies. What are the main uses and limitations of this method of collecting data in psychology?

REVIEW – Long term consequences of deprivation

Michael Rutter and his colleagues have shown that being separated from one's mother is not necessarily any more likely to have harmful consequences than being separated from one's father. They found no significant positive correlation between the length of maternal separation and the amount of anti social behaviour, but did find that families which had the highest amounts of stress were also more likely to have children who behaved badly.

5 So is Bowlby right?

In 1956 John Bowlby was beginning to realise that some of his earlier claims may have been rather too strongly stated. In an article called "The Effects of Mother–Child Separation" in the *British Journal of Medical Psychology* he said that some of the early work on the effects of separation (eg Goldfarb, Spitz etc) sometimes tended to exaggerate. Since the 1970s, quite a lot of doubt has been cast on some of Bowlby's views of the mother and her child.

Alan and Ann Clarke have consistently disagreed with the idea that the first few years in a child's life are as important as Bowlby and others claim. Their objections may be summarised in four points.

1 The Clarke's claim that imprinting probably doesn't exist in all animals, so why should anything like it exist in humans? Quoting evidence from ethology and experiments on goslings, ducklings and other animals is irrelevant to a discussion on human parent/child relationships, they claim.

2 Children who haven't had adequate bonding in early life, can recover later (eg the twins reported by Jarmila Koluchova, the Bulldogs Bank children and many orphanage-reared children who were adopted later in life).

3 Some children have suffered temporary deprivation but show no ill effects later (such as Thomas and many of the children in Michael Rutter's study).

4 Babies don't just need mothers, but can attach to several people (as we shall see in the next chapter).

John Bowlby insisted that (a) the early years are most important for healthy development, and (b) that the mother (or a substitute mother) is crucially important in those years. The Clarkes dispute both these statements. They say "Early experience . . . is no more than a link in the developmental chain, shaping behaviour less and less powerfully as age increases."

Comments on the early research on mother child interaction

Comment

1   Both animals and humans have been studied in various ways to show either that mothers are essential, or that babies can do without them. All the research so far has been used to support either one point of view or the other.

However

It is not usual for any study to give such clear cut results which "prove" that babies need to attach to their mothers, or that they do not. In quoting research evidence in support of either side we may at best be simplifying its conclusions, and at worst, distorting them to suit our argument.

2   A major problem with all this research on children's development concerns the methods they use which usually consist of correlations, case studies, surveys, or experiments on animals. All these methods have their weaknesses for establishing the basis of children's emotional development.

However, apart from natural experiments, there aren't any other methods which can reasonably be used to study children.

3   The case for seeing the "mother/child" bond as all important, and for wanting to keep mothers and children together at all costs, has been criticised for being politically "convenient". During the 1950s it would have suited the government, and men generally, if women had not gone out to work since it would have left more jobs open to men.

This may be true, but the accusation does not necessarily imply that the theory isn't correct of course. Bowlby does not claim to have invented or discovered the existence of attachment, he has merely pointed out the need for it.

REVIEW – Evaluation – the parent/child relationship

We now know that many of Bowlby's original ideas may not be completely correct. Children and babies may be much more "flexible" than he believed, and not all difficulties that occurred during their first five years would lead to emotional disturbance or anti-social behaviour. Regardless of "who is right", without people like John Bowlby, James and Joyce Robertson, Ann and Alan Clarke, and Michael Rutter we would know a lot less about parent child relationships than we do now.

In any field of enquiry people will put forward ideas that seem to fit the facts. These ideas will find some support, and some criticism. For as long as John Bowlby's explanations were thought to be convincing his influence was great. His claims focused attention on the mother child bond probably more than anyone else before him. When criticisms of any theory, and the appearance of alternative explanations outweighs the earlier beliefs, so new insights are gained. Whilst all of Bowlby's claims may not be wholly correct, developmentalists owe him a great deal for inspiring so much debate and research into how children's emotions grow.

Exercise – Evaluating Bowlby's claims

1 What were the main consequences that Bowlby predicted came from breaking the mother child bond?

2 Discuss some of the criticisms that have been made of Bowlby's theory.

4 Attachments and Mothering

Earlier we said that an attachment is a special emotional bond that babies make with their caregivers, but if the attachment bond is broken, children don't automatically become delinquents and suffer emotionally. As Michael Rutter suggests, it depends on when and why the separation occurs. Some American research by Yarrow and Goodwin suggests that 5% of three month olds suffer if they are separated from their mothers, if the break occurs between three and four months 40% of babies will suffer. By six months 90% suffer, and by nine months all will. Babies seem to form their primary attachments from around four to nine months.

The main questions that we shall be looking at here are:

1 How attachments evolve – the role of the child, and the role of the mother.
2 How do we know if attachment bonds are being made and who else can the baby attach to?
3 What lessons can we learn from studies of infant/parent bonding?
4 What are the effects of long term deprivation?

1 How attachments evolve

Attachments are emotional bonds which occur between babies and those people who are most deeply involved with them. To become involved the people and infant concerned must spend some time together, and interact with each other. In order to discover who babies can attach to we must first discover how attachments occur in the first place. The old idea that there is some kind of simple instinctive urge that binds mothers and their babies wouldn't be widely accepted now. We may be born with some instinctive predisposition to form relationships with our caregivers, but these urges are far more flexible than simple imprinting.

Young babies are willing to be sociable with just about anyone who pays them enough attention. After a few months infants are willing and able to let a closer bond emerge. For attachments to occur some of the people who attend to the child, hopefully including its parents, will want to become involved with the child. Over the next few months the infant will grow to trust those people, to feel safe and secure with them, and to regard them as a "*safe base*" from which to explore.

Many psychologists now believe that human infants are born with some skills which allow them to attract and keep someone's attention. These will be useful for interaction. It may be that the child is born with some instinctive basis for various types of interaction.

The child's role in forming attachments

Some animals imprint on the first thing they see. They must have some instinct which tells them that this "thing" will look after them and feed them. In the wild the first thing these babies will see will be their parents who will look after them. Following their parent around obviously has some "*survival value*". Humans rely much less on instincts than most animals do since we have great capacities to learn

Close bonds may develop between the baby and certain people. These people may then become a "*safe base*" from which the child can explore.

"Innate" means inborn, hereditary, something which is genetically transmitted and exists right from birth (or the potential for it does).

and adapt our behaviour. It seems unlikely that we have any genetic programmes which tell us to imprint. Instead we slowly learn who we enjoy being with, and maybe who we can trust. To do that, human babies must be capable of being *sociable*. A great deal of research has been conducted recently, including some ingenious experiments and some detailed observations, on how babies appear to enjoy interacting with other people. Some of their conclusions are summarised here.

Human babies seem to enjoy company. They will give a social smile (ie not just wind!) within a few days of birth, and will start to imitate their mother's facial expressions after just a week or so. They have reasonably good hearing and will turn their heads towards a sound. (Our senses of sight and hearing are closely linked, right from birth.) Babies seem to have an innate preference for looking at things like the human face, and hearing the human voice too.

Over 30 years ago **Ahrens** found that one month old babies will smile at a picture of human eyes in an otherwise blank space. Over the next few months more details such as a nose and mouth are required to make a baby smile, and by five months the picture has to be three dimensional. A smiling baby is likely to encourage the mother to smile and talk to the child.

Over 20 years ago **Robert Fantz** designed some apparatus called a "looking chamber" which allowed babies to be shown particular things, whilst their reactions could be recorded. He showed babies from a few days old various pictures, and he measured the amount of time they looked at each one. He found that they preferred to look at round objects, especially those which were most like a face.

Ahrens and Fantzs' 'face shapes'

Psychologists have known that babies have certain kinds of preferences for the things they look at and listen to. The things they seem to enjoy most are "human".

William Condon and **Lewis Sander** played tape recordings of various sounds, including human speech, to babies from just a few hours old. The babies heard someone speaking American, another speaking Chinese, someone making vowel sounds, and a regular tapping sound. In addition to these tapes they also heard a live adult speaker. The babies reactions as they heard the sounds were filmed. By two days old, these American babies started to move their arms and bodies in time with the speech, whilst not appearing very concerned with the tapping or vowel sounds. This research suggests that humans may be genetically programmed for responding to human speech.

Genevieve Carpenter took a sample of babies between one and eight weeks old, and put them in some apparatus that had a viewing "door" at the top, and a small loudspeaker next to it. The babies saw either their mother's face or a stranger looking through the "door"; in both cases the mother's voice could be heard. By two weeks of age many of the babies seemed to be able to tell the difference between their mother and a stranger, and preferred their mother. The babies turned away when they saw their mother's face in this strange apparatus although they appeared to be interested in their mother's voice. When the mother's face was presented with the stranger's voice the babies looked away and became distressed.

In another experiment, Genevieve Carpenter showed the babies their mother's face, keeping perfectly still, then a "face shape" (a kitchen collander painted pink with three knobs on it to resemble facial features), and finally a shop dummy face. The babies were vaguely interested in the collander and the shop dummy. But when they saw their mother's unmoving face they looked away. Carpenter's experiments suggest that by just a few weeks of age;

a) many babies can recognise their mother's face
b) many babies can recognise their mother's voice
c) they expect the face and voice to go together, and
d) that the face should have movement.

A Summary of Genevieve Carpenter's findings

First experiment

	Mother's face and voice	Mother's face, no voice	Stranger's face and voice	Mother's face, stranger's voice
2 week old baby's reaction	Happy	Unhappy	Happy	Unhappy

Second experiment

	Mother's unmoving face	Abstract face shape	Shop dummy face
Baby's reaction	Restless	Vague interest	Vague interest

Name the main IVs and DVs in these experiments. Condon and Sander, and Genevieve Carpenter, have suggested that human babies are born with very clear preferences for "human" things.

For the first few months this "**sociability**" is only directed towards adults. It used to be thought that children only started taking notice of

REVIEW – The sociable infant

Human infants appear to be genetically programmed to become aware of, and respond to, people around them. They appear to have genetically inherited preferences for things which are human, like voices and faces.

other children when they were about three or four years old. We now know that even babies of 10 to 12 months old will copy and smile at another baby. Given the choice they'd probably prefer an adult, or even a toy, but if neither are available another baby will do.

Exercise – The sociable newborn baby

1 Write a paragraph summarising the evidence so far that supports the view that human babies are genetically programmed to interact socially. Refer to Fantz, Condon and Sander, and Carpenter's research in your answer.

2 What effect is the baby's willingness to be sociable likely to have on its mother? What might it make her want to do?

3 Suggest how the skills discussed in the paragraph you wrote might contribute to "survival value"?

4 What advice would you give a new mother about talking to her baby?

How do we know if the infant is being sociable?

Next time there's a discussion between two people on the telly, and you can see them both, turn the volume right down. Try to tell who's talking, whether the other agrees, whether and how they "butt in" and so on.

Watch two friends talking. When Lee talks to Mick he moves his hands and arms to emphasise the point he's making. Sometimes his voice grows louder or softer, sometimes it goes up in pitch. Mick looks at Lee, sometimes nodding his agreement. He remains quiet until it's his turn to speak. If he wants to "butt in" he'll raise his hands, and his voice. When it's time to go, or to talk to someone else, Lee will let Mick know. Babies and their mothers do much the same sort of things.

Colwyn Trevarthen and **Martin Richards** filmed a sample of five babies for an hour each week for the first six months of their lives. Sometimes the babies were in their cots with toys hanging in front of them, and sometimes they were with their mothers. Their behaviour was quite different in each situation. They explored and played with the toys, but they held a sort of "**conversation**" with their mothers. From around two months of age they would open their mouths when their mother spoke to them, but remained silent, as though they were preparing to reply. A few months later the baby and its mother took turns in their "conversations". When their mother stopped speaking they would make little sounds. This encouraged their mothers to speak again, and again they would wait their turn before "answering". This "*highly elaborate activity*" seems to show that even very young babies are ready, willing, and able, to communicate with their caregivers. The babies weren't communicating in order to make their mothers do anything, such as feed or change them. They appeared to be doing it just for the fun of it. The communication was mutually enjoyable. Moving one's face and body in time with what is going on around us is called **interactional synchrony**. Condon and Sander's sample of babies from just a few hours old showed interactional synchrony with the human speech they heard.

Daniel Stern is an American professor of child psychiatry who has spent many years studying parent child interaction. Although he agrees that there is an instinctive basis to attachment formation, he thinks too much is sometimes made of it. He believes that children develop an

Exchange Games

idea of who they are and what they can do fairly soon after birth through social interaction. He found that by three months babies use the same "face to face" type behaviour as two adults. The babies look for their mother. As she approaches they look away for a moment. Then they look again and hold eye contact. Then they break it. They will smile and move their heads in time to what is being said. If mother is talking and they want to "butt in" they do the same thing as adults do, they raise their hands, heads (and their voices!). They are extremely good at regulating the amount of contact they have. They will let the mother know when they want company, which one of them they want to talk, and when they want to rest. Stern maintains that all this behaviour is purely for fun, for mutual enjoyment, and for sharing each other's experiences.

Interactional Synchrony

People move their heads, hands, arms, and body position to emphasise what they are saying. When they're listening they are more at ease. Babies respond in this way in their "conversations" too. It's called interactional synchrony.

Do you wave your hands around when you're talking, to emphasise the point? How does the person you're talking to look when you're talking? And how does this change when you stop and it's their turn?

Harriet Rheingold and **Judith Adams** suggest that both care-givers and infants enjoy their "conversations". Babies will often stop crying and look around when they hear a human voice.

Not everyone agrees with those researchers who believe that the infant is able to start off, and contribute to, "conversation like" exchanges with their caregivers. Some researchers believe that babies are born with a few primitive reflexes, and that maturation and learning will be necessary before the child is capable of any of the communication skills described by Colwyn Trevarthen, Daniel Stern and others. People like **Kenneth Kaye** argue that whenever an infant behaves in a way that appears to have some social meaning, such as a smile communicating happiness to be with someone, then adults interpret it as though it actually did have this meaning, and treat their babies accordingly. Crying may be a reflexive response to pain or hunger. A parent will interpret the cry, and will treat the child as though it actually were trying to ask for food. Kaye does not believe that tiny babies are capable of many of the social exchanges described earlier.

Babies are said to be quite skilled at regulating the amount of contact they have. How might we observe this?

Not everyone agrees that babies are so sociable. We may misinterpret their sounds and movements as signs of sociability.

69

Very young babies respond to social signals like smiling, and can take turns in their "communication". They seem to enjoy these interactions. Critics of this view say that we exaggerate the infant's social skills by choosing to interpret its behaviour in that way.

If babies are capable of social communication, or if they simply make demands to have their needs met, they will need some means of attracting their caregivers' attention. Crying is a powerful signal.

Exercise – The sociable behaviour of the infant

1 When does "turn taking" in "conversations" begin, according to researchers such as Trevarthen and Richards?

2 What is meant by "interactional synchrony"?

3 Why are babies sociable, according to Daniel Stern?

The mother's role in forming attachments

Since infants don't begin to talk until around their first birthday they must use other signals for communicating their needs. Such signals may include smiling, eye contact, gazing, reaching, and grasping, and (from about six months), babbling. All these abilities are genetically inherited. Adults who are sensitive to these signals may become more deeply involved with their children. One of the most powerful signals an infant has is crying.

So what can parents do about reducing babies crying? **Silvia Bell** and **Mary Ainsworth** conducted a naturalistic observation study of 26 mothers and babies in their own homes for four hours at a time, once every three weeks for the first year of the babies' lives. Some parents tend to their babies as soon as they begin to cry. Others wait a short time to see if the baby will quieten on its own. Some parents even leave their babies for several minutes, believing that the baby will learn that all it has to do to attract attention is cry. The researchers wanted to see if there were any differences between the mothers' responses to their baby's crying, and the amount of crying each child did. They found that babies used crying if everything else failed to attract attention. The mothers who responded quickest and were most attentive to their baby's needs had babies who cried least. The babies were most likely to cry when they were left alone.

During the first year of life babies learn other ways of attracting attention and so don't need to use crying so much, particularly if their mothers have responded sensitively before. As Mary Ainsworth says:

"An infant whose mother has responded to his cries promptly in the past should develop both trust in her responsiveness and confidence in his increased ability to control what happens to him."

Background reading – Crying

On average infants spend about six to seven per cent of their time crying (although it seems like more!) Healthy babies have several different sorts of crying.

There's the "I'm hungry, feed me" cry. It starts with a quiet whimper and becomes louder if food doesn't appear. Then there's the "I'm absolutely furious about . . ." cry. It is louder and more piercing, and harder to quieten. And there's the "I'm in pain, something really hurts" cry. It starts as a long scream, a pause for breath, and another long scream, and so on. A mother will soon learn the difference between them, and what to do for each. There's another type of sound that babies of just a month or so may learn to use. It's the "There's nothing wrong with me, I'm a bit fed up, come and play with me" noise, and isn't a real cry.

Crying is usually the last resort for the child, when all other attempts to attract attention have failed. Babies don't usually just "start to cry" unless there's something wrong. Babies probably don't enjoy crying. Given the choice they'd probably rather smile. Wouldn't you?

Mary Ainsworth uses the term *"the sensitive mother"* to refer to one who is quick to respond to her baby's needs. The babies should feel loved and secure which should help them become more independent later. The opposite of this may also be true, babies who are not sensitively dealt with may tend to become more demanding and clinging.

Sensitive mothers respond quickly when their baby cries. Babies who are being attended to are least likely to cry.

Exercise – Crying babies

A young mother enters the kitchen. She looks exhausted and flops in a chair by the phone. She dials the number of her best friend from the garage where she used to work.

"Hi Cathy, it's Jan. Just thought I'd give you a ring to let you know how its going."

"Great Jan, how's young Peter?"

"He's fine, he's getting quite fat now, but the doctor says he's about right for six months old. I am slightly worried though. He seems to cry quite a lot. I asked Mum and she said that me and my sister used to, it's nothing to worry about. So long as I keep to the routine of feeding him, and putting him down afterwards every four hours he'll learn what to expect and won't be any more trouble. Trouble is, he hasn't quite got the hang of it yet."

1 If you were Cathy, what would you like to say to your friend?

2 Could you think of any explanation for why Jan and her sister cried a lot when they were young?

3 Describe one piece of research on mothering of young babies. Say what method was used and describe the sample. What were the findings, and what do they tell us about young babies?

How important are very early experiences?

Marshall Klaus and **John Kennel** conducted an experiment on contact comfort between mothers and babies in the mid 1970s. They hypothesised that a mother's sensitivity towards her baby may be affected by the amount of contact she had with it immediately after birth. They managed to find 28 expectant mothers and divided them into a control and an experimental group.

The control group underwent the normal routine – seeing their babies briefly after delivery, then six to 12 hours after the usual tests and rest. They had feeding sessions for half an hour with their babies every four hours.

Background reading – What helps a mother be sensitive to her baby?

Here are some possible suggestions.

Support from her husband and family, and sharing childminding. The terry towel covered model was a very important source of contact comfort for Harlow's monkeys. Sensitive mothers could offer lots of "contact comfort" to their babies.

The "surrogates" became a safe base from which to explore. Mary Ainsworth believes that from around one year old human babies will have learned who their "safe bases" are. She says that we have an instinct to attach, which is followed by an instinct to explore. Sensitive mothers will help babies become independent.

The experimental group had more contact. Within three hours of birth they had an extra hour's contact. Then they had an extra five hours a day contact with their babies compared to the control group. Altogether the "extended contact group" had 15 hours extra time with their baby, compared to the controls.

One month later Klaus and Kennel interviewed the 28 mothers and filmed them with their babies (including a feeding session). The extended contact group seemed much closer to their babies generally and held them much closer during feeding. Eleven months later Klaus and Kennel conducted a follow up study. The extended contact mothers still cuddled and soothed their babies more than the controls, and were more likely to say they'd missed their babies when returning home. Their infants too seemed more mature and sociable than the "normal routine" group. They were also physically bigger and stronger. Five of the pairs in each group were studied again at two years, this time focusing on the language used. The differences were still there. The mothers in the "extended contact group" used longer sentences, more adjectives, and gave fewer commands.

Exercise – Klaus and Kennel's experiment

1 What independent variables are being controlled here?
2 What is the size of the sample?
3 Why was a control group used here?
4 What measures of the dependent variable were taken when the babies were a year old? And at two?
5 Summarise the conclusions of this research in your own words.

There has been a great deal of criticism of this experiment, and not everyone accepts its findings. Some of the interpretations were accused of being exaggerated. Similar experiments have been conducted, under strictly controlled conditions, and have found no great differences between extended and non extended contact groups. What we can conclude is that whilst extended contact just after birth may not necessarily have any long term benefits, it is unlikely to do any harm!

Exercise – Mothering

1 Why do babies cry?
2 What advice would you give to a new mother about her child's crying?
3 What does "socially learned" mean?
4 Describe "interractional synchrony"?
5 What did the following researchers conclude:
   William Condon and Lewis Sander
   Colwyn Trevarthen and Martin Richards
   Genevieve Carpenter
   Daniel Stern
   Mary Ainsworth and Silvia Bell
   Marshall Klaus and John Kennel

REVIEW – The sensitive mother

Mothers who put their infants' needs first, and who respond quickly to their baby's needs, have babies who cry less, and who may become the most content and confident children.

6 Are six month old human babies helpless and passive? Give reasons for your answer.

7 What is "naturalistic observation"? How have psychologists used observation to study mother/child interaction?

2 How do we know if attachment has occurred?

By around eight months babies could have become firmly attached to their primary caregiver. There are said to be two ways of telling if a baby is attached to someone. First a baby is said to be attached to someone if it is not afraid of that person, but is afraid of strangers. Secondly, a baby is said to be attached if it becomes upset when the person to whom it is attached is away from it. These two conditions are called **stranger fear** and **separation distress**.

Stranger fear

For the first three months of their lives, babies will smile at strangers; by four months this begins to turn to a stare; and by six months they often "freeze" if approached by a stranger. This fear gradually disappears as the child becomes more independent. Whether babies show stranger fear depends on three factors, whether someone who the baby is attached to is nearby, where the baby is, and how the stranger behaves.

If the baby is being held by its mother it will show little fear if a stranger approaches. If it is on its own in a familiar place it will show fear. If it is with its mother in a strange place it will show fear. If it is alone in a strange place (particularly the open air) it will show less stranger fear, and may even allow itself to be picked up by a stranger. If the stranger approaches slowly, and talks and acts in a quiet, friendly way, the baby will show less fear. If the stranger approaches more quickly and gets too close, tries to pick the baby up, or talks too loudly, the baby will show fear.

Stranger Fear

Exercise – The pattern of stranger fear

1 Under what conditions is a baby least likely to show stranger fear?

2 Under what conditions is a baby most likely to show stranger fear?

3 If you want to speak to someone who is carrying a 12 month old baby, what's the best way to approach them?

The most obvious explanation for why babies show fear of strangers is that the baby is afraid that either it, or its mother, is going to be taken away by the stranger. Babies only show fear of adults they do not know. For some reason they do not show fear of unknown children. Perhaps this is because the baby hasn't much idea of what a "child" is until it is older. Babies develop stranger fear towards other children during their second year.

A baby is said to be attached to an adult if it shows no fear of them, whilst showing fear of others. What "survival value" might stranger fear have?

Babies are also said to be attached if they show distress when absent from their main caregivers. What are the three stages of separation distress that the Robertsons identified? Why did 17 month old John's behaviour change when he was in the residential nursery? Was it simply because he was away from his mother?

"Multiple attachments" means being attached to more than one person.

Separation distress

From around 12 months a firmly attached baby will be upset when it is away from the person it is attached to. The baby will resist anyone else who tries to comfort him. If the separation continues for some days the baby may go through the three stages identified by James and Joyce Robertson.

Making multiple attachments

Being able to measure whether babies have made any attachment also allows us to see the people to whom they are attached. Bowlby claimed that babies have some biological need to attach to their mothers, or at least a permanent substitute. In 1964 **Rudi Schaffer** and **Peggy Emerson** reported on their most important ethological study of 60 Glasgow children from birth to 18 months. They interviewed the mothers once a month and asked them about who the infant smiled at, who it responded to, who caused it separation distress and so on. They found that many of the children were attaching to several people. Where several adults took an interest in the baby, it could attach to them all.

Schaffer and Emerson's study

Schaffer and Emerson's sample went through four stages. For the first six weeks the children had no particular preferences about who they

---

Background reading – The explanations for separation distress

There are a few possible explanations for separation distress.

Association learning:

If an infant has been separated from its caregivers before, and been hungry or wet or lonely during the separation, it may associate those unpleasant feelings with the absence. When the mother is absent again the baby might think it is about to become hungry, wet, or lonely again. Any future absence will remind the baby of these feelings and it will become distressed.

If this explanation was correct, then babies would show the same amount of distress wherever they happened to be when the separation occurs. So John would have been as upset if he stayed at home whilst his mother was in hospital as he did in the nursery for nine days. However this probably isn't true. Babies tend not to show as much separation distress if they are at home when their mother is away as they do in strange surroundings. Association learning can't be the whole answer.

Instinct:

Another possibility is that we have an instinct which tells us that we must be near a caregiver. This instinct declines during the second year. If the baby is separated this instinct is disrupted, and the baby automatically becomes upset. But why then do infants of 10 months or so quite happily crawl away from their mothers to play in a different room?

Schemas:

A third possibility is that, by about 12 months, children are developing the appropriate schemas for "caregivers in places". A schema is an idea of what something is, and how to deal with it. So the one year old baby may have a schema for "mother in sitting room" and "mother in kitchen". That knowledge will allow the baby to feel secure in the living room whilst its mother is in the kitchen and vice versa. If she then goes somewhere that the baby does not have a schema for, it may become upset.

were with. Between six weeks and six months they became increasingly sociable with anyone. By seven months they wanted to be near their main caregiver and started to be wary of strangers. This marks the beginning of the first attachment. Within a month or so of this first attachment they started to attach to other people. Schaffer and Emerson found that each attachment was much the same in quality. The infants responded in the same way to each attached adult. They seemed to use different adults for different things. If they were frightened they generally preferred their mother; if they wanted to play they usually preferred their father. Babies who are attached to several adults can be just as deeply attached to each. As Rudi Schaffer says ". . . being attached to several people does not imply a shallower feeling towards each one, for an infant's capacity for attachment is not like a cake that has to be shared out. Love, even in babies, has no limits." Nowadays most families don't have lots of adults around with time on their hands to spend with the baby. If they did no doubt we'd see many more examples of multiple attachment.

These findings contradicted Bowlby's theory in several ways. Bowlby claimed that there would be a hierarchy of attachments, with mother being at the top. However 20 of the 60 Glasgow babies weren't attached to their mothers, but to someone else altogether. In some families it was the father or another relative, whilst in others it was a neighbour. Secondly, infants don't have any one person who they must attach to. Rudi Schaffer continues "There is, we must conclude, nothing to indicate any biological need for an exclusive primary bond." Attachments could be made to several people.

By seven months 17 (29%) of the sample had attached to two people. By 10 months 36 (60%) had more than one attachment. By 18 months over 50 (87%) had more than one attachment and 25 (30%)

John Bowlby's research and conclusions were well known when Schaffer and Emerson undertook this research. Their conclusions did not entirely support Bowlby's.

Background reading – Theories of attachment

There are a number of psychological theories which try to explain aspects of development. They range from those which claim attachments are instinctive to those which say they are socially learned.

Biological or instinctive explanations These say that the baby has an instinct to bond with the person who feeds and cares for it.

Behaviourist explanation "Behaviourist" psychologists reject the role of instinct. They say that our behaviour is the result of what we have learned in the past. The baby learns who looks after it, and wants to be near that person.

Cognitive theorists Cognition refers to mental events like thinking, remembering, reasoning and so on. "Cognitive" psychologists believe that children develop schemas (ideas) through interaction with the environment when they are intellectually mature enough. Babies will attach to those people who help them to develop positive schemas about security, enjoyment, care etc.

Sensitive responsiveness theory This is Schaffer and Emerson's explanation for who babies attach to. It has something in common with cognitive theory. Babies form attachments to those who are aware of the baby's social needs and interact with them, rather than those who largely ignore them, except when they're crying.

Communication theory This is similar to Schaffer and Emerson's explanation. Children don't like being alone so develop communication skills in order to keep adults near them.

Which of these theories do you think comes nearest to the truth? Or perhaps you have one of your own?

had three, four, or five attachments. In Schaffer's words "There is . . . nothing to suggest that mothering can't be shared by several people."

Thirdly, these attachments weren't different in any way. The infant behaved in much the same way with each person it was attached to. Schaffer and Emerson conclude that attachments are most likely to be formed with those people who are most sensitive to the baby's needs (they call this "sensitive responsiveness"). They do not necessarily attach to those people who spend most time with them.

Exercise – Making attachments

1 What sort of things would you do if you wanted a baby to become attached to you?

2 How do we know who babies are attached to?

3 What advice would you give a new mother who wanted to return to work a year after having a baby?

4 What is the difference between an ethological study and an experiment?

5 Describe one study of parent child interaction that was not conducted in a laboratory. Name the technique used, and the findings made.

Is the attachment process the same everywhere?

The research mentioned so far is from Europe and America. It seems that different patterns of bonding occur in different parts of the world.

An example of early bonding was noted by Mary Ainsworth. She conducted a study of some Ugandan mothers and children of the Ganda tribe. (Uganda is a country in central Africa.) She found that the children showed separation anxiety by five to six months. Ugandan children and mothers spend more time close to each other, right from birth. They have more "skin to skin" contact too. Some research in some poorer countries has shown that mothers are less likely to neglect their baby if they have lots of skin to skin contact. Ganda children sleep with their mothers, and are breast fed, until they are about two years old. They go everywhere with their mothers, carried in a cotton sling. Being separated would be very unusual, so they show more anxiety when it happens.

An alternative kind of mothering is found in the kibbutz. In Israel about four per cent of the population live in large agricultural communes called kibbutzim. There are farms, some light industry, and some shops and offices in each kibbutz. They try to be self sufficient, growing and making enough to keep everyone fully employed. There are about 250 kibbutzim altogether in Israel. Everything should be shared equally between all the people who live in the kibbutz. Everyone works and receives the same wage and a share in the profits. Everyone should be regarded as equal in all respects. There should be no discrimination.

This has important implications for childminding. In order to return to work and start contributing again, the mothers of new born babies

Skin to Skin Contact

In societies where there is even more contact between babies and mothers attachment can occur even earlier than the seven or eight months that we in the West think is usual.

only stay with them for a few weeks. During this time intense "bonding behaviour" usually occurs (lots of cuddling, talking, playing, handling etc.) The mother starts to go back to work, just for an hour or two a day. A trained children's nurse called a metapelet looks after the baby. Gradually the mother increases the number of hours she works and the metapelet is increasing her time with the baby.

By the end of the first year the mother has returned to full time work and the child is living in the Children's House with all the other youngsters. The children spend an hour or so in the evenings with their parents before returning to sleep in the Children's House. The child stays more closely attached to its parents who spend just an hour or two each day with it than they do with the metapelet who's with the child all day. The parents have not abandoned their child in any sense, they just leave the routine of childminding to someone else.

The reason why the kibbutz system works for many children is that it is possible for them to make multiple attachments. Many will start to attach to the metapelet. The very high intensity and quality of the love between the parents and their children makes sure that the children feel wanted and secure. The reason why the children in the studies quoted by Bowlby suffered whilst their mothers were away may have been because the alternative care was inadequate. In the kibbutz the children spend many days away from their parents, and the substitute care is good.

Exercise – Cross cultural data

1 Does the bonding behaviour reported from the kibbutz confirm or reject John Bowlby's explanations? Explain your answer.

2 Does it confirm or reject Rudi Schaffer and Peggy Emerson's findings? Give reasons for your answer.

3 What are the advantages to psychologists of using findings from cross cultural research? What does it allow them to show which they may not be able to show otherwise?

4 What are the problems with comparing data from our society and that from cross cultural research.

5 Discuss one cross cultural study of mothering.

3 Lessons from attachment studies

From what we've seen so far we can draw some conclusions. We know that children need mothering. "Mothering" includes providing for the child's physical needs for food, comfort, and rest. It includes providing a child with emotional security and a sense of trust. And it includes providing social stimulation through play, games, explanations, and social experiences such as going to the shops, or the park.

REVIEW – Multiple attachments

Schaffer and Emerson's classic study of bond formation shows that babies are capable of forming more than one close attachment, and that the mother's role is not as important as some people believed. This means that childminding could be successfully shared between several people.

In the kibbutz babies form multiple attachments with their mothers, their nurses, and possibly even with each other.

REVIEW – Does the same attachment behaviour happen everywhere?

Children everywhere seem to want to form attachments to those people who are most deeply involved with them. The age at which attachment starts varies according to the kind of experiences the child has. Even where childminding is not mostly done by the parents, such as in the kibbutz, babies may still attach to them.

Babies are most likely to make attachments with those people who offer them high quality, meaningful care and affection. Those people who enjoy the child are more likely to be responded to than those who only take care of it.

Also we now know that babies as young as seven or eight months are capable of making more than one attachment. There are obviously differences between individual children, but the usual pattern is:

up to 3/4 months	Babies generally don't mind who is with them.
3–5 months	They start to decide who they feel safe with.
6–7 months	They express their preferences clearly – stranger fear begins. All this time they are attaching to one main person, and "getting to know" a few others.
6–18 months	They start forming multiple attachments if other adults are available and willing.

Further, the success and intensity of the attachment does not depend on the *amount* of stimulation the baby receives, but on the *quality* of it. An infant may form an attachment with someone who is deeply involved in playing with it for just an hour a day (father after work?), and not form an attachment to someone else who cares for the baby physically but doesn't play with it. This quality in the relationship is achieved through play, cuddles (contact comfort), individual attention, exchange games (eg "conversations"), and generally enjoying each other's company. It will provide the child with a sense of trust, security, and the knowledge that it has a *safe base from which to explore*.

Exercise – Lessons from attachment studies.

1 Name three functions of mothering.

2 What advice would you give to parents who wanted to know how to be certain of making a strong attachment with their baby?

3 Do parents make attachments "to" their children, or "with" them? Explain your answer.

4 If "Love, even in babies, has no limits" (Schaffer) what does this mean for sharing childcare?

Attachment in older children

Stranger fear and separation distress slowly disappear in well attached children (so long as the separation isn't for too long!) from around two years of age. Well attached children will be increasingly independent and willing to explore any new environment. They are inquisitive and enthusiastic. By this time they have developed enough language and thinking to enable them to start "experimenting" with their world and seeing what happens. They are able to learn for themselves. New situations and people may cause temporary shyness so some children will seek the security of the safe base (usually just behind their mothers'!). Less well attached children are less adventurous and less independent and will want to stay near their mother. Two and three year olds maintain their close attachments to mother, fathers, and other significant people in their lives. During the preschool period (three to five) they become steadily less clinging. Peer groups (almost always of the same sex) are becoming important, and children start to attach to their peers. Peer groups continue to be important until the child reaches adolescence and begins to prefer the company of one member of the opposite sex to the company of several members of its own! "Boyfriends" and "girlfriends" become attached to each other and will use each other for emotional security and social stimulation.

Exercise – Other attachments

1 Define the term attachment.

2 Apart from our parents, who else might we form an attachment with?

3 When do the two measures of attachment start to decline?

4 What do infants below one year of age need from an attachment?

5 What do three year olds need from attachment?

When attachment fails

We have mentioned some of the problems with insecure attachment. When it fails completely children suffer terribly. For example child abuse is sometimes the result of a failed attachment. The circumstances under which attachments are least likely to be made include those where the "problem" lies with the baby (the first two points below), and those where the parents are responsible (the rest).

Problems with disabled babies In 1974 and 1975 Selma Fraiberg studied some blind babies and their mothers. Blind babies aren't able to join in exchange games, imitating their mothers expressions, smiling back when smiled at and so on. They obviously couldn't recognise their mother's face and smile when they saw her, as sighted babies do. They were more likely to be rejected by their mother for being unresponsive, for example, when the mother of a blind baby enters the room the baby "freezes" so that it can listen very hard. Some of the mothers interpreted this as the baby not welcoming her. Selma Fraiberg has developed a programme for teaching parents how to cope with blind babies, for example, to "read" the child's signals, to talk to the child as they approach it, and putting toys that make a sound near the baby so that it will touch them and so forth.

Problems with difficult babies Some babies simply are difficult to love sometimes. They may be hyperactive, often irritable, or unresponsive. Some adults find it difficult to attach to babies who cry during play sessions. (In America they have a special test to diagnose "difficult" children.)

Some adults simply do not make good parents, particularly if they were abused or unloved themselves.

"Unplanned" babies Children who are the result of unplanned pregnancies are often at risk.

Unaware parents Some parents are inflexible and insist on a certain routine rather than letting the child decide when it's hungry or tired.

Problems with the situation Children in environments such as large families, or with parents who aren't close to each other, or where the housing itself, or the income of the family, is inadequate are also often at risk.

The more of these factors there are, the less likely it becomes that the child will have a firm attachment.

In the early years attachment is an emotional bond from which babies derive feelings of trust. By three or four the child looks for stimulation, as well as care and protection. By the school years the children are becoming more independent and confident, so that they can share their interests and affection amongst friends. During the teenage years the needs for attachment can include members of the opposite sex.

REVIEW – Changing needs for attachment

Children need mothering. This is best provided by people who enjoy being with the child and stimulating it. Dependence on caregivers declines as the child is able to explore and communicate. Children who are securely attached are likely to feel more confident to investigate and experiment with their new world.

Exercise – If attachment fails

1 What differences would you expect to see between the behaviour of an insecurely and a securely attached child?

2 Review the reasons for a child and its parents not forming a secure attachment.

4 The effects of long term deprivation

Most psychologists agree that short term separation produces separation distress in the young child, as described by Rene Spitz and by the Robertsons'. There is disagreement about whether these problems persist. In 1975 J W B Douglas (Director of the National Survey on Health and Development) found that children who had been in hospital (and therefore separated) when they were young, were more likely to become delinquent when they were adolescents. This directly supports Bowlby's theory. The Clarkes' re-analysed his data and found that the reason why many of the children went to hospital in the first place was because of problems of disadvantage in their homes. Many were from poor families, often having a poor diet. Many lived in cramped, overcrowded and inadequate homes. They often played on the street in dirty and dangerous areas. This social deprivation was usually the reason why the children had to go into hospital, and therefore this may contribute quite as much to their delinquency as any maternal deprivation they suffered. Michael Rutter came to much the same conclusion in his studies of adolescents.

Whilst reviewing the case against some of John Bowlby's early ideas we mentioned some orphanage studies which have shown that children can overcome the lack of an early attachment without suffering "affectionless psychopathy". Children raised in orphanages behave like children everywhere for the first few months of life. From around six months their behaviour starts to change. They begin to lose interest in just about everything. William Goldfarb found that children who stayed in the orphanage he studied for the longest time did less well on all the scores he made, but remember there may have been problems with the sampling in this study.

Deprivation of "mothering" will almost certainly have unfortunate consequences if nothing is done to help make up for the deprivation. We mentioned Barbara Tizard and Jill Hodges' conclusions that children who were adopted quite late could, with patience and understanding on the part of their new parents, form loving relationships and enjoy a perfectly normal adulthood. The identical twin boys studied by Jarmila Koluchova seemed to have made an excellent recovery, and the war orphans studied by Anna Freud and Sophie Dann made good progress during the course of their study.

Harlow and Suomi showed that even the most severe privation in monkeys can be overcome with the right kind of treatment. However the laboratory research on animals can be criticised for using small

The effects of short term deprivation will largely depend on the age and previous experience of the child. If the child isn't firmly attached it will not feel the pain of separation so much. The long term effects of separation are harder to judge since they depend on so many more things.

samples, and anyway not being generalisable to humans. The "natural experiments" on the orphanage children can be criticised for having biased samples.

Exercise – Long term effects of deprivation

What sort of advice do you think someone adopting a child who has spent some time in an orphanage ought to be given concerning mothering the child?

Can children from deprived environments recover later?

Harlow and Suomi's monkeys did recover, given the right "therapy".We now know that children can too, if they are placed in stimulating homes and given lots of individual attention. Michael Rutter found many of the adolescent children he studied had recovered from their early deprivation. Wayne Dennis suggests that if the child is below the age of two when the deprivation ends, then it can recover fully. He

Background reading – Why is maternal and social deprivation so harmful?

Here are the main hypotheses:

The maternal deprivation hypothesis This was first advanced by people like John Bowlby and Rene Spitz. They say the child needs a warm loving relationship with its mother (or a permanent substitute). But Rudi Shaffer and Peggy Emerson have shown that babies from about eight months can have many attachments, not just one with a mother.

The stimulus deprivation hypothesis Children need different kinds of stimulation for them to become responsive to their environment. Harlow's isolated monkeys and children raised in unstimulating environments had little to look at or play with. There were no dependable people to show them how to respond socially. There were few toys to manipulate (to learn hand to eye coordination and practise handling skills). There were few opportunities to move around (to develop motor coordination and exploration skills). Altogether there was little opportunity for social, emotional, intellectual, or cognitive development.

The social stimulation hypothesis Some investigators now believe that children need to have their social signals responded to. They use signals like crying and babbling to attract human attention. If this signalling fails, they become apathetic, and eventually give up trying. Sally Provence and Rose Lipton studied a sample of children in an institution who had toys to play with, could see and hear other infants, but they had little contact with adults, ie they were socially deprived, not deprived of stimulation. They became emotionally, socially, and intellectually retarded.

The reason why social stimulation is so important is probably because the stimulation depends on the infant's own behaviour. When the child cries, babbles or smiles, people will interact with it, ie it starts the interaction. This may give the infant some feeling of control over its environment. It becomes more sociable as it learns to use its social signals when it wants to attract other people's attention. The children in the institution wouldn't have their signals responded to, so after a time they would stop signalling since it clearly didn't work. They may develop a sense of "learned helplessness". This may explain why some deprived children are withdrawn and apathetic.

REVIEW – Failed attachments

Attachments can fail for a number of reasons which could originate with the children or with the parents. The effects are emotional disturbance which might affect other aspects of development. Children can recover from failed attachment if there is adequate, high quality, continuous care available.

studied a number of children who had been adopted from a deprived orphanage at various ages. Those adopted after the age of two never fully recovered intellectually.

Other research on children in their normal homes also supports the case for social stimulation. Mentally retarded children from poverty stricken homes are unlikely to have parents who are able or willing to provide the kind of stimulation they need, and the children don't recover. Those in better off homes with better educated parents are more likely to recover.

No one can say for sure that the effects of prolonged early social deprivation are completely permanent or completely reversible. The children in Koluchova's study seemed to recover intellectually and socially, but it's harder to measure emotional development. An interesting version of Harlow and Suomi's "young therapist" technique has been used on a group of socially withdrawn preschool children. Wyndol Furman and his colleagues exposed these children to a series of play sessions with a child who was either their own age, or 18 months younger. The results were just as Harlow and Suomi might have predicted. All the children became more sociable in their normal day care situations, and those who had played with the younger child became most sociable. Although Furman and his colleagues' sample were socially withdrawn they were not "ill" in any sense, but this kind of treatment might be useful for treating even more disturbed children.

Exercise – Can deprived children recover later?

Write an essay to answer the question "To what extent does the available evidence support or contradict the view that the effects of long term deprivation is irreversible?"

5 The Family, Home, and Surrogates

In the last two chapters we have discussed the nature of attachments. We have defined attachment as a close, emotional bond that develops between a baby and some of the people who care for it. We said that it develops from when the baby is around five to seven months old. We suggested that children who are strongly attached feel more confident, and may become more competent, knowing that there is someone who will support it when things are going well, and care for it when things go wrong. There are many other benefits in having strong attachments too. Inevitably not all children are going to have a strong, uninterrupted attachment. In this chapter we will be looking at some of the major issues that can affect a young child's life.

These include:

1 The family, including different types of parenting,
2 Some problems associated with divorce,
3 The effects of care outside the home,
4 And the possibilities for successful fostering and adoption.

1 The family and the parent

The vast majority of people in the West will be born into a family, will be reared by it, and will eventually marry and form a new one of their own. Various people have tried to analyse the "*functions*" of the family, and have concluded that the family reproduces the children, looks after them physically and emotionally, teaches them those things which they must know in order to become useful members of their society, and provides them with a status. **Robert LeVine** studied families from several cultures and concluded that they all fulfilled the following functions which can be described as the objectives or goals of parenting:

The three goals of parenting, and how we achieve them in the West

1 To survive	Parents provide food, warm clothes, and shelter. They "nurse" the child when it is sick, and comfort it when it is unhappy.
2 To become economically independent	Parents teach their children some of the skills they will need to know in order to survive economically. Some parents may pass on the skills of their trade, others may teach their children about business.

What differences might you notice in a new father's behaviour?

(contd. p.84)

3 To learn the norms and values of our culture	Parents socialise their children into understanding about "right" and "wrong", "good" and "bad", and what norms (appropriate behaviour), and values (appropriate attitudes, beliefs etc) are acceptable in its culture.

Becoming a parent usually means taking on certain responsibilities for a new member of society. These include keeping the child physically safe and secure, and passing useful knowledge on to it.

These three goals are arranged according to their importance. Only when the first is satisfactorily achieved will parents begin to pursue the second, and so on. Other people may also be involved later of course. In our society teachers, medical staff, social work agencies, the churches, job training and opportunity agencies, and others may also be involved in the functions mentioned above. In other societies the responsibilities fall entirely on the parents. Parents are almost always more involved with the younger child, and the other people may start to become involved as the child reaches its third and fourth birthdays.

The arrival of a child usually marks some major changes in its parents' behaviour. These changes can affect the parents attitudes and behaviour towards each other, towards friends and relations, and towards any other children they have. Mothers often become more "maternal" and devote most of their time to the infant. Fathers also often start acting differently.

The baby's needs will have to come first, and this can mean a change in the way other family members feel. Older children may start to feel neglected. Their relationship with their parents may become weaker if they think their parents are rejecting them in favour of the new baby. Fathers who are less involved with the new baby may feel left out, and some mothers will be too tired or busy to tend to normal family routines.

Can you think of any other stresses that having a new baby might place on a family?

A baby can be an expensive addition to the family, particularly if one of its parents gives up work to spend time with it. Social engagements may have to be limited if babysitters have to be paid. Having less money, not seeing friends so often, and having to put someone else's needs first all the time, can place great strains on family life. Just about all of the research in "**parenting**" shows that the months and years following the birth of a child can be stressful for all concerned, with some families seemingly unable to cope. If the parents are older and more mature, financially and socially secure, and want, and plan for, a baby, then the stress is least likely to be damaging to the family. Where the parents are younger, possibly unmarried, and the pregnancy is unplanned, the stress is likely to be greatest.

REVIEW – The new baby

Where parents have planned for a new baby it can be a source of great joy to them. Caring for a helpless infant may bring couples even closer. However babies can also be a source of great stress, especially where couples haven't realised the demands babies can make, or where they don't feel that they are able, or want to cope with these demands.

Exercise – Conceptions outside marriage

Conceptions leading to:	1974	1984
A Illegitimate birth (One parent registering)	17%	17%
B Illegitimate birth (Both parents registering)	16%	30%
C Legitimate births (Parents having married)	29%	16%
D Abortions	39%	37%

(Source: Office of Population and Census Statistics July 1986)

1 The trend that less than 20% of births which were conceived outside marriage (reported in *A* above), were registered by just one of the parents has remained stable for many years. Describe the trend (reported in *B*) for both parents having their names included on the birth certificate.

2 If both parents register the child it is likely that they are living together and have a fairly stable family relationship. What trend does the table show for couples marrying after a baby has been conceived?

3 Summarise the problems that younger couples may face with the arrival of a new baby.

Psychological evidence suggests that the goals of successful parenting are more likely to be achieved if the parents are able to show consistent warmth and love, can accept the child for what it is, and use a reasoned approach to discipline.

The effects of early experiences on the child

The vast majority of research in child development shows that the ways in which parents behave towards their children can have a very great effect on almost every aspect of the child's development. We can identify three aspects of the parents behaviour which will have major effects on their children. The first can be described as general *warmth and love* towards the child. For the child of a few months of age onwards parental warmth takes the form of attachment behaviour. Secondly, there is the actual "**child rearing style**" used. Some parents are strict about their children's behaviour, and may punish them quite severely. Others may be highly permissive in what they allow their children to do. Some will be tolerant of some things and not others, some will be inconsistent, and punish the child, then apologise to it. The third factor is the extent to which the parent *accepts the child* for what it is, without imposing unrealistic expectations on what the child should achieve. We will summarise each in turn.

Warmth in the parent

Unfortunately not all children are wanted and planned. Those that are might have parents who are ready and willing to offer them the warmth and love they need. It may be more difficult for a mother to feel the same way towards an unplanned baby. Some children may simply be difficult to love. Hyperactive babies, ones who will not settle to a regular pattern of feeding and sleeping, babies who are uncooperative, and even handicapped babies may all be difficult to love.

We know that parents and children should build strong attachments during the first few years. John Bowlby had claimed scientific evidence to support his view that the early relationship between mother and baby is extremely important for the child to build a sense of confidence and trust. He believes that babies have a hierarchy of preferences, with mother (or substitute mother) at the top, and other family and non family members further down. Babies and mothers will form a bond which must not be broken. If it is broken, usually because mother and baby are separated, then emotional development will be interrupted, and the child will have problems rebuilding relationships later. Other researchers have suggested that Bowlby's view of parenting is too limited. For example, Colwyn Trevarthen and Martin Richards believe that babies are much more flexible in the range of social relationships they can enjoy, and they do not need a single,

Successful parents must show warmth towards their child. By "warmth" we mean that a child enjoys being close to its parent, and enjoys doing things with its parent. The children of warm, loving parents will probably feel that they can confide in their parents too.

Parents who use reasoned explanations, who use discipline in a warm and caring way, and who restrict any excessive aggression in their children seem to be encouraging their children's maturity in several areas of development.

Parents who accept their children's attitudes and ideas, who listen to them and show an interest in what they think and do, are more likely to have children who are more willing to join in, more confident, and more able to be independent.

dominant attachment. Nor will separation from any one person necessarily be devastating if good alternative provisions are made for the infant.

Children of parents who are unable to show warmth and love, and children who were unwanted, tend to be insecurely attached, which can lead to lower levels of curiosity and independence. They may be more selfish and less sociable, have a lower opinion of themselves and their worth, and tend to have a high fear of punishment and parental disapproval. They may constantly seek approval before acting on any decision they have made.

Child rearing style

There's a lot more to bringing up children than just forming attachment bonds, and helping them learn about trust. Parents vary in their attitudes towards how their children should behave, and they may use different sorts of "child rearing style". A number of studies of "child rearing styles" have shown the effect that parents can have on their children's long term behaviour. Mary Ainsworth, a colleague of John Bowlby's, has shown that sensitive mothering, which puts the infant first, seems to be more successful in producing contented babies. Others have noted correlations between sensitive mothers and more independent, sociable, curious children too. Parents who are either too restrictive and domineering, or too easy going and inconsistent, may encourage their children to develop a rather distorted view of the world.

We will discuss two of the best known studies on the effects of child rearing styles and children's social behaviour in the chapter on aggression. Briefly, they conclude that "**permissive**" parents allow their children to do almost anything they wanted to. Their children become highly aggressive. "**Punitive**" or "**authoritarian**" parents disciplined and punished their children a great deal. Their children learn that aggression was an appropriate way to achieve what they wanted although they were used to having other people decide what they should and should not do. A "democratic" or "**authoritative**" group of parents used sensible discipline and restricted their children's aggression, without excessive punishment. Their children were more in control of themselves, and were more advanced in other skills too. They were also the least aggressive of the three groups.

Acceptance of the child as an individual

Parents should accept their children's worth. The children's opinions and ideas should be taken seriously and discussed, so that the child builds up confidence in its ability to make contributions to decisions. The child's ideas should not be overlooked or rejected, just because they are the child's ideas. Parents who accept their children "as they are" do not make unreasonable demands on their behaviour, nor do they set them unreasonable targets to achieve. Rather, they support and encourage the child in whatever direction (within reason) its abilities lie.

Relationships within the family

Apart from how the parent treats the child, how the child sees its own position in the family is also important. The oldest child may feel itself to be more responsible, and more important, since it may be "left in charge", or told to "look after" the younger ones. The youngest child may feel inferior, since its wishes and requests are swamped by those of its older brothers or sisters. Or it may have to fight more to establish its place in the family.

The sex of the child will also be important. One study of the effects of birth order on children suggested that first borns have slightly stronger consciences, are more curious and interested in new things, show more responsibility, and are less aggressive. If the next child is the same sex, and less than two years younger, it would be very similar to the first born. Where the next child was three or four years younger the older child tended to be more aggressive. This may have been because when the new baby arrived the older child may have felt threatened by all the attention that the new baby received. It may have become more noisy and aggressive in order to make people take more notice of it.

Girls who had brothers rather than sisters tended to be more aggressive too. They had clearer ideas about what they wanted out of life, and were more determined to achieve them. They were slightly more intelligent than girls who had sisters too. Girls with older brothers were more tomboyish, and boys with older sisters were less aggressive and less curious.

Older and Younger Children

Exercise – Learning from our parents

1 Name three "goals of parenting", according to Robert LeVine.

2 Name some of the changes that may happen to a couple's life when their first baby is born.

3 Name some of the consequences of an unsuccessful attachment.

4 Here is an extract from Diana Baumrind's description of the authoritative parent.

"The authoritative parent . . . attempts to direct the child's activities, but in a rational . . . manner. She encourages verbal "give and take", and shares with the child, the reasoning behind her policy. . . . She balances her own special rights as an adult [against] the child's individual interests."

Rewrite the extract in your own words.

5 Here is an extract from Diana Baumrind's description of the permissive parent.

"The permissive parents attempt to behave in a nonpunitive, acceptant, and affirmative manner towards the child's impulses, desires, and actions. She consults with him about policy decisions, and gives explanations for family rules. She makes few demands . . . [and] presents herself as a resource for him to use as he wishes, not as an active agent responsible for altering . . . his behaviour."

Rewrite this extract in your own words.

REVIEW – Parental influences

Children acquire a lot of their attitudes and behaviour from their parents. Parents who are warm, accepting, and authoritative in their dealings with their children, may be more able to achieve the three goals of successful parenting, survival, independence, and socialisation.

Divorce is increasingly common in many Western societies. Some social groups are more at risk than others from divorce. This can have serious consequences for children.

2 Children and divorce

Many children spend all or part of their lives away from one of their parents. In America it is estimated that about half of all marriages are likely to end in divorce, and almost half of all children are likely to spend some part of their lives in a single parent family. In Britain and most of Europe divorce rates have been increasing over the last few years. About a quarter of all new marriages in Britain are likely to end in divorce. Some couples are more "at risk" than others. The latest statistics show that the highest rate of divorce is amongst people who have been married between eight and ten years. About 12% of all brides in Britain are under 20 years of age on their wedding day. About three quarters of them are pregnant. Teenage marriages have a very high risk of ending in divorce.

Psychologists have been interested in the effects that divorce is likely to have on the children. Freud argued that the absence of a father during a son's personality development would have disastrous consequences for the child's personality, as we shall see in the next chapter. A girl would suffer less because she still has her mother. Other psychologists say that children learn by observing and imitating their parents, if one parent is absent, then the child will be missing an important source of information about how a member of that sex behaves. The extent of these effects will depend on the age and level of understanding of the child, and should change between the short term and the long term.

Mavis Hetherington has reviewed most of the research on the effects of divorce on children. She claims that just about all children will show some short term distress. For a year or so after the divorce children may feel angry, guilty, afraid, and depressed. She calls this the "**crisis phase**". Younger children may even see themselves as partly responsible, and this can add to their distress. Their behaviour may change as a result of these feelings. Many children become more disobedient and more difficult to handle, whilst the parent who has custody may become more intolerant, bad tempered, and more inclined to use punishment. This may increase the child's anxieties, and lead to more unsettled behaviour. These effects will obviously depend on how close the child (and the remaining parent) was to the parent it has lost. Emotional, social, and cognitive development can all be upset by the loss of a parent. It is usually the mother who has custody of the children and some research has shown that boys who were close to their fathers may suffer more than girls who remain close to their mothers.

The effects also depend on the reasons for the separation in the first place. As Michael Rutter and others have shown, conflict and distress in the home can have much worse effects on a child than simply losing a parent. Even many years after the divorce children may still feel bitter, although studies in America suggest that they do not seem to bear any grudges against either parent. After the "**crisis phase**" comes the "**adjustment phase**" as the child becomes used to life in a one parent family, or life in a family with a new parent if the parent who had custody remarries.

The effect that divorce will have depends on factors like how old the child is, how close it was to the absent parent, and the levels of tension, stress, and conflict in the home already.

Exercise – Divorce

Here are some quotes from some children whose parents were divorced:

Sarah – (aged 10)

"I live with my Mum now, but Dad is here quite a lot too. They don't argue any more . . . and he buys me presents. He has another wife now, but I don't call her Mummy. They tried to explain what was happening when they got divorced. . : . Having parents who are divorced is okay . . . they're friends."

Michael – (aged 7)

"I had to go to court . . . the people asked me questions about what I thought. It went on a long time, and Mum and Dad never spoke. It was cold and I cried. I only see Dad sometimes now. He comes for my birthday and I cry when he leaves. . . . I wish Dad still lived here but I don't think he likes us any more. He doesn't talk to me much, even when we go out."

Andrew – (aged 14)

"No one really cares at school, loads of kids have parents who are divorced. I remember being frightened when they shouted. They probably thought we couldn't hear. We knew exactly what was going on, but they wouldn't talk to us. I hated him for going at first, but we got used to it."

1 Summarise the differences in the way these children are coping with their parents' separation.

2 Do children always suffer when their parents divorce? Explain your answer.

3 Children can often understand a lot more than they seem able to. What evidence is there for this in the quotes above?

4 Children should never be allowed to feel guilty or responsible for their parents' divorce. Is there any evidence that any of these children do?

5 How do you think parents who are planning to divorce could minimise the effects the divorce will have on the children?

Exercise – Divorce in England and Wales

	1961	1971	1981
Divorces granted (in thousands)	25	74	146
Number of individuals divorcing per thousand married people	2.1	6.4	11.9

1 What was the increase in the number of divorces being granted between 1961 and 1981?

2 How many people obtained a divorce in every 1000 who remained married in (a) 1961, and (b) 1981?

3 Name some of the short term effects that parents separating can have on young children.

4 What explanation does Michael Rutter give for some of the long term effects on children's behaviour, apart from their parents separating?

REVIEW – Divorce

Statistically the most usual length for a marriage that ended in divorce in the last few years has been between eight and 10 years. Any children in these families are likely to be young enough to be quite badly affected by the experience. they may feel resentful, angry, afraid, and may even feel partly to blame. However, as Rutter says, a couple whose marriage is full of conflict and bitterness may be better apart. Staying together for the sake of the children is not necessarily thought to be a good policy by most psychologists now, since the children may be hurt more by the conflict between their parents than they would by them separating.

3 Care outside the home

Child rearing is a fairly full time occupation. Bowlby claimed that it was a job which women were naturally equipped to do. In the last 40 years many women, and some men, have increasingly realised that there could be more to being a woman and a mother than just looking after children. Feminists and the women's liberation movements have condemned Bowlby's insistence that a woman's place is in the home with her children. Because of the pattern of unemployment in Britain some women now go out to work whilst their husbands stay at home. It's too early yet to say whether this pattern of childcare is going to have any ill effects on the children.

Apart from being reared full time by one or both parents, there are a number of alternative means of bringing up children. These range from those which give the caregiver a couple of hours a week away from the child, to those which give several hours a day. Some are more successful at recognising and meeting the child's needs. Some children will have a parent, or both parents, who aren't able to manage their child's life because of some temporary difficulty such as illness, a problem with housing, or some problem with the courts. In this case the child may have to be taken into care by the Local Authority.

Some confusion has existed in people's minds about exactly what alternative forms of childcare there are available. Here is a brief summary. For children who usually live at home with their parents there is the local playgroup, to which three to five year olds may go for just a few hours, on one or more days a week. If a mother wishes to have more time away from the child, there are childminders. Childminders often look after people's children for a few hours each weekday. Some may look after older children too, for example during school holidays or if a child is away from school for any reason. The quality of the service offered by childminders varies widely. Some are excellent, others are little more than places to leave a child for a few hours. Nursery schools, which children can attend between about 9 am and 3.30 pm, are run by a relatively few education authorities for their under fives. This has been one of the areas which has suffered major cutbacks in the last 10 years or so.

All the alternative forms of childcare mentioned so far are intended for "normal", healthy children. Some children may live in homes where there is some deprivation. Day nurseries are only available for children who are defined as being at risk or at some serious disadvantage. They are run by some Social Service departments in some areas of the country. In this section we will look at childminding, nursery schooling, and day nursery provision. Later we will look at rather more permanent types of alternative care for children, being "in care", being fostered, and being adopted.

Childminding

Childminders are usually women with children of their own who take other children into their homes for a few hours during the day. This form of childcare could be of benefit to all concerned. It allows the

Do you agree with John Bowlby that women are naturally equipped to be mothers, and to look after the children? Or could men who stay at home bring up the children quite satisfactorily?

Alternative forms of childcare are available in most areas for children whose parents do not look after them all of the time.

mothers to keep their jobs, or whatever engagements they have, the minders are able to earn money, and the children to have another adult to attach to, interact with, and learn from. The child might go to the same childminder for several years and the childminder could be another continuous presence in the child's life.

Childminders should be registered with the local Social Services department who should inspect their premises and see that the facilities available for the children (toilets, heating, ventilation, play area, protection against infectious disease, and so on) are adequate. The child's physical needs and comforts are accounted for. Unfortunately there aren't similar regulations about the child's emotional needs.

In *Minder, Mother, and Child,* **Betty Mayall** and **Patricia Petrie** report the findings of their study of 39 registered childminders in four rather depressed inner city areas in London. Mayall and Petrie believed that the minders they studied were amongst the best available in the four boroughs. They said "We saw no minders living in bad housing conditions, and . . . their accommodation was [mostly] clean and well kept." Most of them had experience of working with children, and most were trained. "Nearly a third of them had had some work experience relevant to childminding [and] more than two thirds had contact with a special social worker who devoted himself or herself to childminder support or training."

Mayall and Petrie observed the interaction between 27 of the children, and their minders, and with their mothers. They were interested to see what kind of activities the children were involved in at the minders, and whether these activities encouraged co-operation, whether the children were being stimulated, and whether they appeared to be happy. Mayall and Petrie also interviewed the minders, to discover what they thought their role was, and the children's mothers to find out what the children were like at home.

Exercise – A study of childminders in the inner city

1 What research method did Mayall and Petrie use in their study?

2 What measures of the independent variable are being taken?

3 How could their findings be validated?

Apart from being brought up at home, some children spend time with a childminder, at playgroup, at nursery school, or at a day nursery. Did you or any of your friends have any of these forms of childcare? What sort of things did you do?

Childminders are usually married women who "look after" someone's child alongside their own.

A 'Minder'

Mayall and Petrie found that the minders were not attempting to act as substitute mothers, neither were they offering the child the chance to form any kind of an **attachment**. Many of the children looked almost **detached**. They seemed to have little real interest in what was going on, and weren't offered any kind of involvement with the minder. Many of the children studied didn't seek stimulation or company. Others were noisier, but there wasn't very much for them to do, and they were there really just to "fill in time". They weren't benefiting much at all. To sum up, Betty Mayall and Pat Petrie found unstimulated children being looked after by childminders who didn't offer them the chance to become very involved. They said "The children spent a low

Mayall and Petrie's conclusions paint a fairly depressing picture. It seemed that an opportunity for the children to have an enjoyable and stimulating experience was not being taken.

level, under stimulated day in unchanging, often cramped, surroundings." Many did not receive the love and attention they needed. Some had experienced frequent changes of minder, and most of their mothers were not satisfied with the standard of care offered.

In the early 1970s a group of people interested in childcare for the under fives came together under the leadership of Professor Jerome Bruner to investigate the state of various aspects of childcare in Britain, and to spread such information as already existed as widely as possible. It was called the **Oxford Preschool Research Group**, and reported on such topics as playgroups, nursery schools, childminding, and day nurseries.

As a part of the Oxford Preschool Project, run by the Oxford Preschool Research Group, **Brigit Bryant**, **Miriam Harris**, and **Dee Newton** studied some childminders in fairly affluent Oxfordshire. They randomly sampled 165 minders from the list of registered childminders, although only 66 were currently minding a child. Between them they were looking after 98 children, so most of the minders were caring for one child who was not their own. The researchers used a questionnaire, an interview, and observations as the main data collection methods. The observations were modelled on those conducted by Mayall and Petrie so that direct comparisons could be made. Bryant, Harris, and Newton found none of the problems of shortage of toys and play materials, or cramped conditions that Mayall and Petrie had found.

Most of the minders Bryant, Harris and Newton studied were reasonably well off, and "housing conditions seemed to us to be very good, particularly in comparison with inner city minders. . . ." Houses were warm, and all but one had a garden, and a nearby park in which the children could play safely. Like those minders Mayall and Petrie had studied, this sample also put their own families needs first. Shopping, cleaning, cooking, and running around after their own children. About three quarters of the children's days at the minders were spent with the minder while she did her chores. Consequently few of the minders found much time for playing with the children, or offering them any specific stimulation.

Bryant, Harris, and Newton conducted observations of the children, both at home and at the minders. They also interviewed the mothers

Background reading – A description of a "typical" minder

She is "married, in her early thirties, with three, or possibly four [of her own] children, and, quite likely, a foster child too. Some of her children are already at school. She has lived in the same area for most of her life, and has parents, brothers, or sisters living nearby. She left school at 15 and went more or less straight out to work until her marriage or the arrival of her first baby, after which she stayed at home, or perhaps worked part time. At some point she

may have worked with children.

She has married a man who is in skilled or semi skilled work, and they are still living together. She feels little stress at being a mother and housewife, and is strongly convinced that she should stay at home with her children at least until they start school. Indeed she may be rather unsympathetic towards mothers who leave their young children and go out to work." (Bryant, Harris, and Newton) and the minders. They found that few minders wanted the mothers to do anything other than drop the child off, then leave. They felt it was their job to look after the children. They did not see any great need to form any kind of a relationship with them, and since they were fairly busy people they didn't have very much time to spend with each child.

Overall the researchers were able to divide their sample up into three groups of children. Only 29% of the children (who were seen both at home and at the minders) were described as being in the "lively" group. 26% were described as being in the "quiet" group. They didn't seem to be involved in anything except repetitive, solitary play, both at home and at the minders. Children who are unstimulated at home are unlikely to find stimulation with a minder. The third group were "mixed", a combination of the other two groups. It was the largest group, with 45% of the sample who were usually unnaturally quiet and good at the minders but quite happy at home. These children could have benefited from childminding, but were not doing so. Overall, almost three quarters of these children were happy and lively at home, but less than a third were lively at the minders.

Better-off parents may employ a full time nanny to look after their children. She could form an attachment with the children in her care, and provide a rich source of stimulation. This is fine so long as the nanny stays for some years, but the child can become upset if the bond is broken when she leaves.

Exercise – Childminding

1 Write a brief paragraph under the heading, "the main benefits of childminding could be . . .".

2 If you have a child that you want to be minded, what steps do you think you should take, in the first instance, to find a minder?

3 Having found one, how might you want to settle the child in? (HINT What did the Robertsons do before having Thomas stay with them?)

4 If attachment doesn't depend on the quantity of time spent with the child, what does it depend on? Briefly explain your answer.

Nursery schools

Nursery schools are run by some Local Education Authorities who employ professionally trained teachers, and sometimes qualified children's nurses, to staff them. Parents and other helpers are also often invited to become involved. Most nursery classes offer preschool children wider opportunities to play and wider social experiences than they might have at home. Playgroups are not usually run by qualified professionals, but rather by groups of mothers. They may hire a local hall, such as a club hut, school, or church hall for a few mornings each week. (Some charitable bodies even run Playbuses to serve families in poor or outlying districts where facilities aren't always available.)

Kathy Sylva, **Carolyn Roy**, and **Marjorie Painter** conducted a study of nursery schools as part of the Oxford Preschool Research Project. They made detailed observations of children's activities in the schools, and assessed the contribution of nursery school experiences to the child's development. In *Childwatching at Playgroup and Nursery School*

Bryant, Harris, and Newton found that childminding seems to work well enough for those children who are happy at home, and who do find stimulation at the minders. It is tolerable for other children, who are content to "fill in time" until they can go home. The opportunities that minding could offer were lost for these children. Those children who are not stimulated at home were unlikely to be stimulated by the minder.

REVIEW – Childminding

Whilst we know that children can make multiple attachments, and that they can benefit from having a variety of adults and children around them, the major studies of childminding show that children are not benefiting in the ways that they could. The reasons for this are not so much lack of knowledge, but more a lack of resources. Parents are unlikely to want to pay enough to a minder to allow her to devote herself to a few children. Most minders take in someone else's child whilst mainly concerned with their own family's needs.

the researchers reported that creative play activities occupied much of nursery school children's time. Some children became absorbed into their own activities and had little time for other children. The children were encouraged to play with paint, to model things, and to engage in pretend play. Most of the children Sylva and her colleagues observed tended to be very active in whatever they were doing. Very few merely "passed time". Many seemed to be enjoying the experiences, and were generally stimulated. However they did not tend to cooperate very much, and their interactions tended to be rather unfriendly, competitive, assertive, or even aggressive.

The researchers classified the children's activities into three broad groupings. "High yield" activites encouraged thinking about, and using, basic reading, writing, and number skills. Large scale construction projects that involved imagination and deduction of certain principles were also found to be of benefit. Those activites that could be described as "moderate yield" included "pretend play" such as dressing up, and role playing games such as being in a shop, or a hospital. Picking up and using smaller objects, like Lego blocks, for small constructions, or jigsaw pieces to attempt to complete jigsaws, could also contribute to general development. "Lowest yield" activities include simpler things such as simple games which do not involve either much skill or much imagination. Can you think of some examples?

The children in Sylva, Roy, and Painter's study seemed deeply involved in their activities, but they weren't very sociable.

REVIEW – Nursery schools

Despite successive governments having recognised the needs of the under fives, and the benefits of nursery schooling, less than a quarter of Britain's under fives are able to attend a nursery school. Teaching and facilities are usually better than those which are available at most minders.

Exercise – Nursery schools

Fill in the spaces in this table which compares the findings of the studies of children at their nursery schools with those at their childminders.

	Childminder	Nursery school
Amount of stimulation		
Degree of involvement		
Amount of cooperation		
Amount of creativity		

Day nurseries

Some children from poor families living in deprived areas may be under-stimulated. They may live in damp, unhygienic houses and have an inadequate diet. For these children some Local Social Services Departments have special day nurseries. (NB don't confuse day nurseries with residential nurseries). Day nursery children from a few months of age, right through to school starting age, spend most of the day in the nursery, usually being busy in the mornings, and resting in the afternoons. A number of these children may have physical, emotional, social, and intellectual problems. They are often undersize and underweight for their age. They may not be very independent and may be untrusting and resentful. They often don't mix well and may be spiteful and aggressive. Their language and thought processes may not be as mature as they should be.

Day nurseries have four main aims. The first is to help the children grow fit and strong, and so they provide nourishing food and lots of physical exercise. A second aim is to try to help children's social interaction, so encourage mixing with other children through playing games and sharing toys. A third goal is to help children's language and communication skills, and try to help intellectual development, by giving them challenging toys such as Lego, jigsaws etc. Finally they attempt to help the children's emotional development, by trying to give the children a sense of belonging.

Some day nurseries are privately run and the children here are often from wealthier homes. These nurseries emphasise educational and social development rather than physical or emotional needs. Those nurseries run by Social Services often have to concentrate on physical and emotional needs since it's impossible to educate a hungry, cold, or insecure child. Other nurseries for deprived children are run by charities, whilst others are run by large institutions such as universities or companies as creches for their employee's children.

A study of day nurseries

Two other researchers in the Oxford Preschool Research Group, **Caroline Garland** and **Stephanie White**, conducted an observation of children at day nurseries. They found that nurseries cater for either physical or educational needs, depending on the attitudes of the staff. Some staff were very child centred and so the needs of the child always came first. They would make sure that the child was fit, well, and happy first, before trying to encourage it to learn anything. In other places staff were more "rule centred". They believed that children do best where there is organisation and discipline. They emphasised the education of the child. Garland and White concluded that care was more important at this young age than education. Making the children (and the parents) feel more secure was the main task.

Exercise – Day nurseries

1 What are the main aims of day nurseries?
2 Who are day nurseries intended for?
3 What sort of things should come first, according to Garland and White?
4 Why?

REVIEW – Day nurseries

Day nurseries are intended for very young children, up until school starting age, who are disadvantaged in some way. They attempt to improve the child's physical, emotional, social, and intellectual skills. Garland and White stressed the need for nurseries to put the child's physical needs before its intellectual needs since children who are uncomfortable or unsettled will not respond well to learning. Not all Social Service departments are able to run day nurseries for deprived children. Some institutions run what they call day nurseries, but these are not intended for deprived children at all. They are more like ordinary nursery schools, and cater for the children of their employees.

4 Children in care

There are several reasons why a child cannot, or should not, stay with its own parents, although it can't ever be an easy decision to take a child into the care of a Local Authority. It is disruptive for the child, and expensive for the Social Services. It is also very upsetting for the child's parents. On the other hand there have been a very few cases where a social worker's reluctance to remove a child has had tragic consequences. Social workers have strict guidelines about the circumstances under which children may be taken away from their natural parents. Mistakes such as those that appear to have been made in the

Children who had to be taken "into care" used to go to orphanages and hostels financed by local authorities. Most now go into temporary foster homes.

Cleveland area, where children were taken away from their parents for suspected sexual abuse, have highlighted the need for extreme caution. Some children have been left with their parents, or returned to them after a separation, and been badly treated and even killed by their parents. Children are often taken into care temporarily, while some problem in their home is sorted out. Some will go home at weekends and so keep in touch with their families. Several Local Authorities try to have children who are "in care" fostered straight away, rather than place them in an institution. Apart from Local Authority homes there are charities such as Dr Barnardo's, and The National Children's Homes, who also look after separated children.

Fostering

Foster parents take someone else's child into their own home, usually for a fairly short period, until it goes back to its usual permanent home, or is adopted. Fostering often involves older children, and new attachments don't generally form between foster parents and their "children". This may be because the foster child is still in close contact with its natural parents. Being a foster parent can be even more demanding than being either an adopting or natural parent. The foster parent knows that the child doesn't, and probably never will, belong to them. They know that they have few rights over the child. Foster parents know that the child will be upset and may take its frustrations out on them, and on their home, especially if the child has spent a long time in an institution before being fostered. Despite trying to do their best for the child, it may sometimes seem resentful and suspicious of them. And they know that they will have to give the child back to its parents, or it may be adopted one day.

Yet many fosterings are successful. One important reason for this is that the new "parents" are so well motivated. They are often experienced in childcare and know what to expect from the children, many of whom don't want to be with the foster parents. Foster parents are carefully chosen by social workers, and fully advised about the benefits and pitfalls of being a parent of someone else's child. They must be very patient, very consistent, very warm, and must surely love children very much. One way that has been used to find out if a fostering has been successful is called a "follow up" study.

Exercise – Substitute parents

Imagine that you were the director of Social Services in your area. You are interviewing some people who want to become foster parents.

1 What qualities are you looking for in them? Make a list and be prepared to explain why each quality is necessary.

2 What advice would you give them about the children they might be fostering?

Follow up studies

A follow up study is a study of adults (or children) who have all shared some similar experience, such as having been fostered. The idea is to

REVIEW – Alternative forms of care

Some children have to be looked after whilst some temporary problem is being sorted out at home. The usual solution is to foster the child, until it can go back home, or until it is adopted into a new family.

Foster parents look after someone else's child, usually temporarily. Some fosters can last much longer, if the natural parents are unavailable to sign a release form.

96

see if there are any differences between what they are like, and what people who have not had the same experiences are like. If there are, it might be that their experiences have caused those differences. For example if people who were fostered had different emotional responses compared to people who were not fostered, then their emotional responses may be the result of having been fostered.

In a follow up study the subjects are asked to recall their early experiences and describe how they felt. Their "new parents" may be asked to describe how the children behaved towards other children, what they were like at school, how they acted towards them etc. The people who had been fostered may be given specific tests to measure their intelligence, sociability, personality and so on.

Here is an example of one follow up study of 40 people born between 1956 and 1957. By the time they were 16 they had all spent at least seven years in a foster home. When they were 20 or 21 they, and their foster parents, were all interviewed by **John Triseliotis**. From the results of these interviews Triseliotis concludes that continuous, high quality care can overcome the problems of maternal deprivation. Those who had been too young to form an attachment before they were fostered had few difficulties, those who were older and had already had one attachment broken, had some problems. Sixty per cent of the children coped well, in spite of the disruption.

Follow up studies have several shortcomings. For example they ask the fostered person to remember their feelings and behaviour from childhood. They rely on the foster parents' memories too. They also rely on the researcher making judgements about how "well adjusted" the subjects are. At best, such studies can only provide correlations. We can never know for certain that what the individuals are like now is the result of having had some experience earlier, such as having been adopted or fostered. They might have become like that anyway. For example imagine that some adult, who had been raised by foster parents, is disruptive in some way. We can't say that the disruption is the result of having been fostered. The adult may have been disruptive as a child, long before it was fostered.

Adoption

Fostering may be a solution for those children who need short term care in a family. Most psychologists agree that the best solution for motherless children, under normal circumstances, is full adoption. Clearly we would like the child to become deeply attached to its new parents. Whether this happens depends on things like how deeply the child had been attached to its natural mother. If the child is a few years old, and was deeply attached, then the loss will be deeply felt. The new parent may have great problems in convincing the child to make another attachment. A child whose trust has been badly broken once is unlikely to give it very easily again. Another factor would be how willing the new parent is to offer such enormous patience, stability, consistency, and security. These things, and many more, will be necessary if an attachment is to be made. A third factor would be the age and maturity of the child. Before babies have learned a strong attachment (before six or seven months of age), a successful substitu-

Follow up studies compare groups of people who have all shared some particular experience with groups who have not. Any differences between them may be the result of the experience they shared.

John Triseliotis found 60% of his follow up study's sample of people who had been fostered appeared to be coping well.

The trouble with follow up studies is that they can only show that some people who have had some experiences sometimes behave in particular ways. They cannot show that the experiences each of us have automatically makes us behave in particular ways.

REVIEW – Fostering
Follow up studies suggest that children can cope with the loss of their parents if the alternative provisions made for them are satisfactory.

tion should be quite possible. At the other end of the age range, older children may find it easier to understand what is happening to them, and may settle into a new home more easily. An American study by Alfred Kadushin found that children of up to 12 have been adopted satisfactorily, and made good loving relationships.

If we can't measure someone's emotional state with any accuracy, how will we know whether being adopted has had any effect. For example, can we say that Sharon's occasional bad moods are the result of her adoption? Is she unapproachable because she misses her real mother? Can you think of any reason why someone might be in a bad mood? Does it have to be anything to do with their parents?

Despite these difficulties, careful observations, interviews with parents, and reports from school and so on are the only techniques that can be used to investigate the effects of substitute mothering. Since it would be impossible to conduct controlled experiments, researchers have to use either follow up studies, or find instances of where children are being offered for adoption or fostering, and observe their progress. (Natural experiments)

Barbara Tizard, **Judith Rees**, and **Jill Hodges** conducted a follow up study of 65 children from deprived families, who had been put into residential nurseries before they were six months old. They hadn't formed strong attachments, and they didn't have the opportunity to form any in the nursery. There were plenty of toys and games and other stimulating materials in the nursery, but the nurses rarely stayed long and weren't encouraged to become too involved with the children. Apart from being fairly noisy, rather afraid of strange adults, and very clinging, the children seemed to be coping fairly well in their nursery.

Between two to three years of age some were adopted, some were returned to their natural mothers (many of the mothers weren't married and hadn't been able to cope previously), and some remained in the nursery (because their mothers couldn't be found so couldn't sign the forms for the babies to be adopted).

Background reading – Can older children benefit from adoption?

During the 1950s and 1960s a number of children from Doctor Barnado's Homes and other orphanages had been adopted at three, four, five years of age, and even older. They made great demands on their new parents, many of whom couldn't cope with the kind of treatment they received from the children, and some of the children had to be returned to the orphanages. Some of the children seemed unwilling to make an attachment so it was assumed that children above one or two years old couldn't be adopted. Bowlby's work was quoted to support this.

There is a more likely explanation for why these adoptions failed. Many of the adopting parents weren't well enough informed about what to expect. Many thought they were adopting a normal child who was no longer a baby. Many social workers themselves weren't trained to be aware of the likely problems. The adopting parents and the children weren't given enough time to get to know each other. The adoptions failed through a lack of information and preparation, not the child's inability to make another attachment to its new parent.

The early years of our lives are important, but not as important as used to be believed. Ann and Alan Clarke have reviewed a great deal of evidence to show that children are capable of adapting to major upheavals in their lives. We also now know that late adoptions can be successful.

Exercise – Fostering and adoption

1 Think of some reasons why a child might be fostered.

2 Think of some reasons why a child can't stay with its natural parents, and so is offered for adoption.

3 Here is an advert from a local paper.

The Astonville Courier   Wednesday 19th Aug

WANTED

A very special family.
Nick is 13 years old and needs someone to look up to.
He's stayed with two families before, but didn't really settle in.
Nick is quiet and plays on his own quite a lot. He is quite shy, and takes time to get to know. We believe the effort would be greatly rewarded. Nick can show a great deal of affection. If you'd like to find out more about Nick, or about becoming a foster parent, please ring Emily Pankhurst on Astonville 393456.

4 What evidence is there in this advert to suggest that Nick may have some emotional problems?

5 What sort of a) behaviour problems, and b) emotional problems might Emily Pankhurst warn anyone replying to this advert to look out for?

6 Imagine your Director of Social Services has asked you to conduct a study into the success rate of adoptions in your area. Write a brief report setting out how you intend to investigate it.

Exercise – The problems of measuring success

1 Try answering these questions about yourself:
When did you first have a "best friend"? Did you often argue with him/her? Did you join in with the other children at school? Were you popular at school? Do you like being alone sometimes? Did you often get nervous and anxious? Have you had many girlfriends/boyfriends, or do you prefer permanent relationships? Do you have a bad temper? Did you cry very often?

2 When answering questions like this, can we be sure that you have understood what the question means? (How often is "very often"?) Can we take your word that you have remembered everything correctly? Or that you've told the truth? Even if we ask your parents to give their opinions of what you're like, will we have an accurate picture of your emotional state?

Here's a brief extract from a case study of a 19 year old who was adopted which was written after naturalistic observation and interviews.

"Sharon is usually calm and in control of her feelings. She is rarely aggressive or self centred, and is popular amongst her wide circle of friends. She expresses her feelings well, and is absolutely truthful. She occasionally has bad moods, and becomes depressed. At these times she is quiet and unapproachable."

3 How scientifically acceptable are such observations?

The Jesuit Fathers (a teaching order of Roman Catholic Monks) have said "Give me a child until he is seven, and I will give you the man". What do you think they meant by this? Do you think it's true?

Barbara Tizard and her colleagues have shown that full adoption seems to be the best alternative for children who aren't able to stay with their natural mothers in a well equipped home. Environmental factors appear even more important for emotional, social, and cognitive development than biological ones.

The success of the adoption seems to depend on things like how far the new parents are prepared to go to show the child that they will love and support it, and that the child is special to those parents.

Barbara Tizard and her colleagues followed up these three groups, and a control group of babies (who had not been in an institution and were being brought up "normally"). The four groups were all studied at two years old, then at four and a half, and then at eight years of age.

At two years old the nursery children were all fairly similar. They were largely unattached. They were quite different from the controls, who were more secure and independent.

By four and a half years some differences between the nursery groups were emerging. Those who had been adopted formed attachments with their new parents, but made great demands on them. They had almost caught up with the controls intellectually, but their emotional behaviour was not as advanced. They were still rather shy and weren't very adventurous. They would cling to their parents, and still showed stranger fear. The next most mature group at four and a half years were those who'd stayed in the orphanage. They received some stimulation, both from toys and from humans. They were often noisy and boisterous. Some weak attachments had been made. The least well developed intellectually were those who had been returned to their mothers. Their families still lived in rather deprived conditions and the children lacked two of the main things they seem to need for healthy psychological development, people who enjoy interacting with them, and things to play with and manipulate. By eight years old the adopted group were still the most advanced group, (after the controls). They had developed strong attachments but were still rather restless and timid. They didn't make friends as easily as the controls, and they were still rather clinging towards their new parents. The lack of an early attachment was still being felt. They weren't able to concentrate on schoolwork for very long either. Those returned to their mothers, and those who had stayed in the orphanage were not as well developed in their social relationships, or intellectual abilities.

Evidence from this and other studies suggests that children can overcome even the most deprived early experiences. Adoption into a family that desperately wants a child, and which is capable of providing the kind of care the child needs, is the best solution for a child from a deprived background. John Bowlby claimed that children need their mothers, and that even a bad home is likely to be better than a good institution. Tizard's study does not support this claim. The children who were returned to their mothers did not develop as well as many of the others who were adopted.

Residential nurseries

Apart from minding, nannying, and other temporary forms of childcare, there are some more permanent ways of looking after children for short periods. Residential nurseries were available in some areas for very young children who were awaiting adoption, or entry into an orphanage. Some children were also admitted for a period of a few days or weeks, whilst their parents weren't able to look after them. If the child's mother had to go into hospital, for example, and no one else was able to take care of the child, it may have been placed in a residential nursery. The Robertsons made detailed observations of the progress of several children who were temporarily placed in residen-

Evaluation of follow up studies

Criticisms

1 The source of information, ie the memories of the adopted or fostered person, and their parents, may not be valid or reliable.

2 They rely on the researcher observing and conducting tests to judge how "well adjusted" the people are. Observations may be partial, and tests may be invalid.

3 Such studies usually rely on seeking correlations.

Advantages

1 What else can we do? It is not possible to conduct controlled experiments on the variables "being fostered or adopted" and adult "emotional responses" in humans.

2 Judgements based on observations and test results are used throughout psychology. Results gained here are no more likely to be mistaken than results gathered in other areas.

3 Correlations may not show cause, but do give an indication of a relationship.

Exercise – Follow up studies

1 What was Triseliotis' sample size?

2 Summarise the conclusions from John Triseliotis' follow up study.

3 Why did Barbara Tizard and her colleagues use a control group in their study?

4 Why did they follow up the four groups several times over the next few years?

5 Briefly describe the development of each of these four groups.

6 Bowlby had claimed that being with one's own mother is the best solution for a child. The study by Barbara Tizard and her colleagues casts doubt on that claim. Other factors, such as the motivation to be with, and to stimulate a child, seems to be more important for healthy development than just being with one's mother. Summarise the evidence for this statement.

REVIEW – Adoption

Barbara Tizard, and her colleagues, have shown that adoption can be a very satisfactory solution. Younger children who have no parents may be offered for adoption. Very young children can attach to their new parents with the minimum of fuss. Older children, who had already formed attachments, may have greater problems. Adoption is still the best solution for motherless children, since all the alternatives seem unable to provide the essential elements of parenthood, warmth, consistency, accepting the child for what it is, and using a sensible, reasonable system of acceptable and unacceptable behaviour.

tial nurseries. Some children would have survived the experience, some might even have benefited from it. The likelihood is that most would have suffered. This was certainly James and Joyce Robertson's conclusion. Factors which would influence the child's experiences include how long the child stays in the nursery, the kind of care available for it whilst in there, and the amount and type of stimulation available.

We have said that children from between approximately six months and five years need to form an attachment bond with their primary caregivers. Bowlby had warned about the terrible consequences of breaking this bond. He warned that a separation of just a fortnight could have permanent ill effects. Even separations of just a few days can have serious short term effects such as poor sleeping, increased temper tantrums, wanting to be carried rather than walking, increased stranger fear, being over affectionate and clinging. James and Joyce Robertson's pioneering work in the 1950s and 1960s showed that this

Residential nurseries are not widely available now, and children are much less likely to be separated from their parents than was the case 20 years ago. A few residential nurseries are attached to orphanages.

A criticism that has been levelled at some of the early work on the effects of separation is that it overlooked a key variable, ie what happened to the child during the separation. As the Robertson's showed, the detachment suffered by some of the children they studied wasn't wholly the result of the loss of their mother, but rather the lack of any permanent substitute.

REVIEW – Residential nurseries

Residential nurseries may be used by children who are awaiting adoption or moving permanently into an orphanage. The Robertson's found that systems of group care had terrible consequences for some of the young children they studied during the 1950s and 1960s. Children in residential care need intellectual and social stimulation as well as warm, consistent, and loving substitute mothering.

experience can be very upsetting for children who were temporarily placed in a residential nursery. Despite fierce hostility from some members of the medical and childcare professions, the Robertson's warnings have now largely been accepted, and every effort is made for young children who have to be temporarily separated from their parents to be fostered.

The type of care available will also have some effect. Many institutions used to employ systems of group care, where a small number of nurses simply looked after a group of children. Inevitably the noisier, more demanding children were likely to attract the most attention. Children who had been in the nursery for a long time would have learned that they must make their demands loudly and insistently if they were to attract the nurses attention.

The child who was placed in the institution temporarily may have been unable to compete. It may feel left out, and may feel its isolation even more. In many child care institutions now, the system of group care has been replaced with a system of individual care. Each child is assigned one, two, or three, particular nurses who are to act as temporary "*attachment objects*". The child may come to feel that "their nurses" are special to them. James and Joyce Robertson's work has shown that many of the problems that young children in brief separation face aren't necessarily caused by the separation itself, but by what happens to the child while it is separated. Being given one special person to form some kind of attachment with may help overcome some of the problems of breaking the bond with its usual caregiver.

Having a few special people to attach to will not solve all the child's problems of course. It is still separated from its permanent caregivers, and it will feel that loss. Three other factors must be mentioned which may affect the child. Firstly the child's age is an important variable. For children below six months, who haven't yet formed a strong attachment, the effects of separation are unlikely to be very harmful. Children over four or five can have the cause for the separation explained to them, although they may not see why they can't stay at home while their mother is away. Children between six months or so, and three or four years, are likely to feel the loss most deeply. A second factor is the willingness and ability of the child's nurses to provide constant love, warmth, comfort, soothing explanations, and reassurance. This isn't always easy, since nursing staff often work very long hours doing very tiring work. A third factor would be the availability and use of intellectually stimulating toys and games. Young minds need to be occupied, and something which challenges a child's imagination and intellect may take its mind off the separation, and make the time seem to pass more quickly.

Exercise – Residential nurseries

1 Why might a child have been put into a residential nursery during the 1960s?

2 What is meant by a system of "group care", and how does it differ from individual care?

6 Freud's Psychoanalytic View of Personality Development

How children develop emotionally will have some influence on how their personalities develop. In this chapter we review Sigmund Freud's contribution to our understanding of personality development. His was one of the first complete theories, and one of the most influential.

Freud spent most of his life constructing **case studies** on his patients, and developing explanations for why their personalities changed. Psychological theories which attempt to explain how people change are generally called **psychodynamic** theories. Freud's was one of the first of these. His particular explanations are usually known as **psychoanalysis**.

In this chapter we will look at:

1 The origins of Freud's theory, and the methods he developed to investigate it.

2 What Freud discovered about the unconscious.

3 The structure of human personality.

4 The stages of personality development.

5 Some evaluation of Freud's approach and explanations.

1 The background to psychoanalysis

One of the earliest and best known explanations for personality development comes from Sigmund Freud (1856–1939).

Whilst studying medicine at the University of Vienna towards the end of the last century, Sigmund Freud had become particularly interested in human anatomy, and intended to do research in human physiology and neurology when he graduated.

Freud had attended some neurology lectures on patients with severe headaches, temporarily paralysed limbs, temporary blindness, and similar symptoms. These are typical of particular disorders of the nerves and muscles. But the surgeons couldn't find anything wrong with these particular patients' nerves or muscles. Freud, and a colleague, Dr Josef Breuer, had some patients with similar problems for which they could find no organic cause. (NB organic refers to the organs of the body.)

Whilst still puzzling over the cause of their symptoms, Freud heard about some work being conducted on hypnosis in Paris by Professor Jean Martin Charcot. Charcot was using hypnotism to show that patients could be made to feel they had certain symptoms such as numbness, paralysis etc. When they were brought out of the hypnotic state they couldn't remember anything about the trance they'd been in,

Sigmund Freud

Here are some suggestions for activities that you may find useful during this section of the course. Collect any articles or newspaper reports, or something similar, on anything involving people with personality or behaviour problems. Make notes from any television programmes you see on mental health. Keep a diary of any dreams you have during the next week.

Freud was interested in physiology and neurology. Physiology is that branch of biology that studies what animal cells, tissues, and organs do, and what they are made of. Neurology is the branch of medicine concerned with studying the nervous system.

Background reading – Sigmund Freud – A biography

Sigmund Freud was born in May 1856, in Frieberg, now in central Czechoslovakia. Freud's father was a rather unsuccessful wool merchant. When Sigmund was three, the family moved, first to Leipzig in Germany, and then to Vienna, the capital of Austria, in the hope that business might be better there. Vienna was dominated by the Roman Catholic religion, and Jews were discriminated against. The Freud family were Jews, and this was to have important consequences for Sigmund Freud later.

Freud's parents encouraged him to be independent and he was always studying. He started school a year earlier than was usual, and did well there. At 17 he entered the medical school of Vienna University. He didn't particularly want to be a doctor, although he knew he could make a living at it if necessary. His real ambition was to do scientific research. He went to as many science lectures as he could. (This is why it took him eight years to finish his degree!) He finally obtained his MD (Doctor of Medicine) in 1881 and started work at a large hospital in Vienna.

Frieberg to Vienna

In June 1882, he became engaged to Martha, with whom he was passionately in love. Like him, she had no money, and their four year engagement was rather stormy. Freud borrowed money from his close friend, Dr Josef Breuer, and even pawned his watch to find enough money to live. He took several jobs at the hospital, and learned as much as he could about the areas he studied. He had to give up the research he was doing and concentrate on earning more money, specialising in neurological and physiological cases. His private patients were mostly poor Jewish people. He worked and saved for four years. By September 1886 he had enough money to marry his beloved Martha.

Freud became interested in the mind, and for almost 50 years he investigated the origins of personality. He developed a theory which was to have lasting effects on psychology in Europe and America (although it had little impact in Russia, China, Africa, and Asia). He wrote several books on psychology. The first, published in 1895, was called *Studies In Hysteria* which he wrote with Breuer. By the 1930s his work was being translated into different European languages, and hospitals were opening psychiatric departments based on using Freudian psychoanalysis.

Freud lived and worked in Vienna almost all of his life. When it finally became obvious in 1938 that the Jews would be further persecuted by the Nazis, the Freud family came to Britain where Sigmund spent the last year of his life working on his final book. He died in September 1939 at the age of 83.

and they had the symptoms that Charcot had told them they would have. Freud wanted to know if hypnosis could work the other way round, ie could a patient with such symptoms be hypnotised into believing that their symptoms had disappeared?

Charcot's Laboratory

Here we have a picture of a number of patients with particular illnesses which don't appear to have any conscious, physical cause. Can you think of any other possible explanation for their illness? HINT There's a clue in the first sentence of this comment.

Do these findings about hypnotism fit in with your answer to the last question? Do they offer any further explanations? Where do these patients' illnesses seem to come from? HINT Look at the last HINT. It has something to do with the causes of the symptoms.

Do you think that there are any illnesses which might be caused by mental events which may be unconscious? Do you know of an example? Check with other people to see if you can find other examples.

Clearly there must be some relationship between the mind and the body. In 1884 Freud went to Paris to study hypnosis with Charcot. During the months he was there he became fascinated by the **"unconscious mind"**. He returned to his patients, determined to develop techniques, like hypnosis, for exploring the unconscious mind.

Exercise – The unconscious mind

A five year old boy named Ounkar was taken to the dentist for his usual checkup. He had been eating lots of sweets recently, and the dentist told his mother he'd have to give the child's teeth a "bit of a scrape". Ounkar didn't like the sound of this. He didn't enjoy the "scrape" either. Ounkar said the dentist had hurt his mouth. When he got home his mother told him he'd have to stop eating so many sweets and then the dentist wouldn't have to scrape his teeth.

Ounkar soon forgot his mother's warning though. Six months later, on the morning of the day of his next checkup, Ounkar was violently sick and had to stay in bed with an upset stomach.

REVIEW – The origin of Freud's theory

Freud had some patients with problems for which there was no organic cause. He called them symptoms of "hysteria". The patients had no conscious knowledge of the cause of their hysteria, so Freud thought the cause must lie in their unconscious. Freud thought the unconscious had a powerful influence on us. He believed it contained deep forces which make us behave in all sorts of ways. He wanted to investigate his patients' unconscious minds.

Freud concluded that the causes of hysteria lay in the unconscious, and wished to find ways of investigating it. Any ideas? We've already mentioned something which could help. HINT Remember Freud's visit to Paris?

Freud made detailed observations of some of his patient's behaviour. Science is very concerned with making observations, and making educated guesses based on them. All scientific investigations must involve observation.

1 Ounkar was genuinely sick and complained of a "poorly tummy". He didn't have any particular illness, and he was fine by teatime. Can you think of any explanations for this "mystery illness"?

2 Would it be possible to check any of your explanations?

If researchers discover some symptom of a disorder that is unknown to science, they give it a name. Bowlby did this when he "discovered" the condition "affectionless psychopathy". Freud described the type of mental disorders his patients suffered as "hysteria". Nowadays we use terms like hysterical neurosis to describe some of the symptoms Freud observed. The term hysteria had been used for hundreds of years, usually to describe "odd" female behaviour. (The term literally means "wandering uterus"!) Can you think of any illnesses that are named after the person who first researched them?

As a doctor Freud could look into someone's throat, or stomach, or chest, but how was he to look into their unconscious minds? Freud was a dedicated scientist and realised that he would have to develop scientific techniques for finding out what was going on in the unconscious.

Exercise – Freud's background

1 Approximately when did Freud start work as a doctor? Was it the middle of the last century, during the second half of the last century, or in the first half of this century?

2 What do neurologists and physiologists study?

3 What does the term "organic" refer to?

4 Why did Freud become interested in hysteria?

5 Name three symptoms of hysteria.

6 Where did Freud think these symptoms came from?

7 Write a paragraph beginning "Freud believed the 'unconscious mind'. . . ."

Techniques for studying the unconscious

Freud thought the human mind was a bit like an iceberg. The tip which shows above the water is the **conscious** part. The **unconscious** part is much larger, and is hidden from view. He developed a number of techniques for investigating the unconscious part. Most were the result of his *"clinical interviews"* with his patients. He started with hypnosis which he had tried to learn from Charcot. However not everyone can be hypnotised, and unfortunately Freud was not a very good hypnotist. Hypnosis seemed to give contradictory results and Freud soon gave it up, saying it was "temperamental". Instead he made some deductions from his observations of some of his patients.

Freud asked some of his patients to talk *freely* about their earliest memories, and how they felt about the people in their lives. If they seemed to run out of things to say Freud would give them key words, like "happiness", "love" or "fear". When Freud asked them a direct question their replies were often fairly predictable, but when they were just talking freely they occasionally said things that were more revealing. Freud thought they seemed to give some clues about what was going on in their unconscious. Several patients mentioned being very frightened of some things. It was as though they were "off their guard" when talking freely, and able to say things which they may not have said otherwise. Freud asked more of his patients to talk freely, and he began to try to piece together their backgrounds. This technique is called **free association** and became a major tool for investigating the unconscious.

One of the earliest, and probably best known of psychoanalytic case studies was conducted by Josef Breuer on a patient referred to as "Anna O". (Her real name was Bertha Pappenheim and she went on to become a well respected social relief worker.) When she was a young woman, she suffered temporary paralysis of her limbs, and was also diagnosed as having multiple personalities. Breuer began Anna's "free associaton" treatment when she was 21. Anna O was a very stubborn, determined woman, and she insisted that talking about her problems made her feel better. She invented the term "*talking cure*" to describe the effects the therapy had on her.

One of Anna O's problems was paralysis of an arm. Breuer thought he had found the cause in something that had upset her a great deal when she was younger. Anna had been looking after her father who was very ill in bed. She worked very hard and was very tired. Whilst sitting in the old man's sick room waiting for the doctor, she imagined she saw a large, black snake slithering towards her sleeping father. This frightened her very much. She tried to stand up and go to her father, but her right arm, which was draped around the back of the chair, just wouldn't move. Breuer concluded that this combination of wanting to protect her father and the fact that her arm wouldn't move, explained Anna's paralysis. She had buried the fear and the guilt she felt about being unable to protect her father in her unconscious, and this somehow caused her paralysis. As Anna began to realise what the things she described meant, so she "got better".

Freud and Brever developed a technique called free association which could encourage their patients to reveal their deepest feelings.

Exercise – Anna O, a case study in hysteria

1 What were Anna O's symptoms?
2 What did Breuer conclude was causing her symptoms?
3 Did Breuer "cure" her? (THINK) Explain your answer.

During a "free association" session one of Freud's patients started to tell him about a dream he'd had. Freud had thought that dreams might be another way of the unconscious "breaking through" into the conscious world, since when we are asleep we are relaxed. So Freud analysed his patients' dreams. He came to the conclusion that during our daily lives there are so many rules and restrictions governing what we can and can't do that we can never be truly free. While we sleep many of these restrictions are cast aside and our innermost thoughts

Freud thought that dreams revealed what was going on in the unconscious. Do you have any recurring dreams? Can you remember what you dreamed last night? We all have a few dreams each night, but we usually forget them quite quickly. Why do you think we dream? Do you think that what we dream is always what we wish would happen?

and wishes can be revealed. Freud believed that dreams reveal what we really want. He said that dreams show our "concealed wish fulfilment".

A Therapy Session

It seemed to Freud that, whilst we are awake and alert, a kind of guardian or censor watches over us, making sure we don't come into contact with anything too upsetting. While we sleep however, our censor is rather "off guard" since little can upset our conscious mind while we are asleep. The parts of the dream that can be remembered may provide a skilled psychoanalyst with the clues as to what the dreams really mean. Dreams are a "window on the unconscious" which, with skilful interpretation, can be understood as signs from the unconscious. Freud described **dream analysis** as "the royal road" to the unconscious.

Apart from dream analysis Freud also noticed that people sometimes say something which comes out all wrong. They are called "**slips of the tongue**". Freud thought that what we actually said was really what we meant. Freud analysed any slips of the tongue his patients made (which later became known as "Freudian slips"). He concluded that these slips of the tongue were also a sign that our guard was down and the unconscious was breaking through.

Freud used a number of other methods to investigate his patients' unconscious minds. For example he examined occasions when people seem to forget things "on purpose", without being aware of what they are doing. He studied their sense of humour to see if there were any clues there about what they thought. Freud used clinical interviews and the techniques of psychoanalysis to develop case studies of his hysterical patients. They relied very much on his own observations and interpretations of what his patients said and did. They weren't just the usual medical case notes that doctors make.

Freud slowly developed his theory of psychoanalysis based on many of the case studies he had conducted over the years, and on the folklore, myths, and taboos of some other cultures which he had studied to see if they contained any familiar themes.

Slips of the tongue may also be the unconscious breaking through into consciousness. Have you ever meant to say something, but when you spoke it came out all wrong? Do you think you really meant what you actually said?

Exercise – A patient's dream

A man was suffering from depression which he said was because he was bored at work. During psychoanalysis he said that he had dreamed about running through a vast desert, on his own. He felt very happy although he knew he had a long way to go. He was looking forward to the journey, and waved and shouted greeting to groups of people as he passed them. In his dream the people looked like animals, some were tied to stakes, others were in cages. In a previous session he had stumbled over his wife's name. Her name was Lesley, but he had distinctly said "Left me". They had been unhappily married for over 20 years, and had only stayed together because of their children.

1 What might a psychoanalyst think the man meant when he said he was enjoying running through a desert on his own?

2 What might the psychoanalyst make of the people looking like animals who were either tied up, or in cages?

3 How might this dream confirm the man's previous slip of the tongue?

4 Comment on Freud's claim that dream analysis was "the royal road" to the unconscious.

Exercise – The unconscious mind

1 Name three of the main methods which Freud used to investigate the unconscious?

2 What is "science" and what is its main method?

3 What are clinical interviews used for?

4 What are case studies?

Write a paragraph beginning "Freud wanted to investigate the unconscious. To do this he had to develop some. . . ."

Exercise – A child's dream

Read this extract from a therapy session.

Analyst: What was your dream about?

Martin: I don't know.

Analyst: But you said it frightened you.

Martin: It did.

Analyst: Can you tell me anything about it?

Martin: I fell over playing and came home.

Analyst: Is that why you were frightened?

Martin: Mummy made it better and kissed me and made it feel warm. Then daddy came in.

Analyst: Does mummy usually kiss you better when you're hurt?

Martin: Daddy says big boys don't need kissing better.

1 How might the therapist interpret Martin's statement that he didn't know what his dream was about?

2 What do you think the therapist might make of Martin's feelings about his mother, and his father?

REVIEW – How to study the unconscious mind

Freud developed the techniques of free association, dream analysis, and analysing slips of the tongue for investigating the unconscious. He had tried to use hypnosis, but wasn't successful. He used clinical interviews to build up case studies of each patient.

Freud had a great interest in ancient civilisations and some of his ideas about the mind appear to have been influenced by it. He was fascinated by archaeology, and, when he could afford it, he bought objects that had been discovered by archaeologists. Although his consulting room and treatment room were small, they were full of his treasures.

Freud derived his ideas about a force for life, and a competing force for death from ancient myths. The concept of the libido still exists in psychology, and in many other people's minds. (Have you heard of it before now? Ask your parents and friends.) Do you know anyone who is always rushing about, who seems bursting with energy? Freud would say they have a strong libido. Libido can be a useful concept in describing some behaviour, but some psychologists reject it. They say our behaviour is the result of observing, imitating, and learning from others. They say that to talk of instincts ruling our lives is wrong. What do you think? Is our behaviour the result of our instincts? Or is it the result of learning whilst growing up? Or both?

2 Instincts and the unconscious

After his return from studying with Charcot in Paris in 1886 Freud began to believe that there were certain *instinctive* forces that rule much of our behaviour. By *instinct* he meant some irresistible biological urge. For over 30 years Freud investigated these instinctive urges. By 1920 he had settled for the existence of two main instincts, one concerned with love and life, the other concerned with death. Many of Freud's ideas were based on ancient Greek mythology which told of Eros, the god of love, and Thanatos, the god of death.

All scientists know that all activity needs some kind of energy to maintain it, eg, cars won't run without petrol, computers won't work without electricity, and your body gets its energy needs from food. But where does the energy to fuel these instinctive urges come from? Freud thought there were a number of sources of "*mental energy*".

The force for life is mostly maintained by the energy which Freud called **libido**. The libido is to do with the amount of energy we put into life and being whichever sex we are. It is a *positive force for survival, reproduction, and well being*. It provides the energy that we need to deal with the tensions that build up when we are frustrated. Opposing this force for good is the force for bad, which Freud calls the **death instinct** or **death wish**. The death instinct is to do with how we deal with aggression, danger, denial, anger, guilt, temptation and so on. It is to do with *negative, unpleasant emotions*. It pushes us towards the state when all our tensions will be relieved, ie death.

Much of our personalities will be the result of a competition between these two forces. Some people will have stronger libidos, and

Background reading – The two instinctive urges

The Libido The force for life takes its energy from the libido. Libido is the main source of our sexual energy which is concentrated on things like survival, worthwhile achievements, love, kindness, and on all the ways in which humans can find expression and fulfilment.

Everyone has libido, but we all have different experiences and grow up in different ways so each person develops a different personality. Libido makes us behave in many ways which relieve pressure that would otherwise build up. When libido is frustrated, emotional problems will occur.

The death instinct or death wish This was the basis of Freud's theory of aggression. He said the origins of human aggression are instinctive, not learned. Death wish is destructive and makes some people want to dominate others. It makes us want to put ourselves in

dangerous situations, and even want to harm those people we hate. (The first people we hate will be our own parents when they start to refuse to let us have things we want!) Freud believed we must transfer these feelings from our parents onto things like toys or furniture. (Children often "take out" their anger or frustrations on toys and furniture.) If the death wish is not released when the frustrations build up, then Freud believed that some personality problems will almost certainly occur later in life. In Freud's later writings he seemed less convinced about the existence of the death wish.

So, according to Freud's psychoanalytic approach, these two instincts are responsible for much of our personality later. Much of our behaviour is directed towards gratifying these basic instinctual urges. The ways in which we gratify these urges changes as we grow.

will be a force for good in the world. Others have dominant death instincts, and will be generally harmful, and even self destructive.

Exercise – Describing libido and death instinct

Here is a list of words which describe aspects of human personality. Have two lists, one headed LIBIDO and one headed DEATH INSTINCT and put the appropriate words in each list. Use a dictionary if necessary.

Brutal, energetic, generous, aggressive, sadistic, sporting, unemotional, hardworking, cooperative, autocratic, withdrawn, intuitive, domineering, purposeful, authoritarian, caring, suicidal, thoughtful, purposeful, aloof, enthusiastic, quick tempered, helpful, quarrelsome.

Exercise – Instincts in the unconscious

1 What do you know about the sample from which Freud drew his data? That is,
(a) Representativeness – What did all of Freud's patients have in common?
(b) Were they a biased sample or a representative sample?
(c) Were they a typical cross section of people of that time?
Yes/No
(d) Selection: How were they chosen as members of a group on which psychoanalytic theory is to be based?
Randomly, systematically, by taking some quota, self selection?

2 Where do libido and death wish come from?

3 Which is (hopefully) the stronger of the two?

4 What is the (very important) missing word in this sentence. "Libido and death instincts will always be in _____, and the strongest will determine our personality."

5 What would the world be like if everyone had a very powerful death wish?

6 What would it be like if everyone's libido was much stronger?

REVIEW – The unconscious mind

Freud knew that we are born with a number of reflexes, for example, sucking. These are instincts, ie behaviour which doesn't have to be learned. He began to believe that we are born with other instincts too. After many years research he concluded there are two important instincts which will determine the way our personalities develop. They will always be in competition, and the strongest will determine our personality. One is a force for good, which Freud called the libido. The other is a force for evil, which Freud called the death wish. The libido should be the more powerful of the two.

Is your libido strong or weak? Answer this question in your head: "The libido and death instincts are . . . ."

3 The structure of personality

Freud's analysis of his patients' problems led him to view the personality as consisting of three related elements. The first is primitive, illogical, and totally demanding. Freud calls it the **id**. This gives rise to the second part of the personality which is a more realistic awareness of oneself and one's world, and is called the **ego**. These two give rise to the third part, which concerns moral feelings, and is called the **superego**.

The first part to appear is the id The id exists right from birth and is the most basic, primitive part of the personality. It can be thought of as being *"the true unconscious"*. Id is mainly concerned with things which ensure that the person survives, and with those things which give it pleasure such as food, comfort, and avoiding pain. Id demands

The irrational id is present from birth. Freud thought that some people would continue to have a dominant id throughout their lives. What kind of personalities do you think they'd have? Find some words that might describe someone with a strong id. Here are a few to start you off . . . Ruthless, determined, inconsiderate, cheating.

Id, Ego, and Superego

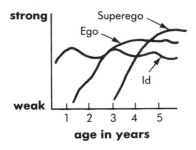

The ego and superego try to find reasonable ways of satisfying the id's demands. Briefly describe what you think someone with a weak superego will turn out like? Now describe an adult whose superego is very strong.

REVIEW – The id, the ego, and the superego

We have three parts to our personalities. The id says "I must be satisfied now." The ego says "I'll work out how to satisfy you." The superego says "You can't do or have it at all, it's wrong." The id is irrational and is based on the pleasure principle. The ego is more realistic, and is based on the reality principle. The superego is less concerned with rationality or reality, and more concerned with moral judgements and censorship. It is based on the morality principle.

that its needs be satisfied by the other instincts immediately and at all costs. Freud said the id operates on the "**pleasure principle**" which means that the child is only interested in things which give it pleasure. The id is irrational and isn't in touch with "the real world".

The ego is the second part of personality to appear For the first year of life the id dominates the child's personality and behaviour. Between one and two years of age children start to use language and begin to learn that they must ask for things. Id is still making demands about what it wants, but parents stop giving in to the child's demands and id will become frustrated.

Frustration of instinctive urges could be dangerous. The child has to become more realistic and realise that making demands which aren't met is a waste of energy. The id is still demanding satisfaction, so the second aspect of personality, the ego, appears. Ego is in touch with the "real world". It is rational and logical. It consists of all that we know, our memories, how we solve problems, how we regard things and so on. It allows the child to realise that talking, explaining, planning, negotiating, asking etc. will be more effective in satisfying id's demands. It relies more on the "**reality principle**".

The superego is the third part of personality By the age of about three we have a child who's unconscious id makes selfish demands for things which will give it pleasure. Ego is trying to satisfy id's demands. For example, the id might demand the satisfaction of food. The ego will know that this demand can be met by taking some food. But taking food without asking our parents may be wrong in some homes, and may result in pain (being smacked).

So we need a third part of personality which will help us know what is right and not right for us, and what we may and may not do. This is the role of the superego. The superego makes sure the ego does not use unacceptable means to satisfy id's demands. It is a sort of censor. It consists of two parts, our **conscience**, and our **ego ideal**. Our conscience gives us feelings of "right" and "wrong". The ego ideal tells us what is good and what we should be like, ie conscience is about "*should not*", and ego ideal is about "*should*". The superego relies on the "**morality principle**". Ego's job now is to satisfy id, without upsetting superego.

A mature personality will be the result of continuing clashes and compromises between these three parts of personality. Sometimes the id will make demands which the ego can't find acceptable ways of satisfying, and the superego will suffer. We feel guilty. Sometimes ego will be dominated by superego, when we refuse to follow our impulses into doing something we know to be wrong. The ego has the most difficult task, trying to satisfy both id and superego. Not everyone will have egos which can cope and they are more likely to develop an abnormal personality.

Exercise – Guilt and the superego

An experiment was conducted on a sample of five children in each of the following age groups: four and five, six and seven, and eight and nine. The researcher wanted to see if those with strong superegos behaved differently from those with weak superegos. One by one they were put in a room with some very expensive looking dolls, a train set, a ball, and other toys. They were told that the researcher's favourite plant (a large rubber plant in the corner of the room) was "sick", and they agreed to watch it for her, in case it wilted. The experimenter left, explaining that she would be next door, in the kitchen.

Some children soon forgot the plant and started playing with the toys. Others lasted several minutes, but eventually took their eyes off the plant. If they ignored the plant for more than one minute the experimenter would release a wire which made the "trick" plant wilt. She quickly entered the room to confront the child, and record its reactions to the "wilted" plant, and to its broken promise. Some of the children felt guilty and apologetic. Others tried to defend themselves by telling lies, and didn't seem to feel guilty at all.

1 What sample size is being tested here?

2 What is the hypothesis of this experiment?

3 What is the dependent variable in this research?

4 Why did the experimenter time how long it took each child to stop looking at the plant?

5 How would those children with strong superegos react to their broken promises?

Exercise – Parts of personality

1 What is the difference between the id and the ego?

2 How does Freud explain aggression in children?

3 Write a paragraph beginning "According to Freud there are three forces which shape our personality. Their roles are. . . ."

4 The stages of development through which we acquire our personality

Before discussing Freud's four main stages of personality development we need to say something about why they occur. Babies put everything they can into their mouths. A baby's mouth is very sensitive and they get some pleasure or satisfaction from this. Freud thought that different parts of our bodies become particularly sensitive as we grow. Freud called these areas **erogenous zones**. Freud thought the libido would concentrate its energy on these erogenous zones. Each one would represent a stage of personality development.

Many of Freud's explanations involve the idea of psychic energy. He imagined that people are born with a certain amount of energy which is gradually used up as we develop. Id, ego, and superego all need a

Babies' lips and tongues are covered in sense receptor cells. Babies of just a few hours old can tell the difference between salt and sugar on their tongues, and they know which they like and don't like! Can you think of any other possible reasons why babies put things in their mouths?

Freud thought the personality would be influenced by the part of the body that was particularly sensitive at the time. These sensitive parts are called erogenous zones. If these sensitive parts received too little, or too much stimulation, then normal personality development will be disrupted, and the personality may become fixated.

REVIEW – Development of personality through stages

As children grow up, different parts of their bodies become especially sensitive – first, the mouth, then the anus, then the phallus, and finally the genitals. Libido will seek expression through these erogenous zones. If too many painful experiences occur the child's personality will become fixated in the stage the child is in at the time.

certain amount of energy. Whenever someone faces a particular crisis, or does something which causes strong guilt or anxiety feelings, this will use up even more energy. For example if id's demands to be fed aren't being met quickly when a baby is less than a year old, this will use a certain amount of energy to cope with. Equally, if the baby is constantly being encouraged to eat, this too will need to be "dealt with". Some energy has to be "left behind" as the child grows, to deal with the feelings of anger or frustration felt at the time.

In the next stage if a child faces a problem with potty training this will require more energy to be "left behind", or as Freud called it, energy is **fixated** on the problem. A parent might be too strict in insisting the child always uses the potty, and may be angry or punish any "accidents". Or a parent may not encourage the child to use the potty, and the child continues to relieve itself whenever it wants to. The more problems the child faces the more energy it will have to leave behind to deal with them. Each of us will have fixated different amounts of energy at different stages in our development, as we faced different problems. An adult's personality will be determined by the different amounts of energy it has "left" to cope with the various fixations that person has encountered.

If someone faces a great many problems during their development they may not have sufficient energy left to go any further. In this case their personality will stop developing at the last problem they met. Being fixated means that the person will continue to seek pleasure or satisfaction through the erogenous zone which it was in when the fixation occurred. A child with some fixation in the oral stage, for example, will be very concerned with its mouth. It may talk a lot, eat a lot, chew its pencil at school, and suck its thumb. Fixation might cause some personality problem later which may have to be dealt with by psychoanalytic therapy.

Exercise – Erogenous zones

Background reading – The erogenous zones

According to Freud the first erogenous zone is the mouth. After a year or two satisfaction results from being able to control the bowels, and the anus becomes the source of the child's satisfaction. From his patients' case studies, Freud concluded that children of just three and four appear to have some kind of "sexual" feelings. Freud called these feelings "pre-genital" sexuality. The phallus becomes the next source of satisfaction after the anus. Real genital sexuality occurs between puberty and adolescence. The stages of personlity development in traditional psychoanalysis reflect these erogeneous zones. They are the oral stage, the anal stage, the phallic stage, and the genital stage.

The Oral stage 0–1/2 years

This is the first stage of personality development. At this age pleasure is gained through the mouth (even where food is not involved). Freud thought we were born with a "feeding instinct", which must be satisfied. No doubt Freud had observed his own and other children putting everything they could into their mouths. Freud said the baby is only aware of its own needs, and will only do those things which give it pleasure or satisfaction. The oral stage is dominated by the "pleasure principle".

According to Freud the libido needs a certain amount of oral satisfaction. Too little, or too much satisfaction may lead to the infant becoming arrested or fixated in this stage. This may result in **oral dependency**. A child who has had too little stimulation will become pessimistic, unable to develop personal relationships, aggressive, often depressed, and will see other people only as objects to satisfy him or her. They will be selfish, uncaring, and untrusting. More recently it has been suggested that too little oral stimulation also produces people who are sarcastic, who smoke, drink, eat sweets, and talk too much! Too much stimulation means that the person will be easily "taken in" (fooled), and will have a high opinion of himself. He'll be excitable and over enthusiastic about things. He'll also be rather dependent on other people and unable to take decisions and responsibility for himself. The right amount of stimulation results in someone who is fairly optimistic and cheerful, and who enjoys other people's company.

REVIEW – The oral stage

Freud said the oral stage is the first stage of personality development and exists for the first year to two years of life. Freud believed we have an instinct to take pleasure from feeding and so the erogenous zone is the mouth. Fixation can occur because of either too much, or too little oral stimulation, ie too little oral stimulation produces an aggressive, depressed, and pessimistic personality. Too much stimulation produces an over optimistic, over dependent, and over excitable personality.

Oral Dependency

Exercise – The oral stage

1 What is the function of the libido?

2 What does fixated mean?

3 How does id become satisfied in the first stage of development according to Freud?

4 What did Freud mean by "oral dependent"? How might such dependency develop?

Write a paragraph beginning "According to psychoanalysis, someone fixated in the oral stage will . . ."

Do you know how old you were when you were potty trained? See if you can find out whether you potty trained easily, or were you reluctant to train? If you have children, how easy were they to train?

Note, there is virtually no evidence for these claims. People with the personality characteristics described here may or may not have been harshly or over indulgently potty trained or fed too little or too much when they were younger.

REVIEW – The anal stage

The anal stage follows the oral stage. The child still derives pleasure from its mouth. During the anal stage the child starts to learn to control his trunk and legs and the anus becomes a source of pleasure. Fixation here can be caused by very strict, or very easy going potty training.

Write a description of "the role of the anal stage in Freudian psychoanalysis."

The anal stage 1/2–3 years

Freud never intended us to think that one stage disappears and another appears. He said "One may appear in addition to another, they may overlap one another, they may be present alongside of one another". In the anal stage the child's behaviour is still dominated by the "pleasure principle". Now satisfaction will be gained from controlling the bowels.

Bowel control is to do with giving and not giving faeces, ie the products of one's own body. The id is demanding immediate satisfaction (ie the child must relieve itself as soon as it needs to), whilst parents are trying to train the child to control itself. Some personality problems might occur if this conflict isn't resolved. The ego, which is more logical than the id, appears now, to help solve this problem.

If id wins the struggle the child will be slow to potty train and its personality may become fixated. This can lead to two types of adult personality. Those who had great pleasure from getting rid of their faeces (the "*anal expulsive*" personality) will be over generous, probably very untidy, will agree with whatever anyone says etc. Those who were forced to give away their faeces (the "*anal retentive*" personality) may become over-possessive, obsessive about things such as tidiness, punctuality, and cleanliness. They may be sadistic and generally miserable.

Between the ages of one and two children start to learn to talk. They begin to realise that they are not the only thing in the world. Id's demands to be satisfied are beginning to fail. Parents will not let their two year olds do everything they want. We need the rational ego to help satisfy the demands of the libido.

Exercise – The anal stage

1 What is the child in the anal stage able to do (which it couldn't do before), that will allow it to be potty trained?

2 What is the id's main function?

3 How is the ego different from the id?

4 Why does the ego appear?

5 Describe someone supposedly fixated in the anal stage.

The phallic stage 3–5/6 years

This is probably the most important stage in the child's personality development, according to Freud. Up until now both boys' and girls' personalities are developing as a result of the strengths of their libido, death instincts, id, and ego. During the phallic stage children will be socialised into learning what is right and wrong, what they should and shouldn't do, and they learn the different ways in which boys and girls are expected to behave.

Freud suggests that children from around three years of age start to have actual (pregenital) sexual feelings about their (opposite sex) parents. The basis for this is quite unconscious. In this stage the child is starting to develop an interest in its own, and its parents' genitals and will experience some kind of sexual feelings. Children often play with their genitals. Unconsciously the boy will start to regard its mother (who first fed it and formed an attachment to it) as a "love object". The girl will unconsciously want her father, since he is big and strong and manly, and is associated with pleasurable genital feelings for her.

Freud called this idea of wanting to have some kind of sexual contact with the opposite sex parent "**The Oedipus Complex**" and said that it can cause "**Oedipal conflict**".

At the same time as unconsciously wanting one parent, each child will, Freud argued, feel jealous of the other one, for example, the boy wants his mother, but can't have her because his father, who he loves, already has her. The son begins to hate his father, and is afraid that his father will punish him, even castrate him, for his feelings. He starts to feel guilty about his feelings and afraid of the possible consequences.

These feelings are negative and dangerous and must be dealt with. All these feelings are unconscious, as is the way the child is going to deal with them. The boy is very frightened by the idea of castration. He may even develop a "castration complex". He begins to be like his father, to act like him, to talk like him, and to think like him. Unconsciously the boy hopes that the father won't be angry with someone who is so much like himself.

This unconscious process of taking on the characteristics of someone else is called **identification**, and it helps explain how boys develop their ideas about what men should be like. If the father is dominant and aggressive the child will have greater castration anxiety and will identify more strongly with his father. This will reduce his fears, but will make him think that boys should be aggressive. Children also develop their ideas about right and wrong (their superego) from identification. We will return to this when we study moral development later.

Socialisation is the name of the process by which we learn the ways of our group or culture. We learn its language, how to behave, what to believe in, and so on.

Background reading – The Oedipus Complex

Throughout his life Freud had been fascinated by ancient history. He knew many of the legends from ancient Egypt, Rome and Greece. One Greek story, written by Sophocles, told of Oedipus, the king of Thebes. Oedipus unwittingly killed his father, Laius, and married a woman called Jocasta, who turned out to be his own mother. When he realised what he had done, he blinded himself. Another legend told of a girl called Electra. Her father, Agamemnon, was murdered by her mother's lover. Electra urged her brother to kill her mother for revenge.

Freud's ideas for the Oedipus (and Electra)

conflict also came from his self analysis after his own father had died. He spent half an hour at the end of each day in self analysis for most of his life, and could remember the feelings of warmth and tenderness that he had for his own mother. His feelings about his father had been very mixed. Although he loved his father, he could remember being afraid of him. His father had been rather strict. His mother would look after him, and he loved her for it. He believed he had been jealous of his father for having so much of his mother's attention.

A phobia is a strong, and often quite illogical, fear of such things as spiders, snakes, heights etc. It results in feelings of anxiety. Do you have any phobias? Ask your friends if they have any. Many people do.

A case study of identification – "Little Hans"

Probably the best known of Freud's case studies is that of "little Hans". Hans' father was a musician and admirer of Freud's, who also worked in Vienna. Hans was born in 1903, and his father soon started to write to Freud to inform him of his son's progress. Freud would reply, interpreting the boy's personality development according to psychoanalytic theory. When the boy was four he developed a phobia of horses.

The streets were full of horses in those days. (The family lived opposite a coaching inn, where horses and carriages came and left all the time.) The boy became terrified of going outside. He said he thought the horses might fall over, they might make a noise, or they could bite him. It seemed that Hans was more afraid of some horses than others. He was particularly afraid of big carthorses pulling heavy loads, like horsedrawn buses. (He'd seen a horse which was pulling a bus fall over when he was younger.)

There are several possible explanations for Hans' phobia. You might think that being frightened by seeing a large horse falling over could cause a fear of horses. He also had a younger sister called Hanna, and he could be jealous of her for taking so much of his mother's attention away from him. He could be pretending to be afraid in order to have more of his mother's attention. Freud was convinced that it was more complex. Since he was four years old Hans would be in the phallic stage, and would be experiencing all sorts of feelings about his mother and his father. Freud thought that the phobia was something to do with the child's identification with his father during his phallic stage. Hans was very fond of his mother, and enjoyed spending time with her. Freud and Hans' father concluded that Hans was afraid of his father and was transferring his fear of his father onto horses. He was afraid that his father would become angry with him for wanting his mother. His father might castrate him for his feelings.

Hans and his father spent a long time talking about the child's feelings. His father used the free association technique. Gradually Hans's phobia disappeared. Freud claimed that this was because he had sorted out his libido's problems.

Exercise

1 Outline Freud's explanation for Hans' phobia.

2 Suggest some other possible explanations for the boy's fear of horses.

3 What does "free association" involve?

4 Outline the main limitations of this method for psychology?

5 How convincing is this case study for Freud's theory?

Freud paid relatively little attention to explaining girl's personality development. He said that girls realise that they have no penis, and that they must have been castrated (by their mothers), who are also castrated. Girls start to hate their mother for that, and for possessing their father. They turn to their fathers for love, and unconsciously hope that this might get their penis back. Girls may develop *"penis envy"* and imagine that taking (possibly their father as) a male lover, and having a male baby will give them a penis of their own. At the same time girls fear losing their mother's love, and so identify with her, taking on her sex roles and moral standards. The fear of loss of love isn't as powerful a reason for identification as fear of castration, so the girl may not identify as strongly with her mother as a boy does with his father. She may not have such a strong sexual identity or superego as the boy, and may overcome her penis envy by concentrating on some other activity such as child rearing or having a career. This explanation has been so severely attacked (particularly by female psychoanalysts) that few people would bother with it now. Freud might argue that a female psychoanalyst is only working to overcome her penis envy!

Freud's idea that all three year old girls are familiar with male sexual organs wouldn't necessarily be accepted now. Many families do not have such sexual liberation! Presumably Freud would claim that a girl without a father or brother will have problems with her identification, since, if she doesn't know about male sexual organs she presumably can't be too envious. If she isn't envious she has less need to identify with her mother.

As we have seen, the superego appears during this stage, alongside the id and ego. It is concerned with moral and ethical feelings. The irrational id is making demands to be satisfied, for example, sexual feelings about the opposite sex parent. The rational ego is trying to find ways of satisfying the id, whilst also trying to discourage its more illogical demands. Now the superego begins to act as a judge between what we should and should not want and do. Superego develops as the child is punished for some things, and rewarded for others. Things which we know are good and will be rewarded by our parents become our "ego ideal".

Exercise – The role of the superego

Two friends, Clare and Paula, are in a large department store, admiring some of the jewellery there. Clare tells Paula that she is going to steal the bracelet she is admiring. She persuades her friend to steal something too. Paula is reluctant, but doesn't want to draw attention to them, so she agrees. Later that day she feels terribly upset about what she's done, and the next morning she posts the jewellery back to the shop anonymously. Clare proudly wears her bracelet to school and isn't at all worried about how she got hold of it.

How might a psychoanalyst explain the differences in Paula and Clare's behaviour?

Fixation in the phallic stage leads to someone who is unreasonable, will think a lot of themselves, will be obsessed by power, particularly in relationships, and will become dominant and uncaring, big headed and a show off. They may have great pride, and even great courage. They may also have sexual problems.

REVIEW – The phallic stage
Between the ages of three and six, boys' and girls' personalities begin to differ. Boys and girls have "pregenital" feelings for their opposite sex parent. This makes them feel rather resentful of their same sex parent, and this leads to feelings of guilt. They resolve these problems by identifying with the same sex parent. If children don't pass through this stage successfully, they may have all sorts of problems with members of both sexes later.

Some boys are very like their fathers, and some girls are very like their mothers. How would you explain this, apart from using Freudian theory. Give some examples in your answer.

Exercise – The superego

During a 30 minute therapy session a 27 year old man made the following collection of remarks. Read them and answer the questions at the end.

"I've always felt that other people don't get on with things. They seem to get sidetracked so easily. I think if you're going to do something, just get on and do it, and worry about the consequences later."

"I never feel comfortable if I'm a passenger in someone's car. People just don't drive safely anymore. I always want to say 'For goodness sake, let me drive'."

"I hate people who pretend to be modest. I think you've got to make as much of your chances as you can in this world."

"I believe a man should be master in his own house. I would never marry anyone who wanted to tell me what to do. I don't really want a wife, you can't trust people."

"It's about time the police got tougher on troublemakers like strikers and students. There's far too many scroungers these days."

"No, I don't think I've ever been nervous of anything."

"Yes, I do wish I was in the government. I could do a lot better than all of that lot. They're too soft and stupid."

1 What is this method of investigation called?

2 Describe a major drawback with it as a means of gathering psychological data.

3 Psychologists from different theoretical backgrounds (which we will study later) would explain remarks such as these in different ways. How might a psychoanalyst interpret such statements?

4 Briefly describe the role of the superego in the development of personality, according to psychoanalytic theory.

Exercise – The phallic stage

1 Outline what is happening during the phallic stage.

2 What is socialisation? Give some examples of the kind of things we learn during our socialisation.

3 Freud said boys and girls start to have "pregenital sex drives". What does this make them want to do?

4 Describe the functions of the superego.

5 What did Freud mean by identification?

The latency period 5/6 years – puberty

This isn't really a stage of development at all, because personality doesn't change very much during it. It is a time of consolidation, of sorting relationships out, of overcoming the Oedipus Complex, and channelling libido's energy elsewhere. Children are going to school, which absorbs most of their energies. They are socialising with (same sex) peers, and directing their energies into sport and games. They

Write a paragraph beginning "According to Freud, the Oedipus Complex is . . ." Mention the process of identification.

120

concentrate on learning the roles which will be expected of them later. The genitals are still the main erogenous zone, but children stop associating them with sexual feelings. They try to have nothing to do with "sex", (including members of "the opposite sex").

Solving the Oedipus Complex and completing the latency stage may be a stressful time for both sexes, and many children don't make it successfully. When they are adults they may be rather afraid of the opposite sex, and uncomfortable with them.

The genital stage 12–18 years

Two very important physiological changes are occurring during the teenage years. Firstly the hormone levels alter as people mature, and secondly, the sex organs are maturing in shape and functioning. If the child has successfully resolved the Oedipus Complex and sorted its feelings out, the result of these two body changes is that the child starts taking an interest in the opposite sex. It's a sort of "*sexual attachment*". They have "crushes" on film stars, their teachers, or even each other. At around puberty children begin to change from being interested in friends of the same sex to members of the opposite sex.

This is a healthy and normal development, according to Freud, but not all societies were very open or approving of sexual relations between unmarried people. This was very true of (Roman Catholic) Vienna where most of Freud's patients lived. Freud was 30 years old before he married, so his own libido must have been rather strained! The libido may want some sexual experience, society forbids it. This can lead to all sorts of frustrations. If fixation occurs in this stage, the adult will find difficulties in relating to the opposite sex. They may be shy and immature.

Exercise – Genital maturity

Anthony is a quiet, reserved man. He doesn't make friends easily because he talks a lot, and is rather shallow. He smokes a pipe almost constantly. He is a very generous person, some people accuse him of trying to "buy" friends. He can be very sarcastic at times, and can have a cruel sense of humour. He is particularly shy with women and blushes easily. His mother and father are both loving and kind, and he always had a good relationship with them.

Anthony is rather lonely, and begins a course of therapy with a psychoanalyst.

1 What kind of diagnosis do you think the therapist might reach, based on the evidence in the passage? (HINT Think about fixation).

2 Can you think of any other explanation?

3 What is the main function of the genital stage?

4 How does libido seek satisfaction at the beginning of this stage, and how does this change?

5 What personality characteristics will fixation in this stage produce?

REVIEW – The latency stage

Between around six to 10 nothing much is happening to the personality. This is more a time for becoming used to people, activities, and situations, and for preparing for the next major step forward, the genital stage.

During the genital stage, from about puberty, we are starting to develop an interest in relationships. Can you remember having any fantasies about meeting film and pop stars when you were younger?

REVIEW – The genital stage of development

During the genital period human beings should reach genital maturity and most of our personality development will centre around members of the opposite sex. Libido will seek sexual expression.

If you've been collecting cuttings or notes on cases on TV, do you think psychoanalysis can make a contribution to explaining any of them?

A summary of Freud's stages of psychosexual development

Stage and Age (approx)	Erogenous Zone	Main Characteristics	Tasks to Achieve
Oral 0–1	Mouth	Main source of pleasure is the mouth, lips, tongue etc. Biting, licking, swallowing etc. The main concern is with immediate gratification of urges so id dominates.	Satisfactory feeding (weaning)
Anal 1–2	Anus	Controlling and not controlling the bowels and bladder. The ego starts to control id.	Potty and toilet training
Phallic 2–6	Phallus	Some pleasure is gained from playing with the genitals. This pleasure is associated with the same sex parent leading to the Oedipus and Electra Complexes. Id demands, ego tries to satisfy id, and superego tries to impose moral choices.	Successfully solving Oedipal conflicts
Latency 6–11	None	Oedipus and Electra identification with same sex parent, and loss of interest in opposite sex. Id, ego, and superego continue to compete.	None
Genital 11 onwards	Genitals	Increasing concern with adult ways of experiencing sexual pleasure.	Good relationships with members of both sexes.

Exercise – Some suggested activities

1 Write down some examples of behaviour that you could look for in junior school children which might indicate fixation in any of the early stages. Say which stage the fixation would be in.

2 Construct a questionnaire which might be used to investigate whether a patient is fixated in any of the four stages.

3 Write this essay: "Describe how children's personalities develop, according to Freud's psychoanalytic approach."

One month **Four years** **Fourteen years**

EGO / ID / repression / superego (values/rules)

Conscious

Unconscious

Three Parts of Personality

When conflicts occur – Defence mechanisms

As we pass through the phallic and genital stages, the three parts of personality will occasionally come into conflict. The irrational id will make demands that the ego and superego will resist. This conflict

---

Background reading – Here is an example of what happens when conflict occurs.

Thirteen year old Fiona is babysitting her one year old sister Angela while their parents are out. Fiona has a couple of friends round, and they are listening to records. Angela has been crying all evening, and Fiona has tried everything she can, but still her sister cries. Fiona wants to be with her friends, and she's becoming annoyed by her sister's crying. She wants to scream "What's the matter, what do you want?" (Impulses from her id want her to shut Angela up in any way she can.) She goes to the crying child and picks her up to soothe her. (Fiona's ego is encouraging her to find a logical way of settling her sister.) Angela quietens for a while, and Fiona goes back to her friends. Soon the crying starts again, and Fiona wishes she could lock the baby in a soundproof room, but she knows it is not the baby's fault. (Her superego is contributing a moral element.) Hopefully their parents will return soon and Fiona's responsibility will end. Her patience is being stretched. Sometimes this conflict is just too much to bear and produces real anxiety.

between the pleasure principle and the reality and morality principles will produce anxiety. Too much anxiety causes neuroses.

Exercise – Anxiety

Anxiety is an unpleasant emotional state which involves feelings of unhappiness, uneasiness, dread, fear, or apprehension. It may include worry about not knowing something which appears to be important.

Can you remember ever feeling very anxious about something? What did you do about it? Did it worry you for a few minutes, a few hours, or a few days? Make two lists of the sort of things that make you "very anxious", and "a bit anxious". You could compare your list with a close friend and see how similar or different you are.

Freud said people have a number of unconscious defence mechanisms which help us reduce anxiety. Defence mechanisms are mental processes which are automatically triggered when anxiety occurs. Here are the main ones.

A Summary of the main defence mechanisms

Repression When conflict occurs between what we want, and what we can have, we may become anxious. Whatever it was that we wanted will be repressed (pushed back) into the unconscious to reduce anxiety.

Rationalising If we do or think something that makes us feel sufficiently guilty we might have to justify our actions to ourselves. (eg "It's not my fault, I thought that if . . .") This is rationalisation.

Projection If we can't admit that we have certain feelings or tendencies we might suspect that someone else has them. (eg "Someone else must have stolen it because I didn't, and I don't tell lies.")

Displacement We displace our own anxiety by blaming someone else for what we have done. (eg "If they put the sweets on a self service counter they're virtually making people steal.")

None of these defence mechanisms are totally successful however.

Sublimation is a more successful defence mechanism whereby we channel our energies into something else which is more worthwhile. (eg "Let's stop worrying about whether we'll pass the exam, let's take up painting.")

REVIEW – Conflict in the personality

If the various instincts and parts of personality can't settle on a way of resolving the demands made on them then the personality will not develop normally. We have a number of defence mechanisms to limit the damage that might be done. They are quite normal and quite unconscious.

Exercise – Defence mechanisms

Can you think of an occasion when you now realise that one of these defence mechanisms may have helped you? Write a brief story of someone (real or imaginary) who used one or more of these defence mechanisms, identifying which mechanism is being used.

Answer these questions from memory.

1 Name three examples of defence mechanisms and say what each of them does.

2 Where do defence mechanisms come from?

3 What causes a defence mechanism to be set off?

Write a paragraph on "Why do we have defence mechanisms?"

Background reading – Some experiments on aspects of Freud's theories

Here are some of the studies which have tried to demonstrate the existence of some of Freud's concepts and claims. Read through them and you'll see just how difficult it is to test these claims.

Yarrow (1954) – one consequence of oral fixation might be thumb sucking. Yarrow studied 66 children and found that those who had spent the shortest time being fed during their first six months of life sucked their thumbs the most later.

Problems with this study – mothers couldn't be expected to remember exactly how long they had allowed their babies to stay at the breast, and many would try to give what sounded like the most acceptable answer. Also Yarrow only asked about thumb sucking, but what about all the other things children could put in their mouths for oral gratification?

Daston (1956) – Freud claimed that people who had great fear of being attacked all the time (caused by a strong Id overcoming a weak ego) hadn't sorted out their identification with their same sex parent, and would have repressed homosexual feelings. Daston mixed words relating to homosexuality amongst "neutral" words, and showed them to a sample of such people, and a control group of "ordinary people". The subjects saw the words for a fraction of a second (using a machine called a tachistoscope). Those with the worries about being attacked did react more to the stimulus words, and Daston claimed this as proof of Freud's claim.

Problems with this study – If they were repressing these feelings then they should surely have shown less response to them, not more.

Skodel (1957) – some Freudians have claimed that men who are fixated in the oral stage will have *oral dependency* characteristics. They will have an unnatural interest in women with large breasts, and will want to be mothered by such women. A carefully conducted experiment studied 169 male subjects' body shape prefer-

ences, and how dependent on others they were, as measured by a Thematic Apperception Test (TAT). The results seemed to point to the opposite of what was predicted! Men who were rather weak and seemed to have greater oral dependency characteristics seemed to respond more to small breasts.

Problems with this study – the TAT is a series of drawings of people in various situations. They can be interpreted in a number of ways. Each subject is asked to say what he thinks is going on in the picture, to "tell a story" about it. The scorer tries to see if the stories have any underlying theme. If so, the theme is supposed to reveal what's going on deep in the subject's unconscious. It is a subjectively scored test, ie the scorer decides for himself whether he thinks there is any theme emerging. Although three judges were used, it could still be coincidence.

Kline (1968) – according to Freud, excessively strict toilet training would result in fixation in the anal stage, leading to obstinacy, meanness, and orderliness. Kline sampled a group of 46 students and investigated correlations between "meanness" (as measured by questionnaires), and a part of a test which concentrated on measuring anal eroticism. There was a moderate correlation, and Kline believed that this supported Freudian theory.

Problems with this study – both tests used leave a great deal to be desired. Many of the questions seeking to discover such personality characteristics as "over concern with cleanliness" seem pretty stupid, for example, one question asked "When eating out do you wonder what the kitchens are like?" What is this supposed to tell us about the personality of the respondent? And what about "Do you regard the keeping of household dogs as unhygienic?" Even if the answer is yes to both questions does that show us anything about anal fixation? And anyway Freud never imagined that anal, or any other fixation was particularly common amongst "normal" people.

5 The strengths and weaknesses of psychoanalytic theory

Freud believed that his research was a major scientific breakthrough in understanding how the human mind works, and how to treat it when things go wrong. And it's only fair to say that many other people did too. Even the great Albert Einstein wrote to Freud in 1932 asking for his thoughts about the future of mankind and could we avoid making war? Freud thought that since we are governed by instinctive urges like the death wish, we probably could not "give up" war. Freud believed the techniques he used were scientifically acceptable, and led to scientifically acceptable conclusions.

The only certain way we can assess the value of science is to see if it stands up to thorough testing. Freud's theories have probably been examined more thoroughly than any others in the history of psychology, although not so much during the last 20 years or more. The problem for psychoanalysis is that many of its ideas cannot be experimentally tested. Various attempts have been made to test some of Freud's specific ideas, although now few psychologists would support some of Freud's more extreme claims about infantile sexuality and aggression.

General criticisms of experimental studies of Freudian theory

1 Studies like these seem to be the result of the following type of approach:
a) a researcher makes some assumption about what Freud said (eg the consequences of fixation).
b) they carry out a study whose results support their prediction, and assume that this supports psychoanalytic theory. Many other hypotheses could equally well explain their findings.
2 Psychoanalysis seems to have an answer for everything and can never be proved wrong. Even Skodel's findings which found the opposite of what was predicted can still be made to fit Freudian theory ie oral dependent men prefer large breasts. They know their feelings are wrong, and this makes them anxious, so the preference for small breasts is simply reaction formation! (NB reaction formation is a defence mechanism whereby people exaggerate the opposite of what they really feel.) How can we evaluate something which seems to have an answer for everything?
3 The statistics used in these studies are generally simple correlations, and correlation cannot prove cause.
4 The research isn't usually repeated, so we can't know whether the conclusions are reliable.
5 Only those studies whose findings are significant are likely to be published. It's quite possible that very many studies are conducted which don't yield the results which would support Freud's explanations. These simply aren't published.

Comments on Freudian psychoanalysis

The attractions of Freudian theory

1 Freudian psychoanalysis has stimulated a great amount of

Some criticisms of Freud's theory

1 Stimulating other research doesn't, of course, mean that

research. Whether they were trying to find evidence to support or destroy psychoanalysis the fact remains that psychologists probably know a lot more because of Freud than they would have done.

2 It provides an explanation for the relationship between childhood experiences and later personality characteristics. Parents could acquire a better understanding of their children's feelings and problems by being aware of Freud's work.

3 It is an "ages and stages" theory, ie it links physiological maturation (age) with psychological changes (stages of development). Many human abilities appear to occur in a sequence. Perhaps personality development does too. Knowing a child's age would allow us to say what is going on in its personality development.

4 It shows the important role of caregivers in development. Children don't just "grow up" quite independent of others. They respond to the things which are close and important to them. As we saw in the sections on attachment formation, Freud is right to emphasise the role of the parent and the child.

5 Freud offers a number of useful concepts, like id, ego, and superego, and like defence mechanisms which do seem to explain some familiar aspects of children's behaviour. And identification has been widely used to explain much of children's early behaviour.

psychoanalysis itself is right. An influential school of thought (which we shall examine shortly) called behaviourism, rejects psychoanalysis as unscientific and totally worthless.

2 Freud's "evidence" for his explanation of how children's personalities grow does not come from experiments or any scientifically acceptable means of data collection. It doesn't even come from observing "normal" children. It comes from the dreams and spoken memory of a relatively small number of people who mostly lived in Vienna, who had some personality "problems".

3 There is no evidence for the existence of the stages of development as Freud described them, and the theory is not predictive. To be of any use psychological theories must attempt to allow prediction of future events. Such "evidence" as there is in Freud's work is retrospective. (ie looking back, therefore explaining what's happening now in terms of what has already happened.)

4 Freud's view of the child is that it is rather helpless and passive. The child "must" try to resolve the Oedipal conflict that it "will" have and "has to" do this by identification. Children are far more active in their own socialisation than Freud suggests.

5 There is no "evidence" to support the existence of such personality dimensions as the id, ego, and superego or libido itself. There's no evidence to prove that anything like the unconscious exists either. Without the unconscious Freud's theory lacks any credibility at all.

REVIEW – Evaluation of Freudian psychoanalysis

It is impossible to experimentally test Freud's claims. This isn't Freud's problem. There are a great many aspects of the human condition that can't be tested experimentally either. He spent a lifetime of dedicated work producing a radically new and different theory. Although some of his earlier claims about aspects of infantile sexuality were, he admitted, rather overstated, he has provided a new and revolutionary view of the development of personality, and uses of therapy. Some of Freud's techniques are still widely used, and some of his insights, for example in the area of defence mechanisms, are still highly regarded. Without Freud's contribution to psychology our understanding of human development would be much poorer today.

6 Freud offered an explanation for sexuality and aggression in early childhood.

6 There is no evidence that all four and five year olds know the biological differences between the sexes, or for the Oedipus Complex. Freud makes much use of the process of identification with the same sex adult. This may occur for a number of reasons that have nothing to do with sexual feelings towards the other parent.

Exercise – Evaluation

Explain what Freud claimed for each of these "features" of personality.

1 The mouth and anus.

2 The Oedipus Complex, castration complex, and penis envy.

3 The unconscious id, the conscious ego, and the moral superego.

4 People repress unpleasant feelings into their unconscious.

5 Dreams convey our real wishes, and are a way of seeing into the unconscious.

Summary of Freudian psychoanalytic theory

Like all forms of activity, behaviour needs some kind of energy to make it work. This "psychic energy" is supplied by two main instinctive urges.

We are born with
  2 instinctive urges (libido & death wish), which provide psychic energy.
They are gratified by
  3 parts of personality (id, ego, and superego)
through
  4 stages of development (oral, anal, phallic, genital)
which reflect the
  4 erogenous zones (mouth, anus, phallus, and genitals.)

Painful experiences may cause conflict between the three parts of personality. Conflict causes anxiety that might threaten our development. It can be dealt with by defence mechanisms, if necessary, by repression. Once repressed some memory stays in the unconscious and may disrupt the personality, and appear later as a symptom of neurosis (hysteria). It must be dealt with by the therapeutic psychoanalytic techniques of free association, dream analysis, analysing slips of the tongue, etc.

7 Acquiring Behaviour – Learning Theory and Social Learning Theory

Freud claimed that children's personalities are partly formed through the process of *identifying* with their parents. He believed that deep instinctive urges direct much of our behaviour. A radically different view for explaining how we learn has been developing, notably in America, for the last 50 years. This approach believes that psychology ought to be much more scientific, and should study people's actual behaviour rather than the supposed instinctive causes of it. This "behaviourist" approach has had a very strong influence on how psychologists view how children learn, as well as on treatments and therapies for children with problem behaviour.

What is learning?

"*Learning*" is a term that we're all familiar with. Most of us "learn something new" every day. Some things are easier to learn than others. It doesn't take much to learn who has the latest "number 1" record in the hit parade. It takes rather more effort to learn to drive a car. Everyone will find some things easier to learn than others, and the kind of things

Humans have a greater capacity to learn, and to act on the results of that learning, than any other animal on Earth. What do you think might be the first thing a baby learns? What do you imagine was the hardest thing you ever learned? What made learning it so difficult?

Background reading – Learning and behaviour

When psychologists study animals and humans they often observe and measure their behaviour. Behaviour is simply what a person or animal does. "Learning" is a mental process that can't be observed. Much of our behaviour is the result of having learned "what to do", but other things affect it as well. For example really wanting to do something may affect how we do it. If you really want to learn to play the guitar you'll work hard at your lessons, and you may learn to play better than someone else who isn't all that bothered about learning to play.

A subject's behaviour is all that can be measured. We can only assume that changes in it are the result of learning, but they may not always be. They may be no more than changes in the person's (or animal's) willingness or ability to co-operate.

Although we can't know whether single cell organisms are capable of learning, we do know that such low level organisms as the flatworm are capable of some learning. For years it was

assumed that most animals, particularly the lower order ones, relied exclusively on instinct. We now believe that most species have some learning ability, ie they can adapt their behaviour to new circumstances after some previous experiences. Circus animals can be trained to do all sorts of things which they wouldn't normally do. As we shall see, pigeons have even been taught to "play" a kind of table tennis.

Higher order animals, such as man, can learn many different kinds of things. This is because a) humans can take in, process, and store a vast amount of information in their heads, b) they can "organise" the information which is being taken in, and that which is to be learned, so that it can be understood and used most easily, and c) human beings can use language to communicate with and teach each other. As each of these skills develops during childhood, so children become more able to learn.

Make a list of some of the things a child does, which it doesn't appear to have consciously learned at all. How would you explain how children acquire these skills.

In your own words, explain "what is learning?"

REVIEW – What is learning?

If a young boy usually behaves in a particular way (eg waits for a parent to button his coat), then has some experience (eg playing at "doing up buttons") which leads to him behaving in a consistently different way, (eg buttoning his own coat), then we might say that he has learned from the experience. Young children learn by repeating actions (like throwing a rattle), by making associations between things, people, and places, and by observing and copying others.

When the term "classical" is applied to a theory it usually means one of two things. Either that the theory was the original which set the standards for those which followed, or that it is rather old fashioned and probably wrong. (The first meaning applies here.) "Conditioning" is a process by which some learning takes place under certain conditions.

that we learn helps to make each of us so different. Babies have a lot to learn, and start doing it from a very early age.

Learning has been defined as "a relatively permanent change in behaviour that occurs as the result of prior experience." For example a young girl who has already had an unpleasant experience at the dentist may do her best to avoid going to the dentist again in the future.

However not all behaviour is the result of previous experience. The very first words you spoke, knowing what you meant by them, and the very first steps you took, were not the result of previous experience. As you practised your walking you were "learning to walk", until eventually you could walk without bumping into anything, or falling over. So we may behave in all sorts of ways. Some of them may be practised until they are "learned".

Perhaps the simplest form of learning is "**associative learning**" ie the organism makes a simple association between something it becomes aware of (a **stimulus**), and some reaction it must make (a **response**). For example you learned to put your coat on (a learned response) when it started to rain (a stimulus in the environment) when you probably weren't much over two years old. Other learning is much more complex however. You couldn't learn about "attachment in babies", or "how to play netball" by simple association.

Some psychologists see the process of learning as a gradual, continuous adaptation to our environment. They argue that every day some new experience alters the way we think about our world. Others, like Piaget, who we will study shortly, believe that the way children think (and therefore the way they learn), occurs in quite distinct stages, each stage marked off from the one before, and the one which will follow.

In this chapter we will examine three theories which may help to explain some of children's learning. They are:

1 classical conditioning.

2 operant or instrumental conditioning.

3 social learning theory.

The first two originated nearly a century ago and were mostly tested using animals as subjects, although they both now have some very important uses for humans. Social learning theory was developed during the last 30 years or so.

Exercise – How children learn

Give some examples of the three ways in which children are said to learn, ie "by repeating actions", "by making associations", and "by observing and copying others".

1 Classical conditioning

The founder of classical conditioning was **Ivan Pavlov**. Whilst doing some research on the digestive system in dogs, Pavlov noticed that some of his older experimental dogs had learned to associate a particular **stimulus** with a particular **response**. He noticed that they started to salivate just as one of his assistants entered the laboratory with their food. Salivation is a **reflex** which is the normal response to food. But were the dogs salivating to the food, or to the sight or sound of the assistants? Pavlov imagined that the dogs had associated the sound of the assistants footsteps, or the sight of the assistant (the stimulus) with the "expectation" of food in their mouths and this knowledge set off their salivation reflex (the response). The younger dogs didn't salivate. Pavlov concluded that they hadn't learned to associate the assistants with the food they brought.

Pavlov decided to investigate how well dogs could learn associations. He set up an experiment in which the dogs' food was presented immediately after a particular sound was made. The two stimuli were being "**paired**". Each "**pairing**" is called a "**trial**". Pavlov used bells, buzzers and a metronome as stimuli in different experiments with different dogs. He constructed some apparatus which measured the amount of salivation in the dogs' mouths, and the amount of digestive juices in the animals' stomachs. These were the responses. After just a few trials the dogs started to salivate when they heard the sound, and before the food was presented. The animals had learned an association between a noise and some food, and that learning set off the physiological reaction of salivating.

You may have noticed that there are two stimuli here. The food, which you might expect to make a dog salivate, and the artificial sounds, which Pavlov controlled. Pavlov suggested that there are also two responses. The reflexive salivation caused by the food, and the learned salivation caused by the sound. He called the food an "**unconditional stimulus**" (US), and the salivation it produced was called an "**unconditional response**" (UR). Animals generally don't have much control over their reflexes. Pavlov proved that they can be

What evidence does this paragraph contain that a careful observer like Pavlov could use to suggest that the dogs salivation was caused by the assistants rather than the food?

Ivan Pavlov

Pavlov taught some laboratory dogs to salivate when they heard a particular sound. How do family pet dogs behave when they hear the rattle of their lead, or someone saying "walkies"? Why do they behave in this way?

Background reading – Ivan Pavlov's biography

Ivan Petrovich Pavlov was born in 1849 in a small village in Russia. His father was the village priest, who sent his son to the nearby church school. Here he took an interest in biology, and eventually went to St Petersburg University where he studied animal physiology. He went on to study medicine, and took a medical degree. After further studies in Germany he returned to Russia and became a researcher and assistant in a physiological laboratory. At the age of 41 he became the head of a laboratory specialising in physiological research. When he was 50 he began to study how certain reflexes (such as salivation) could be triggered by things which were associated with food. Four years later he was awarded one of the first Nobel prizes in medicine.

At this time many psychologists were studying sensations and experiences, dreams and memory, and all kinds of things which went on in the mind. Ivan Pavlov was a dedicated Russian scientist who had little time for such things. He believed that science should be concerned with observing and measuring things, and finding out what caused things to happen. "The mind" couldn't be studied scientifically, so psychology was of no interest to him. He even threatened to dismiss any members of his staff who used psychological rather than biological explanations!

He continued his research into "classical conditioning" for 30 years until his death in 1936.

The food and the salivation are unconditional because they will occur under all natural, normal circumstances. They do not require any special conditions to exist before the stimulus will set off the response. A bell will trigger salivation on condition that it has been paired with some food in the past. The salivation to the bell is therefore conditional upon the bell having been associated with food.

set off by quite artificial means. He called these artificial means (such as the bell, and each of the other sounds in the various experiments) a "**conditional stimulus**" (CS), and salivating to them was called a "**conditional response**" (CR). NB The response is always the animal's salivation. The difference lies in what causes the salivation.

Pavlov's Dogs

Conditioning

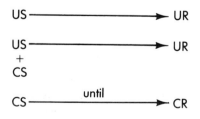

"Elicit" means to make something happen which wouldn't normally occur. In Pavlov's experiments a reflex is being elicited by a sound.

Some principles of classical conditioning

As a very thorough scientist Pavlov was careful to measure and record everything he found. He extended the experiments to see what else could be discoverd. Here is a brief summary of some of the features of classical conditioning that he discovered:

Learning Curves These are shown on a graph and represent the amount of salivation by the number of trials. (Remember a "trial" is a pairing of the US and the UR). As with most graphs, the IV (number of trials) is placed on the horizontal axis whilst the DV (amount of salivation) is placed on the vertical axis.

Stimulus Generalisation Pavlov conditioned his dogs to salivate to different sounds. An animal conditioned to salivate to a bell tuned to the musical note "middle C" would also salivate to bells with different notes without any further conditioning. However as the sounds became less like the one the animal was conditioned to respond to, (a bell producing middle C), so the amount of salivation decreased.

Discrimination This literally means "being able to tell the difference between one thing and another". As Pavlov's dogs learned that other buzzers or bells did not mean that food was about to appear, so they learned to discriminate between those that did and those that didn't, and they only salivated when they heard the bell or buzzer etc, that had been used to condition them.

Extinction This means that the response stops (is **extinguished**). It happens when the animal hears the sound (the CS), but isn't given any food, (the US). After a few trials the CR (salivation) will cease. The animal is learning not to respond when it hears the bell. Pavlov plotted this on an "**extinction curve**".

Spontaneous Recovery This sometimes happens after a learned response has been "extinguished". Every now and again, for no apparent reason, the animal will give the response. For example it will salivate when it hears the bell. Clearly it hasn't completely learned not to expect food. The CR hasn't been fully "extinguished". After a time this spontaneous recovery will disappear, and the response will be "extinguished" again.

Exercise – Some features of classical conditioning

Here are the names of the six principles of classical conditioning described above: 1) reinforcement, 2) the learning curve, 3) generalisation, 4) discrimination, 5) extinction, 6) spontaneous recovery.
Here are some definitions of the principles of classical conditioning:
a) When reinforcement is stopped the response gradually disappears.
b) A line on a graph to show an animal's responses to conditioned stimuli.
c) A response to a given stimulus may also occur to a similar stimulus.
d) Something which increases the likelihood of some behaviour recurring.
e) Occasionally a response which the animal has learned not to give, will recur, for no obvious reason.
f) Subjects can be taught the difference between stimuli which may appear to them to be similar.
You have to fit the definition to the principle by putting the correct letter next to Its number:
1) 2) 3) 4) 5) 6)

Exercise – An experiment on conditioning

Two psychologists wanted to see whether very young babies can be conditioned. They observed that infants of just a day or two old will begin to make sucking motions when they see a nipple. They sounded a tone immediately before some two and three day old infants were (breast) fed. After a very few trials the infants started to make sucking motions when they heard the tone.

1 How old were the infants used in this experiment?

2 What is meant by a "trial", in this passage?

3 Does this experiment suggest that very young babies can be classically conditioned or not?

4 Many reflexes can be classically conditioned. Apart from sucking, what else might be conditioned in children below the age of one?

An Extinction Curve

A Learning Curve

REVIEW – Classical conditioning

Pavlov showed that it was possible to use some neutral stimulus to trigger a reflex such as salivation. Similar stimuli will also cause the response, although to a lesser extent. Animals can learn to discriminate between stimuli, and the response will extinguish if not occasionally reinforced.

2 "Instrumental" or "Operant" learning

Although operant and instrumental learning aren't quite the same, the differences between them needn't concern us.

The key feature of operant conditioning is that the subject behaves in some way which is followed by some "*reward*". The subject may associate its behaviour with the "reward", and so learn to repeat it. The behaviour the animal learns is called an operation or an **operant**. If your dog fetches the stick you have thrown, you "reward" it in some way. Its operant behaviour (fetching the stick), comes first, your behaviour (giving a reward) is a response to it. It may also be a reinforcer for the animal. In classical conditioning the experimenter's stimulus comes before the animal's response (Pavlov's bell rang before the dog salivated). Also, in classical conditioning, only behaviour which is mainly automatic (like reflexes) is conditioned. In operant conditioning just about any behaviour can be conditioned.

In classical conditioning the person doing the teaching does something which triggers some reflex in the animal. In operant conditioning the animal must do something first, for which it will then be rewarded. To obtain another reward it will have to do the same thing again

Early research on operant conditioning

Early this century E L Thorndike put cats (and later other animals) in various "puzzle boxes" which he had made. Outside the box he placed some food. In order to escape and reach food they had to perform some act such as pull some string, or press a treadle. After some time in the "box" (and usually by chance) they managed to pull the string or press the treadle and escape. Next day they were put back into the "puzzle box", and Thorndike timed how long it would be before they

Simplified Graph of Thorndike's Results

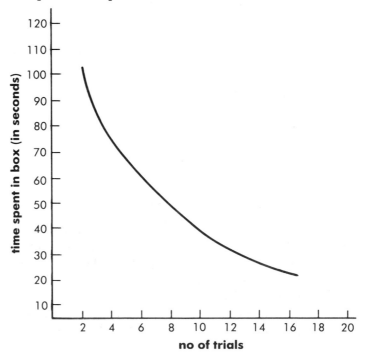

escaped again, having performed the operations of "string pulling", pressing a treadle, etc. After a few "trials" they were able to escape immediately.

Exercise – Thorndike's experiment

1 How long does it take the animal to escape the first time it is put in the box?
2 About how long does it take by the sixth trial?
3 Summarise the conclusions of this graph in your own words.

Thorndike assumed that the animals "learned" the association between a stimulus (for example pulling a string), and a response (escaping and reaching food) because escaping and eating gave them "pleasure". Presumably being in the box was "unpleasant". Thorndike used several species of animals in various "puzzle boxes", and most eventually learned the appropriate operant. Thorndike summarised these conclusions in his "Law of Effect" which he first proposed in 1904. It states that a response will follow a stimulus if it is associated in the animal's mind with "a satisfying state of affairs".

So: "being put in a box",
   (A STIMULUS)
      will emit   "pulling strings",
                       (A RESPONSE)
                       if associated with   "escape and food"
                                                 (SATISFACTION)

Having established this **stimulus–response (S–R)** association, Thorndike then extinguished it, ie stopped giving the reward (freedom and food), although the animal had given the right response, (pulled the string). After a few more attempts at string pulling the animal stopped. Thorndike believed this was because the animal stopped receiving pleasure. As it had learned to respond, so it now learned not to.

Exercise – The "Law of Effect" and animal behaviour

1 In your own words, describe how Thorndike's "Law of Effect" explains his experimental cat's behaviour?
2 What terms would need to be operationalised if this were to become an experimental hypothesis?
3 What are the problems with operationalising such terms as "pleasure" or "satisfaction" in experiments with animals?

One of the most influential psychologists this century must be B F Skinner. During the middle part of this century he developed Thorndike's "Law of Effect". He was unhappy about Thorndike's ideas of "pleasure" and "satisfaction". He thought they would be extremely hard to measure in humans, so how can anyone really know what cats experience as pleasure? They weren't nearly "scientific" enough for Skinner.

In classical conditioning the researcher does something to "elicit" some behaviour from the subject. In operant conditioning the subject "emits" its response without it being elicited. What does "emit" mean?

Thorndike stated that animals will learn to emit some response if giving the response results in something pleasant or satisfying happening to the animal.

B F Skinner

B F Skinner insisted that psychological research must be scientific, and therefore only those things which could be studied scientifically were worth bothering with.

A Skinner Box

Skinner used some apparatus called a "Skinner box" which was similar to Thorndike's "puzzle box", to study the way rats and similar animals learned. Inside the box was a lever and a food tray. Pressing the lever released a food pellet into the tray. Like Thorndike's animals, Skinner's rats soon learned to press the lever. Skinner found that a number of things, apart from food or escaping, would act as rewards, and not all animals would respond in the same way to what Thorndike saw as pleasure giving. (A well fed rat is less likely to regard food as "pleasure" compared to a starving rat).

Skinner used the term "**reinforcer**" to apply to anything which would make the animal (or human) repeat the response. In many societies on Earth money is a powerful reinforcer! Skinner found punishment might act as a reinforcer – if giving a response caused pain then the response soon disappeared. And if giving a response caused pain to stop, this too was quickly learned (and slowly forgotten.)

The nature of reinforcement

The main purpose of reinforcement is to shape, and then maintain, particular behaviour, so a reinforcer can be anything which leads to some behaviour being repeated. The reinforcer may please us per-

---

Background reading – B F Skinner's biography

Burrhus Frederic Skinner was born in America in 1904, and he too became interested in biology. Only when studying it at university did he take an interest in the writings of people like Ivan Pavlov. Whilst Pavlov always regarded himself as a biologist specialising in physiology, because he was using animals, Skinner started to think about applying some of the principles of conditioning to human behaviour. He graduated from Harvard University in 1931 with a doctorate in psychology. He spent a few years researching, before starting to teach and write about what he thought were the principles of learning, and the way psychology should study them. Whilst Pavlov had little time for psychology, thinking it too unscientific, Skinner has devoted all his work, and most of his life, to make psychology scientifically acceptable.

sonally. If you want money and are paid for doing something well, you will have a good reason for wanting to do it well again. We may also do something because we know that it will please other people. The reinforcer here may be the satisfaction of having done something for someone else. This kind of reinforcer probably only applies to humans.

Skinner identified **positive** and **negative** reinforcers. Positive reinforcers may be **primary** (ie the reinforcer is a naturally occurring phenomenon like food or sleep which directly satisfies some physical need) or **secondary** (ie things we have learned can be worth having, such as money.) Secondary reinforcers may be exchanged for primary reinforcers. Reinforcement can also be **negative**. It's not just "nice" things which will make us behave in certain ways. Stopping or avoiding unpleasant ones can also be strong reinforcers too. If the school bully demands a child's lunch money, and pulls its hair until the child gives the money, then the child will give the money in order to escape from the pain. In the future the child may try very hard to avoid the school bully. Negative reinforcement has been demonstrated on some animals.

One final method of changing some behaviour is by using **punishment**. Punishment involves causing some kind of physical or mental distress by either giving some unpleasant stimulus (like a smack), or withholding a pleasant one (like not being allowed to go out for a week). If we know that we will be punished severely for doing something, we are less likely to do it (or more careful not to be caught!)

Operant learning theorists are critical of the use of punishment, saying that all it does is reduce one undesirable response, whilst not replacing it by reinforcing a desirable one. They believe that using reinforcement to increase some desirable behaviour will be more effective than using punishment to decrease some undesirable behaviour.

Skinner experimented with reinforcers. He stopped reinforcing the animals every time they gave correct responses. Instead they were given reinforcement every other time, or every third time. He reinforced some every few minutes rather than every few times they gave a correct

If some act is followed by a "reinforcer" it is likely to be repeated. Reinforcers can be positive or negative. Give some examples of things which you would find positively or negatively reinforcing.

How would negative reinforcement explain the behaviour of the child who had its hair pulled?

Background reading – Negative reinforcement

Here are the steps in negative reinforcement
(a) an animal is being subjected to continuous pain, for example, a rat receiving a mild electric shock through the floor of its cage.
(b) pressing a bar in the cage will turn the electricity off.
(c) the animal presses the bar (by accident probably) and the shock stops.
(d) after a short period the electricity is turned on again.
(e) the animal quickly learns to press the bar! (and who can blame it!!)

This form of negative reinforcement is called escape learning.
A more complicated extension of escape learning is avoidance learning.
(a) a buzzer is sounded immediately before the electricity is turned on.
(b) the animal learns to associate the buzzer and the pain.
(c) the rat becomes very anxious and will soon learn to press the bar to avoid the pain.
(Can you work out what the CS and CR are in avoidance learning?)

response. Skinner taught a pigeon to peck a coloured disc when a particular light came on when it only received reinforcement once in one thousand pecks. The animal seems to know that it will receive a reinforcement sometime, and continues to give the correct response until the reinforcer occurs. There are five possible ways of reinforcing. They are called "schedules of reinforcement".

Schedules of reinforcement

The five major schedules of reinforcement are:

(a) *Continuous reinforcement*, where the desired behaviour is reinforced every time it occurs.

(b) *Fixed Ratio*, such as when every fifth, tenth, or twelfth correct response is reinforced.

(c) *Variable Ratio*, where the number of necessary correct responses is constantly altered.

(d) *Fixed Interval*, reinforcement made once every fixed number of minutes, so long as there has been at least one correct response during that time.

(e) *Variable Interval* where the time between reinforcements is varied.

Although animals are quickest to condition using continuous reinforcement, Skinner found that switching to one of the others made the response harder to extinguish. If the animal isn't led to expect a reinforcement after every correct response, it will give many correct responses before stopping.

Exercise – An experiment on animal learning

Stage One – A rat was conditioned to expect some food powder when she pressed a lever in her cage. After a few hours a red lamp was switched on outside her cage. It stayed on for a few minutes and then was turned off. The rat had to press the lever five times whilst the light was on. She was eventually conditioned to pressing the lever when the red light was on. Occasionally a green light came on, and the animal pressed her bar. Since she wasn't given food she soon stopped pressing the bar when the green light came on. Her feeding sessions were thus controlled by the amount of time the red light was on, and she learned that pressing the lever when the red light was on was the way to receive food.

1 Define the term "reinforcement", as used by learning theorists.

2 What do psychologists call the kind of reinforcer that was first given to the rat in Stage One of the experiment described above.

3 What operant response did she have to give to receive this reinforcer?

4 What schedule of reinforcement was used originally, and how was this changed a few hours after starting Stage One?

5 What feature of conditioning is demonstrated when the animals wasn't given food when the green light was on?

Stage Two – After several days the routine was changed. Food appeared in the food tray at mealtimes, to keep the animal alive, regardless of whether the lever was pressed, or any light was on. At first the rat continued to press the lever, although she eventually stopped. Every now and again she would leap at the lever and press it furiously, often when the red light was first switched on, but she stopped after a few seconds.

It isn't necessary to reinforce an animal every time it gave the correct response. Using one of the other schedules of reinforcement makes the response less likely to extinguish quickly. Why would circus elephant trainers switch to one of the other schedules as soon as their animals were trained to perform some trick?

6 What two features of conditioning are shown in Stage Two?

Stage Three – After a few more days the routine was changed again. The red light would come on and two seconds later a loud whistle was blown. The rat rushed around and tried to climb the bars of its cage. During this frenzied behaviour the animal fell onto the lever, which stopped the whistle. It took some minutes before the animal's behaviour was "normal". Some time later the red light and whistle routine happened again. After a few trials the rat would leap at the lever as soon as the red light came on.

7 What kind of learning is being demonstrated in Stage Three?

8 What is the difference between punishment and negative reinforcement?

Exercise – Can infants be instrumentally conditioned?

A psychologist sounded a bell just as he touched a baby's cheek. Infants have a reflex to turn towards anything which touches their cheek. When they turned their head they were rewarded with a small amount of milk. Two month old babies took around 200 trials before they were finally conditioned to turn their heads when they heard the bell without their cheek being touched. Three month old babies only need about 40 trials. Five month old infants need less than 30 trials.

1 What operant response did the babies have to give in order to be reinforced?

2 What reinforcer was used in this experiment?

3 Construct a table to show the results of this experiment on two, three, and five month old infants.

4 Use the principles of conditioning to explain how an 18 month old baby might "use" its crying as a conditioned stimulus.

Comments on learning theory and conditioning

Good point

1 Pavlov, Thorndike and Skinner's major contribution is not so much what they discovered – much of it had been known for years – but that they applied strict laboratory and scientific techniques to testing behaviour, and found that they worked.

2 Classical and operant theories are clearly described and their principles are not difficult to understand. Reinforcement and extinction, for example, are widely used and understood. Such principles offer clear guidelines for childrearing.

Criticism

1 Experiments conducted on animals under strict laboratory control can't really be generalised to all of human learning. There are many factors in a child's "real life" which affects the way it will behave. Many of these could not be tested in a laboratory.

2 The principles are just too simple to explain all learning. When children experiment with plasticine, sand, water, building blocks, Lego, jigsaw puzzles, etc. they do so for fun, for enjoyment or for the challenge for example. They don't necessarily do so because they've been reinforced in any way.

REVIEW – Operant conditioning

Thorndike, Skinner, and others have shown that many aspects of human behaviour, apart from reflexes, can also be conditioned. Any behaviour which is reinforced, they believe, is likely to be repeated. Behaviour which is not reinforced will extinguish. The reinforcement needn't be continuous. The expectation of receiving some reinforcer will be enough to keep a child behaving in some appropriate way for quite long periods. However not all learning can be explained by reinforcement.

3 Learning theory is practical and avoids references to mental events such as libido, morality, guilt etc. which cannot be observed, measured, or proved to exist. Behaviour is observable, and so are much of its causes.

3 Fun, enjoyment, challenge, etc. are "mental events" and are not observable reinforcers. Behaviour may be observable, its causes are likely to be more complex than can be explained by the principles of learning theory. Anyway Skinner explains why existing behaviour becomes repeated, he doesn't adequately explain where new behaviour comes from.

Pavlov's, Thorndike's, and Skinner's work has been applied specifically to two aspects of childhood which we shall examine later. These are the way some aspects of "problem behaviour" can be "shaped" to become more acceptable, and the techniques and principles of programmed learning that were quite widely used in many secondary schools some years ago.

Exercise – Now answer the following questions

1 What's the main difference between classical and operant conditioning?

2 What was Thorndike trying to discover with his puzzle box?

3 According to Thorndike what acted as rewards for his experimental animals?

4 What exactly does Skinner mean by "reinforcer"?

5 What's the main consequence of reinforcement?

6 What's the difference between primary and secondary reinforcement?

7 How might a parent use positive reinforcement for teaching table manners to a child?

3 "Social Learning Theory" (or "Observational Learning Theory")

Social learning theorists accept that children learn a great deal from reinforcement and punishment, but they claim that children also learn by observing and imitating. If a child sees that someone's behaviour leads to something pleasant happening they are likely to try and copy it, for example, a young child can't reach the biscuit jar in the kitchen. He sees an older child pull up a chair to stand on to reach the jar. The young child may imitate that behaviour so he too can have a biscuit.

This is often called **observational learning**. A child will not simply observe someone, then copy them. Some people will be more important to a child than others, and these people's behaviour is more likely to be copied. The child will **model** aspects of its behaviour on these "important" people. Reinforcement isn't necessary for observational learning, although it is important that the correct behaviour is reinforced if performance is to improve. For example, if standing on the chair results in having a biscuit then the child has a good reason for improving its ability to climb on chairs. If it doesn't receive a reward then there's no incentive to improve.

Each child will observe and copy different aspects of behaviour of different people. Also each child will be reinforced and punished for different sorts of things too. Different parents use different kinds of punishments and rewards, and some parents are more severe or generous than others. If personality is affected by the environment, then each child's personality will inevitably be quite different.

Albert Bandura is a social psychologist who has conducted many studies of who children are most likely to model and imitate. He believes that much of our behaviour, and personality is learned, that is, the result of our nurture.

With various colleagues Bandura has conducted numerous experiments during the last 25 years to see the way in which children modelled themselves on adults. Here is one example.

*Three groups of nursery school children were chosen to watch a short film with three different endings. Each child would see an adult model attacking an inflatable plastic doll (called a **Bobo doll**). He hit it with a mallet, threw it on the floor, sat on it, punched it, kicked it across the room and threw balls at it. At the same time the adult shouted at the doll saying such things as "bang, bang, bang", and "Sockeroo".*

In experimental condition (1) someone came in and gave the adult some sweets for such a good performance. In experimental condition (2) the children saw the model being told off and smacked for his aggression. The third group (the control group) didn't see any reward or punishment.

After watching this performance, the children were given a chance to play with the Bobo doll, and some of the objects (like the mallet) that the adults had used to hit it. Their behaviour was recorded. Those who had seen the aggressive model being rewarded, [condition (1)] and those who hadn't seen any consequences (the control group) were equally aggressive towards the doll (on average they each committed over two and a half aggressive acts.) The group who'd seen the adult being punished [condition (2)] were much less likely to be aggressive (one and a half aggressive acts).

Social learning theorists add observational learning and modelling to reinforcement as explanations of how children learn.

Albert Bandura

Background reading – Why is Observational Learning so widely used?

Bandura claims that most of what people learn is the result of observation and modelling. The reasons for this are:

1 Learning by observing someone else achieve a good result is a lot more efficient than learning by trial and error, or waiting until a reinforcement is given.

2 Many abilities that children master could probably never be learned by simple trial and error. Learning to use a language is probably the best example. Listening to someone, and then incorporating their words or grammar into correct speech is largely the result of observational learning.

Most influential models will be those who seem to have higher status, those who are loving towards the child, and those who are similar to the child.

In general, Bandura and his colleagues found that the aggressive model influenced the behaviour of the children in two ways. Firstly it taught them new ways of being aggressive, and secondly it increased the number of times the children were aggressive in many ways, not just in relation to their toys.

However, several criticisms have been made of such experiments. For example the experiment is rather artificial because in "real life" people are rarely rewarded for behaving aggressively. Rather, in "real life" aggression against people is likely to be discouraged or punished. The children may not have been familiar with Bobo dolls, and may have believed that hitting and kicking them was the appropriate thing to do with them. If so, they weren't necessarily "being aggressive" in their treatment of the doll, they may simply be imitating "appropriate behaviour".

A Bobo Doll

As we said earlier some models are more likely to be imitated than others. Bandura said that if the child is to learn by observation, it must study a model quite closely, and some models are more worth looking at than others. The models who have the most influence will be people who are warm and loving towards the child, or people who have more power, influence, or competence, and people who are similar to themselves (same sex etc.) Some of these will be more important at some ages than others.

Bandura's findings have important implications for childminding. If parents or teachers are not seen as warm, powerful, competent, their influence over the child will be weakened. Other "role models", such as fictional TV characters or pop stars may have influences on the child of which the parent disapproves.

Comments on social learning theory

Good points

1 Bandura accepts that biological factors can affect learning and personality development, but he emphasises the importance of situational variables.

2 Social learning theorists show that particular role models (people likely to be copied) can make learning more efficient.

3 The theory explains why some people are more influential than others over what children learn, and how their personalities grow.

4 Social learning theorists see a child's personality being the result of it modelling its ideas as well as its behaviour on various adults.

5 It emphasises how social forces act on the child, making it behave or think in one way or another.

6 It explains "how children learn".

Critical points

1 Some psychologists claim that our genes determine certain characteristics, such as gender behaviour or aggression.

2 Children are all different and even if they see the same role model they may interpret its behaviour in quite different ways.

3 Children don't automatically copy the behaviour of people who may appear to be influential. Their behaviour may be the result of trial and error, misunderstanding, or have no apparent cause at all.

4 If true then children's personalities would be constantly changing, depending on who they were modelling at the time. This view isn't widely shared by psychologists.

5 It pays little regard to what the child makes of all these influences. Many psychologists claim that children are rather more actively involved in their own learning. (Bandura has modified the original theory to take account of this.)

6 It doesn't describe what children are capable of learning at different ages.

Exercise – Social learning theory

Some psychologists arranged for four samples of five to seven year olds to hear and see an adult model. One group heard and saw an adult being charitable and saying that it was good to donate things to poor children. These adults then gave some valuables to charity. A second group heard the adult talking generously, but then didn't give anything away. The third group heard an adult saying it was alright to be greedy, asking why they should give their money to anyone else. They then refused to donate. The fourth group heard the greedy adult talking, but then saw him being generous.

The children were each then given some tokens which could be changed into sweets, and asked if they would like to donate some of them to needy children. Here is a histogram displaying the results.

REVIEW – Social learning theory

Albert Bandura has shown that children can learn from observing and modelling. This is a very efficient way of learning how to do complicated things. The people who are most likely to be copied are those who are powerful, competent, kind to the child, or are rewarded for behaving in some way.

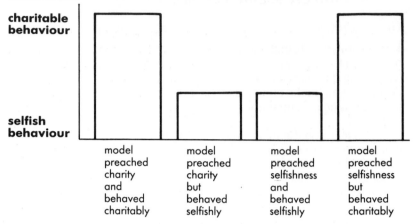

Children's behaviour after being exposed to different kinds of model

charitable behaviour

selfish behaviour

| model preached charity and behaved charitably | model preached charity but behaved selfishly | model preached selfishness and behaved selfishly | model preached selfishness but behaved charitably |

1 Which experimental groups resulted in the most generous behaviour and which the least generous?

2 What factor seems to be the most influential in determining these children's levels of generosity?

3 Are these findings consistent with social learning theory? Explain your answer.

4 Children of parents who smoke are much more likely to smoke themselves. True or false?

5 According to Bandura, why do children model some people rather than others?

8 Changing Problem Behaviour

Is it "normal" for a child to wet the bed occasionally? Is it "normal" for a child to tell a lie? Is it "normal" for a boy to fight another boy, or for a girl to call another girl names sometimes? Your answer to each of these questions is probably "It depends on the circumstances". It would be very convenient to think that people were either "normal" or "not normal". Of course this simply isn't true. Most people have done something in their lives that others might describe as very odd indeed. As we grow our behaviour changes. Something that was unfortunate, an accident, or "only to be expected" from a three year old, might be regarded as a problem if a six year old behaved in the same way.

For various reasons not all children will grow up to behave in the ways that we might describe as "normal" or "well adjusted". For example, temporary, or permanent separation of a child from its parents can result in emotional difficulties, conflict and stress in the home can lead to anxiety, parents who model aggression tend to have aggressive children, and an unstimulating environment can lead to retarded mental development. Children may suffer from intellectual, emotional, personality, or social problems. Such problems may gradually disappear on their own, may stay throughout childhood, or may become worse until the child must receive some kind of treatment.

Nearly all children have minor "problems" at some time. For example they may be over active, have temper tantrums, constantly seek attention, tell lies, talk too much, act aggressively and destructively, sleep badly, are disobedient, refuse food and so on. Most grow out of these difficulties. But some problems can persist, or become more serious. Children who are extremely shy, or very aggressive, who have severe temper tantrums, or continue bed wetting, may create difficulties for themselves, for their parents, teachers and others. Something like 15–20% of children have some problem which will need special help at some time. Therapy may be the best answer for children with severe problems. The type of therapy given depends very much on how the therapist sees the cause of the problem.

Even "problem" children are a lot more like "normal" children than they are unlike them. For example a child who has reading difficulties may be quite as good at other tasks as other children. Even quite severely mentally retarded children may have been fairly normal babies, and have learned their attachments and so on in much the same way as normal children.

Some widely used therapies have developed out of some of the principles of classical conditioning, B F Skinner's learning theory, and Sigmund Freud's psychoanalytic theory. Classical conditioning has given rise to a number of techniques, generally referred to as **behaviour therapy** which is used in the treatment of certain kinds of phobias and other fears. Skinner's work has been developed into rather different kinds of treatments, called **behaviour modification**, which can be applied to all sorts of learned behaviour, whilst Freud's

Problems?

Most children have some minor "problem behaviour". For most of them it will be temporary, and treatable.

145

Background reading – Changing views of mental and social problems

Some Stone Age skulls have been found with small circular holes which were deliberately cut in them. Some archaeologists believe that these holes were made while the unfortunate person was still alive, to let "evil spirits" out. During the Middle Ages mentally disturbed people were also thought to be possessed by demons, and they suffered all kinds of tortures to free them from the wicked force within them.

By the 1500–1600s some doctors started to believe that mentally disturbed people were ill, not possessed, and asylums started to be built. These were pretty desperate places. Often patients were chained to their beds for years on end. All sorts of awful devices were invented for restraining their disturbed behaviour.

Earlier this century people started to realise that cure would be better than restraint, although strait-jackets and locked rooms were still used as late as the 1950s. We now know that mental illness can be caused by a number of social and chemical factors, as well as biological ones. About 10% of us are likely to suffer some kind of mental "breakdown", and need some "treatment" during our lives. Mental problems may well be temporary and quite curable.

The causes of many of the problems that children suffer can be divided into three categories.

a) Some babies are born with problems caused by genetic abnormalities. Down's Syndrome, for example, is caused by there being an extra 21st chromosome, so the baby inherits 47 chromosomes instead of the usual 46.

b) Something that happens to the mother during pregnancy, such as an accident, or catching some infectious disease, can also lead to abnormal development, and problems for the child later.

c) Other problems are caused by factors during childhood (such as having some kinds of disease), or by upbringing.

Psychologists are concerned with investigat-

One Early Treatment!

ing problems caused by factors in the child's upbringing, whilst medical researchers are concerned with the other problems.

Most traditional approaches see the cause of the child's problem coming from within the child itself, and they seek a "cure" to the particular problem. For example Freud argued that children must resolve the problems that arise during the Oedipal Complex if their personalities were to develop normally. Others believe that many of the problems that children suffer may be caused by difficulties in the home, school, or even society itself. For example R D Laing is a psychiatrist who has written a number of books on the origins of mental problems. Laing argues that many families force children to obey petty rules which may be of little benefit to the child. Some parents may use a great deal of physical punishment to control a child's behaviour. According to Laing it is often the family, not the child, which needs therapy.

ideas have led to **play therapy** for use with some children. Here we will review:

1 Classical conditioning's behaviour therapy.

2 Operant conditioning's behaviour modification.

3 Freudian psychotherapy.

1 Behaviour therapy

In Chapter Seven we saw how classical conditioning had been developed by Pavlov, leading to the establishment of certain principles of learning such as generalisation, discrimination, and extinction. Pavlov found that he could teach an animal to associate a neutral stimulus such as a buzzer or bell with a stimulus such as food that normally produced a reflexive response such as salivation. Pavlov was able to elicit the reflex by just giving the neutral stimulus – ringing the bell produced the salivation.

People are able to learn many more associations than animals are, and we do not always need actual, physical rewards. Just knowing that we are succeeding may be a sufficient reward for adults and older children. If someone knows they have a "problem" they may see "getting better" as a reinforcer. Here are brief descriptions of some therapeutic techniques which have been developed out of classical conditioning.

Systematic Desensitisation "Systematic" means in an ordered way, and "desensitisation" means becoming less sensitive towards something. This technique can be used with adults and older children. Someone who is over sensitive to the presence of spiders, for example, may suffer uncontrollable fear or panic when a spider is in the same room. The therapist discovers what is the most frightening contact with the spider that the person can imagine, and what is the least frightening. The person is then taught how to relax, then is gradually exposed to the object which produced the anxiety, starting at the least upsetting type of contact. For example they might start by being shown a drawing of a spider. When they can relax In the presence of this the

Classical conditioning showed how associations between various kinds of stimulus and response could be learned. Pavlov developed some "principles of learning" from his studies of classical conditioning. What do these "principles of learning" mean: Generalisation, discrimination, extinction, spontaneous recovery?

Systematic Desensitisation

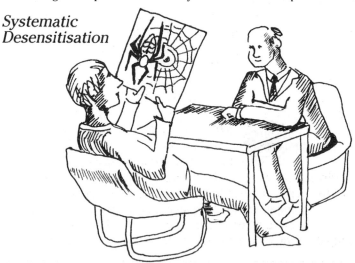

Systematic desensitisation gradually replaces the phobic reaction with relaxation.

Implosion therapy rapidly replaces the phobic reaction.

Aversion therapy replaces a pleasant response with an unpleasant one.

next most worrying thing will be shown, perhaps a photograph of a spider. When they can relax with this the next object, perhaps a small, live spider in a tightly sealed jar, is placed in a far corner. When the subject is relaxed the spider may be brought closer, until finally she or he can control their feelings towards spiders. With a child it wouldn't be practical to teach them relaxation exercises, however it might be possible to substitute some other reinforcer, such as being given some favourite foods as the anxiety producing object is slowly brought closer.

Implosion therapy Here the sufferer is made to face the thing which causes it the anxiety without either relaxation or being gently exposed to it. The panic reactions will eventually subside, and the response should extinguish. The greatest of care will be necessary in using this technique, particularly if it is to be used with children. A child with school phobia may be made to stay at school all day until its fear of school eventually declines.

Aversion Therapy In aversion therapy some punishment is given for undesired behaviour. It is not widely used by child psychologists! The idea is to weaken the association the person has made between some "bad" response, such as taking illegal drugs, solvent abuse and so on, and an inappropriate emotion such as pleasure. The person is faced with the thing that gives them pleasure at the same time as something unpleasant is happening. For example giving an emetic drug to someone makes them feel sick, and eventually will make them vomit. At the same time as these feelings of nausea are being experienced the person is in contact with the object that previously gave pleasure or satisfaction. One example of aversion therapy is giving an alcoholic a drug which will make him or her feel ill if it comes into contact with alcohol. Knowing that having a drink will result in vomiting should make the person learn a connection between alcohol and nausea. With children a mild form of aversion therapy has been used to "treat" bedwetting. The child sleeps on a special sheet that can detect any sign of wetness. As soon as the child starts to urinate the sheet sets off a mildly unpleasant buzzer which should wake the child quite quickly. The child should soon learn that not waking voluntarily when its bladder is sending messages that it needs relief will result in being rudely woken.

REVIEW – Behaviour therapy

Classical conditioning has been used to treat a variety of adult and children's disorders, notably things which produce anxiety or fear such as phobias. It is often used in conjunction with other therapies too, particularly for learning which has been strengthened over many years.

Evaluation of behaviour therapy

Good points

1 Pavlov showed how associations between various kinds of stimulus and some reflexive response could be learned.

2 Pavlov's detailed scientific investigation led to the establishment of some therapies for dealing with people who have phobic reactions to certain objects or events.

Criticisms

1 Learning associations between neutral stimuli and reflexive behaviour does not explain how or why the majority of our behaviour occurs.

2 The therapies therefore will only apply to a limited range of problems, such as phobias.

3 The therapies can be effective.	3 The therapies can be expensive since they may take a long time. With some disorders, such as acute anorexia nervosa the time isn't available.

2 Behaviour shaping and behaviour modification

Skinner's ideas about learning and behaviour were discussed in Chapter Seven. They were developed out of E L Thorndike's "Law of Effect" which stated that if something pleasant or satisfying followed some act, then that act was likely to be repeated. All sorts of things can satisfy or please people. Just about every day parents and teachers use smiles, nods, encouragement, rewards, and attention to reinforce good behaviour in children. Punishments are also used to *shape* children's behaviour.

Skinner's techniques involve "*behaviour shaping*", and "*behaviour modification*". Their principles are not difficult to understand, and, in theory at least, not difficult to put into practice. Behaviour shaping involves deciding what behaviour we want to teach to a child or animal, and gradually building up to it.

Behaviour shaping

Behaviour shaping simply means changing someone else's behaviour until it resembles the kind of behaviour you want. We might look disgusted, or ignore someone who has behaved badly, or we may punish them in some way. We hope that showing them our displeasure will stop them from behaving badly. Or we may smile and say something which means "well done" to someone who has acted in a way that we approve of, hoping that this will encourage them to repeat their behaviour. We all use these reinforcers every day to *shape* the behaviour of people around us. Skinner developed a version of this which is called **behaviour shaping by successive approximations**. Using behaviour shaping by successive approximations Skinner taught pigeons to play a version of ping pong. Two pigeons are reinforced for standing in the right places on a model ping pong table. When this behaviour is conditioned reinforcement will only be given if they allow a ball to hit a part of their bodies whilst standing on the right place. When this is conditioned reinforcement will only be given if they hit the ball with the upper part of their bodies. Later reinforcement

We all use operant conditioning techniques to teach our pets and children how to behave. Many children use conditioning to "train" their parents too. Can you think how?

An Experiment in Operant Conditioning

Background reading – the basic assumptions that learning theorists make

(a) since behaviour is the only thing that can be measured, and
(b) science should be about measuring things and establishing how one causes another, so
(c) behaviourists reject the role of instinct, the mind, emotions, personality etc., claiming that

all these are caused by experience and are observable only through behaviour so
(d) all behaviour will be the result of previously reinforced responses which will extinguish if reinforcement stops.

Can you see why Skinner calls his approach "behaviour shaping by successive approximations"?

will only occur if they hit the ball with their heads, and later their beaks must be used to hit the ball if they are to obtain a reinforcement. Finally they will have to move towards the ball, and hit it in the right direction with their beaks in order to be reinforced.

Behaviour modification

Behaviour modification attempts to extinguish "problem behaviour" in favour of "normal" behaviour. It is not concerned with the causes of problem behaviour, only with the actual behaviour itself. Here is a summary of the procedure using the example of a five year old who hardly ever shuts up!

In order to modify some aspect of behaviour it will be necessary to: a) precisely define the behaviour that needs to be reduced, for example, amount of talking, talking when eating, talking when in the car, talking in the shops etc; b) identify and define each aspect of behaviour that is to be increased, for example, being quiet for a few moments (since these last two statements are opposites, any change in one of them is bound to produce a change in the other); c) identify what is reinforcing the "problem" behaviour, for example, the pleasure of being the centre of attention, and change it, either by ignoring or punishing the undesired response, at the same time as reinforcing "appropriate" behaviour, for example, ignore the child when it is talking. Eventually it should be quiet for a few moments. Pay attention to it after such a silence. When the child realises that it must be quiet before it gets a response it should learn to talk less. It should be possible to get the child to lengthen the silences by witholding the reinforcer until there have been longer periods of silence. This procedure must be applied consistently by all the adults the child seeks attention from, for example, parents and teachers must all be willing and able to join in with the therapy. Frequent checks must be made to measure the length of time for which the child is talking. These will be compared to the length of time the child was talking before the "treatment" started. Only this way will we know if the treatment is working.

Of course there'll always be some children (and adults too) who just do not seem to respond to this kind of treatment. For example the child here may continue to chatter away regardless of how the teachers and parents ignore it. It may not even notice the way it is being treated, or the treatment might even lead to more talking! Another possible type of treatment is modelling therapy, and is based on the Social Learning (or Observational Learning) theory developed by Albert Bandura and his colleagues. The child is shown examples of people behaving in the desired way, and sees them being rewarded for doing so. People who are behaving in an unacceptable way are seen being punished for doing so. So our talkative child will be shown (perhaps a film of) someone being praised and given sweets for keeping quiet, and a talkative child being told off and not be given any sweets.

Here are some examples of "behaviour to be decreased"; shouting, being destructive, being greedy, bed wetting, being disobedient. What should replace them?

Neither the traditional behaviour modification, or modelling approaches will be appropriate forms of treatment with all children. In this case more extreme remedies may be necessary. One example sometimes used with children who are excessively aggressive or destructive, for example, is "**time out**". In "time out" the child should be told that its behaviour isn't acceptable and that it will have to change. If it doesn't change the child is going to be made to stay, on its own, in some particular place, for a specific period of time. It needn't be a very long time, although five minutes can seem a very long time to an overactive child! The child may not necessarily understand what it is being told, or be prepared to do anything about it. If it is shouting and screaming and throwing things around it could be a waste of time even trying to explain what is about to happen. In which case it will be put somewhere, physically picked up and put down if necessary, completely on its own. The place where the child is to spend "time out" must, of course, be safe and have the minimum possibility for the frustrated child to hurt itself. The child must be left in that isolated state for the full five minutes, or whatever length of time was decided on, no matter how hard it might be for parents and teachers to do this to a child. After five minutes the child will be released only if its behaviour is acceptable. Rather than set a fixed time limit some therapists might prefer that the child should be released when its behaviour has been acceptable for a certain period of time in "time out".

A child who has developed its destructive behaviour over a period of time will not usually give it up so easily. In fact its behaviour in "time out" may well become worse. Frustration at being "locked up" will add to the problems which are causing the child to behave aggressively or destructively. The child may scream all the more, and may attempt to destroy its surroundings, or even hurt itself. The therapist and parents must resist this at all costs. Giving in to the child now must only be considered under exceptional circumstances such as the child being in serious danger of doing something dangerous. Eventually the behaviour will become acceptable and the child will be released from "time out". It may well start its unacceptable behaviour again, possibly straight away, perhaps as a sort of punishment for having been locked up. If the child becomes aggressive and destructive again, it will go back into "time out".

"Time out" is sometimes used as a last resort for a child whose behaviour is so badly disturbed, yet is known to be mentally "normal". The child is locked away somewhere for a given period. It can create great anxieties in the child's parents.

Exercise – An example of behaviour modification

A four year old boy named Jasvir spent most of his time at playgroup sitting down. The adults tried to encourage him to move around, but without success. A psychologist suggested that having so much adult interest shown in him was reinforcing Jasvir's behaviour. The adults were instructed to ignore him completely when he was sitting down, and speak to him when he was standing. He was observed for 30 minutes each day and the number of minutes spent sitting or standing was noted. Here is an extract of the record which was kept of his behaviour.

	Unacceptable Behaviour (Sitting)	Acceptable Behaviour (Standing)
Day one	23	7
Day five	24	6
Day nine	19	11
Day fifteen	14	16
Day twenty one	11	19
Day thirty	5	25

Skinner developed his ideas about behaviour modification out of his studies of the effects of operant conditioning on shaping behaviour. This view maintains that since all behaviour is learned, problem behaviour must be the result of the unfortunate pairing of a response with a reinforcer. To correct the behaviour it is necessary to find that reinforcer and remove it. Then the problem behaviour will extinguish. At the same time "good" behaviour must be reinforced.

1 What explanation does the psychologist suggest for Jasvir's behaviour?
2 What recommendation does the psychologist make?
3 Why is it necessary to keep a record of Jasvir's behaviour each day?
4 Does the extract of the record shown here support or contradict the psychologist's suggestion?

Comments on behaviour modification

Advantages

1 The technique is not difficult to understand, and fairly easy to teach to parents, teachers, and others involved in dealing with "problem children".

2 Several kinds of "problem behaviour" have been successfully treated by behaviour modification.

3 Behaviour modification can be successful in changing problem behaviour.

4 Behaviourists remove the reinforcer that is maintaining the problem behaviour.

Disadvantages

1 It is extremely time consuming and demands almost the full attention of the parent or teacher. The temptations to give up are enormous, particularly if the child's behaviour worsens in the beginning.

2 It is unlikely that "all" human behaviour has been learned. If some behaviour is the result of biological forces it may not respond to operant conditioning.

3 Behaviour modification treats problem behaviour. It does not attempt to find or treat the cause of that behaviour.

4 Much of children's learning seems to occur without the need for any observable reinforcer. For example some may be the result of simple trial and error.

Background reading – Behaviour modification with older subjects

The Token Economy. This is a technique applied to groups of patients in some wards in some mental hospitals, rather than as a single treatment for one patient. The idea behind it is that some mental patients can learn "good" behaviour. In the outside world good work should be rewarded by good pay. So patients are given jobs to do around the hospital, for example, cleaning, working in the laundry, and kitchen. When they work well they were "paid" (given coloured counters which represented money). These tokens could be exchanged for books, magazines, food, a better bed, even weekends out of the hospital! This technique has been used to teach some patients to read, take exercise, behave socially etc.

Biofeedback. With carefully placed electronic sensors, it is possible to see and hear the functioning of some of our internal organs – for example, heart beat, stomach contractions etc. It is also possible, by concentrating on them, to control them. Wekiss and Engel (1971) let certain of their heart patients listen to their own heart rates. The patients knew that they were "high risk" for having a heart attack. They learned to control their heart rate by concentrating on it. After release from hospital four were able to reduce their heart rate at will, and one still could, to some extent, 21 months later.

3 Freud and Psychotherapy

Play therapy has been developed from Freudian views of personality development. The main terms we use here were explained in Chapter Six so look back if there's a term you don't understand.

Freud said that if something which is making us anxious can't be removed we will use some **defence mechanisms** to protect ourselves from it. Perhaps we might bury it in our unconscious. If the anxiety remains unsettled it may appear later as some **neurosis** needing to be dealt with by psychoanalytic therapy. Some series of problems during our childhood may have caused our personality to have become arrested or fixated in one of the stages of development. This will limit the extent to which any future development can occur. The cause of this fixation must be found and removed by **psychotherapy**, so that development can quickly catch up, and become "normal".

Psychotherapy generally means using just about any (legal) technique that either makes the patient actually better, or at least think they feel better. It can be applied to any mental, emotional, or behavioural disorder. Psychoanalysis specifically uses the techniques developed by Freud to investigate and interpret the unconscious mind.

Freud's therapy was to use the techniques of psychoanalysis to explore the unconscious. Eventually, he believed, he would find the memory of some incident which probably occurred during one of the stages of personality development. It would probably have produced a great deal of anxiety at the time. This could have caused the **libido** to become fixated. Encouraging the patient to face whatever caused the anxiety will help her or him to overcome it, and the hysterical symptoms should disappear as the libido is freed.

Exercise – Starting analysis

If patients said something about their past which an analyst thought was interesting, he might ask a question. Write down five questions that Freud might have asked a patient during treatment, giving the reasons for the questions.

Psychotherapy and children

Psychoanalysis is much more than a theory of development, it is a therapeutic technique for curing problems. For adults it uses the techniques of analysing their dreams, slips of the tongue, and free talk. These techniques do not work with children.

Play therapy

Since the usual psychoanalytic techniques weren't suitable for studying children, another technique had to be found. Freud himself never really investigated this, but other psychoanalysts, starting with Freud's own daughter Anna, (who followed her father into psychoanalysis), did. (With Sophie Dann she studied six war orphans at the Bulldog Bank which was described in Chapter Three.) Psychoanalysts believe that children express all their concealed emotions through play, just as adults are supposed to through dreams, so play therapy would involve letting the child be itself.

Freud believed we have very many defence mechanisms which are unconscious, and perfectly normal ways of dealing with anxieties. If the anxiety is too great it can lead to repression.

What is a "neurosis"?

Freudian psychoanalysis was intended to free anxieties which had become repressed in the unconscious.

What was Anna O's problem? What caused it, according to Breuer and Freud?

Why wouldn't analysing children's mistakes in speech be much of a guide to their unconscious?

Children spend a lot of their time playing. Play is often used by children for expressing their emotions, as well as for developing other skills.

Play becomes a "window" through which the skilled analyst can see the child's unconscious. Having seen the child's problem being acted out through play, the therapist tries to help the child to see it too – to "make the unconscious conscious" to the child. As Freud said, "where the id was, let the ego be." The id is the primitive unconscious, which is the source of energy for all our instincts. The ego is rational and logical.

There are several versions of play therapy, but they can be loosely grouped according to their main purpose. These are for diagnosis and for treatment.

Play Therapy for Diagnosis (Diagnosis is the process of categorising various symptoms as belonging to various diseases and putting someone with particular symptoms into the appropriate category of disease.) The child is invited into a playroom full of toys, and encouraged to play with whatever it wants for as long as it wants, and how it wants. The therapist encourages the child, but doesn't suggest to the child what it should do. This is called "**non directive therapy**". The therapist doesn't question the child, but lets it "become itself". A good therapist responds to anything which the child says or does which shows that the child is becoming aware of its "true self" through expressing its feelings. (NB different play therapists go to different lengths to encourage self expression. Some are less "non directive" than others.)

A Therapy Playroom

Background reading – An application of Freud's techniques

One of Freud's last students in Vienna was Bruno Bettelheim. He was put into a concentration camp by the Nazis and there he saw many horrific things. He felt afterwards that he needed all his knowledge of psychoanalysis in order to survive. When he was released he went to America where he was appointed the head of a school for very severely disturbed children. He used Freudian techniques of allowing free expression, and letting the child feel that no one was trying to trap it and that adults could be trusted. About four in every five children who went to the Orthogenic School (Orthogenic means getting straight, right from the beginning) was able to leave and lead normal lives. However even this totally child centred version of psychoanalysis couldn't "cure" all the children.

Play Therapy as Treatment Children are encouraged to "play out" their frustrations and tensions in the playroom. According to psychoanalytic theory "normal", healthy children use play activities to help them sort out their understanding of things which are going on around them. For example through play they can "*relive*" experiences which they weren't able to fully understand when they first had them. Some emotions may be too painful to be dealt with all at once. Through play children can *regress* to some earlier time, and go through the events again, both in their imagination, and in the play activity. They use real or imaginary objects to *symbolise* the real world, and playing with them is like "*playing through*" whatever is really going on. Negative feelings can be *displaced* onto dolls or imaginary people, and any emotions which the child still can't deal with can be successfully *sublimated* through play.

Joyce Robertson used a version of play therapy with the children they looked after; including "Thomas", a 28 month old child who they fostered for 10 days whilst his mother was having a second child. Joyce Robertson used some simple props to show Thomas what was happening to his mother, and to him. She had a "mummy doll" in "hospital" where she was "resting". "Daddy" visited her and came to see "Thomas". Soon "mummy" would be "all rested" and would come to see "Thomas". "Mummy" gave "daddy" a kiss for "Thomas", and "Thomas" would send a kiss back to "mummy". Thomas wanted Joyce Robertson to play this game several times, and it may well have helped him understand what was happening.

Psychoanalysts have developed a number of versions of play therapy to deal with particular children's problems.

An example of play therapy

Virginia Axline is an American play therapist who reported on a six year old boy called Dibs who she had studied in 1964. Her book, describing her therapy, is called, *Dibs: In Search of Self*. It provides an excellent illustration of one technique of play therapy.

Dibs was a five year old American child who was attending elementary school. His teachers found him rather mystifying. They couldn't really decide whether Dibs was backward or not. He didn't seem to be able to do many of the things that the other children could, and this gave the impression that he was mentally retarded. Then sometimes he would do something that suggested that he was really quite intelligent. He had never really been friendly with his teachers, although they had tried to establish a good relationship with him. He was a rather lonely child, and tended to shy away from all the other children and the teacher. As Axline said, "If he thought anyone was watching him he quickly withdrew into his shell."

One very obvious problem was that Dibs never seemed to want to go home after school. He "backed into a corner of the room and crouched there, head down, arms folded tightly . . ." He had "always behaved this way when it was time to go home." When Dibs' teacher went across to him, to encourage him to get ready to go home, he screamed and fought not to go. He tried to scratch and bite with all his strength. Something about home obviously upset him very greatly.

In the play therapy sessions Virginia Axline allowed Dibs to slowly explore the playroom. She used a "non directive" technqiue, so didn't interfere with Dibs' exploration in any way. She didn't make any

Not Joining In

Dibs' 'Treatment'

suggestions or comments about his activity unless he invited her to contribute. Even then she merely confirmed what he had already said. She didn't show surprise, approval, or disapproval at anything he did. As Virginia Axline said ". . .I wanted him to learn that he was a person of many parts, with his ups and downs, his loves and hates, his fears and courage, his infantile desires, and his more mature interests." There was a sandbox, and a number of toy cars and trucks in the playroom. He would play with them in many inventive games. There was a dolls house and a number of dolls too. Dibs gave the mother doll long walks around the park, watching the birds, flowers, trees, and even the water in the lake. The sister doll was taken out of the dolls house. He said "the sister is going away to school. They have packed the bags and sent her away from home and she goes far away all by herself." The father doll was often treated quite differently from the rest. It didn't go out of the house to the park. "He didn't want to be bothered." A soldier doll, possibly representing the father, was repeatedly buried in the sandbox. Dibs took the boy doll from its room in the dolls house, after the father doll had "unlocked the little boy's room." Dibs moved the boy doll outside the house, although he didn't take the doll far away. Dibs broke down and cried that he was sometimes locked in his room. It emerged that the child's father wasn't very tolerant of Dibs, and Dibs was sometimes locked in his room. This upset him very greatly. After some time spent in play therapy Dibs seemed more in control of himself and his emotions. It seemed as though he had worked through all his feelings of hate and despair, of loneliness and sadness. Virginia Axline claimed that he understood his feelings better, having been allowed to express them, especially to himself, and was more in control of himself. He could understand, control, and cope with his feelings. His attitudes and behaviour slowly improved as did those of his family.

Exercise – Play therapy

1 Virginia Axline used "non directive" therapy. What does this mean?

2 Think of some emotional problem a child might have. What kind of play materials might be useful to have around?

3 What do you think Axline means by "his infantile desires"?

Comments on play therapy

Psychoanalysts believe that:

1 Causes of "problems" can be found in the frustration of instinctive urges in the unconscious mind.

2 These problems can be successfully treated by play therapy helping the child to understand the problem that is causing its anxiety.

3 Once a child has understood what is causing its problem behaviour, the behaviour will disappear. The child has been successfully "cured".

4 Children use play in many ways, which helps their personalities develop.

Criticisms of Play Therapy

1 It isn't possible to test ideas about repressed anxiety causing childhood problems.

2 The therapy cannot be measured for success since any number of factors, such as the personality of the analyst or the fact that an adult is giving individual attention to the child could have brought about the same behaviour.

3 What exactly is "success" when we are talking about a child's problems? It cannot be defined (or measured) precisely.

4 Play therapy could only work with those children who are young enough to play with toys.

Exercise – Therapy

1 Identify three problems in childhood that may affect personality development.

2 Where do childhood problems come from, according to Freud?

3 Why do play therapists use non participant observation?

4 Do you think a very destructive, aggressive child could be treated by play therapy?

5 How were the six war orphans at the Bulldog Bank "treated"?

Write a short "essay" summarising the usefulness and limitations of play therapy.

REVIEW – Psychoanalytic therapy

Freud's techniques for investigating the unconscious turned out to be useful tools for diagnosis and treatment of personality disorders in adults. Many psychoanalysts throughout Europe and America still use free association a great deal in their treatments. With children the main psychoanalytic technique is play therapy. This involves watching the child, and encouraging it, to play out its problems. Once they are "in the open" they may be dealt with. However it isn't certain that any change in the child's behaviour that does occur is the result of the therapy.

Jean Piaget

9 Jean Piaget's Theory of Cognitive Development

As we have seen, B F Skinner has explained some of the principles of learning. We can apply these principles to a number of areas of psychology, notably when dealing with "problem behaviour" in both children and adults. Skinner's contribution to psychology has been vast. In our ordinary daily lives we all know that some things are easier to learn than others. We often say that those people who seem to be able to learn things quickly are more intelligent than other people. It isn't always clear what this means though. Some people seem very "intelligent", but have trouble with the simple things of life! In this chapter we will be looking at a very different way of understanding how children acquire knowledge about their world from the **stimulus–response** explanation advanced by Skinner. During the last 50 years Jean Piaget has developed a theory of *how* children learn about things. He believed that it would be more useful to study the ways in which children *take in* and *use* information, rather than *how much* knowledge or "intelligence" they are supposed to have.

In this chapter we will be examining the main features of Piaget's theory. However we start with how it came about.

1 We see the background to his theory.
2 Then we examine his biological view of behaviour.
3 We describe Piaget's belief that cognition is the result of adaptation.
4 We will examine the stages Piaget proposes for intellectual development during childhood.
5 We examine other research into some of Piaget's ideas.

Jean Piaget has probably conducted and stimulated more research into how thinking develops in children than anyone else. He disagreed with those who saw intelligence comprising one or a number of fixed characteristics that could be measured. Unlike most biologists and psychologists earlier this century Piaget did not believe that intelligence was fixed at birth so saw little point in trying to measure it. Instead he researched into how logical **thinking** develops in children, and has suggested a way of understanding how children acquire and use information from their environment. This is Piaget's basic idea: our senses take in information about things around us, our brains process and store this information, and our behaviour changes as a result of it. This process is called **cognition**.

1 The background to Piaget's theory

Piaget's biological background led him to believe that every animal's genetic makeup prepares it to live and behave in certain ways. For

Piaget's pioneering work into the way children take in and use information (cognitive development), has had enormous impact on our understanding of children's mental development.

REVIEW – Piaget's approach

Jean Piaget was a biologist and zoologist working in Switzerland earlier this century. He believed that biological principles and research might reveal much about some aspects of mental, cognitive development. He had noticed that children didn't use the same rules of logic for solving problems as adults do, their thinking was consistently different. Piaget decided to find out why.

example fish inherit gills which allow them to breathe under water. They can't live out of water. Birds need to be able to fly, so nature has provided them with wings. Giraffes have long necks which allow them to reach the new shoots which grow at the top of bushes. The older leaves further down are eaten by the smaller animals. Anteaters have long snouts with longer, sticky tongues which they can flick into anthills. Moles eat worms and spend much of their day burrowing. Their front paws are well adapted to digging. Each of these animal species can only survive in the environment nature intended it to. A polar bear wouldn't survive in the desert, and there aren't any zebra at the North Pole! But one animal manages to "cheat". Humans have learned to adapt. Answer these questions and you'll see how.

'How do humans "cheat"?'

1 How do polar bears cope with their freezing climate? How do Eskimos?

2 If we can't get a giraffe to clean the bedroom windows what can we do?

3 If we need to dig the Channel Tunnel must we recruit an army of moles? Why not?

Background reading – Jean Piaget's biography

Piaget was born in Neuchatel, Switzerland on 9 August 1896. He was a brilliant scholar, particularly in science subjects. Before he was 10 he had made a detailed study of birds, fossils, and mechanics, and had his first article published on the subject of sea shells at the age of 11. He had published 20 scientific papers on molluscs (snails, oysters, limpets etc.) before he was 21.

Piaget also read articles and books on religion, psychology, sociology, and philosophy throughout his adolescence. He studied biology at Neuchatel University, and graduated in 1916 at the age of 20. Two years later he had written a most detailed study of the mollusc, for which he recieved his PhD, and had written a semi-autobiographical novel at the same time. He wasn't particularly interested in children at this stage.

He started to become interested in psychology in 1919 and worked in psychological clinics and laboratories in Zurich and Paris. At first he was interested in Freudian psychoanalysis and thought that biology might help explain aspects of psychological development. Whilst studying clinical psychology at the Sorbonne (a famous university in Paris) in 1920 Piaget helped in the standardisation of intelligence test procedures

at Alfred Binet's laboratory in Paris. Piaget wasn't very interested in intelligence tests, and standardising a test was very repetitive and boring. However Piaget started to notice that five and six year old children seemed to give the same wrong answers to particular questions. It seemed to Piaget that the children weren't just guessing. They were using rules of logic to solve their problems. These rules were not the same as the ones that adults use. In other words Piaget started to believe that children are not just "little adults" in the way they think, and that there might be stages in the development of the intellect just as Freud had claimed there were stages in personality development.

Piaget had learned the "clinical method" of talking to patients, asking them questions, and observing their behaviour. He used this method to study the children who were doing the tests. He asked them questions like "Why does it rain?" Obviously the children weren't going to know the answer, so what would they say instead? He asked a sample of children from each age group between three and 12 to see if their answers had anything in common.

It soon became clear that children below the age of about seven years used different principles to base their judgements on compared to

4 If we want to explore the sea bed shall we train dolphins to go down, and tell us all about it when they surface? How else could we find out?

Piaget applied the same principles of adaptation to human cognitive development.

If we want to study the development of any human skill a good starting point is birth. Piaget noted that human infants are born with a few **reflexes** which allow us to survive the first few months and years. A reflex is any action which is triggered by some particular stimulus. If dust blows near your eye you will blink. If you feel very cold you will shiver. If you touch something extremely hot you'll withdraw your hand. The individual cannot control its reflexes, they are therefore **involuntary** responses to particular stimuli. These reflexes are the result of our first "**mental structures**".

Breathing, crying, smiling, and looking are all behaviour that children have at birth. Breathing is the constant response to needing air, crying may be a reflexive response to being upset or in pain. Smiling starts as a reflexive response to some activity in the child's brain. Looking may be a response to hearing something of immediate importance. We tend to think of reflexes as set, fixed patterns of

Jean Piaget applied the biological principle of adaptation to human mental development. He thought that there would be biological structures in our brains which would represent our knowledge. The first structures represent the reflexes which humans have at birth. Can you name any of the reflexes which we are born with?

(Background reading continued)

older children. For example, they appear to think that all things have life, and therefore have feelings. A child may well say "naughty table", if he's just walked into it and hurt himself. His mother might console him with "David smack naughty table". Piaget called this idea that everything has consciousness "animism".

Piaget was also studying some children who had mental problems, at a hospital in Paris. They couldn't answer his questions so he had to find another way for them to express their ideas and abilities. He gave them materials like clay to manipulate. The kind of things they did with it gave him the idea that the way they think and behave also changes with age. Piaget wrote some of his findings down, hoping that others would take up his research, whilst he returned to studying pond life! However Piaget was offered the job of Director of a famous Institute for research on children in Geneva, Switzerland which he took in 1921 at the age of 25. He intended to spend about five years researching in psychology. He was studying children's language development, reasoning, and moral development, as well as intelligence as such, and publishing some of his preliminary findings. To Piaget's surprise several well known psychologists started to regard him as an authority on child development.

Piaget had married Valentine Chatenay in 1923 and they had their first daughter, Jacqueline, in 1925. With his wife's help he began to investigate how Jacqueline's thought processes developed. This continued with the birth of their second daughter, Lucienne, in 1927, and their son, Laurent, in 1931. Piaget kept detailed diaries on the development of each of his children's cognitive development.

Piaget spent 50 years studying children, and has had enormous influence on the way people now regard how children think. Read this list of the positions Piaget held, and you'll see what his influence was during the middle part of the twentieth century.

He was the Director of the International Bureau for Education between 1929 and 1967, Director of the Institute for Educational Sciences at the University of Geneva from 1933 to 1971, Professor of Psychology and Sociology at the University of Lausanne from 1938 to 1951, Professor of Sociology at the University of Geneva from 1939 to 1952, Professor of Experimental Psychology, University of Geneva from 1940 to 1971, Professor of Developmental Psychology at the Sorbonne from 1952 to 1963. He died in 1980.

behaviour which we have very little control over. They are also very fast since the brain is not informed until after the response has begun. It is this speed of response which lets us drop a very hot object before it has time to burn us badly. Almost all reflexes seem to have one thing in common – some "survival value" – that is, in some way, they help us to protect ourselves.

Three things might happen to a reflex. They may stay for life (eg breathing), they may disappear altogether (eg touching the hand makes it open or close), or they may be modified into some other piece of learned behaviour (eg the grasping reflex becomes the deliberate use of the hand for picking things up etc).

Exercise – Reflexes

1 What is a reflex?

2 Name three reflexes that exist during infancy, but not during adulthood.

3 Why are we born with some reflexes?

Background reading – some human infant reflexes

Babies have many (possibly 50) reflexes, but not all infants show all the reflexes to anything like the same extent.

Two of the earliest reflexes to occur are breathing and crying. (Fairly obvious survival value here!) Crying may help the new born infant to "breathe in" during the first moments of life. Later the baby will use crying to tell its caregivers that it is not entirely happy. Crying is not a way of preparing for talking, except it might help in exercising the voice muscles. When the child is a little older, crying is used when all else the baby can do to attract attention has failed. Crying stops being reflexive when the child starts to use it deliberately.

Smiling takes much longer to establish than crying. During the first fortnight babies smile during sleep, but not much when they're awake. Either way they are probably not always smiling to show pleasure at anything going on around them. Smiling is often simply the result of some brain activity stimulating various facial muscles. At some time between six weeks and three months, the baby will start using its smile to show pleasure. By the third month the smile, like deliberate crying (both of which are being used to attract attention), stops being reflexive and starts being social.

The looking reflex begins right at birth. As soon as the baby opens its eyes its visual system is sufficiently well developed to allow it to see, for example, being able to follow and focus upon an object within minutes of birth. No learning is necessary.

During the first few days babies usually show "the doll's eye reflex", ie if you turn a baby's head round when its eyes are open, its eyes tend to turn rather more slowly. By the end of the second week this reflex will have disappeared.

Other reflexes include sucking, which is clearly an essential reflex for feeding. Babies can move their lips to the correct shape, and use their lungs to suck. A reflex which is sometimes used by doctors to check normal development is called the Moro Reflex. This occurs when a baby's head is supported with one hand and its body with another, then lowering the first hand will result in the baby's head falling because it is too great a weight to be supported by its neck muscles. When the head falls, the baby raises both hands upwards, cries, and stiffens its shoulders. Another reflex concerns a baby's hands. When the baby's fist is clenched a touch on the back of the hand results in the hand opening. If the open palm is touched with a finger it will be grasped.

2 "Invariant Functions" and "Variant Structures"

Just as birds can fly, and fish can swim, human beings have the ability to think as part of their genetic inheritance. According to Piaget thinking develops in the same way, and through the same sequence of stages in all humans. It starts off in the baby as very simple mental structures called **schemas**. The first schemas are for reflexes. Thinking is only really concerned with the information which is picked up through the baby's senses, and with learning to control its movements. For the first few years thinking is mostly concerned with the child's own needs and wants. A young child's thinking is quite illogical, and young children can't see things from anyone else's point of view. By around the age of seven the child starts to think about its own actions and their consequences for other people. As the child reaches puberty it should start to develop logic and reasoning, and starts to think what things "ought to" be like. According to Piaget this sequence is "fixed" and all children will go through it in the same order. It isn't possible to skip a stage. Piaget describes the sequence as "**invariant**"; it cannot vary.

Every individual has had different experiences. We've mixed with different people in different places, at different times. Even identical twins can't have had exactly the same experiences. Since we each learn through our experiences we must all know different things, and similar things in different ways. Each person's cognition is the result of countless ideas, or "mental structures" in their heads, and must be "**variant**".

There are two sorts of these **variant mental structures**. These are called **schemas** and **operations**. Schemas are "mental representations" or ideas about what things are and how we deal with them. You have schemas for "eating with a knife and fork", "crossing the road", and "buying things in shops". We don't all have schemas for "eating with chopsticks", "swimming", or "being a shop assistant". As soon as a baby develops a schema it will be applied to all things, for example, a baby soon finds that it can grasp some things in its hand. It will now try to grasp everything. By "trial and error" it will find that this isn't possible. So its "grasping schema" will gradually be refined into schemas for "graspable objects" and "non graspable objects". Later on it will develop schemas about playing games, speaking, passing exams, driving a car and so on.

The second type of mental structures are called **operations**. They allow us to combine schemas in an orderly, sensible, logical way, for example, the schema for gazing will be combined with the schema for reaching, and the schema for grasping in order to pick up a rattle. As the child grows, and its experience broadens, so it will be able to handle increasingly difficult operations. Operations take place in the imagination. They allow older children to imagine "what" might happen "if" something else was to occur.

Schemas and operations occur as we interact with other people and things in our environment, that is, they are mostly learned.

Reflexes are the first schemas. Thinking develops within a few months. Piaget claimed that human thinking develops in a fixed sequence of stages. Remember that Skinner would disagree. He would argue that development is a continuous process.

Since we develop cognition from our experiences, and everyone has different experiences, so everyone will have different levels of cognition. Do you have any areas of well developed cognition?

Schemas are ideas and plans we have for dealing with things. Operations refers to the way we can combine schemas and modify our ideas, mental states, thoughts and so on. What schemas are being combined in the activity "riding a bike"?

REVIEW – Functions and structures

All human beings are born with a few reflexes which may help them to survive, and then use their senses to help them to adapt to their environment. The way in which we are able to adapt goes through an invariant sequence. We all have different experiences and so all have different kinds of cognition. The mental structures which make up our cognition are variant. Piaget believed that cognition isn't something which can be measured since it is totally individual.

We must take in and understand (assimilate) any new information which applies to a schema we have, then we must modify or extend (accommodate) the existing schema with the new information. How would this process apply to "playing the guitar"?

3 Learning as a process of adapting to the environment

Piaget believed that "intelligence" was all about making appropriate **adaptations** to things around us quickly and efficiently. By adaptation he meant a way of taking in, processing, and using new information in an appropriate way. If a five year old girl wants to design and build an office block from Lego bricks, she must know which pieces to pick up. She must look at the Lego blocks in front of her, and realise what she needs to do first. This process of taking in the main elements of the situation is called "**assimilation**". She chooses the various pieces and puts them together in an appropriate way. Some blocks fit together in the way she thought they should. This makes her knowledge about how Lego fits together even more certain. However some blocks do not seem to fit together as she thought they would. She'll have to modify some of her schemas about building with Lego. Piaget called this process of extending and modifying schemas "**accommodation**".

In order to adapt her way of thinking about what she is building, the child must **organise** her experiences in some way. For example she may recognise that she is running out of Lego blocks. She will combine this experience with the knowledge that there aren't any more blocks, and switch to building something which needs fewer blocks. Without some "**mental organisation**" we're going to find it difficult to learn from our experiences. This mental organisation obviously involves intelligence, memory, etc. Fortunately much of our early mental organisation is automatic. Babies seem able to combine certain schemas and behaviour to achieve particular ends without ever having been taught what to do – for example, a nine month old boy sees a favourite toy, recognises it, decides he wants it, crawls to it, reaches for it, grasps it, takes it away with him, plays with it etc. There must always be a balance between assimilation and accommodation. The child mustn't take more in that it can practise, use, and come to understand. The child needs to do these things to fully accommodate the new information. Too much stimulation produces confusion because the existing information hasn't been accommodated when new information is being added. Piaget calls this balance "**equilibrium**".

Organisation is the general principle that all living things seem to have of making what seems like the most sensible use of whatever knowledge, skills, or functions they possess.

There must always be a balance between information which is being assimilated, and the accommodation that is already occurring. This balance is called "equilibrium". If a child tries to take too much information in all at once it will become more confused than it was to begin with. Has this ever happened to you?

Background reading – An example of adaptive behaviour

A child learns that if he pulls the cork out of a bottle he can drink the contents. He has assimilated the schema "pulling at the top of a bottle to open it". He will now apply that schema to all bottles, including screw top ones. He will eventually realise that his earlier schema doesn't work and that it only applies to certain bottles. Accommodation is this "finding out and modifying existing schemas" process. Clearly it is a very active business. The child must explore, discover, experiment. The first schemas consist of a small number of actions and perceptions. Later the child is able to let one thing (eg a word) stand for another thing. He doesn't need to be so active any more but can think more, for example, an infant must turn a box round in his hands in order to see what it looks like from the other side. A 10 year old can imagine what it looks like, without touching it, and could probably even draw what it looks like.

> ## Piaget's Model of Cognition
>
> **1** Invariant functions
> (What all people do)
>   (a) Organisation
>   (b) Adaptation: assimilation and accommodation
> **2** Variant structures
> (Which each of us develops individually)
>   (a) Schemas
>   (b) Operations

Exercise – The structure of cognition

1 Explain in your own words what Piaget meant by the terms schemas and operations.

2 What did Piaget mean by assimilation, accommodation, and equilibrium?

3 What is adaptation?

REVIEW – Adaptation

Piaget sees "intelligence" as adaptation. Having met some unfamiliar event, object, or experience for example, we try to understand it in terms of our existing schemas. When we assimilate this new experience our cognitive mental processes try to fit it in with the most appropriate schemas. The new perception may modify existing schemas, or cause other schemas to join together. This new set of schemas will then be applied to the next situation.

4 Piaget's stages of intellectual development

1 Birth–Two years: The sensory motor stage

Piaget observed several very young babies, particularly his own three children very closely indeed. Much of what he regards as the functions or purposes of the sensory motor stage are the results of these naturalistic observations and interpretations. Piaget claimed that most of the infant's first schemas during its first few weeks of life are to do with movement. Much of the baby's behaviour is **reflexive**. Some particular stimulus appears, such as something touching the baby's face, and its reflexive response is to turn its head towards the thing which is touching it. This reflexive schema provides a solution to this experience. After the first few weeks of life the baby will learn to use some of its muscles and limbs for movement, and will begin to understand some information from its senses. Piaget calls these first ideas which babies develop about how to deal with their world "**action schemas**". The baby is totally "**egocentric**" and unable to take anyone else's needs or interests into account.

The baby starts to learn about objects and what they can be made to do. The baby is assimilating and accommodating lots of information about itself, its world, and the people in it. It begins to understand how one thing can cause another, and begins to acquire some simple ideas of time and space.

Even babies of less than a year old can show some "intelligent behaviour". For example, imagine a ten month old girl sees, and wants, her rattle. Suppose the rattle is resting on a cushion. The infant

According to Piaget "egocentric" refers to the way a child's thinking is dominated by its own ideas. The child "centres" on its own actions, its body, its knowledge. It can't take other aspects of a situation, or other people's ideas into account.

will reach for the cushion, and pull it towards her, until it is close enough for her to grasp the rattle. She has used the cushion as a "tool" to reach what she wants. Quite a large amount of "*intelligent behaviour*" is to do with inventing and using "tools".

Each infant builds up a *mental picture* of the objects around it based on its knowledge of what it can do with them, for example, sucking them, shaking them, throwing them etc. By about eight months of age the baby becomes more interested in the objects for their own sake. They feel them, study them, and try to do other things with them. A great deal of the baby's experience is concerned with objects. It doesn't matter too much what the object is: what's more important is that the baby should be able to explore it, to see what it does, and what the infant can do with it. Existing **action schemas** have to be expanded to take account of these new assimilated experiences.

Piaget studied babies' reactions to objects which they could see, and then which were hidden from them. For example the baby may be looking at its rattle. The rattle is slowly covered by a cushion. Although the infant has seen the cushion, the baby seems to lose all interest in the rattle. Piaget concluded that the infant behaves as though it believed that an object which is out of sight no longer exists. By eight to twelve months old the babies did continue to look for the hidden object. Piaget concludes that they must now have learned that an object is still there, even though it can't be seen. Piaget called this ability "**object permanence**".

Piaget's view of object permanence has been challenged by other researchers. For example Tom Bower has spent many years studying the visual abilities of babies and young children. In several ingenious experiments he has shown that one to four month old infants have some idea of object permanence. The skill may even be innate. Bower knew that infants learn a great deal by simply looking, and that they can see quite well right from birth.

He showed infants an attractive toy placed on a table in front of the child. It could be hidden from the infants view by a screen sliding in

---

Background reading – An experiment to demonstrate object permanence

Two researchers named Mundy–Castle and Anglin sat a sample of four month old infants in front of some apparatus consisting of two "portholes", A and B. An object travelled in an elipse in a clockwise direction so that it entered porthole A at the bottom and moved towards the top, and entered porthole B at the top and moved towards the bottom. For the rest of the time it was hidden behind the screen.

The researchers watched the infants' eyes. After a few revolutions they started to "follow" the object round the elipse, anticipating where it would appear next. These four month old infants seem to have object permanence.

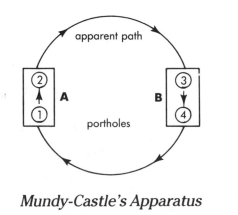

Mundy-Castle's Apparatus

front of it. The toy could be left there, or removed before the screen slid away again. If the babies had knowledge of object permanence they would expect the toy still to be there when the screen was removed. When they saw it again they would continue to look at it. The older ones might even smile. If the toy had been removed they would show surprise. They would be expecting to see something that wasn't there. Most of these one to four month old infants were surprised when the screen slid back and the toy was missing. Bower claims that they must have object permanence several months before Piaget believed they had any schemas for it. Bower believes that several perceptual skills may be innate, as we shall see shortly.

Exercise – The sensory motor stage

1 Name and describe the first of Piaget's stages of intellectual development.

2 What is meant by "object permanence"?

3 At what age did Piaget believe object permanence was achieved?

4 Outline one piece of research into the existence of object permanence in young babies. Identify the age of the babies studied, and the apparatus used.

2 Two–seven years: The pre operations stage

Earlier we defined Piaget's use of the word "*operations*" as meaning "combining schemas in an orderly, sensible, logical way". In this second stage of cognitive development children's thought processes are developing, but are far from "logical" (in the adult sense). The thinking of two to seven year olds is *Pre Operational*.

Piaget used the clinical interview technique with several hundred children to discover any similarities in the way they think. He was always looking for average or typical modes of thinking (and has been criticised for having no interest in children whose thinking was different from "the average"). The clinical interview consisted of asking children questions (in language that they could understand), and interpreting their answers. Towards the end of this stage Piaget did use some formal experiments. The main features he identified in this stage were "**symbolisation**", "**egocentrism**", "**animism**", and "**moral realism**".

Symbolisation is allowing something to stand for, or symbolise, something else. Anything which we allow to stand for something else can be a symbol. A red traffic light is a symbol which means "stop". The "thumbs up" sign is a symbol standing for agreement. Words are symbols too. During this stage a child's vocabulary of words will be expanding. As such symbols expand they allow the child's imagination to expand as well. This is best seen in children's play.

Exercise – Symbolisation

Think of some play activities for which knowing words like "house", "sun", "mummy", "car", "tree", "dog", etc. will help a child of two years old to use its imagination.

REVIEW – Sensory motor stage

For the first couple of years children are developing basic egocentric schemas which allow them to practise and master sensory and motor skills. They achieve object permanence during their first year, so must be able to tell the difference between themselves, and other people and things around them.

Symbolisation is the ability to think in ideas, and use words to express those ideas. It stimulates the child's imagination.

All pre operational children are usually **egocentric** in the way they think. They can only see things from their own point of view, and imagine that theirs is the only point of view that anyone could hold.

One of Piaget's experiments to show egocentrism

Piaget had three model "mountains", made of papier mache. Each mountain was a different shape and colour, and each had different things on the top. One had a cross, like a church, one had a hut, and one was covered in "snow". The child sat with the three mountains in front of it, and a doll was placed behind the first. The child was asked, "What can the doll see?" The child was shown a number of pictures of the mountains from various viewpoints, including the one the doll could actually "see", and what the child could see from where it sat. The doll was moved in front of the second, and then the third mountain. Again the child was asked which of the pictures represented what the doll could "see". Children up to about seven years old usually chose the picture representing what they could see from where they were looking. Only later do children learn to imagine that they are looking from the doll's viewpoint. Seeing things from a different perspective can only happen when a child can stop centring on itself (being egocentric), and can imagine something else to be the centre of attention. This ability is called **decentring**.

The third feature of the pre operational stage which Piaget identified is "animism". "Animism" is the belief that everything that exists has some kind of consciousness. A car which won't start will be described as being "tired" or "ill". A high mountain will be thought of as "old". A

Piaget's Mountains

child who has hurt himself colliding with a chair will happily "smack" the "naughty" chair. Animism can also be explained by the fact that the child's thinking is still egocentric. Since children can't see things from anyone else's point of view, so they will assume that everyone, and everything, will be like themselves. Since they have emotions and can feel pain and pleasure, so they believe that everything else can too.

The fourth feature which dominates the way children think in the pre operational stage is the way they view moral issues. This too can be explained by egocentric thought. "Moral realism" is the belief that the child's way of thinking about what is right and wrong will be shared by everyone else. Being egocentric they can only focus on one aspect of a situation at any one time. They develop a respect for rules and insist that they must be obeyed at all times. They can't take anything else, like motives, into account.

To discover how children of various ages regard rules, Piaget played marbles with quite a lot of them. He asked them questions like "What are the rules of this game?", "where do these rules come from?", "what would happen if I did . . . (something which would break the rules as explained by the children?")", "must everyone obey these rules?", "could anyone change the rules?" etc.

Exercise – The pre-operational stage

1 What is the name of the method of investigation which Piaget used to investigate children's ideas about rules called?

2 What do you think might be the advantages and disadvantages of this method of collecting information on the way children think?

3 Summarise the main differences in the ways that sensory motor and pre operational children think.

4 What did Piaget mean by egocentrism? Describe one of Piaget's demonstrations of egocentrism.

3 Seven–eleven/twelve years: The concrete operations stage

Thinking is becoming "operational". This means it is becoming more rational and "adult like". This takes from around seven years of age to well into the teenage years. Piaget divides this period into two stages which he calls the stage of **concrete operations**, and the stage of **formal operations**. During the concrete operations stage children can think "logically" if they can manipulate the object that they are thinking about. In the Formal Operations Stage they can manipulate their thoughts, and don't need the real object.

During the concrete operations stage egocentric thought declines. So does the belief in animism. Up until the beginning of the concrete operations stage Piaget claimed that children's ideas about objects were dominated by how those objects appear. Something which looks heavy will be thought of as being heavy. So a balloon which is fully inflated will be described as being very much heavier than one which is only half the size because it's only half inflated. According to Piaget children gradually learn that objects are not always what they appear to

REVIEW – The pre-operational stage

Thinking in the pre operational stage is egocentric, illogical, and dominated by animism and moral realism. It will gradually become more logical and less egocentric as the child learns to symbolise.

169

be sometime after their seventh birthday. This skill is called "**conservation**". Children learn to conserve things like number, weight, volume, mass, length etc.

Conservation

According to Piaget a five or six year old child cannot conserve. One experiment to demonstrate this allows the child to adjust the amount of liquid in two identical tall thin jars until the child is satisfied that each jar contains "the same amount to drink". The child then sees the experimenter pour the liquid from one of the tall jars into a shorter but wider jug. The child is asked whether the tall thin jar and the shorter, wider jug still hold the same amount of liquid. Most pre operational

---

Background reading – Some examples of experiments on conservation skills

Conservation of number

The child is shown two rows of apples and agrees that they contain the same number. The apples in one row are then spread out, and the child is asked if either of the two rows now contains more apples. A child who cannot conserve will say that the "spread out" row must contain more apples.

Conservation of length

A child is shown a stick and a piece of string of equal length. The string is then curled and the child is asked if the stick and the string are still the same length. A child who cannot conserve length will say that the stick is now longer than the string.

Conservation of mass

The child agrees that two balls of clay contain the same amount of clay. One of the balls is then rolled into a "sausage shape" and the child is asked whether they both still contain the same amount of clay. A child who cannot conserve will say that the sausage shape must contain more clay than the other ball because it looks as though it contains more.

Conservation of area

Two identical sheets of cardboard have wooden blocks placed on them in identical positions. The child agrees that both sheets of cardboard have the same area left uncovered. One of the sets of blocks is then scattered around the cardboard and the child is asked if they still have the same area left uncovered. The "scattered blocks" seem to cover more area to the child who cannot conserve area.

Conservation of Liquid

Conservation of Plasticine

---

children will say the tall jar contains more liquid because it looks bigger. Their thinking is dominated by the appearance of things, and don't realise that the volume or mass of an object does not change just because its appearance changes.

Conservation occurs when children are able to take in several features of the objects they are looking at all at the same time. Because they now have "*operational*" thought they can start to imagine "what if" something were to happen, then it was reversed. For example a child who has operational thought is shown a stick and a piece of string laid out alongside each other. The child sees the string being curled up, and is asked if it is still the same length as the stick. The child will see what the string looks like now, but can also mentally reverse the operation of curling the string, and so realise that it is still the same length as the stick.

Children are usually more familiar with some objects than with others, and these are likely to be the things the child conserves first. For example children become aware of numbers from quite a young age. They learn to count and do simple arithmetic almost as soon as they start school. They usually need "real (concrete) objects" to count. A six year old's teacher might well ask what happens "when we take three apples away from five apples?" By around the age of seven many children will have learned to conserve number. They no longer need the actual apples to count. They will probably know that the row containing the apples which have been "spread out" still has the same number of apples as the other. By nine or 10 years of age most children should have learned enough about weight to be able to conserve it, and by 11 or 12 years old most children will understand volume. Children become more "logical", according to Piaget, between the ages of seven and 12, but only if they have the real object near to them, to look at or touch.

Ask a child in the pre operational stage "which is the most, ten fives or five tens?", or "Which is the heaviest, a ton of feathers or a ton of coal?" They usually say that the coal is heavier. If you asked for any explanation they'd probably say that a feather is lighter than a piece of coal.

Reversibility

Having learned to conserve, children will slowly realise that if whatever was altered in the conservation exercise was reversed, things would be as they were to begin with, for example, in the conservation of volume experiment, using the different shaped water containers, a child who is capable of **reversibility** knows that there would still be the same amount of liquid if the contents of the small jug was poured back into the tall jar.

According to Piaget the concrete operational child's thinking is becoming logical and is using mathematical principles. It is characterised by conservation, reversibility, and decentring.

An extension of conservation is reversibility. This is the knowledge that things would be returned to normal if we reversed the steps we took to conserve.

Exercise – Conservation

1 What does Piaget mean by conservation?

2 Outline one experiment which Piaget used to demonstrate conservation.

3 Explain what is meant by decentring?

4 Piaget claims that there are differences in ways of thinking between children in the pre operational stage, and the stage of concrete operations. Summarise the changes which Piaget noted.

REVIEW – Concrete operations stage

Children in the early years of the concrete operations stage can solve mental problems, so long as they have real objects to check what they are doing. During this stage children learn conservation and reversibility and become more able to see things from other points of view.

4 Eleven–sixteen plus years: The formal operations stage

REVIEW – Formal operational thinking

Teenagers in the formal operations stage are usually able to think more abstractly than younger children. Being able to manipulate thoughts means children start thinking about a wider range of issues, including ideas like honesty, morality, and freedom. They can see other people's point of view, and can take their reasons for their behaviour into account.

From around puberty the ways in which many children think change again. They become more "adult like", and can rely more on ideas rather than needing real objects to manipulate. Most children learn how to work some things out in their heads, without having to see the real objects. As we saw, a seven year old will learn addition and subtraction by counting numbers of apples, sweets, or blocks of wood etc. By 12 most can do some mental arithmetic. Teenagers start to think about moral and philosophical issues too.

Piaget argued that the changeover from concrete to formal operations takes several years to become fully established. But do all people reach this last stage? Some recent research shows that quite a number of adults never do. Correlations have been found amongst some adults between the variables "low scores on IQ tests", and "not appearing to think in formal operational ways". There are also cross cultural differences. In some societies children are not reared to use the same rules of what we in the West think of as formal logic.

Comments on Piaget's theory

Piaget devoted most of his life to making us aware of the cognitive development of children, rejecting totally the previous belief that children are merely "little adults". Many people believe that his theory is the most comprehensive and detailed analysis of the way children think that exists to date. He has shown that children are naturally curious and willing learners who need stimulation. Like any good theory Piaget's has stimulated an enormous amount of research, and inevitably some questions and criticisms will be raised. Here are some of the main ones.

Criticism

1 Piaget claimed that children spend the first ten years or so not able to use the rules of logic which most adults are supposed to use. (You might think that someone who was considering

Comment

1 Countless hours of careful research led Piaget to this conclusion. He may have regarded himself as an exception to the general rule.

Background reading – One of Piaget's tests for formal operational thinking

Someone old enough to have reached the formal operations stage is shown a number of weights which can be hooked on to the end of a piece of string to make a pendulum. The youngster is allowed to choose the length of the string, the weight to be attached, and the height at which the weight is to be released. She or he has to work out which of these three factors, or which combination of them, determines how quickly the pendulum swings. The way to do this is to alter one of the variables (weight, length, or height) whilst keeping the other two constant, and see if it has any effect. Children in the pre operational, or concrete operational stages will randomly alter the variables and find it difficult to solve the problem. Someone who uses formal operational thought will soon realise that the length of the string is the determining factor – the shorter the string, the faster the pendulum swings.

scientific issues whilst still a child himself would have had a more optimistic view of children's ability to think logically and abstractly!)

2 Piaget suggested that logical thought develops from about puberty. Several studies have shown that many adolescents and adults are not all capable of logical thought.

3 Piaget was probably mistaken about the timing of when children can do certain things (such as conservation). Researchers like Jerome Bruner have shown that five and six year old children can be taught to conserve if they are encouraged to think things through for themselves.

4 Peter Bryant has shown that many of Piaget's tests were too complicated for many of the children to understand. Bryant simplified some of Piaget's experiments and found that children under five were capable of logical thought when they knew what was being asked of them.

5 Piaget's main method for finding out about children was the clinical interview. This can be rather vague and open to the interpretation of the interviewer.

6 Some researchers, such as the "behaviourists", suggest that development does not occur in stages but is gradual and continuous.

7 Piaget did not make clear what makes one "stage" end and another begin. (This criticism is also levelled against Freud's theory.) Presumably children are constantly adapting to new information—assimilating and accommodating it. Why should there be particular stages?

2 Piaget was attempting to find the main stages of development that most people pass through, and the ages at which they occur.

3 Piaget did accept this criticism, and modified his views about the ages at which the different kinds of thinking occurred. He had thought that children's mental abilities changed at particular ages, that is, 2, 7, and 11. These seemed to fit the ages of the children he had observed and tested who were capable of understanding the various games and tests he used.

4 Piaget simply gave children particular objects and asked them to answer specific questions. This may not have been the most sophisticated research, but it was amongst the first to study children's cognitive development.

5 Piaget was aware of the problems of "leading" the child, but children still say and do things for many reasons, particularly when a strange person is watching them and asking them questions.

6 A number of other aspects of maturation, such as motor skills (crawling, walking, running), and language (babbling, single words, and sentences) do appear to occur in stages. Cognition might too.

7 Piaget maintained that there are distinct stages, each stage following from the previous one. They partly reflected the child's state of maturation. Different skills would develop in each stage.

8 Piaget is said to put too much emphasis on the role of the intellect in development and thus overlooks the effects of the child's emotions and motivations, personality etc.

8 This isn't entirely fair, Piaget often makes reference to "the whole child". But Piaget was a biologist primarily concerned with exploring the maturation and functioning of mental structures.

9 Some of Piaget's terms such as "equilibrium", "schema", "accommodation" etc. are criticised for being rather general.

9 Piaget needed general terms which could apply to how human thinking is organised, since thinking is so abstract and varied.

10 There is no firm evidence that Piaget's concepts, no matter how loosely or accurately defined, actually exist. Piaget observed children's behaviour, and made assumptions about the organisation of mental functioning, which he then named.

10 Most scientific enquiry involves scientists making educated guesses about the existence of things, which they then try to prove. It is necessary to give them a name in order to discuss them with others.

11 Piaget was always looking for what the average or typical child could do and so ignored the great variations in the ways individual children think.

11 Whilst he was aware of individual differences he didn't consider that trying to understand them would help his general theory.

12 Piaget concentrated on children's interactions with their environment, mostly when they were alone. Latest evidence suggests that their social development with others has a great deal to do with their cognitive development.

12 Piaget offered the first radical alternative view of how children's thinking develops. His early ideas are bound to be refined and improved greatly.

5 Other research into some of Piaget's ideas

One of the major criticisms that has been levelled against Piaget's conclusions is that his methods were complicated, and led to him underestimating younger children's abilities. Here are a couple of the best known studies.

An experiment by Martin Hughes

In the mid 1970s Martin Hughes constructed a game with a "policeman doll" and a "boy doll". Each doll could be moved to various positions around two walls which joined in the middle to form a cross. The idea was to involve the child in the game, and draw on its previous experience. The child was asked questions like "Can the policeman see the child if we put him here?" And "put the child doll where the policeman can't see him". Most children will have had some experi-

Hughes' Doll Experiment

ence of "hiding" so this game should appeal more than asking them to make guesses about a doll looking at three "model mountains". Very few of the children made many mistakes, and Hughes would explain to them where they went wrong if any did. Piaget didn't give the children many opportunities to ask questions, or to explain where they were going wrong. Hughes' conclusions were quite surprising. Almost all of his sample of three and four year olds could imagine themselves in the place of the policeman, and of the boy doll. Hughes introduced more dolls, and more walls. The children still gave the correct answer. Hughes has shown that children of three and four could decentre and show reversibility.

An experiment by McGarrigle and Donaldson

McGarrigle and Donaldson changed the context of one of Piagets conservation experiments so as to involve the child more. They sampled four and five year olds, asking them to watch a glove puppet (called "naughty teddy") spreading out a row of sweets whilst not moving another row. The children had agreed that there were the same number of sweets in each row before "teddy" started being "naughty". They knew that there were still the same number afterwards. Many of the children may have seen "naughty teddy" as a game in which they could become involved, and something they could understand. When an adult had moved one of the rows they said that something had changed. But this may have been *because* it was an adult who moved one of the rows. A child's experience of adults is that they are always changing things! Few were fooled by the glove puppet.

In response to a number of studies such as these Piaget did accept that children as young as five could start the concrete operations stage.

Despite all of the criticisms we have mentioned, Piaget's contribution to our understanding of children's cognitive development has been enormous. Psychologists have been retesting, and confirming many of his ideas for years. Even where valid criticisms have been made without someone of the intellect, energy, and enthusiasm of Piaget we would know far less than we do today about the way children think. One final criticism suggests that there is another stage, after the stage of formal operations, which Piaget didn't identify. It describes the highest level of thinking. In this "stage" thinking is abstract and highly sophisticated. Only the greatest thinkers reach this stage. Some who did might include Einstein, Freud, and, of course, Piaget himself!

'Naughty Ted'

REVIEW – Evaluation of Piaget's theory

Piaget's research was a major breakthrough in the way we understand children's thinking, and his ideas have dominated cognitive psychology for nearly 50 years. Many other psychologists have confirmed his conclusions, others have challenged them. His ideas have stimulated a massive amount of further research, all of which increases our knowledge of children's development.

Exercise – Evaluation of Piaget's contribution

1 Describe the main methods which Piaget used in his research.

2 What is a "stage theory" of development?

3 Outline two criticisms that have been made of the way Piaget conducted his research.

4 Describe and evaluate four criticisms that have been made of Piaget's explanations of cognitive development.

10 Children's Moral Development

An important part of the **socialisation process** is learning what is "right" and "wrong". Each society has rules and laws governing what is "right" and "wrong", or "good", and "bad". In Europe, for example, we accept that one man may be married to one woman at any one time. In some Arab countries some women may have several husbands, and some men may have several wives. People in all societies can only live at peace with each other because they agree to live by their society's rules.

Socialisation is simply the name of the process by which we learn those things that we must know in order to fit in with the rest of the people in our society. We must learn to speak the language, learn the customs and habits of our society, and learn about the acceptable ways in which we must think and behave.

Exercise – Moral development

How do you think a person knows about right and wrong? Here are some possible sources of knowledge.
Instinct, Inner knowledge, God, Upbringing, Commonsense.

1 Are there any other sources of knowledge that you think could be included in this list?

2 What percentage of our knowledge of right and wrong would you imagine comes from each of the items in the list?

Most people probably acquire some sense of morality during their childhood. Some people will have very strong ideas about "proper" behaviour, others will be less concerned about doing and saying "the right thing". For example those delinquents who John Bowlby described as suffering from "*affectionless psychopathy*" had very little concern for "moral" or "decent" behaviour. The process by which children acquire their sense of morality has been explained in quite different ways. Freudians see it as the result of identifying with a parent in order to resolve some of the conflict that children feel during the *Oedipus Complex*. Behaviourists see children as little adults who will learn appropriate behaviour by a combination of *reinforcement*, *imitation*, and *punishment*. Cognitive psychologists see moral judgements developing as children's cognitive skills develop generally. Socially cognitive psychologists see it developing as a combination of cognitive development and social interaction. The result of our moral development is that we acquire a **conscience**.

All societies have developed rules about "right and wrong". Many of the rules have been made into laws which all the people should obey. Can you think of any "rules" which we agree to obey, which aren't legally required.

Exercise – Conscience

1 Define the term "morality".

2 What is meant by "conscience"?

3 Where do our "consciences" come from?

A conscience is a set of moral principles that we each develop. We usually try to live by these guidelines. In the past some people believed that the conscience was "the voice of God", but now many psychologists see it as something we each acquire as we are socialised.

Just because we have a conscience, we don't always live by it, especially if the rewards for not doing so are great, or the risk of being caught is slim! In psychology we are interested in questions like "where do children's ideas about morality come from?" "When and

Psychologists have concentrated on different aspects of how children develop ideas about right and wrong. Freud concentrates on the origin of moral feelings, Piaget and Kohlberg explain moral reasoning, and behaviourists explain moral behaviour.

how do children learn about moral ideas?" "What kind of moral thinking are children capable of at different ages?" Four theories which attempt to answer questions such as these come from Sigmund Freud, Jean Piaget, Lawrence Kohlberg, and learning theorists such as Albert Bandura. Freud is concerned with the emotional components, Piaget and Kohlberg are concerned with the cognitive elements, and Bandura tries to explain the social and behavioural aspects.

In this chapter we will be examining these different explanations. We will:

1 Review Freud's psychodynamic explanation.
2 Examine Piaget's cognitive explanation.
3 Note Kohlberg's development of Piaget's views.
4 Examine the main behaviourist theories.

1 Freud's psychoanalytic theory of moral development

Sigmund Freud once said that one of the hardest tasks facing any parent was the moral development of their children. Freud attempted to explain the growth of personality, and was interested in how children felt about "right and wrong". Freud claimed that the personality mainly consists of three unconscious parts, the id, the ego, and the superego. For the first year or two the primitive, unconscious id dominates. It makes demands which must be met. In the child's unconscious the ego tries to modify some of id's demands and find rational ways of achieving them.

During the phallic stage of development children begin to have unconscious, incestuous "*feelings*" about their opposite sex parent. These "*feelings*" will make the child feel aggressive towards the same sex parent. For example the boy may see his father as a rival. He will have unconscious "*feelings* of hostility towards his rival. He may be afraid that his father will punish him for his feelings, his father may even castrate him. Hostility towards someone the child loves, and the fear of punishment, will produce feelings of guilt and anxiety. Freud suggested that the superego would be an unconscious force which would help us to set our own standards of acceptable feelings and behaviour. The superego is involved with overcoming these feelings by making the boy identify with his father. If the child loves his father, and

---

Background reading – People's attitudes towards right and wrong

In a survey conducted (in 1970) for the Independent Television Authority a sample of adults were asked "How do you think a person knows what is right and what is wrong?" Here is a summary of their answers:

Conscience, Inner self, or God	43%
Upbringing	28%
Commonsense	16%
Instinct	13%

It seems that many people think that "Upbringing" and "Conscience" are quite separate. Many psychologists claim that conscience is the result of upbringing.

is deeply attached, the tensions caused by his feelings will be stronger, so the need to identify will be even stronger. Also, if the father is very dominant, very demanding, and seems threatening to the boy he will feel a stronger urge to identify.

By "**identification**" Freud meant the process by which a child is seen to "take on" the attitudes and ideas of its parent, to become like the parent, so that their personalities are supposed to become similar. When a child identifies with its parent it's as though the child became like (a smaller version of) its parent. This smaller version of the parent is represented by the child's superego. The child's ideas about its parent's standards of "good" behaviour become a part of the child's **ego ideal**. What the parent seems to think is "bad" behaviour becomes a part of the child's "**conscience**". If the child does anything "wrong", which it knows would hurt its parent it would be, in effect, hurting itself.

To a lesser extent girls identify with their mothers. The girl knows that she can't be hurt in the same way as the boy, since she already appears to have been castrated, and so her fear of her mother may not be as strong. However she is afraid that her mother may stop loving her, and so identifies with her.

Freud saw these identifications occurring to resolve what he called the Oedipus Complex for boys, and the Electra Complex for girls. (A "complex" is a group or collection of, in this case, unconscious feelings, desires, ideas, wishes etc.) They draw the child towards its opposite sex parent, and make it want to eliminate the same sex parent. If the tensions and conflicts that these unconscious urges produce are not resolved satisfactorily, the child may develop some neurotic disorders later.

The superego is described as having two parts. One is a sort of "conscience". It punishes us when we do wrong by making us feel guilty and uncomfortable. The other part contains the ideal moral code that we think we ought to live by which Freud called the "ego ideal".

According to Freud, during the phallic stage children are unconsciously drawn towards their opposite sex parent, and feel hostile towards their same sex parent. This produces unpleasant feelings. How does Freud explain how these feelings are resolved?

Exercise – Evaluating Freudian psychoanalysis

Try to remember as much of the evaluation of Freud's theory in general as you can. Make two lists, one headed "contributions", and the other called "criticisms" and see how many points you can remember.

Exercise – Psychoanalytic explanation of moral development

1 According to Freud a child's family will have an enormous influence on its moral development. Write a paragraph explaining the role of the superego and identification in Freud's theory of moral development.

2 Freud explains how children acquire their moral feelings. What other aspects of morality are there, apart from feelings?

REVIEW – Freud's explanation of moral development

A child in the phallic stage will identify with its same sex parent, to overcome its Oedipal conflict. Through identification it accepts its parent's views of right and wrong.

Comments on Freud's ideas

Before reading the evaluation of Freud's ideas on moral development you should look back to the evaluation of Freud's general theory at the end of Chapter Six.

Good points

1 Freud offered one of the first, and most complete explanations for the development of moral feelings in children. It was central to his whole theory, and claimed that one of the three parts of personality, the superego, developed to guide children's moral behaviour.

2 Freud's theory suggests that children of three and four years old would be more likely to imitate the moral attitudes and behaviour of the parent with whom they are identifying than anyone else.

3 According to Freud children learn their moral norms and values from their same sex parent.

4 Freud claimed that children would have resolved their Oedipal problems by the age of six or seven, and would be morally mature by then.

Bad points

1 Other studies of moral development do not show much support for any of Freud's ideas. For example the claim that boys have stronger superegos than girls, and therefore are less likely to behave "badly" than girls seems to be the opposite of the truth!

2 Children do not usually start to understand and imitate the feelings of one parent more than the other until they are older than the three or four years that Freud suggested.

3 If so, how could boys being raised by their mothers in one parent families learn their moral code? Yet they do.

4 There's little evidence for that either! Eight, nine, and ten year olds can still have all sorts of confused moral feelings, for example about their family (see Chapter Five).

Other psychoanalysts do not agree with Freud's explanations of moral development, and Freud himself modified his own ideas several times.

A Naughty Child?

2 Piaget's view of moral development in Children

Freud sees the child as a rather helpless and passive receiver of other people's views. For Freud boys acquire moral feelings in a desperate attempt to protect themselves against their fears about what their fathers might do to them. Girls are supposed to identify with their mothers who have already punished them by castration. Piaget sees children being much more actively involved in their own learning about the world than Freud did. Since cognition develops through the four invariant stages which we studied in Chapter Nine, moral reasoning should follow a similar course.

Piaget used a number of techniques to investigate how children think about rules, honesty and truthfulness, "right" and "wrong" (justice), motives, and punishment. For example he played some games with children to investigate their thinking on "rules", and he told children stories which could be interpreted in different ways, to see if they could understand about intentions. He observed the way

Piaget's cognitive view sees the child as an active partner in its own cognitive development. The child will apply the same rules to learning about moral issues as it does to learning about many other issues.

they played and he conducted experiments, to see how their thinking on moral issues changed. Here are some examples.

Exercise – Piaget's main stages

Here are the names of the main stages in Piaget's cognitive theory. You have to fill in the gaps.

Name	Age	Main features
Sensory Motor		
Pre Operational		
Concrete Operations		
Formal Operations		

Children's views on rules

Piaget played games of marbles with many Swiss children. Young children usually invent their own rules when playing marbles, so Piaget asked them about where the rules came from, and whether they could be broken or changed. He played marbles with children of various ages who were in each of the stages of development he had identified. He found that their thinking on rules tied in with their general stage of cognitive development.

Two to three year old **pre-operational** children used no rules at all, but played with the marbles in any way they wanted to at the time. (This is an example of **egocentric** behaviour.) By four or five years of age they were starting to imitate each others games, although they were still largely egocentric. When they were taught some of the rules of marbles they followed them without question, as though the rules were absolute law and couldn't be broken or changed at all. The

Piaget playing marbles

children seemed to accept that rules are made by authority figures such as adults, and they must not be broken at any cost. If they are broken, punishment will be immediate and severe. This did not stop individual children changing, amending, and breaking the rules for their own advantage, whilst trying to resist anyone else's attempts to change them!

Children in the stage of **concrete operations** still obey the rules, but not quite so slavishly as they had before. They accepted that rules were there for the players' benefit, and could be changed, so long as the change was fair to everyone. (Children can now **decentre**.)

Exercise – Egocentrism and decentring

1 Explain what the terms "egocentrism" and "decentring" mean, according to Piaget. (Look them up if you have to.)

2 Name three games that young children play, which demonstrate their egocentrism.

3 Name three games that operational children play, which demonstrates that they are able to decentre.

4 Write a few sentences summarising the way that pre-operational, and concrete operational children regard rules.

Piaget's research into honesty and truthfulness

To investigate children's attitudes towards lying, cheating, stealing, and similar "wicked" behaviour, Piaget developed a new method of investigation, the "story telling" technique. For example he would tell children of various ages two stories. One concerned a child who deliberately told a lie that had minor consequences. The other told of a child who accidently said something which wasn't true, which had a major consequence, for example:

Story A A little boy says that his dog is as big as a horse, and the postman won't come to their house because he knows he will be eaten alive.

In this story the untruth is so silly that no adult would begin to take it seriously.

Story B A little boy tells his father that their dog has just run off down the street. He waits until his father is ready to go out and search for the animal before saying that it hasn't really run off at all, but has been taken for a walk by his mother.

In this story there is a deliberate lie. Pre-operational children here are judging how wicked something is by how big a lie it is. They judged the child in Story A) to be more wicked than the child in Story B) because what he said was obviously a long way from the truth. What the child in Story B) told his father could have been true.

Piaget found that pre-operational children can't take account of someone's intentions either. Here are two more stories:

Story A A little boy stole a loaf of bread from a shop to give to his friend who was very poor and was starving.

Story B Another boy stole one cake from a shop, not because he was hungry, but just because he fancied a cake.

In the first story the dishonest act was committed for a good reason, in the second it was committed for a selfish reason. However "a loaf of bread" is larger than "one cake", and pre-operational children judge by appearances. Being egocentric they can't understand "intentions'. Many claimed the child in Story A) was more wicked than the child in Story B).

By the time children acquire operational thought they are able to take other things into account when making judgements. They could see that deliberate lying is worse than exaggerations or accidentally telling an untruth. They can see that consequences of an act aren't the only things to judge by, but intentions must also be understood.

Exercise – More examples of the kind of stories that Piaget told

Story A A boy called John is in his room, when he is called to dinner. He enters the dining room, but doesn't know that there is a tray with 15 cups on it, just behind the door. The door knocks the tray over and all the cups are broken.

Story B A little boy called Henry decided to have some jam one day when his mother was out. He climbed onto a chair to try to reach for the jam jar which was in a high cupboard. Whilst stretching up he knocked over a cup which fell to the floor and smashed.

1 Which would you say was the naughtier child?

2 Why?

3 Would a pre-operational child say John or Henry was the more wicked?

4 What do pre-operational children base their judgements about right and wrong on?

Piaget described the pre-operational stage (from around two years old to around seven years old) as "the stage of **heteronomous morality**". "Heteronomous" means "controlled from the outside". In this stage children aren't able to decide for themselves, and assume that all control comes from other people. Children in the operational stage (after seven years of age) acquire "**autonomous morality**". Autonomous means "controlled from within". They are able to make their own choices about good and bad behaviour.

A Summary of Piaget's stages of moral development

1 The stage of heteronomous morality (up to seven or eight, or even older)

Piaget claimed that in this stage children believe that all rules are fixed and unchallengeable. Any wicked act which broke any rule would be punished immediately and severely. Behaviour will be judged by its consequences. Breaking one cup whilst taking jam is certainly wicked, and the child should be punished. But if a child is being good and accidently breaks 15 cups, this seems worse than breaking just one cup. Piaget claimed that children in the pre-operational stage seem to think that the more things that are broken, or the bigger the mess that is made, the naughtier the child is being, and therefore the more severe the punishment must be. Piaget also found that the pre-operational child is unable to understand alternative interpretations which do take motives into account. They think that an act is bad because it will lead to punishment.

2 The stage of autonomous morality (from seven or eight, or even later)

Children begin to learn that rules can be changed by experiment and trial and error. Other people's decisions can be challenged. Punishment for "wickedness" is not inevitable and it is possible to "get away with" things. Children in this stage said that the child who did something wrong by accident, or with good intentions, should not be punished. From seven years old children begin to realise that breaking one cup whilst being wicked will be much worse than breaking 15 cups by accident. Children in this stage often think that punishment should be made to "fit the crime". For example, someone who kicks a ball through a window should be made to pay for a new window. That way they'll learn the value of being more careful about where they kick the ball in the future.

Comments on Piaget's theory

Piaget's work is still regarded as a revolutionary step forward in the way we understand how children think. Many attempts have been made by other researchers in Europe and America to test and refine Piaget's ideas and methods. There does seem to be considerable evidence that children's moral reasoning does change with age, and distinct stages of development do seem to eixst. However Piaget's methods have been criticised, and if the method isn't totally acceptable, the data it gathers may not be wholly acceptable either. This is particularly true for younger children. Many may not really have understood Piaget's stories, and what children say in response to a story told by a strange adult may not be what they really think.

Piaget claimed:	*However:*
Heteronomous stage children cannot take other people's intentions into account.	Piaget told children stories and asked for their responses. He did not investigate whether the children understood the point about intentions that the stories made. If all they understood was that one child broke 15 cups and another broke one cup it's not surprising that they thought that the first child was more wicked than the other. Recent research has shown that even three year olds can take someone's intentions into account when making judgements, if the intentions are explained to them.
and	
Heteronomous stage children have absolute respect for rules.	There's more than one sort of "rule", and even three year olds respond differently to them. They think a child who breaks "moral rules" such as not hitting, spitting, scratching, stealing etc should be punished as Piaget said, whereas a child who breaks

"social rules" such as not staying in it's seat at playschool, or not eating all its food when it hasn't specifically been told to, aren't nearly as wicked. The respect for "moral rules" occurs in younger children than Piaget imagined, and the respect for social rules is much more open to negotiation than Piaget claimed.

One of the criticisms we made of Piaget's cognitive theory in general was that his methods weren't as precise as they could have been. They led to some claims being made about what children can and cannot do which were rather pessimistic. Latest research on moral development shows that children can take other motives into account, when they understand what those motives are, and they do not see all rules as being equally important. Despite these criticisms we still owe a great deal to Jean Piaget. His pioneering work has led to much more realistic ways of understanding children's moral development.

Exercise – Piaget and morality

1 Outline Piaget's explanation of how children view rules.

2 How do children's ideas about people's intentions change, according to Piaget, and why does this change occur? (HINT What can older children do that younger ones can't?)

3 What does Piaget mean by "heteronomous morality" and "autonomous morality"?

4 At what age does the change from one to the other generally occur according to Piaget?

REVIEW – Piaget's theory of moral development

Piaget identified two stages of moral reasoning, which correspond to his pre-operational and operational ways of thinking. The pre-operational child uses moral ideas which are imposed on it from the outside. They use heteronomous morality. Children who are capable of operational thought are able to make and change their own views of right and wrong. They use autonomous morality. Some modern research criticises some of Piaget's methods which led him to underestimate the abilities of the child.

3 Kohlberg's cognitive theory of moral development

Kohlberg asked some children and adults to respond to a series of stories about people facing "**moral dilemmas**". (A dilemma is a problem which has two or more solutions, each of which is somehow "wrong".) In each story the subject could choose to support the moral rights of some authority, or could support some deserving individual whose needs were fair and just, and weren't being met. After hearing each story the listener was invited to say what should happen to overcome the difficulty. This meant they had to make a choice between either obeying a law or rule or someone in authority, or taking some action that conflicts with these rules. In probably the best known

Background reading – Lawrence Kohlberg's view

Since the late 1950s Lawrence Kohlberg of Harvard University has extended and refined Piaget's views. He agrees that moral development is one aspect of general cognitive development, and develops in stages, just as Piaget claimed that the rest of cognition does.

Kohlberg's 'Thief'

of Kohlberg's moral dilemmas someone chooses one of the alternatives, and the listeners are asked about what should happen. Here is a summary of it.

A woman was very near to death from a particular form of cancer. There was a type of radium that a chemist in the same town had recently discovered which might save her. The drug had cost a great deal of money to make, but the chemist was charging ten times as much as it cost for just a small amount of it. The sick woman's husband borrowed all the money he could to buy the drug, but it only came to half of what the chemist wanted. He told the chemist that his wife was dying and asked him if he could have the drug cheaper, or even have the drug now and pay the rest of the money later. The chemist refused, saying "I discovered the drug, and I'm going to make money from it." The man was desperate, and later on he broke into the shop and stole the drug.

Kohlberg asked "Should he have stolen the drug?"

Some of the sample said that theft is wrong and the thief must be severely punished. Others said that the man shouldn't be punished very severely since he was trying to save his wife. Kohlberg was not particularly interested in the actual answers, but rather how each person explained or justified their answer. Kohlberg asked them questions like "should the husband be punished for stealing the drug?" "did the chemist have the right to refuse to sell it to the man?", "should the police arrest the chemist for murder if the woman died?", "should the chemist be punished more if the woman who died had been a very important person?" etc.

Exercise – Story telling

Like Piaget, Kohlberg is using the story telling technique to investigate the way children and adults think.

1 What did Kohlberg's stories ask the listeners to choose between?

2 Why may "story telling" not reveal what the subjects really think?

Kohlberg identified about 30 aspects of moral thought which develop through three distinct levels of moral reasoning. Each level contains two stages. Everyone passes through them in the same order, but not everyone achieves all the stages.

In the first level, the **level of pre-conventional morality**, children respond to "rules" which they see as being imposed by authority figures such as parents or teachers. Rules must be obeyed simply to avoid punishment or to obtain some personal reward or benefit. If you asked a girl at the beginning of this level why she should eat all her food she would say that it was because she'd be punished if she didn't. Anyone in the level of pre-conventional morality would not be concerned with why the husband in Kohlberg's dilemma stole, they would only be concerned with the consequences of the theft. Their thinking would follow these lines: the husband stole, stealing is wrong, what he stole was important therefore he must be severely punished. Later in the first level children behave in the way they do because the child expects some personal reward. Now the child eats all her food so that her mummy will be pleased with her. In one survey Kohlberg found a substantial number of 10 year olds were still thinking in ways typical of the first level of moral reasoning.

At the second level, the **level of conventional morality**, children try to obey the rules laid down by others in order to be praised or recognised for "being good", "being nice", "being friendly", etc. They start to be able to take other people's intentions into account. Everyone who reaches the second level of moral thinking would either say that the husband should not be punished, because he was trying to save his wife, or that he should be punished because the chemist needs to be protected from people like him. Judgements seem to be made on the basis of what "most people" would think. Later, people at this level start becoming concerned with society being kept in good order. Anyone who steals should be punished because they upset the order of society in which most people do not steal.

Not everyone reaches the third level, the **level of post conventional morality**. It involves each person deciding just what is right and wrong for themselves as individuals, and always trying to live by their own rules. People who had reached the third level said that other factors ought to be considered, such as why the chemist was unwilling to sell the drug, and that the government should make such drugs available to everyone who needs them. Thinking is more concerned with justice and injustice, changing bad rules, comparisons with other society's ideas etc. The last stage is only reached by a few. They have developed an individual set of principles, beliefs, and codes of ethics which they apply to other people's behaviour, according to that individual's particular situation. They have firm ideas about equality and inequality, freedom, individual rights and responsibilities etc.

The level of pre-conventional morality is generally associated with young children, but some older people may occasionally behave in such a way. Can you think of an example, either real or made up?

In the stage of conventional morality people start to accept that people must not be judged only by their behaviour, but also by their intentions. They may also become concerned with the smooth running of society.

In the last stage people develop individual principles of acceptable and unacceptable behaviour, both for themselves and for others. Not everyone reaches this stage.

A Summary of Kohlberg's stages of moral reasoning

Kohlberg suggests that there are three levels of moral thinking, each having two stages.

Level I The Level of Pre-conventional morality

Stage One: Children are only concerned with the outcome of some behaviour. They aren't able to take motives into account. They are mainly concerned with avoiding punishment.

Stage Two: Children judge things in terms of what gives pleasure to them or their favourite people, toys, pets etc.

Level II The Level of Conventional morality

Stage Three: The individual is very concerned with trying to win approval from others.

Stage Four: The person will insist that there are rules which must not be disobeyed. If these rules are broken, then punishment will certainly follow. Children's ideas about guilt usually start during this stage.

Level III The Level of Post conventional morality

Stage Five: People at this stage start to become aware of the

	interests of the wider community, and of the individual. They may start to see that the needs of the whole community may sometimes be of greater importance than an individual's needs.
Stage Six:	This is the level of the deepest moral principles and conscience. Some deeply religious or philosophical people, and people who think deeply about events, such as some politicians, may use these principles. Relatively few people reach this stage.

According to Kohlberg, people pass through these stages in the order shown. For example, it wouldn't be possible for someone to show much consistent understanding of the wider community's needs (Level III, Stage Five), before being very concerned with its own (Level I, Stage One). However, even someone who has shown that it can think in the more advanced ways may occasionally revert back to the type of thinking typical of some earlier stage. The opposite also seems occasionally to be true. Children who think at a certain stage are sometimes able to understand, and be persuaded by, the kind of thinking typical of someone one, or even two stages, above the child. This is usually only specifically to do with one issue. They do not apply the principles to their wider thinking until they have passed through the stages outlined.

Comments on Kohlberg's approach

Kohlberg's stages of moral development do seem to reflect changes in children's cognitive development. However a number of criticisms have been made.

Criticism

1 Kohlberg has examined how children make moral decisions, and how they justify them. This doesn't explain how they actually behave in the "real world" when faced with a moral dilemma of their own. Their actual behaviour varies, according to how the child sees the actual situation it is in at the time. Certain behaviour would be acceptable in one situation and not in another.

2 Other research suggests that there may be some differences in the way that boys and girls see moral issues. If we acquire our consciences through socialisation, and if there are any differences in the way we socialise boys and girls, then it is not surprising that each sex's reactions to moral issues will be

Comment

1 Kohlberg is interested in the way children make and justify their moral judgements. Their explanations may not always reflect what they would really "do" in real life, but Kohlberg was not primarily interested in their behaviour, but in their powers of reasoning. Kohlberg claims that story telling is an acceptable means of investigating moral reasoning.

2 Whenever we begin some research we try to operationalise and limit the key variables. Kohlberg concentrated his research on boys in order to obtain an overall impression. Initially he asked 10, 13, and 16 year old boys to respond to his "dilemmas". When the research on boys had provided a model for

different. Perhaps a fuller theory of moral development will need to explain any differences between the sexes.

3 Some psychologists claim that Kohlberg underestimated the ways in which young children see moral issues. This was partly because of the methods he used. They relied heavily on the children's understanding of language, and their ability to communicate their ideas in words. The children may not always have understood the stories, and may not have been able to express their ideas in words.

4 Social learning theorists have shown that children will often imitate the behaviour of certain models in certain situations. If so, then moral behaviour cannot pass through the stages of cognitive development outlined by Piaget or Kohlberg. A theory which explains the growth of moral thinking may be more valuable if it also explains children's moral behaviour.

moral development research on girls could begin. Other people are comparing girls and boys moral reasoning.

3 There are very few ways in which children's moral development can be assessed. Facing them with real problems in real life would be unethical. Telling them stories may be the next best thing. In which case the stories have to be sufficiently detailed for the dilemma to be made clear. The boys tested were between 10 and 16. Their language should have been sufficient for them to express their ideas.

4 Children will behave in certain ways, imitating important models, under certain conditions. Reinforcement and modelling are indeed strong influences. This doesn't mean that children's moral reasoning does not pass through identifiable stages however, since younger children's statements and their behaviour do not always match!

REVIEW – Kohlberg's theory of moral development

Kohlberg extended Piaget's two stages of moral thinking into six stages, in three levels. The first level child will reason in ways designed to bring it pleasure and avoid punishment. During the level of conventional morality the child's reasoning makes it do things which bring it praise and satisfaction. Many people never really leave this stage. Those that do pass into the level of post conventional morality. They see and do things for the general good of the wider community, and are concerned more with wider social justice. Kohlberg does not tie his stages of development to particular ages in quite such a rigid way as Piaget had. He accepted that people would reach the stages at different ages.

Exercise – Kohlberg's theory of moral development

1 What is a "moral dilemma"?

2 Outline Kohlberg's three levels of moral reasoning.

3 Discuss some of the criticisms that have been levelled against Kohlberg's theory of moral development.

4 Evaluate one method used to study children's moral development.

5 What is meant by a "stage theory" of moral development?

4 Behaviourist theories of moral behaviour

Whilst Freud emphasises children learning to adopt their parents' moral feelings, and Piaget and Kohlberg show how children apply their own rules to making moral judgements, behaviourists emphasise the role of the parents as trainers of behaviour. Behaviourists claim that all behaviour is a result of reinforcement, possibly modified by punishment, although modelling has also been shown to be effective.

Fit these six words together so that they make three pairs – Freud, Piaget, Behaviourists, reasoning, feelings, behaviour.

The effects of reinforcement

As we saw in Chapter Seven, the effect of reinforcement is to increase the likelihood that certain behaviour will occur again. All parents, teachers, and animal trainers use reinforcement to teach particular behaviour. The first stage is to decide exactly what we want the child to do, for example, to be generous and caring towards others. Every time the child acts in a thoughtful or considerate way it is praised and encouraged. Eventually it shouldn't be necessary to continually reinforce the child since children will eventually learn to reinforce themselves. Knowing that they have performed something to their own satisfaction should become a reward in itself.

Exercise – Reinforcement

How might a parent teach a child to help look after a younger brother or sister? Identify the reinforcers used, and say what schedules of reinforcement might be employed.

The effects of punishment

We would all agree that rewarding "good behaviour" is likely to cause more "good behaviour". But will punishment act as a deterrent, and decrease "bad behaviour"? Behaviourists do not generally favour the use of punishment, since it only seeks to reduce some bad behaviour, rather than trying to replace it with some "good". According to behaviourists, at the very best, punishment will discourage someone from doing something. It doesn't show a wrongdoer what to do, only what not to do. Also, if bad behaviour goes unreinforced it is likely to extinguish by itself.

Background reading – When is punishment most likely to be effective?

Most research shows that punishment can be effective for developing morally acceptable behaviour if certain factors apply, for example, if the "wicked act" is punished just before, or just after it occurs! That is, a child who is about to do something which it knows is wicked will probably have some feelings of anxiety about doing it. This anxiety will be reduced after the wicked act has occurred. If the child is punished whilst this anxiety is at its height, the child should learn a strong association between the anxiety involved in being wicked, and the anxiety of being punished. This is an example of classical conditioning. Any plans to be wicked in the future should remind the child of its anxiety, and hopefully stop it from wanting to behave badly.

Children should never be punished more severely than is necessary to stop them behaving badly again. Severe punishment may well stop some behaviour from occurring again, but it will make the child afraid of the person who punishes it severely. The child will try to avoid that person. This is simply "avoidance learning". This will reduce the influence the punishing adult had over the child, which is precisely the opposite result from the one intended.

Parents and teachers must be consistent in what they punish children for. A child who sees that its behaviour has upset a loved one, and might stop that person loving the child, is less likely to be wicked again.

After about the age of three years children should be able to understand simple explanations. Explaining why the child is being punished can strengthen the effectiveness of the punishment.

Exercise – Punishment

Why do behaviourists generally reject the use of punishment for modifying "bad" behaviour?

The effects of modelling

Albert Bandura's "**social learning theory**" emphasises the way children learn by observing and modelling their ideas and behaviour on important people they see around them. Mothers and fathers will be especially important to the young child. Unlike Piaget and Kohlberg Bandura doesn't see moral development occurring in any particular sequence. Instead children behave in the ways they've seen others behave, particularly if those others are important to the child, or if they have been rewarded for behaving in that way previously. For example if a child observes its parents behaving in generous ways, it is more likely to behave in a generous way itself.

REVIEW –
Behaviourists views of moral development

Children's responses to moral decisions depend on their previous experience of similar situations. If influential models have been seen behaving in some way, the child is likely to behave in a similar way.

Comments on behaviourist views of moral development

Good points

1 Behaviourists see learning moral behaviour in the same way as they explain learning any other behaviour, largely as a consequence of reinforcement. If "good" behaviour is reinforced it is likely to be repeated.

2 Punishment isn't generally necessary, or effective to extinguish "bad" behaviour.

3 Children also learn by observing and modelling the behaviour of important models they see around them.

Criticisms

1 Human learning and human behaviour is much more complex than animal behaviour, and requires more than simple reinforcement to explain it. Children may still behave "badly", even when they have previously been reinforced for behaving well.

2 Punishment can be an effective deterrent if it is given in a sensitive, caring way.

3 Imitating an important model's behaviour isn't to be confused with learning their attitudes to moral issues. Young children are egocentric and may have little idea of the effect of what they are doing.

Moral behaviour varies according to the situation a child is in. A child who is generally truthful and honest may cheat and lie in some circumstances, and a generally wicked child may sometimes behave like a saint. Their behaviour does not change just because their thinking may be passing through different stages. Instead it depends on factors like how the child sees the situation, whether it has previously been rewarded or punished in similar situations, and whether it has seen other, influential models behaving in some way.

Exercise – Behaviourist explanation of moral development

1 Summarise the three factors which are likely to influence a child's moral behaviour, according to behaviourist psychologists.

2 Put a tick in the appropriate boxes here:

MAJOR THEORIES OF MORAL DEVELOPMENT

	Stage theory	**Continuous development**
Freud		
Piaget		
Kohlberg		
Behaviourism		

11 From Playing Alone to Going to School

As children in Western countries, most of us played with toys and games. We had dolls and construction sets, swings and skipping ropes, footballs and plasticine. We painted and drew, played hide and seek, and tried to solve puzzles. We've been in teams, and amazed our friends with the tricks we've learned. However, not all children have enjoyed these experiences. Not all families have the money to buy toys and games, and many children do not attend well equipped schools. In some countries children are expected to work as soon as they are old enough, whilst in others there are different types of play activities. For example children in America are encouraged to be individualistic and competitive whilst children in Russia are encouraged to work and play as a team, not as individuals.

For the first few years children are largely egocentric in the way they play. Some may become more sociable if they attend playgroup. At around five years of age children's lives are going to change again, as they start to go to school. *Learning through play* will gradually be replaced by *being taught*. Piaget's view of how children learn will have implications for both the meaning of play, and for the early years in school. Skinner's ideas about learning and reinforcement have been applied in some specific ways in the secondary school.

In this chapter we will be looking at:

1 What play is, and why children spend so much time and effort on it.

2 How play changes during childhood, and whether boys and girls play in the same ways.

3 What play means to children who have some emotional or behavioural problems.

4 Piaget's explanation for the functions of play will be examined next.

5 Whether attending playschool or nursery will be of any benefit to children.

6 Going to school for the first time.

7 Social factors in schooling.

8 Piaget's ideas on "discovery learning".

9 Skinner's use of "programmed learning".

1 What is "play"?

Let's try to define "play". Adults might say that "play" is something we do for fun which shouldn't be taken too seriously. Children often take it very seriously. They may concentrate on something for quite long periods, and practise it over and over. For example learning to roller

Think of some answers to these questions before going any further. What is "play", and why do children do it? What kind of "play activities" might help a child develop, and in what ways? How might playgroup and nursery school benefit the child?

Think of some examples which illustrate "the ways in which children play may have important consequences for other aspects of their development."

REVIEW – Differences in play

During the first two years children are finding out about things, people, and themselves largely through play. Their play is solitary, becomes parallel and associative around three years of age, and they learn to share and co-operate after three. Boys play with the noisier, more adventurous toys, girls are generally quieter, preferring more "domestic" type play.

Imagine a group of children playing hopscotch. Is it possible to say whether they are passing time, developing social skills, or developing cognitive skills? Or could they be doing all three?

skate may take a great deal of time and effort, yet children do it "for fun". When parents tell their children to "go out and play" they usually mean "go and pass some time in a pleasant way". But the ways in which children play may have important consequences for other aspects of their development. For example skipping and chasing each other may be fun, but also helps build concentration and healthy muscles. One dictionary says that play means to *move around in a lively manner*. Another says play includes activities with *no other goal than enjoyment*. Others say play is activity which has *no serious point to it*. Psychologists would not totally agree with these definitions.

Why do children play?

Our ideas about why children play have changed quite a lot during this century. There are at least three views of what play is for. The first was the old fashioned and non psychological view that play was just a way of passing time for babies and young children until they were old enough to work. Secondly Piaget offers the view that play contributes to cognition. Thirdly learning and social learning theorists say that play is for practising, and learning those skills that we will need as adults. Freud suggests a fourth possibility, play may help children to overcome potential problems, for example, some Oedipal conflict.

Play almost certainly caters for all of these things. As we shall see, some play activities do merely "pass time" in a fairly pleasant way, some activities do encourage cognition, whilst others allow us to practise adult skills.

Exercise – Children's pastimes

Sue and John are studying GCSE psychology. As part of their project on changing fashions in children's pastimes they make a list of the toys and games they used to enjoy. Make four lists with these headings:

Developing Muscles and Co-ordination	Developing Cognition	Developing Co-operation	Passing Time

Sort their pastimes into the most appropriate list(s).

Reading books and comics, playing football, Cowboys and Indians, Skipping, Brownies, building things with blocks, jigsaws, races, playing with the dolls house, playing cars in the sandpit, riding a scooter, lying in bed, puzzle books, adventure playground activities, marbles, games like draughts and chess, train set, rounders, children's crossword puzzles, hide and seek, making model aeroplanes, watching TV, dressing up games, hopscotch, watching adventure films at the cinema, table tennis and snooker, riding a tricycle, riding a bike, colouring books.

Children, and many other young mammals, spend much of their time playing. One reason for this is that they learn a great deal through play. Social learning theorists like Albert Bandura say that children will observe and imitate adults and build this into their play. A child who does something "adult like" is likely to be reinforced. Children certainly have a lot to learn about their world. There are three categories of "things to learn" during childhood.

Exercise – What each child must learn

DEALING WITH THINGS, OTHER PEOPLE AND OURSELVES

(a) Each of us must learn how to deal with *things*. Infants will manipulate just about anything they can get their hands on. If they can't touch an object they will stare at it. As they grow older they will experiment with larger objects such as building blocks, and materials which can be used for something, like water, playdough (the modern equivalent of clay or plasticine), or sand. Most teenagers enjoy the challenge of investigating things, solving puzzles, and practising skills like swimming. As well as learning what to do children must also learn what not to manipulate. Young children should be discouraged from investigating sharp knives and boxes of matches!

(b) Each of us must learn how to deal with *people*. Infants learn about who they can rely on from their caregivers. They may continue to show fear of strangers until they are a few years old. Children don't take very much notice of other children until they are three years of age, or older. Until then they play mostly on their own. If there's nothing else to play with, a baby will touch and explore another baby. A two year old is more likely to ignore other children unless they are in its way, or try to take one of the toys it is playing with. Then they'd be aggressive. After about three years old a child who is aggressive or spiteful may find that other children do not want to play with it. One who is more willing to share its toys will be more popular. Older children learn to co-operate in team games and learn about loyalty and competition.

(c) Each child must learn about *itself*. From around the age of seven children are becoming more aware of themselves, and the effects they can have on things around them. We all learn something about what we are like from the ways that other people treat us. If lots of people want to be friends with us it might be because we are pleasant to be with. "Friendly" behaviour will be reinforced, "unfriendly" behaviour should be extinguished. As children play roles in games, they learn about how other people see them, and this influences their ideas about themselves. When there are disagreements, children have to learn to compromise, and this may alter what they think they are like.

1 Name some games or pastimes that you would associate with a child of
a) 12 months, b) 3 years, c) 8 years, d) 14 years.

2 Which of the following groups of people will be important to a child of
(a) 12 months, (b) 8 years, (c) 14 years: Parents, teachers, friends?

"Mammals' are animals who have a spine, who suckle their young, who have hair (rather than feathers or scales etc), who breathe using a diaphragm etc.

REVIEW – What is play?

Play allows children to practise the skills they will need as adults. They must find out about dealing with things, how to deal with people, and who and what they are themselves.

2 How play changes as we grow

According to some psychologists, infants and toddlers are totally egocentric. They will only play games with their parents as long as the game pleases the child. When the child is bored it will turn its attention to something else, regardless of the other players. Generally play is a fairly **solitary** pastime for children up to about two years of age.

From around two or three years old children start to take some notice of each other. They sometimes try to join in another child's game, whilst trying to stop another child joining in their own. Even two children who were playing the same game and sitting right next to

Noisy Boys and Quiet Girls

The way children play reflects the way their general behaviour develops, from egocentrism to co-operation.

each other would not usually be "playing together". For example two girls might be playing "nurses", each with her own doll. They may be playing right next to each other, but each is playing her own game quite separate from the other. This is an example of **parallel play**. Parallel play begins as an extension of *solitary play*.

During the next year children engaged in parallel play become increasingly aware of each other. They occasionally touch or take each other's toys. They occasionally "invade" each other's space, or might bump into each other. They begin to communicate with each other. The communication will usually include talking. One child may explain its game to the other. Slowly the other may be drawn in. This is called **associative play**.

Eventually most children start to **co-operate** and share their games, although solitary, parallel, and associative play do not disappear altogether. Some children seem less willing or able to join in and co-operate with others, and they will continue their solitary type play, sometimes even for years to come. All children may prefer to play on their own sometimes. Co-operative children may take on roles, copying TV characters perhaps. They will use simple props, like furniture or bits of wood or metal, imagine them to be something else, and invent a whole, complicated drama around them. The "game" can last for several days. Some games can involve aggression, often against an imaginary enemy.

Four stages in young children's play activities

Age	Type of play	Main features
0–2	Solitary play	Toddlers live in a very private world. They play with things in all kinds of inventive ways, exploring and trying things out.
2–3	Parallel play	Although aware of each other's existence, children aren't able to co-operate for very long since each is still thinking egocentrically. They will play alongside, but not with each other.
3+	Associative play	The awareness of the other child is increased as they start to communicate.
3+	Co-operative play	As children start to be able to take other people's wishes and needs into account they start to become more sociable. They gradually learn that co-operation can lead to new and interesting things to do and games to play. They start to be able to make "best friends" out of people who live near and have similar interests, although they can also "fall out" just as quickly!

Sex differences in young children's play

From the time they are three most children know which sex they are, and that the other sex is different from them in some way. They also seem to prefer the company of members of their own sex. Boys usually choose the more adventurous, noisy active toys and activities such as the climbing frames and construction sets. Girls often play with quieter toys and activities, like "the shop", the Wendy house, painting, and sewing. Boys tend to be more independent than girls too. They play further away from the teacher, and are less likely to ask for help than girls. The two sexes don't mix very well. Some teachers have tried to encourage boys and girls to mix, and play each others games, but the children themselves have resisted. By the time the children start school the two sexes are very firmly divided, and any child of one sex who seems to want to play with the other sex's toys will soon be discouraged.

Try to find out what you and your friends' favourite pastimes were when you were around five years old. (You might ask your parents.) Compare them to the favourite pastimes of members of the opposite sex.

What explanations have been put forward to explain these early sex differences in behaviour?

Solitary and Parallel Play

"Play" seems to be a very complex phenomenon, and a lot harder to define than you may have thought. It will mean different things to different children at different ages. What we can say is what play is not. It is not "simply to move around in a lively manner", neither is it "activity with no other end than enjoyment", and it is not "something which has no serious point to it."

Some psychologists would talk about "the serious business of play". What do you think they mean?

3 Play in severely maladjusted children

There are a number of ways in which children's development can go wrong. Severe maladjustment may be the result of genetic disorders. Autism and Down's Syndrome are examples of genetically inherited diseases. Or maladjusted behaviour may be due to a problem during pregnancy, birth or socialisation. For example a child who isn't allowed to mix with other children because his over protective mother thinks he is "fragile", or "delicate", may remain emotionally dependent on his mother. Other children may have some particular learning difficulties which may stop their play being as normal as that of other children.

REVIEW – The nature of play

"Play" can mean hard work, as well as passing time, as children acquire the cognitive and social skills which they will need later. They learn about what objects are for, and what they can do with them, about other people, and about themselves. This takes place gradually as children stop their solitary play, go through parallel play, and start becoming sociable. Sex differences in play can be seen in many playgroup and nursery school children. Not all children are lucky enough to enjoy this "normal" development, and for some, such as severely maladjusted children, play may be very restricted.

Children with symptoms of mental retardation have been extensively studied in America by Ann Brown and Joseph Campione. Their observations of the cognitive skills of such children have important implications for how these children play. Remember that Piaget claimed that children's play contributes to their cognitive development too.

Here is a summary of Brown and Campione's main conclusions, and the implications they might have for the child's play:

1 Retarded children think more slowly than other children. They do not immediately see connections between things that other children might.	Board games such as Snakes and Ladders, Ludo, and Junior Scrabble may not be so easily understood by children who are slow to learn.
2 They have slower reaction times.	Games like table tennis, cricket, football etc. will be more difficult for children who take longer to react.
3 They need to hear detailed instructions several times before they begin to understand what any game is about.	Any game which involves rules which are very complicated may never be fully understood.
4 They cannot apply the knowledge and skills they have acquired from one situation to another one.	Skills which apply to one kind of activity may not immediately be seen by the child as relevant, or worth trying to apply to another.

Many seriously maladjusted children can, and do, learn. It's just that the learning of most skills will take longer, and will need far more practice and help from others.

Exercise – Play in one example of maladjusted children

So far we have been looking at the patterns of play usually found amongst children in societies like our own. But even in our societies not all children will play in the ways we've described. Some children will suffer mental or physical handicaps, or will be emotionally or socially maladjusted. One of the most extreme and tragic forms of maladjustment in childhood is autism.

Autistic children are severely emotionally withdrawn. They seem preoccupied by their own thoughts and feelings, and barely notice other people. Their play will usually involve a small number of objects such as a toy, an item of clothing, or their blanket. They will want to keep it close to them. They will often repeat the same movement over and over again. For example an autistic child might sit on a chair and rock backwards or forwards for hours on end. Or they may turn a toy round and round in their hands for hours. One movement that is even more distressing is when an autistic child bangs its head against a wall for hours.

Autistic children strongly resist any change in their environment. Often they will not go out, and would not explore any new objects which a "normal" child would. They do not usually talk, and if they do it's rarely more than a simple two-word sentence. They often avoid looking at other people. These things mean that social exchanges during play are usually impossible.

1 Name some of the characteristics of play that normal children enjoy.

2 Look back to the list of pastimes that Sue and John could remember enjoying from their childhood. Which of these could severely autistic children enjoy?

3 Outline some of the differences in the play of "normal" and "mal-adjusted" children.

4 Piaget's view of play

Several psychologists have studied children's play. One influential theory which looks at the role of play in cognition comes from Jean Piaget. Piaget claimed that a child's cognition develops through four main stages. During each stage the child is mastering certain ways of thinking which are more advanced than the ways it could think in the previous stage. For the first few years children are fairly egocentric in their thinking. They improve their abilities to assimilate and accommodate new information as their schemas expand. Sometime around their seventh birthday children learn to decentre.

According to Piaget, cognitive, and possibly intellectual, development would benefit greatly from play. Piaget believed that there would be different kinds of play activities amongst children in each stage. For example the child's first tasks are to learn movement and interaction with its immediate environment. Piaget identified three types of play.

Play in the sensory motor stage

During the first two years play allows children to explore and manipulate their environment, mainly to see how they can master it. Early play consists of repeating actions that give the baby pleasure. Some of this play will be quite solitary, some will involve "give and take" and "exchange games" with adults. During the first few months the child learns hand to eye co-ordination, what it can reach, grasp, pick up etc. By 18 months most children can walk and control their movements quite well. They will also be able to use some words, and understand a lot more. They will be learning something new about their environment and the people in it practically every day. Piaget said these first two years were for "**mastery**" or "**practise**" play.

What does Piaget mean by "schemas", "assimilation", and "accommodation", "egocentric", and "decentre"? If you're not certain, go back now and read Chapter Nine on cognitive development again.

Background reading – An example of mastery play

Throwing a rattle out of its cot and having an adult pick it up and return it may be helping the child expand two important types of schemas. Firstly it develops muscle co-ordination schemas for reaching, grasping, lifting, and releasing the rattle, and mental schemas for recognising the object to be thrown, and that its action can cause a reaction in someone else.

Play in the pre-operations stage

The changeover from playing alone during the "**mastery play**" stage to playing with other people is gradual. At first children may use other people (rather as objects) in their early games. By the end of this stage other people are important partners in play. By about two years of age a child can let one object stand for (or "**symbolise**") something else. A box can be a car, a stick can be a pencil, a doll can make someone who has it into a parent etc. Children often play "pretend" games when they make believe they are someone else. For example, wearing a box on one's head might make a child into a policeman or a nurse. They see how other people respond to the role they are playing, and this helps them to "try out what it feels like" to be someone else. Sometimes they invent an imaginary friend, who has a name, who sits by them at mealtimes, and who even shares their food!! Piaget called the kind of play that goes on in this stage "**symbolic**", or "**make believe**" play. Children in this stage must be encouraged to think and do things for themselves. They can be helped to find the right way of doing things, but they learn best when they learn for themselves.

Play in the concrete operations stage

Singing nursery rhymes like "Ring a ring a roses" and dancing around in a circle is useful for developing motor co-ordination, for being sociable, and for having fun. By the time children reach the concrete operations stage, from around seven years, they are capable of far more advanced activities than these. Children who can decentre can take other people's feelings and needs into account. They make up their own rules about things which might seem like a good idea to them. They learn about rules which are imposed on them by others. They become more sociable and cooperative. As they learn to use rules of logic and reasoning, they can understand the point of playing games with rules that affect themselves and the other players. They learn about sharing and about rights and responsibilities. Piaget calls this kind of play "**play with rules**".

Background reading – An example of symbolic play

A psychologist could investigate whether children use play to settle any emotional difficulties they feel. A five year old girl could be told that she has to do something which she doesn't want to. She must, of course, obey. This creates an "emotional crisis" which she must overcome. Here's an example.

It's lunch time and Kerry's mother has called her in to wash her hands. Kerry was happily playing an elaborate game with her friends and she didn't really want to stop. Having hurriedly washed her hands Kerry sat down and ate some of her soup. After a few mouthfuls she said she had finished, and could she go outside to play with her friends again. Kerry's mother said "no", she could not go out until she'd eaten all her soup. Kerry finished the soup very reluctantly. An hour or so later Kerry might be observed with her doll. She might play the part of an adult who was making the doll finish all her food. This symbolic play may be helping Kerry to understand what happened to her, and how to deal with these feelings.

Piaget's three stages in young children's play activities

Age	Stage of Intellectual Development	Name of Type of Play	Main Features
0–2	Sensory motor	Mastery or practise play	"Play" lets children explore and manipulate their environment, mainly to see how they can affect it. They must master the skills of muscle and limb control, so they can attract the attention of their caregiver.
2–7	Pre-operational	Symbolic or Make believe Play	The child's play reflects its increasing experiences and imagination. Children pretend to be someone else, imitating their behaviour, and seeing how others respond. They are also learning how to communicate symbolically through language.
7+	Concrete operations	Play with rules	The child learns about rules which are imposed on it by others. It is now becoming sociable, and, as it learns to use rules of logic and reasoning, it can understand the sense of playing games with rules that affect itself and the other players. It learns about give and take, and about its, and other people's rights and responsibilities.

Exercise – Expanding schemas through play

A report of an observation in a local playgroup

Sheila is four years and three months old. She is playing in the sandpit. Other children are also playing in the sandpit, but each seems to be in their own little world. Sheila is trying to build a sandcastle. She has a bucket

Play seems to reinforce the cognitive experiences the child is having. Mastering early sensory motor co-ordination may help the child with its symbolisation which will encourage imagination. Imagination and symbolisation encourage co-operation, and co-operative play may provide help towards decentring. At each stage, imagination should be encouraged by parents, teachers, and other adults. Toys and games should develop problem solving skills, muscle development, hand to eye co-ordination etc. Play helps assimilation and accommodation best when a child responds to some demand made by his environment (eg parental rules). Play is essentially active.

which she half fills with sand. When she turns it over the sand just falls into a little heap. She tries this several times and the same thing keeps happening. She doesn't seem to be very pleased with it. Mrs Hawkes notices that Sheila is beginning to become frustrated, and is about to give up, so she goes over to "help". She doesn't make a sandcastle for Sheila though. She tries to explain that the bucket needs to be full, and she shows Sheila what she means. She shows Sheila how to turn the bucket over quickly. I didn't think Sheila understood what Mrs Hawkes was saying, but when Mrs Hawkes left, giving Sheila the empty bucket, the child filled it to the top, turned it over very firmly, patted the bottom of the bucket, and she made a sandcastle. She seemed very pleased, for a moment. She looked at it, touched it, walked round to the other side of it and looked and touched some more. She seemed totally fascinated by it. I thought she was going to play with it but she didn't. She looked at it, smiled, and slowly and deliberately knocked it over.

1 What is the name of the technique used for collecting this data?
2 What is the sample size?
3 Why didn't Mrs Hawkes simply help Sheila to build her sandcastle?
4 What do you think the phrase "Each seems to be in their own little world" in the third sentence means?
5 How would a Piagetian psychologist explain Sheila's behaviour when she made her sandcastle?
6 What is "associative play"?
7 How could the reliability of these observations be checked?

5 Will playgroup and nursery school experiences help development?

As we said in Chapter Five, playgroups are run for younger children, usually by some of the mothers. Nursery schools take older children and are usually run by more experienced staff. The kinds of activities that we would expect to see at each may be slightly different. At playgroup and nursery school children can come together to play with different toys, in different ways, alongside different children. Some activities will be clearly organised and will have to work to some kind of a timetable. Others can be less restricted, and the child can be encouraged to express its ideas more freely. Some materials will be more useful for this than others. Playdough, water, sand, and paint are some of the more expressive materials

Background reading – Playdough

Playdough is used in many playgroups and nurseries now. It can be bought commercially, but isn't difficult to make. Mix a cupful of flour, half a cupful of salt, and a cupful of water together in a saucepan. Stir a tablespoonful of cooking oil and two tablespoonfuls of cream of tartar and some food colouring into it, and warm the pan over a low heat. Stir the mixture until it lifts away from the sides of the pan. Let it cool, and it makes a cheap, harmless and creative plaything.

What children do with their play objects changes as they pass from playgroup and through nursery school. These changes may reflect changes in their cognitive development. For example young children start by exploring and experimenting with playdough. They want to know what they can do with it. As they grow they seem to enjoy the sensations that playing with playdough can give. They derive pleasure from seeing and feeling it change shape. The next stage is to make the playdough into something (perhaps by accident at first). It might be "a dog", or "a house". Finally they realise that the shape that they have made is a model of what they are calling it, that is, it's a "dog shaped" lump of playdough, not a real dog.

Water contains just about all the elements from which children can build up their experiences. It has form which can be moved around, can be contained in differently shaped containers, can be coloured, made into bubbles, can be "got into", floated on, and even drunk. It can be silent, or make noises, it can be poured, spilled, mopped up, wrung out, and thrown away. Water has many qualities that can stretch young imaginations.

There have been a number of studies of children's play, both at playgroup and nursery school, and out of it. In general the research hasn't come to any really firm conclusions. Some studies suggest that going to playgroup has positive benefits for social development, others say the benefits are for cognitive development. Still other writers say that, since we don't really know what the purposes of "play" are, we can't really know if "play" at school is going to do anything useful. It certainly is not possible to separate the benefits of these early experiences. Improving sociability, practising skills, and developing cognitively are closely inter linked.

Exercise – Children's play

Two psychologists made a half hour videotape of the play of five boys and five girls between three and five years old at playgroup. They also filmed five nine year old boys and five nine year old girls. They wanted to see if there were any sex differences in the sociability of the two sexes. They averaged how many minutes each group spent, during the half hour, in the following activities:

Number of minutes spent in three activities

		BOYS		GIRLS	
Age		3–5	9	3–5	9
Playing alone		19	2	16	1
Playing alongside other children		8	2	7	1
Playing with other children		3	26	7	28

1 What was the total sample size used in this study?

2 What was the hypothesis being studied here?

3 What type of play was most common for the playgroup children?

4 Which group spent the longest amount of time playing together?

5 Outline the way children's play changes from around the age of seven, according to Piaget.

John Shea observed some three and four year old children during their first 10 weeks at a nursery school. He operationalised five dimensions of "sociability". These were, aggression, rough and tumble play, how far the child was from any other child, how far it was from the teacher, and how often it spoke to or played with another person.

Some of the children began by only attending two days a week. Some attended three days a week, whilst others attended all five days a week. Over the 10 weeks just about all of the children went through the same kind of behaviour pattern. They all started off by staying near to the teacher, and were wary of each other. Some children were occasionally physically and verbally aggressive towards the others. These usually resulted from disagreements over toys. As the weeks went by this behaviour changed. The children were more content to play farther away from the teacher, and nearer to each other. They were less aggressive too.

The children who went to school for five days a week became more sociable most quickly, those attending for two days a week took the longest to become more sociable.

Exercise – A study emphasising the social benefits of early schooling.

1 What do you think the hypothesis of John Shea's research was?

2 What research method was used?

3 What does "operationalising" (in the second sentence) mean?

4 Outline Shea's conclusion.

5 What do the terms "social development" and "cognitive development" mean?

Kathy Sylva, Carolyn Roy, and Marjorie Painter conducted some research for the Oxfordshire Preschool Project. They wanted to see what play activities would be most useful for developing a young child's cognitive development. They conducted naturalistic observations of 120 children aged between three and five, and made detailed recordings of what each child was doing, whether this was solitary play or involved others, whether it included talking and listening, what materials were used, whether the child appeared to be deeply involved in trying to solve something, or whether it was just passing the time. They evaluated each activity for the contribution it made to social and intellectual development. Kathy Sylva and her colleagues concentrated on what they called "**complex play**" which involves the child in some thought and action that stretches them. This is different from "**simple play**" which merely passes some time.

Kathy Sylva's study suggests that children benefit from a balance between doing things in their own way (free play), and being organised, for example, to listen to a story, or all do art (structured play). This can be achieved by well run playgroups. Children learn from things which have a specific end, for example, completing a Lego house, making something with plasticine, or solving a jigsaw. Playgroup children work well in pairs since children learn much from each other. A variety of adults should be encouraged to be involved with the children, since children seem to learn best when adults are providing models, and suggesting alternative ways of doing things when the child becomes stuck and is about to give up. Overall they found that playgroups could be of great benefit to stimulating cognitive development.

Exercise – Play activities

1 How might materials like playdough and water be used at playgroup to help children's cognitive development?

2 Name some materials or activities that could stimulate playgroup children's social development.

3 What types of play activities may be most likely to stimulate cognitive development?

4 What kind of play activities are least likely to be stimulating for cognitive development?

5 What advice would you give to the organiser of a new playgroup?

Exercise – End of topic test on play

1 Draw three columns with the headings "Mastery Play", "Symbolic Play", and "Play With Rules". In each column write some examples of the kind of things you would see if observing a child in each of the three stages.

2 Explain how Piaget's view of play fits in with his general theory of cognition.

3 What are solitary play, parallel play, associative play, and co-operative play? Give an example of each type of play.

4 How does the play of "maladjusted" children differ from the play of "normal" children?

5 Why do some psychologists refer to "the serious business" of play?

As we said, we do not know exactly what play does for social, emotional, personality, or intellectual development. Remember Harlow's monkeys who, after maternal privation, were allowed group therapy? Playing certainly helped their emotional and social development. Children probably use play in slightly different ways too. Freud, and others, believe that some children use play to "construct" their problems, and this will contribute to their personality development. For example a child in the phallic stage of development may be experiencing Oedipal conflict and anxiety. It may construct a story or drama in its play, with symbols to represent itself and its mother and father. Playing its game may help it come to terms with its feelings.

6 Learning and school

Children who have been lucky enough to have attended playgroups will become used to the idea of "going out" to play and learn in the

As children grow their play activities will change. They will use the same materials, but in different ways, probably reflecting changes in their cognitive development. Playgroup and nursery school allow them to experience a wider range of toys and materials than most could at home. Having other children around seems to help social development too.

When children start school, sometime after their fourth birthday, they have to make some important adjustments to their world. They must adjust physically, socially, and in how they learn.

company of other children. They should be more aware of others, and able to co-operate more. All children must start going to some kind of school from the age of around five in Britain. When children first go to school several very important aspects of their lives change. There is a physical change – they leave home for several hours each day, and go to a new place, they must find their way around and learn the routines of the school day. Even those who attended playgroup will have new routines to learn. Social aspects of their lives change too – they will be mixing with new people, adults and children. Hopefully they will overcome these changes to their routines in the first few weeks. Another major change comes later. It involves mental changes, to do with learning. Before starting school children learn things through play, by imitating others, by modelling, by reinforcement, by trial and error, by accident, and occasionally by being taught. At school the emphasis is going to be on "*being taught*". They will "*be taught*" new skills like simple arithmetic, reading, and writing.

Some children make the transition from home to school without difficulty. They seem to enjoy the challenges, and benefit from the experiences. For other children the change does not go smoothly. Some of the reasons for this can be explained by their early socialisation. Those who have been encouraged to be independent, active, and curious, are more likely to do well in school than those who have not. Psychologists, sociologists, and others, have researched many of the factors that affect children starting school. They include how old the child is, and what its personality is like, how its parents have prepared it for the challenge of school, what teaching materials are used in the school, what the teachers expect of the child, what the child thinks of the teachers and what subject is being learned.

7 Some Social and Cultural Issues affecting schooling in Britain

When children first go to school

The child's first class will probably contain 20 or more children. Each is an individual with individual needs and abilities. At home each child will probably have been treated as an individual. If it was curious about something there was always someone around to ask. If it was asked a question it could just "shout the answer" back. Many researchers, including Freud, Skinner, and Bandura, have all claimed that children acquire at least some of their attitudes and behaviour from their parents. Either by identification, reinforcement, or modelling children "become like" their parents in many respects. They will also speak the same language as their parents. Some parents will have prepared their children for school by telling them to enjoy it, and to be active and ask questions. Other parents will tell their children that they must be "quiet" and "good", or they'll be in trouble. Some of the children will be inquisitive and interested in what's going on, others will be quiet and shy.

All children do not have the same expectations of school. Do you know how you responded to school during your first year or so?

What the first school offers the child

A single teacher can't teach 20 individual five year olds. If many of them are asking questions at the same time, trying to play with things, and getting in each others way, then we'd have a lot of noise, very little actual learning, and an unsafe classroom. There must be some organisation. There must be rules which will govern the children's behaviour. For example teachers usually insist that children put their hands up if they know the answer to a question. They must not "speak out", as they might at home. Otherwise some children will dominate and others will be left out. One of the most important things the school first offers the child is discipline. According to Piaget children who can't yet decentre will accept rules which are imposed on them by others.

Children must conform to the teacher's rules. Some will find this easier to do than others. Those who conform may be regarded more favourably than those who do not.

Younger Children in School

What teachers expect of children

The teacher will define what is meant by "success in school". A "successful child" will be one who accepts the teacher's authority, who is polite and well mannered, who does what she or he is told, and who learns the material expected of her or him. An unsuccessful child will be one who is reluctant to conform, whose "individuality" is interpreted as silliness or rebelliousness, and who doesn't fit in with what a teacher defines as a "good pupil". A number of studies have shown that teachers respond differently to children who they have interpreted as "able", and to those interpreted as "less able". They smile more, are friendlier, use a lower tone of voice, and give more opportunities to do well to "good" pupils. When a child who a teacher has defined as "low ability" doesn't answer correctly the teacher will probably ask another child. When a higher ability child answers incorrectly the teacher may provide some more clues and encourage the child to try again.

Teachers form opinions about which children are "better than" others, and they may not always respond to each child in an identical way.

The child's social class may be one factor in explaining its attitudes to schooling. What attitudes did your parents take to your schooling?

Exercise – Going to school

1 Name some of the ways in which pre school children learn.

2 Name some of the changes that will occur in a child's life when it starts to go to school.

3 What sort of things can parents do to help their children start school?

How do teachers define success

Schools have been defined as middle class institutions. To put it very simply, the "middle classes" are people who work in office type jobs. Teachers, insurance agents, doctors and bank managers are all members of the middle classes. Lorry drivers, plumbers, gardeners, and electricians are described as belonging to the working classes. Sociologists claimed that "typical" middle class people had different attitudes and beliefs compared to "typical" working class people. For example middle class parents were more likely to see the benefits of a good education for their children. They would take more interest in their child's progress at school, and help more with homework etc. "Typical" working class people were more likely to see education as useful for learning basic skills, but leaving school at 16 and "getting a job" was more important.

Middle class teachers, it was argued, had more in common with middle class pupils, and would be more likely to define them as "good". Many of the books, films, visits and other educational materials which were used in schools tended to have more in common with middle class backgrounds than working class or with many ethnic

Background reading – Teachers' expectations and pupils' performance

In the mid 1960s, Lenore Jacobson and Robert Rosenthal conducted a now famous study on teacher/child interaction in a Californian elementary school. We briefly mentioned it in Chapter Two. They told the teachers about a new kind of intelligence test which wouldn't just measure intelligence, but would actually predict it. Knowing what a child's intelligence was going to be could be of enormous benefit to teachers. The pupils were given the tests, and, based on the results of these, each teacher was told that five of the children in their class would become "rapid bloomers". Jacobson and Rosenthal claimed that the teachers would expect these children to make good progress in school. Rosenthal and Jacobson returned eight months later and retested all the pupils, and, sure enough, many of their predictions were proved correct. Not only did most of the "rapid bloomers" make significant gains in their I.Q.

scores, but their record cards showed that the teachers thought they had made very good progress in, for example, reading skills.

In fact the "rapid bloomers" were simply a 20% random sample that Jacobson and Rosenthal had taken from each class' register. Jacobson and Rosenthal claimed that the improvement in these children's performance in school must be explained by the only real difference that existed between them and the other children, that is, their teachers expected more of them than of the others. Some concerns have been expressed about this study. For example some of the teachers claimed that they couldn't remember who the "bloomers" were, so couldn't have treated them differently. The study still suggests that teachers do have considerable influence over some aspects of their pupils' progress.

minority backgrounds. Working class children, and children from many ethnic minority backgrounds, may not share the teachers' ideas about the importance of high achievement in school. They were more likely to be defined as "*poor achievers*".

Why do some children do better than others in school?

Once defined as "someone who should do well", or "someone who will not make much progress", the teacher may treat the child accordingly. If teachers have low expectations of someone's ability they are less likely to "push" them. Where teachers have high expectations the children are more likely to do well. Many sociological studies have linked these teachers' expectations to the social class of the child. The researchers are not suggesting that teachers deliberately favour some children and discriminate against others. It's just that teachers seem to treat some children differently, often without having any idea that they are doing so.

Exercise – A study of teacher/child interaction

Here are some extracts from an observational study of two children, Robert and Jamie, made by Roy Nash in Edinburgh, Scotland, in 1971. Nash is making the point that it's not necessarily the child's background that teachers use to make their judgements, but rather their early perceptions of the child's abilities and personality.

Robert: A ten minute observation of a fairly typical primary-school day. . . . Most of the class are doing project work. Three boys still seem to be doing English. This means they haven't finished quickly enough. Teacher looks over to them. "Robert, you could be doing an excellent drawing for me, but you're so slow with your English." Robert looks glum. He puts down his pencil. It looks like he's finished at last – or given up. He goes to teacher who is telling Albert what a "lovely wee fire" he has painted. She sees Robert standing a little behind her, not drawing attention to himself. "Ah, now you can help me here" she says. She leads him over to the model tray. "We're going to have the mountains either side, and that's going to be a wee pass. Are you very good at making mountain shapes?" Robert looks doubtfully at the heap of papier mache. "No?" asks teacher. "Well I'll get someone else to do them then." She tells him to do a picture instead. Robert goes back to his desk. He looks about, sees that he hasn't got any paper to do his picture on, and decides to finish his English. A couple of minutes pass. "Anyone still doing English?" calls teacher. Robert raises his hand. "Oh, come on Robert" she says.

1 What is Robert doing when nearly everyone else is drawing or painting?

2 Most of the children would find drawing and painting more interesting. What did Robert do to try to get something more interesting to do?

3 What was the teacher's response to Robert over the model mountains. How would you explain her behaviour?

4 What does the teacher tell Robert to do, and what is his response?

5 The observer concluded that Robert isn't very happy at school. What evidence for this is there in the passage?

Teachers may not necessarily be aware that they are favouring some children over others. Did any of your teachers seem to have any "teacher's pet"?

We have discussed many of the special terms that Piaget and Skinner used in previous chapters. If you're not sure about any of them refer to the relevant chapter.

Here is a ten minute observation of Jamie.

> . . . Jamie is waiting in the queue at teacher's desk. He talks to Iain. Teacher takes his book. "Right" she says. Then "Some of you are not using very sharp pencils. I can hardly read it." Quickly she corrects his work. "Jamie, there you are." Jamie takes his book. . . . One of the boys in the queue asks him a question, and Jamie pauses for a moment to talk to him. Teacher asks who is talking? "I just can't concentrate with this noise, whoever it is", she says. There are about 20 children now around teacher's desk. The noise grows louder again. Teacher warns the class. "Shirley, I don't want that shrieking", she adds. Jamie works hard for three to four minutes . . . (teacher) gives instructions about the project she wants them to do. "Everybody is going to write diaries of a western pioneer family." . . . She looks around to see who has finished their English. "Right" she says, "Jamie, you pick your wagon." Jamie grins and stands up, and makes a great play of picking his friends who move over to his desk.

1 How does the teacher respond when Jamie's pencil is blunt, and when he is talking?

2 How does she respond when Shirley is talking?

3 Why is Jamie allowed to "pick his wagon" and what does he feel about it?

Having decided "what a child is like" the teacher treats the child accordingly. The teacher is quite unaware that she is treating the two children differently. As Nash says, ". . . it is possible to see that the teacher regards Jamie in more favourable terms than Robert. Jamie she sees as: forthcoming, easy-going, industrious, confident, interested, quiet, boisterous, and bright. By contrast Robert is seen as a worrier, talkative, and tending to be emotionally disturbed, lazy, lacking confidence, shy, and with a low I.Q." (What evidence can you find for the teacher regarding Jamie as: "forthcoming, easy-going, industrious, confident, interested, quiet, boisterous, and bright"?)

Psychological contributions to ideas about schooling

Whilst others have been interested in issues concerning the school as a social and cultural environment, the main areas of research in psychology have concentrated on answering the question "how do children learn?" If we knew this then teachers could use their time more efficiently, children could learn more easily, and potential learning problems could be reduced. One major contribution has come from Jean Piaget, and others, who see learning as one part of a general development of cognition. The main application of this approach has been to primary schooling. The other major contribution is made by learning theorists like B F Skinner, who say learning is the result of reinforcement. These ideas have been more widely applied to the secondary school.

8 Piaget's theory – Discovery learning

Piaget was interested in the way children think. He was interested in the following questions. Why did the standardisation sample of children for an intelligence test he was working on consistently give the same wrong answers? Where did children's natural curiosity come from? Why will a seven year old keep on making the same mistake without realising it? Why can't a child realise that Michael being taller than Sean, and Sean being taller than Lorraine, means that Michael has to be taller than Lorraine too. How could we discover what children think about, and how do the ways they think differ from the ways adults think?

Piaget was fascinated by biology, and speculated about human brain structures. He thought there must be some biological structures in the brain which expand as children grow and gather more experience. These "**schemas**", as he called them, develop through a fixed sequence of stages as children find out about their world. Piaget saw the way these schemas develop changing at about two, and seven years of age. After seven the child's thinking starts being "**operational**", that is, able to accept adult rules of logic. Before seven their thinking has quite a different logic.

Moving from pre-operational to operational thought from around six to eight years of age probably marks the greatest change in a child's cognitive development.

Exercise – Piaget and learning

1 Write a brief summary of what Piaget meant by "schema" and "operations".

2 How do children up to the age of about seven, learn, according to Piaget?

3 What did Piaget mean by "symbolic play"?

Discovery learning

Piaget didn't make specific recommendations for what should happen in school, but it isn't difficult to apply some of his conclusions to education. His approach is generally referred to as Discovery Learning. He insisted that children learn by acting on things, by using them in all sorts of new and different ways. As we said before, children are naturally curious and are well motivated to discover things for themselves. Children ask all kinds of questions which seem quite sensible to them. They arrange and play with their toys in all sorts of ways which parents might not begin to understand. Since children actually enjoy learning, nursery school teachers have an excellent opportunity to help them.

The role of the primary teacher in discovery learning

Firstly teaching should not emphasise "passing on knowledge". There'll be enough time for that later, when the child is able to think

Why do you think some supporters of Piaget's might think "nursery school *teacher*" wouldn't be a very accurate description?

more widely. Since children are naturally curious, and they learn by manipulating objects and materials, teachers should provide them with "new" things to master when they seem to have learned as much as they can from the existing materials. The materials should be provided in the amounts that children can manage. Discovery learning is a very active process and children must be given all the stimulation they can act upon. This does not mean that the child is to be "pushed". According to Piaget schemas will develop as the child masters and accommodates the skills involved. Children need time to practise and shouldn't be hurried.

Secondly, children can learn from each other, so they may be seated in pairs, or even small groups for some activities. Some activities need more than one child, and children often imitate each others speech and behaviour, especially if they see their partner receiving some benefit. Cooperation and learning to share are important skills which can only be learned from others.

Thirdly, the teacher must be aware of which stage of development each child is in, and know what skills each child has acquired, and will be preparing to acquire. The materials and resources provided should be designed to help the child achieve mastery of the tasks of

---

Background reading – Cognition and the under sevens

Here are some of the differences between preoperational and operational thought.

1 Children below about seven years of age cannot think about numbers and space in the same ways that adults do. They think that things always are what they look like, for example, if we show a pre-operational child 10 model farmyard animals which are spread out, and 10 which are bunched together, they will say that there are more animals in the first group than in the other group. Tall, thin containers look as though they hold more liquid than shorter containers. However other experiments suggest that children under seven can think in these ways, and their major problem may lie in their use of language. Bryant and others suggest that children have difficulty in expressing ideas about, for example, "more" or "less". However they can be taught to think in these ways, and carefully designed experiments will show that they do have the ability to conserve. For example McGarrigle and Donaldson's use of "naughty ted" allowed over 60% of their sample of four to six year olds to demonstrate their ability to conserve number. Hughes found that younger children could decentre too.

2 Piaget has also shown that young children cannot understand time, movement, and speed, for example, age is confused with size – bigger things must be older. A car about to overtake another will be described as going slower since the car in front is thought of as being the fastest car!

3 Nor do children understand space. Squares, triangles, and circles will all be copied as much the same shape. In children's paintings some rules that they have learned will be applied rigidly, ie trees grow at 90 degrees to the ground, so even if the painting shows a hill, the trees will still be at 90 degrees to the ground!

Children seem to start with the basic elements of understanding and gradually add to them until they grasp the whole idea. Piaget says that these schemas are formed and developed through manipulation, ie through the child handling materials like paper, water, sand or plasticine. They must discover for themselves, by trial and error, such things as "what goes with what", and "what happens if . . . ?", and "how does that work?". This process of discovery is essentially active. The children must actively participate, using their sense organs to the full. Mastery and symbolic play will help develop schemas of how to deal with things.

that stage. This is generally known as "**the readiness approach**", and does not try to force children to learn. Development will only occur when the child is ready for it. As the child nears the end of one stage teachers should prepare it to achieve the skills of the next stage. The changeover (called "**stage shift**"), when it comes, should be smooth. For example after the age of six or seven the child will be starting to think operationally. One aspect of this is the ability to conserve number. The teacher might provide things which can be counted, moved or put together to help prepare the child for conservation of number.

Teachers should show children that there are other, possibly better, ways of achieving something when the methods the child is using cannot possibly succeed. When the child has achieved the concrete operation stage it must be taught skills like doing arithmetic using actual objects such as beads.

Older Children in School

If these are the roles of the teacher, then the role of the child is to actively and enthusiastically explore, manipulate, play, and develop techniques for solving problems. The child should respond to its own curiosity which is stimulated by the things in the school. Most of all the child has to find out for itself.

Comments on Discovery Learning

Good points

1 Piaget's theory of how cognition develops in children was based on many years of patient investigation, and is a breakthrough in the way we think about children's intelligence. It provides us with a series of ages around when children's style of thinking changes from pre-operational to operational.

Comments

1 The idea that children's style of thinking changes at around seven could be regarded as a major breakthrough in our understanding. Other researchers have cast doubt on some of Piaget's methods, and therefore on any conclusions derived from them. Children are capable of thinking in more advanced ways than Piaget believed before the age of seven.

REVIEW – Discovery learning

Piaget claims that cognitive development, learning, and intelligence are all closely related. When we are young they will be affected by how we act on, and with, objects and people around us. Children below about 10 years learn best when they learn for themselves. When they are cognitively ready they will start to learn about things like time, space, number, length, mass and volume. Discovery learning suggests that teachers employ the "readiness approach" to help children pass through the various stages of cognitive development.

Do you think there are some things which may be very difficult to study scientifically? For example, do you think scientific psychologists could study "love"?

2 It provides a logical and practical guide to what children in various stages of development should be able to understand. Parents and teachers can put Piaget's theory to practical use in the way they deal with children.

3 It provides a model for the approach of teachers in the first school in terms of what signs that a child's thinking is changing to look out for.

2 Children aren't all the same, and any rigidly applied theory will be inappropriate for some of them. General guidelines can be useful, specific "do's and don'ts" are less so.

3 Being ready to help children pass through the various stages of cognitive development would be helpful if we knew precisely what children in each stage were capable of, and exactly when each child was passing through it. We are unlikely ever to have such information.

Exercise – The readiness approach

Daljit was six and a half years old when she asked her teacher "when is Christmas"? It was October, so the teacher explained that it was in eight weeks time. Daljit thought for a moment and said "there are seven days in a week." Her teacher said there were, and asked the girl when a day started? Daljit replied "when I get up." During the next week Daljit asked several questions about time. She wondered why we start school at nine o'clock? She knew why we went home at 3, it was to have something to eat! She asked why her teacher looked at her watch. Daljit's teacher started to bring the large cardboard clock out of the cupboard and put it near to Daljit. Daljit seemed interested in numbers, and in time. Daljit's teacher started to show her how to "tell the time".

1 The teacher's behaviour here is an example of "the readiness approach". Explain what this means.

2 Why did Piaget think that it wouldn't be possible to teach a younger child "how to tell the time"?

3 Outline how "discovery learning" fits in with Piaget's views about cognitive development.

4 Outline the roles of the teacher and the child in discovery learning.

5 Give one example of how you could use discovery learning if you were helping at a junior school. Mention some of the materials you'd use, and say what you think the child will learn from them.

9 Learning theory

As we saw in Chapter Seven, Skinner is not very interested in the possible existence of biological structures (in this case "schemas"). He doesn't think scientific psychology should be too concerned with things which can't be proved to exist. His careful scientific measurement of how reinforcement and punishment can bring about learning is very different from Piaget's view. Skinner says that learning is the result of living in a particular environment and behaving in particular ways. Any behaviour which is reinforced will be repeated, behaviour which isn't reinforced will be extinguished. This is the principle on which the whole of operant conditioning is based.

Skinner showed that even quite complicated behaviour could be "**shaped**". *Behaviour shaping* refers to the way in which learning theorists try to change certain behaviour. It was discussed in Chapter Eight. In school the "thing to be learned" is mainly the contents of our lessons. Maths, English, history, geography, and the other lessons, all consist of information that children need to know. Skinner developed a method which would present the information which had to be learned in each lesson, give the child a chance to learn it, test its knowledge, and offer a reinforcement for a correct answer. This has become known as "**programmed learning**" and many attempts were made to use it during the 1950s and 1960s.

Programmed learning

Programmed learning involves individual learners, either with their own text, worksheets, teaching machines, or with their own computer terminal or similar machine. Several different types of programmes have been developed but they all follow much the same general procedure.

The topic to be learned is stated, and all the items which are relevant to it are broken down into their smallest parts. Each part is arranged logically in order, usually in a series of "frames". The learner reads each frame in turn. At the end of each one there will be some question to answer, or perhaps some problem to solve. When the information on the frame is learned, and the correct response is given, the learner will be given immediate feedback, telling them if they are right or wrong. Skinner said that telling a learner that she or he has the right answer is the positive reinforcement which will encourage them to try to answer the next frames correctly. The frames form a logical sequence and when each has been mastered, so the overall lesson will have been learned.

Skinner's original version was the linear programme. A fairly small amount of information was given, and was followed by a question that would be almost impossible to answer incorrectly. The correct answer was given immediately after the child's response anyway. Skinner thought it was important that the children should make as few errors as possible because the error might accidently become reinforced and learned. The reinforcers would be the children's success in operating the machines, and knowledge of their results as they followed the lesson, although the occasional "well done" could appear after the answer. If the learners achieved about 80% or more correct answers they would be allowed to go on to the next lesson. If they achieved less than this, then they would have to go through the present one again. The reason for this is that each lesson to be learned depends to some extent on knowing the previous lesson. If someone scores less than about 80% they probably won't know the information well enough for them to be able to base the next learning required by the next frame on it.

Programmed Learning

Exercise – Programmed learning 1

The Linear Programme

FRAME 12

The most powerful way to reinforce a learner is after every correct response. This is called "continuous reinforcement".

Reinforcing a learner after every correct response is called

_____

continuous reinforcement. If this is what you wrote, well done.

FRAME 13

However it isn't necessary to reinforce continuously. We could use a schedule of reinforcement whereby all children are reinforced sometimes when they give the correct answer.

A "schedule of reinforcement" is when all children are reinforced _____ when they give the correct answer.

sometimes

FRAME 14

A positive reinforcement will be anything the learner finds pleasing. Just knowing that the correct response has been given may be sufficient positive reinforcement. This is especially true with older learners.

Anything the learner finds pleasing will be a _____

positive reinforcer

The small amount of information that Skinner's frames gave, and the type of questions asked, didn't really let students think about what they were learning. They just responded, rather like a robot. Many subjects at school require the student to think, and to use their knowledge. They must apply the principles which they have learned for one situation, to any other which is similar to it. Learning is more to do with application of principles than regurgitating knowledge. A development of Skinner's linear programme was made by Crowder to overcome this criticism. It was called the *intrinsic* or *branching* programme. This is more complex, but more flexible, and it's more like how a "real teacher" behaves. The learner is given a fair amount of information in the frame. Where Skinner gave learners a couple of sentences, Crowder gave them a paragraph or two. They were then asked a question and given a number of possible answers from which to select the correct one. This is more like a multiple choice exercise. Unlike Skinner, Crowder allows for the possibility that students will make some mistakes. When learners make a mistake they will receive more information which should help them make the correct choice.

Exercise – Programmed learning 2

The Branching Programme

FRAME 27

The most powerful way to reinforce a learner is after every correct response. This is called "continuous reinforcement". Do you think that teachers continuously reinforce every correct response in every child?

YOUR ANSWER _____

FRAME 27 – THE RESPONSE: Very unlikely indeed.
If you said something similar to "very unlikely", go on to FRAME 28.
Otherwise go to FRAME 99

FRAME 99
If you thought it might be possible to reinforce every correct response you may have been thinking that there was only one child per teacher. In most classrooms there are many children, and teachers can't pay equal attention to all of them all the time. Go back to FRAME 27 and try again.

FRAME 28
Positive reinforcement will be anything the learner finds pleasing. Just knowing that the correct response has been given may be sufficient positive reinforcement. This is especially true with older learners. Children may need something more "concrete", such as sweets or stars.
Which of the following would be positively reinforcing for a ten year old:
(a) a sweet, (b) a gold star, (c) being smacked, (d) being made to stand in the corner.
    YOUR ANSWER _____

FRAME 28 – THE RESPONSE: (a) and (b) are the most likely to reinforce 10 year olds. If you agree, go on to FRAME 29.
Otherwise go to FRAME 100

FRAME 100
If we punish a ten year old we are showing him that we disapprove of whatever he was doing, but it doesn't provide any positive information about what the child should do. Positive reinforcement should increase the likelihood of something happening, not decrease the likelihood of something else happening. Go to FRAME 28

Many criticisms have been made of the branching programme. Most are the same as would be made of any multiple choice test, ie they encourage "guessing" rather than trying to "work out" the right answer. Very little of "real life" consists of multiple choice situations, so to use this as a learning device is a long way removed from reality. It reduces the "activity" of the student leaving it rather passively awaiting information, rather than, as Piaget insists, taking an active part in learning. This leads to a general criticism of "programmed learning". It doesn't explain how children *learn* at all. It explains how they may be *taught*. All it says about learning is that it is a change in behaviour that comes about through some previously reinforced response. Some critics argue that this claim is simply untrue.

A Comparison of linear and branching programmes

	Linear programme	*Branching programme*
Theorist who developed the approach	Skinner	Crowder

	little information in short frames	fair amount – quite long frames
Amount of information in each frame		
Any extra information?	not available	plenty available
How difficult to complete	easy	rather harder
Likelihood of giving wrong answer	unlikely	much easier to go wrong

There are other variations on the linear and branching programmes.

Comments on Programmed Learning

Advantages

1 Both the teacher and the learner know exactly what is expected from the lesson. It has been carefully planned and the objectives to be achieved are clearly stated.

2 The learner "learns through doing", ie she or he takes an active part in problem solving and achieving their goals. We usually learn best when we actually have to do something, rather than just hearing someone else telling us about it.

3 The learners can proceed at their own pace. Some people naturally work faster than others. Some people will absorb some things quickly and other things less so.

4 The teacher can monitor each individual learner's progress. If someone runs into problems in understanding a particular frame or topic, the teacher will be there

Disadvantages

1 Programmed learning isn't of much use for teaching subjects, like art or music appreciation, literature, or anything which involves essay writing, ie where the learners have to think for themselves. Therefore it tends to be used in remedial teaching, and lower school teaching. The GCSE tests what you can do, and what you understand, not just what you know. Programmed learning isn't very useful for teaching these skills.

2 Not all subjects can be "taught through doing". Programmed learning only puts across the specific subject that the programme is about. It can't broaden experience as classroom teachers can.

3 Computers, language laboratories, and teaching machines can be very expensive to buy, maintain, and run. The programmes take a great deal of time and effort to prepare. They must be thoroughly checked, and this can make them very expensive. Having different children at different stages in their learning can be wasteful of the resources.

4 Teachers can't watch all the children at once. Those children who have finished and are waiting for the teacher could be bored and tire of the teaching

to explain it to the individual. "One to one" teaching is often more effective than "group teaching" because the teacher can respond specifically to the particular, individual problems.

5 Programmed learning can be useful for those subjects which can be broken down into small elements that could fit into a "frame". The basics of foreign languages, for example, can be taught in this way. Larger schools and colleges have their own "language laboratory" where this sort of thing goes on. Simple mathematics can also be taught in small steps that fit into frames. Some basic remedial teaching of reading has also used programmed instructions.

machine, the subject, and even school itself.

5 The programme is fixed and inflexible. It can't be changed or modified in any way. If the learner doesn't understand something the programme can't offer other examples in the way that human teachers can. This is particularly important in remedial teaching.

REVIEW – Programmed learning

Skinner showed that animals would learn fairly complicated behaviour if the task could be broken down into its smallest parts, which were arranged in order, and if he reinforced each successive part of the skill as it is learned. He applied the same principles to children's learning in school. Frames of information include a simple question. If answered correctly the learner has immediate feedback and immediate reinforcement. Crowder developed a branching programme where more information is given and the child has to think a little more before responding (or guess!)

Exercise – Two ways of teaching maths

Two parallel classes in a large school were chosen to take part in research into various ways of teaching maths. It was judged that both classes contained children of equal ability. One class was taught in the usual way, with teachers explaining, and getting children to do examples, and correcting any mistakes as they occur. They were called the "traditional group". The other group learned from a computer programme that had been written specifically for teaching maths at this level. They were called "the programme group". At the end of the course the two groups were tested to see how well they had understood the topic. Here are the percentage raw scores for each group:

Traditional group: 67, 49, 45, 72, 39, 76, 51, 34, 82, 43, 62, 84

Programmed group: 65, 71, 77, 56, 44, 56, 88, 72, 66, 71, 72, 84

1 Why was it necessary that each class should contain children of equal ability?

2 Find the range and mean average of the two groups and state which of the two teaching styles appears to have been most successful.

3 Describe what is meant by programmed learning.

4 What theory is it based on?

5 Discuss the strengths and weaknesses of programmed learning.

6 How might programmed learning be used in a classroom to teach reading or mathematics?

How do discovery learning and programmed learning compare?

Both Skinner and Crowder's approaches are radically different from Piaget's. Piaget's "cognitive development theory" aims at explaining the stages of development that children's abilities for mental processing pass through. Hence sensory motor stage children can only think in certain ways, preoperational children can only manage certain ideas etc. Skinner's "learning theory" argues that children are basically little adults, and the reason why they aren't able to understand certain things, like conservation, is that they haven't learned enough about those things yet. Piaget claims they will find things out for themselves when they are ready. Skinner's approach suggests that children will generally learn things, if reinforced in some way for doing so. Piaget's approach has been thought to be more relevant to primary school children, Skinner's has been applied more in the secondary school. If Piaget is right then learning in childhood will happen when the child is ready, willing, and able to learn. If Skinner is right then children will learn something when they are taught it. Now that every primary school has access to at least one computer, and some good educational software is being produced, perhaps younger children may benefit from some kind of programmed learning.

A Summary of the main differences between discovery and programmed learning

Piaget believed that children find out for themselves.	Supporters of programmed learning expect children to sit in front of machines and receive knowledge.
Piaget's approach seems more appropriate to the nursery school. Teachers should provide a safe, stimulating environment for children to learn in.	Programmed learning seems more applicable to the secondary school.
"Teaching" should be relaxed, informal, and encouraging.	Teachers should provide the programmes and monitor the progress.
Piaget believed children will motivate themselves to learn since they are naturally curious.	Teaching must get across a fixed set of knowledge.
Children will learn when they are ready and able to do so.	Skinner and Crowder believe all learning needs some kind of reinforcement, such as knowledge of progress.
	Children will learn what the programme reinforces them for learning.

12 The Nature of Intelligence

In Chapter Nine we saw that Piaget argued that we acquire our knowledge through interacting with our environment. However this doesn't mean that if everyone had the same environment they would end up with the same knowledge. Some people are more likely to learn more things, and learn them more quickly, from the same environment, than others. Take 2 four year olds in the playground. Rachel is curious and interested in the sand and water, in the dolls and skipping ropes, and in the puzzles and books, and becomes involved with them and uses them inventively. Mary is more likely to be found banging a drum, on the rocking horse, or messing around with the paints. It seems that the activities Rachel chooses are more likely to encourage imagination and intellect than Mary's choices. Even if both girls played with the same things, they could still benefit in different ways. If Rachel benefits more, could we describe her as being "more intelligent" than Mary?

In this chapter we will be looking at early and modern ideas about intelligence and intelligence testing.

1 We start with the most obvious questions, "what is intelligence", and "what is intelligence testing"?
2 We will look at the development of intelligence testing and I.Q.
3 We note differences in "intelligence" between boys and girls.
4 We will review the use of intelligence tests in school, and their limitations.
5 We will study the "nature nurture" debate as it applies to intelligence, and visual perception.

1 Defining intelligence

Intelligence has been one of the most thoroughly researched areas in psychology during the last 100 years, but we still can't either define it precisely or measure it accurately. To put it simply, intelligence is that marvellous skill that humans (and to lesser extents some other animals) use to allow them to *adapt to their environment*, and *adapt their environment to them*. When man first climbed a tree to escape from an enemy he was adapting himself to his environment. When he first made a shelter to protect him from the weather he was adapting the environment to him.

Exercise – Defining intelligence

1 Write what you think the definition of intelligence is, if possible compare it to someone else's definition.
2 Look "intelligence" up in a dictionary and see how close your definition came.
3 If you have more than one dictionary look it up in the others and see if all the definitions a) have things in common, and b) have things which others don't.

REVIEW – What is Intelligence?

It is almost impossible to give a simple definition of "intelligence" because it consists of so many different skills. However, a stimulating environment seems to be involved in developing it.

There has always been disagreement amongst psychologists about precisely what intelligence is, where it comes from, and if it can (and should) be measured.

The Penguin Dictionary of Psychology concludes:

". . . intelligence will be what it has always been 'the ability to profit from experience' and . . . what it has become 'that which intelligence tests measure'."

Exercise – Developing intelligence

Explain, with examples, what is meant by this quote from the background reading "Some factors in developing Intelligence". "Another important factor [in developing intelligence] will be the parent–child relationship, for example, how much the parent talks to the child, how much interest generally the parents take in the child."

2 Intelligence testing

How can we measure intellectual development? The area of psychology which deals with the "testing" of human abilities is called **psychometrics**. We must say, straight away, that some psychologists do not believe that trying to "test" someone's intelligence is worthwhile. Piaget, for example, totally rejected the idea of "intelligence testing" since he did not believe that "intelligence" is a "thing" which can be tested and measured.

Exercise – What does intelligence consist of?

Many modern psychologists are suspicious of intelligence tests, since they do not believe that "intelligence" is a thing which can be measured.

So far we've mentioned several factors which are involved in intelligence. Write down as many as you can. Look back if you can't remember them all.

Intelligence tests involve someone sitting down for some time working through a series of questions. They need subjects who can stay alert for some time, who understand language, can read and write, and who

---

Background reading – Changing ways of looking at intelligence

During the nineteenth century intelligence was thought to consist of several separate factors such as reasoning, imagining, remembering and so on. Early this century L L Thurstone suggested it consisted of two factors, "g" or "general" intelligence, which we applied to everything we did, and "s" or specific intelligence which we applied to particular skills. The inventor of the first intelligence test (Alfred Binet) thought intelligence consisted of our potential for imagination and insight, reasoning and adaptability, and judgement. His tests were designed to measure them. Later others argued that intelligence consists of just three main factors, learning ability, how to deal with new and different information or objects, and how

abstract ideas are handled.

D O Hebb suggested that much of the difficulty in defining intelligence came about because people were confusing two aspects of intelligence a) the potential which we are born with, and b) the intelligence which actually does develop. Hebb identified three types of intelligence. Intelligence A is genetically inherited (part of our genotype), and cannot be measured. Intelligence B is that part of A which does develop. It is socially learned and may be measured. Intelligence C is that which intelligence tests measure. Hebb said that genes provide the basic potential for intellectual development, environment provides the stimulation for that potential to be reached.

can follow instructions. Babies and young children can't do these things, and so aren't given intelligence tests as such. Instead their progress is measured on what are called **developmental scales**.

Developmental scales

These are a range of tests and procedures which try to measure the progress of infants and preschool children towards passing certain developmental "milestones". They involve getting the child to do something and rating its performance, or getting it to talk and answer questions, and measuring its verbal skills, for example, since a six month old infant can sit up without support, any six month old who can't do this will be "behind". The score a child makes on a developmental scale is called a "**development quotient**" or "**DQ.**"

Developmental scales are used to judge a child's progress in acquiring physical, social, and intellectual skills.

Some examples of developmental scales

1 The Gesell Developmental Scales

This was the first organised attempt to describe children's perform-ance in the areas of motor skills, adaptive behaviour (ie co-ordination, alertness, problem solving), language development, and personal–social development. During the 1920s and 1930s Arnold Gesell and his colleagues observed hundreds of children to establish "**age norms**" of what average children were achieving at given ages. There are two sets of scales, one for infants, another for preschool children. Gesell's scales are simple descriptions and do not allow us to make predic-tions, nor do they suggest anything about the origin of intelligence or the factors which affect it.

Background reading – Some factors in developing intelligence

1 One important factor is the ability to use language. The child can interpret and react to its world much more quickly and effectively when it can ask questions, understand answers, and obey instructions or advice. Someone tell-ing a child "Don't go near the fire" and explain-ing why not, is better for learning than trial and error! From language comes one of the major sources of man's superiority over the animals, his ability to reason.

2 Ideally we need well developed sense organs to provide a variety of information. Serious defects in one sense can be overcome (eg what a blind person cannot take in through sight may be compensated for by taking information in through well developed hearing and sensitive touch). Serious defects in two or three senses may limit intellectual potential.

3 A healthy nervous system and the ability to control our muscles and limbs may help us explore our environment, and this may contri-bute to intellectual development. A fully func-tioning body isn't essential at all however. Many highly intellectual people are physically hand-icapped in some way, including some eminent writers and academics.

4 Intellectual development may also depend on the "richness" of the "learning environment" – that is the opportunities available at home and school for stimulation from things like "educa-tional toys", materials like paint and plasticine to manipulate and experiment with, exciting and enthusiastic schools, "good" books and so on. Evidence suggests that children who do not have these things may not develop intellectually as well as others.

5 Another important factor will be the parent–child relationship, for example, how much the parent talks to the child, how much interest generally the parents take in the child.

2 The Bayley Scales of Infant Development

Nancy Baley's scales are probably the most widely used now particularly in America. They consist of three types of test aimed at measuring infants from two months to 30 months of age.

(a) There is a "**mental scale**" which measures things like aspects of perception, learning ability, following direction, searching for a missing toy, memory, and simple problem solving.

(b) The "**motor scale**" measures co-ordination skills such as are used in sitting, walking, manipulating objects, throwing a ball or climbing stairs.

(c) The "**infant behaviour record**" rates social and personality development, persistence, attention span, etc.

3 McCarthy Scales of Children's Abilities

These are aimed at children between two and a half and eight and a half years. There are 18 tests in all which rate children on scales for verbal skills, perceptual skills, mathematical skills, memory skills, and general cognitive skills. Cognitive skills are usually taken as a measure of intellectual development.

4 The Wechsler Scales

David Wechsler has devised a whole series of intelligence tests which are very widely used today. The Wechsler Adult Intelligence Scale (WAIS) was modified for use with six to 16 year olds as the **Wechsler Intelligence Scale for Children (WISC)**. The **Wechsler Preschool and Primary Scale of Intelligence (WPPSI)** is for children below six years. The Wechsler Scales give two scores, one for **verbal ability** and the other for **non-verbal performance**, and they do correlate positively with educational performance generally.

Evaluation of developmental scales

There isn't a very positive correlation between children's scores on many developmental scales (their DQ), and their scores on intelligence tests, or their achievements at school, or any other way of measuring their intellectual skills. This has led to considerable criticism of the usefulness of developmental scales. However, yet again, this illustrates the problem of drawing conclusions from correlations. The reason why the correlation isn't strong is probably because developmental scales and intelligence tests aren't measuring the same sorts of abilities. Developmental scales for infants and children measure motor skills, memory, perception, social and personal development etc. Intelligence tests try to measure more abstract things like verbal reasoning, seeing relationships in time and space, choosing and applying appropriate principles to solving abstract problems etc. We shouldn't necessarily expect there to be any correlation between them.

Developmental scales are useful for diagnosing any particular areas of difficulty a child is having at the time, rather than any kind of prediction for future intelligence. Backwardness in motor development, problems with perception, difficulties with the manipulation of objects, may be caused by physical, neurological problems which will need to be dealt with by doctors or therapists. Further, children do not develop at the same rate. A child might be advanced in motor skills, but be retarded in language skills. Some of the tests on the Bayley Scales have been found to be accurate predictors of future language performance.

Administering developmental scales is expensive because they take time and skill to do. Therefore only children who are thought to have something wrong with them are given the tests. Many American and British institutions which deal with children have some screening procedures which may be administered by nursing staff.

Exercise – Developmental scales

1 What's the difference between positive correlation and negative correlation?

2 What are Developmental scales used for, and why?

3 Say, in your own words, why scores gained on developmental scales may not be good predictors of scores on Intelligence tests.

Intelligence tests

The term "intelligence test" is really very misleading since "intelligence" is not one single thing which can be measured. Instead, an intelligence test is simply a test of a sample of abilities. Many tests exist. Some are individual tests (where one person is tested by one tester). Others are group tests (where larger numbers of people can all be tested by one tester at the same time). Which type to use depends largely on what the results are to be used for. To survey the progress of all children in a class requires one kind, to evaluate the extent of brain damage in a particular patient requires another.

The first intelligence test was designed by Alfred Binet in Paris in 1904. The French government had asked Binet to devise a way to identify "below average ability" French school children. It was thought that having low ability children in a class might hold the average and bright children back. These "below average" children could be sent to special schools, otherwise there would be nowhere else for them to go, apart from home. If they stayed at home they wouldn't have received any formal schooling at all. Binet believed that mental ability matured as the body matured so he spent many hours doing naturalistic observation and experimentation to find out what children of various age groups could do. He produced a long list of skills which most five year olds had mastered, another list of the typical abilities of six year olds, another for seven year olds etc. These skills included things like reasoning and deduction. Such tests as Binet's do not attempt to measure the whole of a child's intelligence, just some aspects of it. Binet never claimed that his test could assess general intelligence, or that it could be used as a general test for all children. It was simply a practical way of discovering children who had some learning problems in some particular skills such as arithmetic, or language.

REVIEW –
Developmental
scales
Intelligence tests are used on those children who are old enough to understand what is expected of them by the test. Developmental scales are used with younger children to judge whether certain aspects of their development are proceeding normally. They can provide useful indicators of any areas in which children are not making good progress.

The first intelligence test was used to measure French school-children, but was developed for use elsewhere.

Other researchers either overlooked these reservations, or tried to overcome them. Binet's original test was modified at Stanford University in America for use with American school children. The "Stanford Binet" test gave an individual score for each child. It soon became popular and has been revised many times since it was invented and is still used today. It consists of a series of "subtests" which are arranged from easiest (for youngest children) to hardest (for older children). There are subtests for every half-year from two to five and a half, then for each year from six to 14, and then there are four adult levels. The idea is that an average person of a given age could pass all the tests for those younger and the same age, but none of the tests for someone older.

For example, an average 13 year old could pass all the tests which are meant for 12 and 13 year olds, but could not pass any of the tests for 14 year olds.

Of course some children would be able to pass some of the older children's tests, whilst others couldn't pass all of the tests for their own age group. Binet used a simple formula to give each child a score. He distinguished **chronological age** (CA), which is ones actual age in years and months, from **mental age** (MA) which is worked out from the number of correct answers given to the subtests.

Intelligence tests often assess someone's mental age or "MA". This is compared to their actual, or "chronological age", or "CA".

Example 1 If a five year old girl (CA = 5) could do all the tests of a "typical" five year old, she would have an MA of five. This would make her perfectly average. If she could do all the tests of a five year old, and all those for a five and a half year old as well, she'd have an MA of 5.5. She would be well above average.

Intelligence and I.Q.

A German psychologist called William Stern invented the concept of the **intelligence quotient (I.Q.)**. He found that dividing one's actual age into one's mental age would give a figure which could be used to express one's intelligence. So the formula mental age/chronological age = I.Q. was invented.

Example 1 Someone who was four years old, but had a mental age of four and a half would have their I.Q. worked out as: 4.5 (MA) / 4 (CA) = 1.125. 1.125 isn't a very attractive way of communicating a measurement of someone's intelligence, so two further steps were taken. The number could be expressed more simply by rounding it down to two decimal places, for example, 1.13, and it would look much neater if we could lose the decimal point, so Stern multiplied it by 100. This produced an I.Q. of 113. Stern expressed Binet's findings as the formula:

$$MA / CA. * 100 = I.Q.$$

REVIEW – The Intelligence Quotient

Someone's I.Q. is discovered by dividing their age in years and months by their mental age, rounding it to two decimal places, and multiplying it by 100. It is expressed by the formula MA./CA.*100.

Example 2 A 17 year old who can answer all the tests for someone of 17, but none of the tests for anyone over 17 will have an I.Q. of 17 / 17 * 100 = 100. The average I.Q. score is 100.

Example 3 A child of five with a mental age of 5.5 would have an I.Q. of 5.5 / 5 * 100 = 110.

Recent evidence suggests that the "average I.Q." has increased since Binet's time, by about 13 points. As people's diet, housing, and experience of life has improved, so has the average I.Q..

Exercise – I.Q.

1 What is the difference between mental age and chronological age?

2 Briefly describe how an I.Q. score is calculated.

3 What would be the I.Q. for a seven year old who could do the tests for six year olds, but none of the tests for older children?

4 Find the I.Q. for a six year old who can do all the tests for six year olds and below, but no others.

5 What is the I.Q. of a four year old who could do all the tests for a five year old?

These I.Q. scores do not show the "amount" of anything which someone has. Someone with an I.Q. of 125 doesn't have 125 "units" of intelligence. They are simply a way of indicating someone's average stage of mental development, as measured by the particular test.

The "normal distribution"

If we have a massive population, for example, the 1000 million people who live in India, and we measured how tall every one of them was, we'd find that a few are very short, and about the same number are extremely tall. Some would be smallish, and about the same amount would be tall. The vast majority would, of course, be of "average height". There is a statistical device called "**the curve of normal distribution**" which allows us to predict more or less what percentage of the population will be of any particular height. Binet assumed

REVIEW –
Intelligence tests

We do not really know all of the many mental abilities which make up what we call "intelligence". Intelligence tests are tests of a sample of these mental abilities. Different tests will probably sample different mental skills. To describe someone as having a particular I.Q. score can be quite misleading since it only describes a score they made on a given test. That test only tries to measure those abilities that its inventor thought constituted "intelligence".

Background reading – The normal distribution for I.Q. scores

If we plotted the normal distribution curve on a graph it would look something like the diagram below. This is called the "bell shaped curve" or the "curve of normal distribution".

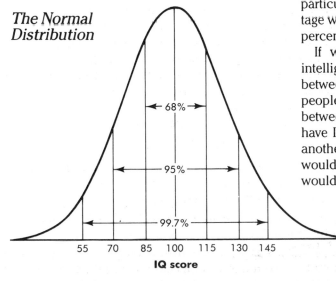

The Normal Distribution

68%

95%

99.7%

55 70 85 100 115 130 145

IQ score

If the distribution of intelligence in the population really did follow this curve we could make some interesting predictions about the percentage of the people who would grow to particular heights. We could say what percentage would be between 90 cm and 110 cm, what percentage between 180 cm and 210 cm etc.

If we could apply the same principle to intelligence then 68% of people would score between the I.Q. range of 85 to 115. 95% of people score between 70 and 130. 99.7% fall between 55 and 145, whilst only 0.3% would have I.Q. scores at the two extremes. To put it another way, three children in every 2000 would have I.Q.'s below 55, and another three would be geniuses with I.Q.'s over 145.

However the idea of normal distribution is only a statistical model. It is unlikely to exist with such accuracy in real life.

that there would be roughly equal numbers of very intelligent people and very dull people, the same number of fairly bright and fairly dull people. He thought intelligence would also follow the curve of normal distribution.

Exercise – Normal distribution

1 What percentage of people would have I.Q. scores within 15 points either way of the average score?

2 How might the government benefit from being able to predict how many children are likely to be educationally subnormal, or extremely intelligent?

3 Gender and I.Q. scores

The amount of intelligence children have, and their good progress in school are positively correlated. However high intelligence is not the only explanation for why some children achieve more than others. Another major explanation for why some children do well and others do badly is that some are well motivated and others are given low expectation of achieving very much. An intelligent child who does not expect to do well in school may actually achieve less than a child who isn't as bright, but who believes she or he can do well. Some research indicates that, as children pass through their schooling, girls increasingly underestimate their abilities, and boys increasingly overestimate theirs.

Although there are no differences in the average score for boys and girls, there are some slight differences in particular skills. None of the differences are very marked, and there are many exceptions to them. Some of them do not appear until the teenage years. Up to about the age of six girls are slightly ahead in basic arithmetic although boys take over some time after that age. Girls develop language skills slightly ahead of boys, on average, and stay slightly ahead. By the time they reach adolescence boys are slightly better at "artistic type" abilities such as thinking about abstract shapes, whereas girls are slightly better at verbal reasoning such as solving word puzzles.

There are two possible reasons for these slight differences.

a) It is possible that there are differences in the ways in which boys' and girls' brains are organised. This reflects the nature side of the nature/nurture debate. The "language centres" may be slightly more efficiently organised in females, whereas the parts of the brain concerned with processing numbers may be better in boys. This explanation seems fairly unlikely however, because the overall differences are small, and there is tremendous variation between individuals.

b) Boys may be socialised into thinking in terms of science, mechanics, and things which involve numbers. This reflects the nurture view. Girls may be encouraged to be more talkative, more sociable and co-operative, and generally to use language more.

The importance of parental expectations and roles on children's achievement has been studied by Jacquelynne Parsons. Parsons asked

There are slight differences in the skills which boys and girls score more on. The differences are not great. The explanation for why boys and girls achieve differently may be because parents expect them to be good at different things.

some American parents of secondary school age children for their attitudes to various school subjects. Most of the parents said that they thought maths and science subjects were more important for boys than for girls. They also said that they thought that maths was easier and more enjoyable for boys than for girls. Parsons found that the children's expectations of their abilities were in line with their parents' expectations. Girls, who had similar abilities and scores in maths compared to boys, said that they didn't think they had the same potential or aptitude as the boys claimed. When girls did well at maths their parents said that it was because they had worked very hard at maths. When boys did well their parents said that they had ability. Such attitudes were bound to influence the children's perceptions of their ability.

4 Intelligence tests in school

Binet's original instructions were to design a test that would sort children into the most appropriate school for them. I.Q. tests are still used for this purpose today, particularly in America. Before school starts a child may be given some kind of diagnostic test if there are any doubts about its ability. I.Q. tests may be given to school children who seem to be too intelligent for the work that their peers are doing, or to those who can't keep up for some reason. In either case the child's score may be one of (many) factors which are considered when deciding whether they should be moved to another class or another school. In Britain's comprehensive school system we tend to use tests only for diagnostic purposes.

Comments on intelligence testing

Here we ask a series of questions to discover the value of intelligence testing.

i) What do I.Q. tests measure?

We've said that it is extremely difficult to define "intelligence" so psychologists often assume that it means "that which intelligence tests measure", eg logical problem solving, numerical ability, verbal reasoning, ability to understand time and space etc. Many psychologists now prefer the term "intelligent behaviour". At least this can be measured to some extent.

   Intelligence tests do not measure the whole range of abilities that people have – merely a sample of them. Here are a few examples of some of the skills which modern I.Q. tests do measure. (The answers are at the end of this section on intelligence, before the part on perception.)
(a) Seeing relationships between series of things, for example, What is the next letter in the sequence A D G J? Or in the sequence Q P M L I?
(b) What do pairs of words have in common? for example, wood and coal, or apple and peach, or ship and car.
(c) Putting the words in a scrambled sentence into the right order, eg "school back we Monday it's so go tomorrow to".
(d) Vocabulary, eg find a word which means the same as stake and mail. Which is the odd one out: tootap, prinut, tintek, otrrac?

REVIEW – Gender differences in intelligence

There are very small differences in intellectual skills between boys and girls. If an intelligence test is being given which has items which emphasise a skill that one sex has more than the other then it may be necessary to have slightly different marking systems for each sex's scores. Parsons suggests that parental influences affect children's performance and that boys are encouraged to do well in those subjects which will be better rewarded.

(e) Unscrambling words. Which of these towns is not in England? Grothnib, Yuqtora, Drifcaf, Hercest, Sheeldiff?

Other skills which are tested include memory span, number ability, copying shapes, finishing sentences, pointing out illogicalities, following a maze, doing a jigsaw, assembling coloured blocks in a particular pattern etc.

All that I.Q. tests really measure is our ability to deal with items in the particular test.

ii) Are intelligence tests accurate

To be accepted as accurate:

(a) I.Q. tests must be **standardised measures of psychological functioning**. This rather grand phrase means that each item on the test has been given to many hundreds of people (called the **standardisation sample**), who have been chosen (by stratified random sampling) to include a representative cross section of the population (men, women, white, non white, rich, poor, old, middle aged, and young). If the standardisation procedure is accurate, then an average person of any given age should make an average I.Q. score of 100. (Or perhaps 113 now.)

(b) I.Q. tests must be **reliable**, and **valid**. See Chapter Two for definitions and explanations of these terms if you can't remember them.

(c) Questions must be clear and easy to understand so that there's no confusion amongst the people taking the test as to what they mean.

Regrettably some tests fail in one or more of these areas, and none are completely accurate. They give an indication of a general level of ability.

iii) What are the main criticisms of I.Q. tests

(a) To use an "intelligence test" assumes that there are some particular abilities which make up "intelligence", and which we know about and can measure. Not everyone agrees.

(b) According to Binet, each child's intelligence was fixed at birth and intelligence would be distributed "normally" throughout the population. Many psychologists dispute both assumptions.

(c) I.Q. tests do not measure all the skills we may have. One child may be especially good at verbal reasoning and vocabulary, and less good at numeracy (ability with numbers). Another may have good numeracy, but not be so good with language. If the test has lots of questions which involve verbal reasoning then the first child will have an advantage. To give one I.Q. score is, therefore, misleading. (Many mentally retarded people have some exceptional abilities, for example, painting and music.) The belief that "intelligence" consists of many abilities has led psychologists to devise many tests of specific ability such as aptitude tests for things like mechanical ability and musical capabilities).

(d) I.Q. does not remain constant over time. The reasons for this are that our abilities vary according to the environment we grow up in, and an individual would take different tests which measure different skills. There is no reason to imagine that your average score for one set of skills when you are six years old should be the same as your score for some different skills when you are 20 years old.

(e) If intelligence was something we were born with, which couldn't change, and if I.Q. tests were accurate, then it wouldn't be possible to be trained to pass an I.Q. test (eg the old 11 plus exam which was used to help decide which children should go to grammar schools or secondary moderns.) Many primary school children were "taught" how to tackle the 11 plus. I.Q. tests try to measure some of the skills someone has, but don't indicate anything about where such skills come from.

(g) The relationship between the examiner and the child might well affect the child's performance. The examiner may not always appear to be friendly and sensitive to the child.

(h) The mood the child is in, whether or not it feels that it wants to co-operate etc. can be particularly important with younger children. Just because a child doesn't do something correctly in an artificial test, doesn't mean she or he can't do it correctly.

(i) I.Q. tests do not always work satisfactorily with people from different cultures. Different people speak different languages, have different norms and values, have different early experiences, and have different expectations. The tests may be biased in favour of children who have the same sorts of background as the people who set the test. In Europe and America this tends to be white, middle class people.

(j) They are not accurate!

At best I.Q. tests can only measure a range of abilities. At worst all they may measure is how good someone is at doing I.Q. tests! They are sometimes unreliable measures too. Many factors can influence a child's performance on an I.Q. test, quite apart from its intelligence. They are still sometimes useful for measuring general ability or for showing up areas of particular need. However they do also run the risk of having someone "labelled" as intelligent, or below average, etc and such labels may be hard to break away from.

Exercise – Evaluation of intelligence testing

1 What is an I.Q. test?
2 What do I.Q. tests measure?
3 When applied to intelligence testing, what do the terms "reliability", "validity", and "standardisation" mean?
4 Outline the main uses of I.Q. tests in schools.
5 Outline the argument against the use of I.Q. tests in schools.
6 Suggest two possible explanations for why girls tend to do slightly better than boys on tests of verbal fluency.

5 Advantages and disadvantages of using intelligence tests

For using I.Q. tests in school:

(a) The main advantage of an I.Q. score is that it gives an idea of the child's present level of intellectual ability.

(b) It also gives a useful indication of a child's specific abilities, for example, verbal, reading, numeracy etc, which the psychologist and teacher may find useful.

(c) Any areas of particular weakness can be identified and the child can be given special help.

Against using I.Q. tests in school:

(a) The main disadvantage is that the tests are usually constructed, given, and marked by middle class people who have attitudes and beliefs that may not be shared by all people, that is, they are biased in favour of one culture (or subculture) over others. In America studies have shown that non white children score 10 to 15 points less than white children (although there are no real differences before the age of two or three). Some of the reason for this may be biased testing.

(b) Once labelled as "dull" or "slow" a child may be treated as "slow" and, for example, put in the lower ability groups at school. Here the child may be under stimulated.

6 The nature/nuture debate

6a Is intelligence genetically inherited or acquired socially?

The "nature" side of the "nature/nurture" debate claims that intelligence is genetically inherited. The "nurture" side claims it is largely the result of the amount of stimulation in the environment in which someone grows up.

Although we can't measure intelligence very accurately, no one would deny that some children seem more able to do certain things than others. We've all heard people say that one child seems very bright whilst another is rather slow. An important question is, how do these differences between children happen? There are two obvious possibilities. Intelligence could be acquired genetically, and therefore would be fixed at birth. If so there's nothing much we can do to alter it. Alternatively it could be acquired socially. If so then changing the amount of stimulation a child has would alter its intellectual abilities.

Exercise – Nature/nurture

Some psychologists, who believe that intelligence is socially acquired, are asked to advise a school for children with I.Q.'s of less than 70. Many of the children there have learning difficulties with basic skills like simple arithmetic.

1 What is the average I.Q. score?

2 What sort of recommendations might the psychologists make?

We will review the arguments for the nature and nurture case here.

The case for heredity

This argument can be traced back to Charles Darwin. Darwin was a famous nineteenth century biologist who found a mass of evidence to support his view that all species of living thing on the earth, including human beings, would have to evolve in order to survive. Those species which could not evolve would die out. He thought that most of the differences between most members of a species were the result of differences in their genotypes, and this would include the differences in intelligence between people. Alfred Binet supported this view. Here is some of the evidence for their claims.

1 Many human characteristics are fixed at birth

At conception in humans a male sperm fertilises a female ovum. The resulting egg contains 23 chromosomes from the sperm, and 23 chromosomes from the ovum. Each chromosome consists of thousands of genes, each of which carries some information about how parts of the body will be formed. There are genes for the colour of our eyes, hair, and skin, for our sex, eventual height, and shape, and for what we will look like. The "mix" of each parent's genes determines a number of things about the individual, long before it is born.

Intelligence may be one of the things determined by our genes. During pregnancy, however, some things could happen to the mother which might also affect the child's intelligence. For example taking certain drugs, suffering from particular diseases, or having some kinds of accidents could all affect how the foetus develops.

2 Selective breeding

Racehorse breeders try to put their best mares and stallions together so that their foals might inherit their parents' speed. Most animal breeders try to mate their adult animals so that their offspring will possess the characteristics which the breeders want to emphasise. We hear people say that a child has got "her mother's eyes" or "his father's chin". But these are physical characteristics. Can we selectively breed other characteristics too? Can we breed "intelligent animals" to see if their offspring are "more intelligent"? In the late 1950s two researchers called Cooper and Zubeck took a sample of rats, and put each in turn into a maze. They counted the number of mistakes each made, and timed how long it took them to complete the maze. Those who made the fewest mistakes were called the "maze bright" group, and were only allowed to breed with each other. Those rats who made most mistakes were called the "maze dull" group, and they were only allowed to breed with each other. After a few generations the descendants of the "maze bright" group were much better at running mazes than their ancestors were. The descendants of the "maze dull" group were much worse than their ancestors at running mazes. Different temperaments (fearfulness, aggression, sociability etc.) have also been selectively bred in animals.

There are two problems in using selective breeding as evidence for the "nature" case. Firstly we can't really know what "intelligence" means in animals. It certainly can't be compared to human intelligence. Secondly inter breeding in humans seems more likely to produce a child with some disability than to produce a genius.

3 Identical twin studies

For every 1000 babies born, about 12 will be twins. There are two types of twins, identical and fraternal. **Fraternal twins** occur when two male sperms fertilise two female ova at the same time. A fertilised cell is called a zygote, and fraternal twins are called **dizygotic twins** (**DZ** for short). Two babies develop in the womb. The only other thing they have in common is that they are born at about the same time. They are just like ordinary brothers and sisters. **Identical twins** occur when, for some unknown reason, the single zygote divides into two, virtually identical, halves. They each have the same chromosomes carrying the same genes. Because they come from a single zygote they are called **monozygotic twins** (**MZ** for short). MZ twins must have just about identical genotypes. If intelligence is the result of our genotypes, then MZ's must have just about identical intelligence.

Probably the best way to discover the effects of the environment and of genetic inheritance, is to study the I.Q.'s of four groups of people. Two groups need the same heredity and different environments, the other two need the same environments and different heredity. If the

Intelligence may be one of the human characteristics which we acquire as a result of genetic transmission from our parents. It may develop as the foetus develops. A foetus is a developing baby between the third month of pregnancy and birth.

It would obviously be immoral and probably impractical to selectively breed human beings. Selectively breeding physical characteristics like speed of running or the length of an animal's tail is not the same as trying to breed mental characteristics like "intelligence".

If we found that monozygotic twins who were reared apart had similar I.Q.'s this might prove that intelligence is inherited.

I.Q.'s of the people who share the same environment are similar, then we could say that intelligence is largely determined by the environment. If those with identical heredities have similar I.Q.'s, then intelligence is mainly genetically acquired.

Exercise – Genetic inheritance

1 What do MZ twins have in common?

2 What do DZ twins have in common?

3 To be absolutely sure of the influence of heredity and environment we would need the following four samples:

MZ twins		DZ twins	
Reared together	Reared apart	Reared together	Reared apart
(same heredity, same environment)	(same heredity, different environments)	(same environment, different heredity)	(all different)

Explain why testing the I.Q.'s of these samples should help us to solve the "nature nurture" debate on intelligence.

It isn't difficult to find people who have grown up in the same environment. Most twins do, to a large extent. Finding people with identical genotypes (ie identical twins) isn't so easy. A small number of identical twins who have been brought up separately have been found. They have been studied in three main surveys. All three found a high correlation between each member of the pair of twins' I.Q. score. This supports the idea that intelligence is innate. We will return to this idea later.

Exercise – Correlating the intelligence of family members

A number of studies have tested the intelligence of various family members. Here is a summary of their findings:

Study by	Newman	Sheilds	Erlenmyer	Nichols	Jensen	Wilson
MZs reared together	0.91	0.77	0.89	0.87		0.80
MZs reared apart	0.67	0.76	0.75			
DZs reared together	0.64	0.57	0.60	0.63		0.45
Siblings reared together			0.46		0.55	0.45
Siblings reared apart			0.35			
Parent/child			0.44		0.50	
Foster parent/child			0.31		0.20	

The studies that have been conducted on family members do find that identical twins, with similar genotypes, have similar I.Q. scores.

(NB siblings are simply children of the same parents, ie brothers and sisters.)

1 How many investigators have studied MZ twins' I.Q. scores, according to this table?

2 What does correlation mean?

3 Which family members had the most similar I.Q. scores?

4 Which family members have the lowest positive correlation in their I.Q. scores?

5 What figure expresses no correlation at all?

6 What is the average correlation amongst the studies of a) identical twins reared together, b) identical twins reared apart?

7 Summarise the evidence presented in the table which supports the influence of heredity.

Not everyone agrees that the similarities in monozygotic twins, whether reared separately or together, is evidence that intelligence is a result of heredity. Leon Kamin has summarised the evidence against this view. He says that probably the most widely quoted of the studies which found a high positive correlation between the I.Q.'s of MZ's reared apart was conducted by Cyril Burt. Burt's work has been questioned, and although no proof exists that his research was flawed, he has been accused of inventing some of his data. Kamin suggests that we should ignore this study. He also claims that those who were separated were often reared in very similar homes, and treated in similar ways. They may have been reared separately, but they weren't reared differently. For example two thirds of the twins in the Shields study were actually raised by the same family, one twin by its mother, the other by her mother, sister etc. Most were treated similarly, attended the same school, and saw a great deal of each other.

Another problem Kamin identified is with the nature of the I.Q. tests the twins were given. In each of the studies the twins were given different I.Q. tests, some of which were not properly standardised for the group taking the test. For example most of the twins in Newman's (1937) study were female (as were the majority in each of the studies quoted). Newman used the (1916) Stanford Binet test which hadn't been properly standardised for adults, or for females.

A final problem concerns the unrepresentative nature of the twins studied. Most had answered advertisements in the media asking for twins who had been reared separately to contact the researchers. Each sample was therefore self selected. Self selected samples are unlikely to be typical.

Studies which have found that identical twins do have remarkably similar I.Q.'s are not scientifically acceptable. Their authenticity, validity, or use of statistics have all been found to be suspect.

The case for the environment

The case for the environment appears to be rather stronger than the case for genetics. Animals and children whose environments have been changed and whose I.Q. has changed, provide support for the argument that environmental factors affect intelligence.

1 Impoverishment and enrichment studies

If intelligence is the result of the environment, then someone brought up in an "**impoverished**" (unstimulating) environment would not be capable of very intelligent behaviour. "Enriching" (improving) the environment should lead to an increase in their intellectual skills.

a) **Animal studies** Psychologists could not deliberately impoverish

It is possible to alter animal's behaviour by interfering with their environments. Giving them practise with some materials will improve their performance. But an animal's responses to some test situations does not tell us about the origins of human intelligence.

children's environments for the same reasons that we discussed earlier when looking at maternal privation.

As we saw earlier with Harlow's 1960s experiments, the same restrictions did not apply to animals. The rhesus monkey experiments involved very severe privation. The privated, impoverished monkeys did behave very differently from the "normally reared" monkeys. However there are some problems with applying these findings to human intelligence. Here are two of the main problems: what exactly do we mean by "intelligent behaviour" in monkeys and other animals? Secondly, can we generalise from the behaviour of animals to the mental functioning of people?

Exercise – Impoverishment

Write a paragraph reviewing the main reasons why we cannot conduct research involving privation and impoverishment on children.

b) **Studies of Children** Studying animals isn't really of much use in untangling the role of "nature" or "nurture" in intellectual development in humans without facing all sorts of practical, moral, and ethical problems. We can't deliberately manipulate children's environments. We could see if there are any differences in intelligence scores between children raised in "deprived environments" (eg children in orphanages where there are few facilities) with those in enriched environments (eg children in orphanages where there are many facilities). This would be a natural experiment. If the average I.Q. score for children in well staffed and well equipped orphanages is greater than that of children in poor orphanages, then it may be that the environment affects the intellect.

This still wouldn't "prove" that environment has a greater effect on us than heredity, because we could not match the children (or monkeys) in the different institutions for the key variables like age, intelligence, health, etc. If those children in the better equipped orphanage did turn out to be more intelligent than the others, they might have been more intelligent to begin with. A number of such studies have been conducted however, all finding much the same results: environment has a major effect on intellectual growth.

2 Orphanage studies

a) Wayne Dennis

Until 1956 adoption of "foundlings" (illegitimate children) or those whose mothers could not cope was not legal in the Lebanon. In 1955, just before adoption was legalised, Wayne Dennis measured the intelligence (D.Q. and I.Q. as appropriate) of a group of children in the deprived environment of a Lebanese orphanage. Their average score was 53. (NB the "average" D.Q. and I.Q. score is 100.) Dennis also measured the I.Q. of some teenagers who had been in the institution for some years, and found that they too had I.Q.'s well below average. An impoverished environment did correlate with poor intellectual and social development in the children, ie those children raised in the least well equipped orphanages had the lowest D.Q.'s and I.Q.'s.

After 1956 many of the children were adopted, some by American

Improving children's environments does lead to an improvement in their intellectual responses, so environmental factors must be important.

couples. Fifteen years later Dennis traced and retested the children. Almost all the children showed an increase in their scores, those who were the youngest when they were adopted showed the greatest increase. Dennis suggests that Lebanese children, who are adopted by two years of age, could catch up with normally reared children. If adopted after two their intelligence stayed "behind" by the number of years spent in the orphanage after the age of two. A child adopted at five, for example, would remain around three years behind in its intellectual development. Dennis suggests that around two years might mark the end of the sensitive period for intellectual development for these children. He says ". . . there is a period near the second birthday which is critical with respect to complete recovery from the effects of . . . deprivation upon intelligence. Those adopted before age two recover completely . . . among those adopted later there is a marked persistence of retardation."

In his study Wayne Dennis found some correlations between the amount of stimulation in a child's environment and its intellectual development. But remember, positive correlation does not prove cause.

If impoverished environments hold back child development, then enriched environments should encourage it. Dennis provided increased stimulation for some orphanage children – giving them more to play with, things to watch etc. He found that the extent to which the child progressed was determined by its state of maturation – more stimulation would not improve motor or intellectual skills unless the child was maturationally ready.

b) *Skeels and Dye*

Harold Skeels and his colleagues have conducted a number of studies of children whose environments have changed. Most showed a corresponding change in their intelligence. In a 21 year longitidunal study of two groups of children, Skeels and Dye found that those who lived in the most stimulating environments increased their D.Q. and I.Q. scores over those who did not. Skeels knew about two children in a state orphanage in America who were so backward it was decided to put them in a special institution for backward children. One had an I.Q. of 35, the other's I.Q. was 46. A few months later they were retested, and now showed dramatic increases to 87 and 77 I.Q. points respectively. It seemed that the other children in the institution, and the staff, "mothered" them and gave them lots of stimulation and attention. Within two years both children were fostered, having I.Q.'s which were just below average. This observation suggests that intelligence can be influenced by the amount of stimulation a child's environment contains.

Skeels and Dye decided to test this more thoroughly. They found the D.Q.'s of 25 nineteen month old orphans in a rather deprived and overcrowded orphanage where there was little to do or see. Thirteen of them had such low D.Q.s that they were considered "unadoptable". They were then moved to an orphanage for slightly subnormal older girls who cared for the children for much of the time, acting like "substitute mothers". Eighteen months later the babies D.Q.s had risen on average by 28 points, from around 60 to nearly 90.

The 12 babies who remained in the first orphanage acted as a kind of control group. They lost up to 26 D.Q. points. Their D.Q.'s were now the same as the first group before they were moved – around 60. Two

Skeels and Dye's studies seem to support the "nurture" side of the "nature nurture" debate. But it is important to point out that I.Q. tests are notoriously unreliable and D.Q. tests for very young children aren't necessarily testing intelligence.

and a half years later the differences were still there, and when Skeels tested them again when the two groups were 21 years old those from the "better" environment were still ahead.

Koluchova's longitidunal study

Do you remember Jarmila Koluchova's report of the MZ twin Czechoslovakian boys who'd been kept isolated from 18 months to seven years old? Their D.Q.s were very low when they were found, but by their middle teens their I.Q. scores were 100 and 101.

3 Operation Headstart

During the 1950s and 60s in America, many children were leaving school with very little education and no qualifications. Many came from the ethnic minorities and the poorer home backgrounds. The fact that they were unqualified, and the general shortage of decent jobs for unskilled people meant that many were living on Welfare benefits, and some were turning to crime.

An anthropologist called Oscar Lewis suggested that their lack of success in education was due to the fact that many lived in deprived neighbourhoods which did not have the usual facilities like libraries, parks, theatres etc. (An anthropologist is someone who studies the relationships people have within their culture.) These children often spoke their own native language at home, so their American "English" was poor. Lewis concluded that their culture was deprived when compared to that of "normal" American children. This deprived or impoverished culture would hold those groups of children back in later life, which would be bad for them, and quite possibly bad for America as a whole since they would end up in the dead end jobs, or on Welfare, or in prison!

In response to this, and as a part of a much wider government policy to combat poverty, called the "War On Poverty", the government made a massive attempt at enrichment, to improve the culture of these children. It spent 17 billion dollars on a series of programmes of "compensatory education" for disadvantaged children. Some of the programmes emphasised social development, some emphasised cognitive development. The general aim was that 100 000 "deprived" children would receive some preschool remedial education. One of the best known programmes of compensatory education was "Operation Headstart" which started in the summer of 1965.

Most of the children in the American Operation Headstart programmes came from poor homes which lacked many of the basic necessities. Their diet was often inadequate too. Project Headstart was based on the idea that their culture wasn't as good as the "native" American culture, and proposed to make them more like "normal" Americians.

The people running Headstart often had different ideas about what the children needed. Some of the centres were very "education centred", with children being taught discipline as well as basic skills. Others were more "child centred", trying to help children be more sociable, co-operative, or confident. Most of the children in Headstart and similar programmes would go on visits to parks, and have people come into their neighbourhoods, even into their homes and teach them about road safety and where to play. They had extra teaching in English and maths, they received free medical and dental checkups, and generally encouraged to absorb the competitive atmosphere that dominates American schools. In this way, it was argued, they would be academically as prepared for junior school as their native American classmates, and they would be able to join in the games, the competitions, the individual achievements etc, too.

Most of the children benefited from their early enrichment. However, once they were in school many of the Headstart children started to fall behind their better off classmates. Many coped better than they may have done before, at least for the first few years of schooling, but very few actually improved very much by the end of it. By nine or 10 years of age, the vast majority had slipped behind their better off American counterparts.

So why didn't more of the children who went through these compensatory education programmes improve in their schooling? Perhaps, the influence of the home and family as the child grew was greater than the influence of spending a few hours a day in the programme when it was young. Those Headstart programmes that involved parents did seem to be more successful than others. Enrichment only seems to have any real chance of success when all the areas of one's life are affected, for example when a child is removed from one institution, such as a poor orphanage, and reared by loving parents. A few extra hours of "enrichment" could not begin to outweigh the disadvantages of being brought up in a poor, deprived environment.

4 Twin studies

It is common to find similarities amongst identical twins. To have so many similarities seems to demand that genetic pre-programming does have a role to play in understanding some human behaviour. However many of these similarities could be explained by coincidence, and most have little to do with intelligence. Using a basement for woodwork, owning a dog called Toy, tinting one's hair the same colour, liking and disliking similar things etc do not prove anything

Some critics argued that Operation Headstart probably failed to produce many lasting effects because children's intelligence is determined at birth. It's more likely that Headstart wasn't the success that many hoped it would be because the children spent most of their time in the home environment that lacked the kind of intellectual stimulation they needed.

Background reading – Operation Headstart

The number of children who could benefit from Headstart was about five times greater than the government had realised, and the first year's cost came to 96 billion dollars. In all about half a million people were involved in Headstart at over 4,700 centres. There were 100 000 doctors, dentists, and teachers for a start!

Over the next few years the numbers increased still further. There were 200 000 more children in the scheme by 1967.

By the late 1960s doubt was being cast on the success of Headstart. A study in 1969 found no differences in the educational performance of children who'd been through Headstart compared to those who hadn't. Funding for the scheme was not increased further, and the number of people involved started to fall. Some psychologists started to reject the idea that intelligence can be altered by changing environmental factors, and that it was, as Binet said, fixed at birth.

Over nine million children have now been through Headstart, and although there are still more poor people now in America than ever before, it seems that Headstart does have some long term benefits that couldn't have been realised in 1969. In one study it was found that Headstart children were less likely to appear in the crime statistics, more likely to finish college, less likely to become pregnant before marriage, less likely to need to live on Welfare benefits etc. It was estimated that if all these things are costed, for every thousand dollars spent on preschool provision the community saves four thousand dollars later on not having to pay Welfare, and not needing so many policemen, jails etc.

Twins may be socialised to emphasise their similarities. They may learn to accept and expect that they are similar, and must remain so. They share the same environment even more so than normal brothers and sisters.

about identical genotypes.

And what about all the differences between the twins that we aren't told about? Perhaps one twin was a deeply religious person and the other was an atheist. Perhaps one twin always started the day with a large glass of carrot juice and the other twin hated carrot juice. We are only told about the "startling" similarities, which imply that there must be something mysterious about them.

Peter Wilson has gathered and analysed the available information on twin studies (published in his book *Twins* in 1981). He is not convinced by the genetic nature of the similarities. He suggests that mothers treat identical twins in very similar ways, doing the same things with both of them, dressing them in similar clothes, and emphasising all the similarities between them. Once established this early bond may be hard to break. The individuals are treated as a unit and similarities in their behaviour, tastes, expectations etc. may well stem from this. The twins may become dependent on each other, and their socialisation will not be "ordinary".

Exercise – Twin studies

1 Does the fact that some identical twins have a number of similarities mean that their intelligence will also be similar?

2 Some similarities can be explained by "statistical coincidence". What does this mean?

Conclusion

Trying to "untangle" whether human intelligence is the result of genetic or environmental factors is a) impossible, and b) a complete

---

Background reading – Twin studies

Scientists at Minnesota University, USA, have been studying monozygotic twins for 15 years. Many striking similarities have been found amongst the 20 or so twin–pairs so far studied. Here is the case of some twin boys – adopted within two months of birth. Both married a girl called Linda, divorced her and married a girl called Betty. One twin named his first son James Alan. The other names his Alan James. Both children had owned a dog named Toy.
Both had worked in the same type of jobs.
Both spend their holidays at the same place.
Both chain smoke the same cigarettes.
Both have vasectomies.
Both have had two heart attacks.
Both have had haemorrhoids.
Both have basement workshops and do wood-work.
Both had the same favourite subject at school.

Both have white benches built around the trunk of a tree in their gardens, etc, etc.

Other twins show striking similarities. A British pair bought the same type, make and colour of diary for the same year – even filled out the same pages! Another pair had both fallen down stairs in the same year and injured their ankles. Two others, both tinted their greying hair the same shade of auburn, both enjoy the same two authors, both fell down stairs at the same age, both met their future husbands at town hall dances, both laugh compulsively, both suffered miscarriages with their first babies, then both had two boys followed by a girl, both hated Maths and games at school, both had been Girl Guides, both loved ballroom dancing. When they met for the first time since they were adopted, they turned up wearing identical dresses.

waste of time. There's little doubt that both environment (nurture) and heredity (nature) are involved. One useful explanation of the origin of intelligence sees our genetic inheritance as a rubber band. People who could be intelligent have long rubber bands, less bright people have shorter bands. The environment which we grow up in decides whether our band is stretched.

It is obviously true that we inherit certain potentials for developing intellectually from our parents. It is also true that whatever potentials we possess will not develop unless they are stimulated by factors in the environment.

Exercise – The rubber band hypothesis

This graph shows the effects of environment on genetic potential. The length of the rubber band represents the potential for intellectual development which is fixed at birth. The amount of stimulation in someone's environment will determine how intelligent they actually become.

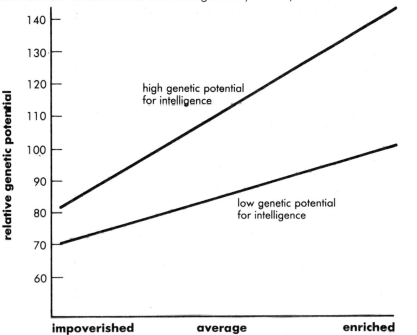

The Rubber Band Hypothesis

Enriching the environment for someone with a low genetic potential could lead to an increase of something like 30 I.Q. points. Someone with a higher genetic potential may be able to improve by up to 60 I.Q. points.

1 What is the average I.Q. score?
2 Can someone with a low genetic potential ever achieve a higher IQ than someone with a higher genetic potential?

Background reading – Statistical coincidence?

There are about 4,300 million people on earth. Many of them are bound to have some similar characteristics. There are 14 900 000 000 000 000 trees. Many of these will be similar, yet we are not surprised at this. There are estimated to be about 3 000 000 000 000 000 000 000 000 000 000 000 000 000 000 000 000 000 000 000 000 000 000 000 000 000 living things on this planet. Similarities and coincidences should occur. The chances of winning the football pools are 1 in 22 000 000, but every week some people win and we are not surprised at this. You have a very much greater chance of being struck by lightning than of winning the pools. It's only 1 in 2 million!

3 What sort of things provide "enrichment"?

4 Outline Skeel's findings from the 25 orphanage children he studied.

In view of these findings, some people have wondered whether we could create a perfect environment, and teach all parents to use ideal child rearing methods, so that every child would develop its full potential for intelligence, being co-operative and caring and all the other human qualities that many parents find desirable. Unfortunately this isn't realistic, for the simple reason that we all have different genotypes, and different things stimulate different people in different ways.

Answers to the intelligence test items

Answer	Explanation
a) M	A [B C] D [E F] G [H I] J [K L] = M
H	H I J K L M N O P Q are from the alphabet. Reading backwards we have Q P, missing the next two gives us M L, missing the next two gives us I and H.

b) Wood becomes coal if left long enough under pressure.
Apple and peach are both edible fruits.
Ship and car are both forms of transport.

c) It's Monday tomorrow so we go back to school.

d) Post means the same as stake and mail.

e) Kitten

        tootap = potato
        prinut = turnip
        tintek = kitten
        otrrac = carrot

Cardiff isn't in England
        Grothnib = Brighton
        Yuqtora = Torquay
        Drifcaf   = Cardiff
        Hercest   = Chester
        Sheeldiff = Sheffield

6b The nature/nurture debate on visual perception

Those psychologists who emphasised the importance of biological inheritance claimed that intelligence was a result of the genes we inherit from our parents. Those who support the learning theory approach claim that intelligent behaviour is the result of learning in our environment. Piaget's view of cognitive development seems to combine the two. Most modern psychologists might conclude that "intelligence" is some kind of genetically transmitted potential whose development appears to be influenced by the environment. Would the same be true of other aspects of human development? Such visual skills as the ability to recognise certain shapes, to perceive depth, to realise that objects stay the same size when they are nearer to us or further away, and the ability to judge distance may all have some "survival value", and may be present at birth. Or they may be there, but need some experience to allow them to develop. Or perception may be a combination of both.

The Nature view – Perception is innate

Pattern Perception

Do infants perceive objects as wholes? Do they have any preference for looking at one shape or texture rather than another? The main work in this area has been conducted by Robert Fantz beginning in the 1960s. He started with some chicks which he hatched in total darkness. Since chicks will peck at grain soon after birth, and before they could have learned that grain is their food, it seems reasonable to assume that they have an instinctive knowledge of what their food looks like. So Fantz gave them 8 different shaped objects and recorded the number of times they pecked at each of them. The objects were different shapes, from a small "ball shaped" object, similar to a grain, to pyramid shaped objects. The chicks pecked 10 times more at the round objects than the ones which didn't look anything like grains. Fantz concluded that chicks innately recognise round shapes and objects with three dimensions. This supports the nature view that shape recognition in chicks is innate. Since chicks rely much more on instinct, and are much more mobile than human infants, it isn't really surprising that being able to recognise "food" would be genetically inherited. Like "following the first thing they see", knowing what food looks like should have considerable "survival value".

The question which arises from this research by Fantz concerns whether human infants have any kind of recognition for things which could have "survival value" for them? Fantz tested some human infants. He suggested that he could decide whether the baby liked looking at one thing or another by observing babies' eye movements, facial expressions, and body movements. If they stared and looked happy when shown one object, and looked away and became restless when shown another, then the baby must be able to perceive the form of these objects, and to prefer one to another.

To test this he designed some experimental apparatus called "**the looking chamber**". It consisted of a cot above which various objects could be suspended, and a viewing hole through which the baby's face and eyes could be observed. Objects were to be presented in pairs and the infant's reaction to each object in the pair was measured. Fantz tested 30 infants at weekly intervals, from when they were one week old, to when they were 15 weeks old. He showed them a number of shapes and patterns such as a "bulls eye" pattern, stripes of various textures, a cross, a "chess board" design, plain triangles, and plain squares. Fantz found that even the youngest generally preferred the more complex shapes such as the bulls eye and the chess board. This suggests that some degree of form perception may well be innate.

Fantz claimed to have shown that babies can perceive form or pattern from one week of age and that they can see objects of increasing complexity over the first six months. Next he investigated

The nature–nurture debate has been raised over some aspects of human visual development. Visual perception means making sense of information received through our eyes.

Fantz's Chicken 'Food'

Fantz showed that chicks can instinctively recognise "food shaped" objects. Why might this have survival value? Is there any reason to suspect that anything similar might exist in humans?

Fantz's 'Looking chamber'

Fantz's "looking chamber" experiments suggested that young babies do seem to prefer looking at complex, round shapes. These might appear to be "face shaped" to the child.

whether babies have a preference for the human face, as opposed to other shapes. (You may remember from Chapter Three that Ahrens had suggested that they did.)

Exercise – Form perception

1 How did Fantz measure the babies' ability to recognise and show if they preferred any particular patterns?

2 What sample size was used in this experiment?

3 What IV's are used here?

4 What is the DV and how is it measured?

5 What does Fantz conclude about the origin of form perception?

6 Can you think of any potentially confounding variables in either the patterns presented, or the way in which they are presented?

7 Outline some of the main difficulties in using babies as subjects in experiments such as this.

The human neonate's preferences for looking at the human face

Fantz had three pictures which he could show to babies in the looking chamber. The first was a "face" with black features painted on a pink background. The next was the same as the first but the features were all jumbled up, and the third was a pink "face shape" without any features, except the top part was black (to resemble hair).

Fantz sampled 49 infants, from just four days old, up to six months old. He showed them the three "faces" in every possible combination. Most of the infants ignored the face without features. The six month olds barely glanced at it. The children up to about three and a half months of age seemed interested in the "scrambled" face. However the infants all seemed slightly more interested in the picture that most resembled a real face. The differences weren't great, but enough for Fantz to conclude that babies do have an innate awareness of, and preference for, the human face. This claim aroused considerable interest among ethologists who claimed that babies have innate capacities to recognise, and therefore attach to, their caregivers.

Criticism The difference between the babies' reactions to the "face" and "scrambled face" were not very great, and other researchers have used Fantz's methods and repeated his experiments, but either do not obtain the same results, or explain them in other ways. For example some found that very young babies had no preference for one picture over any other, and any that did were simply preferring symmetrical patterns to jumbled ones.

Older babies did seem to prefer the face shapes, but by then they could have learned to associate the human face with food and comfort. Anyway the pictures which Fantz showed to the babies were rather unrealistic two dimensional drawings of "faces" coloured pink and black. They didn't really look like human faces at all.

Perhaps the reason for the error in Fantz's early work was his method – just because a baby looks at one shape more than another doesn't have to mean that it prefers one over another.

REVIEW – Pattern perception

Fantz claimed to have shown that very young babies can only perceive a certain level of detail, but this increases over the first months. He claimed that they have an innate preference for looking at the human face, but this claim has not been confirmed.

Exercise – Pattern perception

1 Summarise Fantz's experiment to demonstrate infants' abilities to recognise certain shapes.

2 Summarise the main criticisms of the basis for these claims.

Depth, distance and direction Perception

If humans do have some innate preference for looking at round "face like" shapes, do they have any other innate visual skills? The ability to perceive depth has been demonstrated in a number of newborn animals. The classic experiment in depth perception was conducted by Eleanor Gibson and Richard Walk in 1960.

Gibson and Walk constructed some apparatus known as the "visual cliff" which consisted of a glass shelf which had a "shallow side" and a "deep side". Checked cloth could be seen just under the glass on the shallow side, and at some depth on the deep side. Some newborn animals were placed on the shelf, and Gibson and Walk noted whether they would wander all over it, or would prefer either side. Most of them would not walk over the "deep side". Even one day old chicks never strayed onto the "deep side". Lambs and kids placed on the "deep" side refused to stand, and kittens either froze or circled backwards aimlessly. Rats base their depth perception more on touch, by using their whiskers rather than on vision. They wandered across either side. But when their whiskers were trimmed, and they were forced to use vision, they then wouldn't move onto the "deep" side. This seems to confirm the view that animals have innate depth perception.

Gibson and Walk also put some human infants on the visual cliff apparatus. Thirty-six infants between six and 14 months of age were studied. They were placed on a ledge in between the "shallow" and "deep" sides. Their mothers called them alternatively from one side, then from the other side. Nine infants refused to move at all, but the 27 infants who did would crawl to their mothers over the "shallow" side, and only three would crawl over the "deep" side. Some crawled away from their mothers when called from the "deep" side, others just cried because they couldn't reach their mothers. Some of the infants fell onto the glass on the "deep" side, and started to crawl towards their mothers, until they looked down. Once they saw the checked cloth at some distance below them they became very distressed. Before looking down these babies were presumably using their sense of touch, which told them that the surface they were crawling over was safe. As soon as they looked down their sense of vision must have overruled their sense of touch. Even in infants vision is a most powerful channel of information.

Gibson and Walk don't claim that this experiment proves that depth perception is innate in humans. The experiment needed infants who could crawl, so they had to be about six months old. A great deal of learning takes place during the first six months of life so the babies could have learned depth perception. Gibson and Walk did say that the results support their view that depth perception is innate in animals.

Gibson and Walk's visual cliff experiment has shown that depth perception is innate in some animals. Does knowing this help us to resolve the nature nurture dispute in humans? Explain your answer.

The 'Visual Cliff'

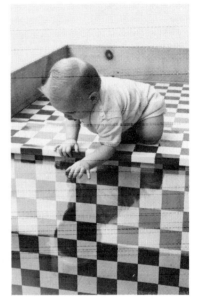

What does Gibson and Walk's "visual cliff" apparatus need the baby to be able to do? How might this confound any claim that this experiment supports the "nature" view?

Background reading – How do we perceive depth?

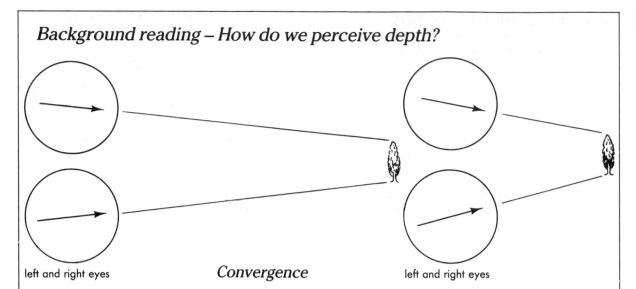

left and right eyes   *Convergence*   left and right eyes

Our eyes are set about 6 cm apart. The "picture" we receive from each of them is slightly different. This is called retinal disparity. You can see this by looking at something quite close to you first with one eye, then with the other. If you look at something from a distance then the "pictures" are very similar. The part of our brain which is mainly responsible for interpreting what we see (the visual cortex) compares the pictures it receives from each of our eyes, and judges how similar the pictures are. The more similar the picture is, the further away the object we are looking at must be.

Information from the muscles which move the eyeball is also sent to the brain, for example, if an object is close to us, our eyes turn slightly inwards. If it is more than about 50 metres away, they look straight ahead. This turning of the eyeball is called convergence, and it can also give us clues about how near the object we are looking at is.

Our eyes and ears have one ability that our other senses do not. They exchange information with each other, so if the thing we are looking at makes any sound, that sound could help us judge its distance from us.

There are a number of clues in the environment which may help us to perceive depth. Gibson and Walk suggest that motion parallax is one. This refers to the way in which nearer objects seem to move more quickly than distant objects. When driving at night the moon doesn't seem to move at all, but the houses at the side of the road whizz by. If your brain is sent messages that some object hardly seems to move, whilst it knows that you are moving, then it may reason that the object is some distance away.

Other clues to depth include "relative size". If you see a horse and a double decker bus in the distance, and they look the same size, the horse must be closer to you. You know that horses are smaller than buses. "Interposition" is where one object blocks the view of another. It must be nearer. "Shadowing" provides another clue. If one object casts its shadow onto another whilst the light is coming from the observer's position, then it must be in front.

Relative Size

Exercise – Depth perception

1 What was the sample size for children?

2 What was the purpose behind the visual cliff experiment?

3 What was the DV in this experiment?

4 What evidence is there in the passage to suggest that perception may be innate in animals?

5 Explain why these findings may not be used to solve the nature nurture debate on depth perception in humans.

Exercise – Cues to perceiving depth

Summarise the evidence which has been used to show that depth perception is innate?

Tom Bower's research into the visual abilities of young babies

Distance and direction

Tom Bower has investigated babies' abilities to judge distance and direction. Doctors use the baby's "defensive reaction" to test whether babies are blind. An object is moved towards the infants face. If the infant is blind, there will be no reaction. If, however, the infant can see the approaching object, it will try to move out of the path of the object. It will also lift its hands as if to protect its face. It is possible that the child is responding to the rush of air towards his face as the object approaches. To test this more thoroughly Bower arranged an experiment with three experimental conditions.

Condition (1)

A cube is moved towards the baby's face at the same time the air around it is displaced. This produced the classic "defensive" response.

Condition (2)

The air was displaced, but there was no object. The babies made no attempt to protect themselves.

Condition (3)

The object was moved towards the baby, but the air was not displaced. (The baby saw a film of the travelling object.) This produced no reaction at all.

Babies can tell the direction of an approaching object well. They become disturbed if objects appear to be heading straight for their faces, but do not show concern when the same object would miss them, even by just an inch or two! The "defensive reaction" is also probably innate. This would make sense since it could have considerable "survival value".

These experiments also illustrate some of the limitations of the baby's visual system. It can take in a great deal of information, but cannot process that information as quickly as an adult, for example, in the "defensive reaction" experiment, if the object was heading for the

Gibson and Walk's experiment showed that very young animals appear to have innately acquired abilities to judge depth. The babies they used on the visual cliff were six months old however, and during that time they could have learned about depth and distance.

baby at any great speed, then it didn't respond at all. The information would probably have been sent to the brain, but the brain isn't mature and well organised enough to respond very quickly.

Size Constancy

An orange held half a metre from your eyes will cast quite a large image on your retinas. The orange held two metres away will cast a much smaller one.

Yet we know that it is still the same orange, not a satsuma which has suddenly appeared! This is known as size constancy. There are other visual constancies, of course. You know that something doesn't change its shape just because you see it from different angles. You know the colour of your front room curtains, whether you're passing them on a sunny day, or returning home in the middle of the night. They appear to be different colours; you know that they are not.

In 1966 Tom Bower conducted an experiment to investigate whether size constancy was innate or learned. A supporter of the nurture side would argue that young infants would not show size constancy because they would not have had time to learn it. A nativist would argue that the baby would show size constancy because it is an innate ability.

A sample of babies of just a few weeks old were used. Each in turn is placed on a table in a comfortable cot from which it could see a screen. Behind the screen is a 30 cm cube. It is set one metre away from the child.

When the screen was moved and the baby saw the cube it was reinforced. Bower used operant conditioning to teach the child that if it turned its head to one side when it saw the cube (or when it became bored of looking at the cube) it would be rewarded by its mother playing "peek-a-boo" and tickling it. [See Chapter Seven for an explanation of the terms used here.] After several trials the baby would be conditioned to turn its head towards its mother when it saw the 30 cm cube. Now the 30 cm cube was moved back to three metres from the child, and the number of head turns was counted. It was still the same cube. In the third condition the original cube was removed and one three times as big was put one metre from the child. Bower knew that a cube three times as big (90 cm) set three times as far away (three metres) would cast the same size image on the retina as the original cube. So in the fourth condition the larger cube was placed at three metres. If the baby perceives this new cube to be the same as the original cube it should turn its head for its reward.

The four experimental conditions therefore are
(1) a 30 cm cube at one metre
(2) a 30 cm cube at three metres
(3) a 90 cm cube at one metre
(4) a 90 cm cube at three metres.

In each experimental condition the number of times the child turns its head for a reward can then be used as a measure of how similar the child thinks each cube is to the one it is conditioned to look at.

If babies are born with size constancy they should respond most to 1) and 2) since these conditions use the original cube. They should respond rather less to 3) and least to 4). If they have to learn size constancy then they should respond most to 1), then most to the one that cast the same size retinal image (condition 4)), then condition 3), and least to condition 2).

Here is a table of Bower's results.

Experimental Condition	Number of correct responses
(1) 30 cm at one metre	98
(2) 30 cm at three metres	58
(3) 90 cm at one metre	54
(4) 90 cm at three metres	22

These results seem to support the nativist view – babies are born with size constancy. As the baby could recognise the original size cube at different distances it also suggests that depth perception (or a form of it) is innate.

Bower's Experiment

Exercise – Bower's experiments

1 Summarise the conclusions from Bower's "distance and direction" experiment.

2 What would Tom Bower's hypothesis for this experiment have been?

3 What would Tom Bower's hypothesis for the size constancy experiment have been?

4 Explain the method Bower used to teach the babies to turn their heads.

5 Explain the nurturist prediction (given above) for the DV.

6 Explain what the results actually show.

REVIEW – Size constancy

Tom Bower used very young infants to show that they seemed able to judge size, shape, and distance. This is further confirmation that these sorts of visual skills are innate.

Several experiments have shown that humans can make an adaptation to an altered experience, but the adaptation may not be visual. The subjects may well have learned to cope with an altered visual experience.

REVIEW – The Nurture view

Studies showing that humans can make some adjustment to a perceptually distorted world provide further evidence of just how well integrated various aspects of the human sensory system are. We can adapt our behaviour to suit the distorted world. However adapting our behaviour is not the same as adapting our vision. Even if adults could learn to make visual adaptations to distorted visual perceptions, that doesn't mean that babies have to learn to adapt to a "normal" visual world.

The Nurture view – The case for learning

If perception had to be learned, then someone who had been unable to see, and who then had their sight restored, would take some time to learn to recognise all the things that normal people take for granted. For example a "sighted" person would recognise things like a double decker bus, a dolphin, a block of flats, a mountain, and an aeroplane from photographs of them. Someone who has just had an operation to give them their sight may not. It will take them some time to learn what the various things they can see are called. However just because adults can learn visual skills like recognising objects and judging distance, this doesn't mean that babies have to learn them.

If visual perception in humans is learned, then humans should be able to learn to change their behaviour if their visual experiences are changed. The following experiments suggest that this is the case.

Stratton (1897) wore a lens over one eye, which turned his view of the world (through that eye) upside down. He kept the prism on for eight days. He covered the other eye with a patch, forcing him to look through the lens. By the fifth day he was able to walk around without bumping into things. While he was moving around everything looked "normal", but as soon as he stopped, and concentrated on an object, it appeared to be upside down.

J and J K Peterson (1938) used inverting lenses on both eyes of a sample of people, and found similar results to Stratton. Eight months later they retested their subjects and found that they adapted to their upside down world more quickly than before. They soon returned to behaviour they had learned during the first trials. So humans can learn to adapt – but maybe not fully. In the Peterson's experiment, even after two weeks not all of the subjects had fully adapted to their new world.

Kohler (1962) wore a variety of goggles with lenses which distorted vision in a number of different ways. Some had differently coloured lenses, some turned the line of sight slightly to the left or right etc. After a few hours of wearing each of his "distorting lenses" he was able to adjust to cope with his changed visual experiences.

There are some criticisms of these "**readjustment**" studies. Human beings do seem able to make some adaptation to changes to their visual experiences. However these adaptations may not be "visual adaptations" at all. They may be simply learning what to do to compensate for the visual distortion. For example seeing something which you know is set off to the left by a few degrees will not stop you learning to point at it accurately. It may not be new visual learning though, it may be simply adapting your behaviour. Some of our senses, such as our sense of balance and the senses which respond to muscle and limb movements are generally described as our "body sense", or "**proprioception**". Proprioception adapts to altered vision. When the Peterson's subjects learned to move around they were adjusting to an upside down world, not seeing one which was the correct way up.

Combining the two views – The need for genetics and learning

So far we've seen evidence which seems to support either the nature view, or the nurture view. Few psychologists now would disagree with the idea that visual perception relies on both genetics and learning. For the first few months of life the baby's visual system isn't fully developed. The nerves carrying information about what the infant is looking at in the visual areas of the brain, aren't as well insulated as they will become. This results in "interference" (like a radio that isn't quite tuned properly). Some of the signals are lost, others get confused. As the baby's visual system matures so its ability to see and perceive will improve.

Despite these limitations babies can see fairly well right from birth. We can do tests to measure how far a baby can see, and even what sort of things it can see. This supports the nature argument. We cannot know what it makes of the things it sees. Genevieve Carpenter showed that by two weeks of age a baby may recognise its mother, and will expect her face to move and change expression. Other research suggests that babies of just 36 hours will recognise and imitate certain facial expressions under certain conditions. Clearly early experience is necessary for the infant to make sense of what it can see.

Other evidence for the need for both innate factors and experience comes from studies of animals who have been deprived of various kinds of visual experience.

Deprivation studies with animals

A N Reisen (1950) deprived one male and one female chimpanzee of sight for their first 16 months of life, except for some short (45 second) periods each day when they were fed. When exposed to light at 16 months they showed the following reactions: their pupils weren't as open as normally reared monkeys, they were frightened by sudden intense light, they did not blink when sudden, threatening movements were made towards their faces, and they showed no interest in their toys unless they touched them with some part of their bodies.

One chimp then had longer periods in the light until it was 21 months old. It developed normal sight. It could recognise objects, had good "hand to eye" co-ordination etc. The other chimp was kept in darkness until 33 months. When exposed to normal light it behaved in the same way as it had earlier. Its abilities improved slightly over the next few weeks, then declined.

It seems that chimps (and presumably other animals) need light during the first year or so, for their eyes to develop normally. If this is correct, then it would be necessary to rear subjects who can see light, but not see objects. Reisen reared another chimpanzee who was made to wear a translucent mask which allowed one and a half hours of diffused, unpatterned light to enter the eye each day. (Like looking through greaseproof paper.) The mask was removed at seven months. This chimp also did not develop normal sight.

However Reisen's experiments were often carried out on very few (and sometimes only one) subjects and so we must be cautious about any generalisations we make from them. Some of Reisen's operationalised experimental procedures can be questioned, for example, the chimps reared in darkness had 45 seconds a day (feeding time) of

Reisen's results suggest that patterns are needed as well as light for normal visual development. In other words environment (nurture) is necessary for the development of normal visual perception.

light. Maybe this was enough to allow the development of some visual abilities.

Colin Blakemore and Grahame Cooper (1966) reared kittens in large drums so that they could only see vertical or horizontal black and white stripes. The critical period for kittens developing visual skills was thought to be from three to 15 weeks of life. Their visual abilities were tested from when they were five months old. At first they did not recognise anything with edges that were different from the ones they'd grown up with. Those brought up to see only vertical lines weren't supposed to be able to see horizontal lines. They bumped into anything which had no vertical lines, such as a pencil waved horizontally across their path. This does not mean that responses to lines are purely environmental. It could be that the cat's ability to respond to vertical lines and horizontal lines is there at birth, but the cells which respond to horizontal lines may not have developed. There is a problem with the design of this experiment however. No doubt many of the playful kittens would have rolled around and moved their heads to different angles, during the time they were allowed to see the stripes. The result is that they would be seeing stripes at different angles. Some independent judges couldn't tell which of the kittens had been raised amongst vertical stripes, and which amongst horizontal stripes.

Richard Held and Alan Hein (1965) designed some apparatus to overcome the problem of the cat's movement. They wanted to see if their bodies, particularly their paws, affected visual development in kittens. Their apparatus, called "**the kitten carousel**", gave two

Blakemore and Cooper suggested that the visual system needs a variety of shapes and patterns to stimulate it. Their experimental subjects could have received such stimulation.

Kitten Carousel

kittens the same amount of the same type of visual experience. They were linked together by a series of pulleys and strings.

One kitten (called the active kitten) could move around inside a drum and its actions were transmitted to the other kitten (called the passive kitten) through the pulleys. The kittens were given three hours' exposure to light on the apparatus every day for several weeks. When tested for "paw to eye co-ordination" it was found that the active kittens were far superior. For example after 30 hours' exposure all the active kittens could put their paws where they wanted. None of the passive kittens could. Experience in the environment seems necessary for "normal" development.

There is a problem with these kinds of experiments. We cannot say that deprived animals do not perceive, only that they do not act as if they perceive. We have studied their behavioural responses to various forms of deprivation, but haven't begun to study their visual experiences.

Held and Hein's kitten carousel experiment still does not prove that nature nurture debate either way. Their results were not entirely conclusive, and we can never know exactly what the animals could perceive.

Conclusion

A newborn's skills such as depth perception, size constancy, and pattern recognition are impressive. Most of the research seems to support the "**nature modified by nurture**" view that most psychologists hold today. We are not so interested nowadays in what skill is innate or learned. Instead we are more interested in what skills babies can have, and how we can encourage our children to use their skills to their greatest advantage.

Humans are born with a number of skills that will develop if their environment allows them to develop. Babies have other skills that we can only guess at. Even very young babies will imitate their mother's facial expressions. But when mother sticks her tongue out, and baby imitates, how can it possibly know what part of its mother's face is being "funny". How does it know that the thing which is sticking out is a tongue, and how could it know that the thing in its mouth, which it has never seen, is also a tongue. Why should the baby *want to* imitate its mother anyway? Why does the baby want to be sociable? Perhaps that's innate too. Many researchers suggest that it is.

REVIEW – Combining the two views

Several animal studies have shown that parts of the visual system need a variety of changing visual experiences, and interaction with the environment, in order to mature. Both nature and nurture are needed for the full range of visual skills to be developed.

Exercise – Is perception innate or learned?

1 Summarise the evidence for each side of the nature/nurture debate on size constancy.

2 Describe some of the evidence from studies of animals which suggests that the environment may be necessary for the development of visual perception.

3 Describe three different techniques that have been used to study the perceptual skills of babies or young children.

A boy shouting

13 The Development of Language and Communication

The study of the origins and development of language is called "**linguistics**". Until quite recently it was not really considered to be a part of psychology at all. Those who supported the "nature" side of the "nature nurture" debate would claim that language was an ability that humans developed when they were maturationally ready. It was used for communication and had little to do with topics concerning the human mind and human behaviour which psychologists were interested in. However Piaget, and others, have emphasised the importance of the child's own contribution to its socialisation. Children should be actively involved in exploring and discovering things for themselves. The ability to ask, to find out, and to share knowledge will help children to expand their understanding. During the first two years of a child's life it will become mobile, and so actively able to explore, and it will learn to talk. Both these achievements will transform the seemingly rather helpless infant into a sociable and inquisitive human being. Like Piaget, Jerome Bruner has spent many years studying children's cognitive development. Whilst Piaget emphasised the child's interaction with its environment as the main factor in intellectual development Bruner goes further than Piaget in stressing the importance of language in intellectual growth. He refers to "*symbolic representation*" as one of the most important ways in which we come to understand our world. Bruner argues that the ability to organise ideas into those which are more, or less important, and to know "what goes with what", would contribute just as much as a stimulating environment. Language would be essential in organising ideas. Largely because of the work of researchers such as Jerome Bruner, Jean Piaget, and B F Skinner, the study of language is now seen as an important part of psychology.

In this chapter we will be interested in

1 What exactly language and communication are,

2 How psychologists study them,

3 The "stages" of language development in children, and

4 The main theories to explain language,

5 Whether only humans can use language, or whether any animals can be taught to communicate.

1 What is language

Let's start with a definition. To put it simply, language is an organised system of symbols which humans use to communicate. These symbols can be spoken, signed (so called "deaf and dumb language"), or

We've all heard dogs barking, cats meowing, birds singing, and cows mooing. Compare these sounds to what you'd hear in any park or school playground where children are playing. What do you imagine that the animals are trying to communicate? What are some of the things that the children may be communicating?

Write a two sentence definition of "language". Then look it up and see how close you were.

Try to answer these questions yourself, then try them on your family and friends. Make a note of whether they could answer all the questions.

Are the hand signs that dumb people make to each other "language"?
Is there any such thing as "body language"?
Are the flags that ships fly signalling distress "language"?
Is Morse Code "language"?
Are the ways in which we talk to computers "language"?
Can animals such as dolphins use "language"?
Is it possible to say at what age babies stop "babbling" and start using "language"?

All spoken languages consist of phonemes, which are the basic sounds, and morphemes, which are groups of phonemes which have some meaning in the particular language.

What do the following communications mean, and how exact is their meaning?
The red flag flying at the seaside?
A green traffic light?
The "thumbs up" sign?
A dog barking at another dog?
A "No Smoking" sign in a classroom?
A "Keep off the Grass" sign in the park?
A "DANGER KEEP AWAY" sign on an electricity generator?

Children shouting

The earliest method for studying children's speech was by keeping detailed diaries. This method does give a longitudinal record, but generalisations made from the small and biased samples used may not be very helpful.

written down, such as handwriting, printing, or braille. Spoken language consists of sounds like "f" and "ish" (which are called **phonemes**) which, when combined, have meanings like "fish" (which are called **morphemes**).

Communication is rather easier to understand. It is the transmission of something (usually some message or some meaning), from one place to another. The meaning of the communication may be vague, or precise.

Our ability to use "language" is one of the main things which separates us from the rest of the animal kingdom. As far as we know, humans are the only species which have the ability to use *language*. Various animals have been studied, most widely known may be dolphins, to see if they use anything like a language system. Many animal species *communicate* with each other. If one zebra senses a predator it will start to run. This is taken by the rest of the herd to be a sign to run too. The first animal is communicating with the others, it isn't "talking" to them. When the honey bee performs its "figure of eight" dance back in the colony it will rattle its wings together in a way which communicates to the others that a useful source of pollen is to be found in a particular direction. Dolphins appear to have some high pitched sounds which they use to communicate simple messages to other dolphins. Each species seems to be equipped with just as much ability to communicate as they need in order to thrive in their environment. Humans live in very complex environments, and have very complex relationships with each other. Perhaps we are the only species which "needs" such a sophisticated communication system as language.

Exercise – What is language?

Write a paragraph beginning "The difference between language and communication is . . ."

2 How do psychologists study language development

During the nineteenth century some people started to take an interest in how language develops. They listened carefully to growing children's "speech", and kept careful diaries of what they said. Piaget used the *diary method* a great deal for studying the cognitive development of his own three children in the 1920s and early 1930s.

The diary method does have some advantages. It is longitudinal, often lasting for the first five or six years of the child's life. It is conducted by someone who knows the child well, who knows "what it means by" whatever strange thing it is actually "saying". The child will behave "normally" with someone it knows, and the recording is a complete record since it can include every day in the child's life. But it also has some severe disadvantages too. The record may be "patchy", not covering all of the child's speech, and a study of one or two or three children cannot be representative of all children. Most of the diary keepers were well educated and so provided rather "better" models for their children to learn from than might many parents from the poorer groups in society. Parents may not be the most reliable people to study their own children, and whilst they are writing down what the child has said, many other words and sentences may be missed.

During the 1950s and 1960s tape recorders became more widely available and affordable. The *tape recording method* allowed several children of the same age to be recorded, and an "average" made of their abilities. The children could be visited every week or fortnight, and everything they said, for example, during one hour, could be recorded. What was being measured was how far the children had advanced along the road to achieving "adult type" speech. Sometimes children were brought into the laboratory so that situational variables like distractions (toys, sounds, smells etc) could be controlled. But children may not respond "naturally" in a strange laboratory as they would in their normal environment. Even in their home, when a "strange" researcher is present children may not respond normally. Remember "stranger fear"?

Speaking can be an efficient way of communicating ideas. However it's not the only means of communication that we have. When you say "I'm cold" that's a very simple way of communicating what you are feeling. But we use much more than just speech to communicate. If you are turning blue, or shivering you probably do not need to say anything at all. When a toddler tries to reach for its beaker, most mothers will probaby understand that the child wants a drink. If it screws its face up having taken the first sip the child doesn't need to say that the drink doesn't taste very pleasant. We all use **non verbal cues** such as facial expressions, body position, gestures etc to aid communication. ("Non verbal" means "without speaking", and a "cue" is something that prompts someone into doing something.)

If someone asks "How are you?" and you smile back, doesn't that answer the question? And you haven't used any words at all! We can only really know what the child is communicating if we can see what non verbal cues it is giving us. Hence *videotaping* is now widely used. Each film can be analysed by several researchers. Jerome Bruner used this approach to observe how babbling seems to help in play, which will, in turn, aid language learning later. Filming the whole scene will allow researchers to analyse both the verbal, and the non verbal components of communication. However it can be fairly time consuming, and expensive.

Listening to, and analysing, children's "normal" speech is not the only means of studying linguistic development. Psycholinguists have devised a number of *psychometric* tests such as *comprehension* tests which ask the child to choose from a number of pictures or objects the one that the researcher is naming. Unfortunately young children can only pay attention to a very few pictures or objects at any one time. Another type of test discovers the child's knowledge of the rules of grammar such as plurals, tenses etc.

The tape recorder allowed more "scientific" analysis of more children, but can only record what children say, which isn't always what they mean.

REVIEW – Methods of studying speech

As in many aspects of science, the way we study something is largely determined by the technology we have to study it. Charles Darwin and Jean Piaget used diaries to record their children's development because that was what they saw as the best method available to them. The tape recorder was widely used in the 1960s, as it became available. The video and some deliberate tests are the main techniques used now.

3 The main stages of language development

For something to occur "in stages", there must be a period of time when some activity is occurring, which gives way to another period when some different activity occurs. According to Freud our personality develops through four main stages, each dominated by some unconscious urges concentrating on an "erogenous zone". Piaget claimed that cognition also develops through four stages. Each of the stages he identified is dominated by a different type of thinking. Here we are suggesting that language occurs in stages too. You may remember that not everyone accepts that human abilities occur in "stages" at all. Behaviourists such as Skinner, for example, argue that our various abilities simply "unfold" as we gain experience and receive various reinforcers.

Children all over the world are thought to follow the same sequence in acquiring language. We will describe it as consisting of three broad stages.

The pre-linguistic stage – From birth to about twelve months

The first few months of life are dominated by the infants' "heredity" and need for "maturation". What do each of these terms mean?

Using the voice requires quite a complicated arrangement of skills. We must control our breathing, face muscles, tongue muscles, have ideas about what we want to say etc. It will take babies a few months to acquire these things. However, that doesn't mean that neonates have no knowledge of language and communication. William Condon and Louis Sander showed that by just a few hours after birth babies seem able to distinguish speech from other sounds, and they may even have a genetically acquired preference for listening to human speech. Studies of brainwave activity in babies suggest that the human voice stimulates the "language centres" in the left hemisphere of the brain, whilst music sounds stimulate areas in the right hemisphere, just as happens in adults. So babies are probably able to *discriminate* (tell the difference between) the human voice and other sounds, although that doesn't necessarily mean that the baby would know what it is listening to. Heredity and maturation dominate the first months.

Most babies start babbling by about six months. All over the world babies are likely to babble just about all the sounds which exist in any language.

Between two and six months babies start "**babbling**", that is making sounds that are similar to human speech, but not just the sounds that the baby will have heard around it. It is not simply imitating what it has heard. Some of the sounds that babies make do not occur in the language which their parents use, and which they will have heard around them. For example British born babies will make sounds that only occur in Japanese or Chinese. They have never heard these sounds before. Babbling is probably a genetically acquired response, but it can have some communication value, and can be modified by social learning.

Producing Language

A great deal of evidence now exists to show that babies benefit from social interaction. We know that children in the deprived orphanages studied by people like Wayne Dennis and Howard Skeels (see Chapter Twelve) had poor language development. We also know that infants seem to enjoy human companionship. Dan Stern has shown that babies of just a few months old move their bodies in *interactional synchrony* with human speech. Infants must wait a few months before they are maturationally ready to start making "speech like" sounds, and before they are able to start learning their particular language. These first months of life are known as the period of **pre-speech**.

During the first year of "pre speech" the infant is maturing and developing some of the ideas which it may want to communicate in language later.

Colwyn Trevarthen and Martin Richards filmed five babies, once a week, from birth to six months of age. Each baby sometimes had a toy hanging in front of it, or was with its mother. The mothers were asked to "chat" with their babies. Trevarthen and Richards wanted to know if there would be any differences between the baby's behaviour towards the toy, and towards its mother. They noticed that from about six weeks old the baby's behaviour changed when its mother was present. The babies moved their hands differently, the expressions on their faces changed, and the tone of their voices altered. They moved their lips as if trying to speak, and took turns at "speaking" with their mothers. Trevarthen calls this "elaborate activity", "pre-speech". This encouraged their mothers to respond, and so the "conversation" went on.

Even though the child can't talk, this doesn't mean it can't communicate. Several studies of parent child interaction claim that communication is an important part of their interaction.

The early, innate responses, like babbling and hand movements, were modified by interaction, with the mother. Such social relationships may modify other innate tendencies too.

Exercise – Reciprocity

1 What are Trevarthen and Richards looking for in this observational study?
2 What is the sample size, and what are the independent variables?
3 What dependent variables were being measured?
4 What is meant by pre-speech?

One explanation of how babbles become words emphasises the importance of selective reinforcement. Those sounds which are selected to be reinforced are likely to be used by the child, whilst those which are not are less likely to be repeated.

After six months babbling increases, reaching its peak at around 10 months. Jerome Bruner filmed the interaction between some mothers and their babies, and noticed that communication is an essential feature of their play. Before about nine months children will be quite passive in games like "give and take". Mother does all the giving of an object such as a toy, the baby reaches out and takes it. From about nine months the infant becomes more active, and will offer the toy to its mother. By 12 months mothers and babies are equal in the amount of "giving" and "taking" they do. Bruner suggests that games such as these give children ideas about taking turns which they will practise later with language.

By 10 months many babies are stringing sounds together such as "popopopa", "babababa", and "dididi". It may be that parents reward their children when they make "English type" sounds and don't reward them when they don't. The child may associate the making of some sounds with the warmth and comfort shown by its mother. This is mainly the explanation which learning theorists like B F Skinner would support. It may explain how children acquire some aspects of speech. The babbling sounds that are most often rewarded (or "reinforced") will be those which sound most like human speech. At the same time the baby's vocal organs and nervous system are maturing, and the baby may begin to enjoy imitating sounds it hears around it. (NB Daniel Stern has shown that babies are very sociable almost right from birth.) Quite a lot of language skill is acquired through imitation (eg when talking to a man infants' voices are usually a little louder than when talking to a woman!). They must have heard that men speak louder than women, so perhaps they are imitating what they think is the right way to speak. Babbling also seems to reinforce itself. Babies may well enjoy hearing their own noises! Profoundly deaf babies start to babble at about the same time as "normal" babies, but stop after a few months. This may be because they can't hear themselves, and so can't reinforce themselves.

REVIEW – The first twelve months

The first few months are dominated by the biological needs of "getting used to life". There's a great deal for an infant to learn, such as how to use various muscles and limbs. Babbling starts as a biologically inherited activity which probably isn't intended to convey any meaning, although it may be "shaped" later into having some meaning for itself and its caregivers. Caregiver/child interaction may prepare the child for important aspects of language, for example, taking turns.

Exercise – The pre-linguistic stage

Construct a two column table with the heading "The Pre-Linguistic Stage". Head one column "Up to six months", and the other one "Six months to one year". Write three of the baby's main skills in each column.

The first words – From one to two years

Babbling is mainly for amusement and doesn't appear to communicate anything very much. From about 10 to 12 months two important changes occur. Firstly the infant is mature enough to have control over its vocal chords, tongue, breathing etc, which it needs for speech. And secondly, the cognitive structures in the infant's brain are mature enough to accept that a sound it hears or makes can stand for something it "knows about". So when a mother makes a sound like "BALL" she actually means the thing the infant rolls along the ground.

Here's the total vocabulary of a child of 12 months

WORD	REFERS TO
kaa	mother, juice, bottle, or milk
gaga	"No"
papa	doll, rattle, "buggy", blanket

Most children start to use their first words from around their first birthdays. The first words they learn will be for people or things which they are most familiar with.

These sounds can be thought of as "one word sentences" or holophrases, (this period is sometimes called the holophrastic stage.)

The first words children learn are for things which are most familiar to them, "mam", "dada", "milk", "juice", "doggie", "bath" etc. All children, no matter which language they're learning, seem to have one thing in common – they all make pronunciation mistakes. (If language was genetically inherited they shouldn't make many mistakes.)

Early mistakes

Inevitably when we first learn anything we will make some mistakes. The most common mistakes babies make concern making the word sound correct so that other people can understand what the child is saying, and applying the word to the correct thing which it describes.

Mistakes with pronouncing words

When babies first learn to talk they often double their syllables. "Baba", "mama", "dada" are all quite common words for a child of 18 months. The reason for this mistake might be that the child cannot hear the adult saying the words "baby", "mummy", or "daddy" very clearly. Another reason is that some adults seem to want to teach children the wrong word. Adults may well say "moomoo" when the child sees a cow, and the child will be taught this incorrect pronunciation. Secondly some sounds are quite simply easier to make than others. Babies will use words that have sounds which they have mastered, and will avoid using words which are difficult to say. These first words are often ordinary words reduced to their simplest sounds. For example since "s" is a difficult sound to make, "smack" becomes "mack", and "spoon" becomes "poon". Some children will continue to simplify difficult words until they are four or five years old. And of course some sounds are simply more enjoyable than others for children to make. Sounds which vibrate the vocal chords such as b, d, and g, are often substituted for the less pleasant p, t, and k. So "pie" becomes "bie", and "toe" becomes "doe".

Mistakes with applying words

Babies frequently **overextend** the meaning of the words they use. Having learned the word "dog" and associated it with the family's pet labrador, they will then apply the word to anything which has some similarities to a dog, for example, four legs and a tail. So horses will be called "dog", as will cows and sheep. Just because a child describes oranges, plums, and tomatoes as "apple" this doesn't mean that it doesn't know exactly what an apple is. It just doesn't know the words "plum", "tomato" etc, and "apple" is the nearest to it that it does know.

Here are some examples of overextension from one child's vocabulary:

Babies often make mistakes in pronunciation and in correctly applying the words they know to the objects or events they describe.

Word	First applied to	Later applied to
da	father	all men, boys, some women.
baw	ball	toys, most fruit, stones.
mil	milk	all drinks, bathwater, urine, the sea, a goldfish

Babies also **underextend** some words. Having learned that a dog is an animal, for example, the child believes that all animals must have the same characteristics as a dog, for example, four legs etc. Fish and birds clearly can't be animals! Having learned that "grass" grows in the child's garden the child will **underextend** the word so that grass can't grow in the park too.

Exercise – Early errors

Write a paragraph summarising the main errors that children make in their early speech.

Background reading – Why do children make mistakes?

Eve Clarke proposes the *"semantic features hypothesis"*. ("Semantic" loosely refers to the "meaning" something has.) She says that the child identifies one or two of the main features of an object, for example, its shape, colour, smell, sound, weight, etc. So "da" first applies to "father", father is tall and moves, talks etc. Height and movement are two "semantic features" of things called "da". Therefore all tall things will be "da", particularly if they are people. As the child grows it is capable of using more features to define a word.

Katherine Nelson proposed the *"functional similarities hypothesis"*. ("Functional" refers to what something does.) She says that a child learns what someone called "da" does. Anyone else who does the same thing will be "da".

Richard Prawat and Susan Wildfong conducted an experiment to test these alternative hypotheses. A group of three and four year olds were shown some familiar objects like a cup, which were being used in unusual ways, for example, having cereal poured into it. If the "semantic features hypothesis" is correct then the children will still call it a cup, because it looks like one. If the "functional similarities hypothesis" is correct they will call it a bowl, because that's what it is being used for. The results seem to confirm Eve Clarke's "semantic features hypothesis". Other research conducted on two year olds supports this hypothesis.

How would the semantic features hypothesis explain why a girl calls her buggy, her mother's car, and buses, lorries, and vans, "brm brm"?

How would the semantic features hypothesis explain a three year old who sees a cow for the first time and calls it "doggie"?

Think of some other things, apart from a cup and cereal, that Prawat and Wildfong could use to test these two hypotheses.

Children learn what words mean long before they can use the word themselves. If asked, many nine month old infants could point to "daddy", "the milk", "the clock" long before they could say any of those words. Learning to talk will take some time. From the day it starts to learn about language the child builds up two kinds of vocabulary, an active vocabulary, which consists of the words it can use, and a passive vocabulary, which consists of the words it knows but can't use. From the time a child uses its first words it takes another three or four months to learn to use another 10 words. After this the rate of learning speeds up very greatly. By around two years many children have a vocabulary of about 50 words, although it's impossible to say exactly just how large an average child's active vocabulary is. Different studies give different averages and not all children develop language at the same time. It's not uncommon for children of 14 and 16 months not to have said their first word. On the other hand some children speak their first word at seven or eight months.

Learning the first words marks a great achievement in communication. The child can make requests, state its preferences and dislikes, etc. But single words do not allow complicated ideas to be expressed. Try explaining the following observation by using a few single words. . . . "A red haired boy was being chased down the road, in his pyjamas and bedroom slippers, by an angry policeman. He tripped on a loose kerbstone and fell into a large, green furniture van that was parked in the road." The best a child could do might be "Boy, run, hit, fell."

Exercise – The first words

1 What is an "active vocabulary" and a "passive vocabulary"?

2 Make a list of the things a child who knows some words can do which will help it to become more sociable and independent.

The first sentences – From around two years onwards

From around 18 months to two years children start to combine their words into simple two word "sentences". They tend to leave out some words which do not necessarily add anything to the meaning of the sentence. The result is called **telegraphic speech**. They also start to use **grammar**. Grammar is the rules of a language. It includes things like putting the words in a sentence in the correct order so that they mean what the child wants them to mean. It includes the correct use of tenses, meanings of words, sound of words etc.

Exercise – Grammar

Spot as many of the grammatical errors as you can in this passage from a nine year old speaker.
"One day I was playing in the grounds an' I seen a mice. I frightened of mices so I run to find Michael. He's older 'n me an' he catched the mice . . . the mouse. My dog would eat them if I fetched her but she had to go away for a blind dog. She'd eat."

Even before babies can use words themselves, they have some understanding of what some words mean. They have both "active" and "passive" vocabularies.

REVIEW – The first words, or the holophrastic stage

All children make mistakes when they first use words, and they learn new words quite slowly (although their passive vocabulary is much larger than their active vocabulary). Learning some words allows the child to interact more, which will help it become more sociable and independent later.

The first sentences appear between 18 and 24 months in most children. They have to learn how to make the word sounds, what they mean, and what order to put them in. These things are to do with grammar.

To begin with children's speech has a limited number of "themes". These include action, possession, place etc. Some adult conversation is still dominated by these themes!

Children's first speech has several main themes. They talk about actions such as what has happened to what – "me hit ball", "me fall", "car go bang". They seem obsessed by *possessions* and who owns what – "my teddy", "daddy pen", "mummy car". They are also concerned with the *place* of things – "cup in box", "car in garage", "mummy outside". They also learn about *repetition* – "more milk", "go again". They *label* things – "that teddy", "this one", "this car". They learn about "*nonexistence*" – "beads all gone", "no more apples", "all gone now". Some are able to express their feelings, and to say what they want and do not want.

This list represents what just about all two and three year old children can do, regardless of which language they are learning. Perhaps we are all born with the same basic mental structures for such things as action, possession, location, repetition, naming things, and nonexistence. Or perhaps these are "going on" around the child so it is most likely to be aware of them. The earliest two word sentences have been spoken by a child of 10 months, the average age is about 18 months, but it's not uncommon for children of 24 months not to have spoken a two word sentence.

Exercise – Cross cultural studies

Let's imagine that some psychologist was interested in whether children in other cultures spoke their first words and sentences at the same ages as they do in Europe. Imagine she puts adverts in three national daily newspapers in three countries, asking for mothers to fill in a questionnaire. She may have received 250 replies from mothers from one society, 150 from another, and 100 from the third. The table on page 265 summarises her "findings".

Background reading – Grammar

Here are some examples of the use of grammar.
Word order
No one is certain why babies seem to use two of the basic rules of grammar as soon as they start to join words together. They rarely make mistakes, unlike when they are learning pronunciation. Firstly they seem to know that the subject of a sentence usually appears before the word which describes what it is doing. For example a baby will say "I go", and is unlikely to say "go I". Secondly babies correctly put words which describe before a thing they are describing, for example "big lorry" is rarely said as "lorry big". It may be that they have heard adults using these rules in their own speech.
Adding morphemes
As we said earlier, morphemes are the smallest parts of language which convey some meaning.

Children start to learn that adding an "s" makes a word into a plural, so "dog" becomes "dogs". Also "ed" makes it past tense so they learn "dream" becomes "dreamed". Some common mistakes are "runned", "sleeped", "eated", "tooked" etc.
Semantics
Semantics refers to the meaning of words. A two year old with a vocabulary of 50 words or so may not be able to say that "Alexandra has fallen off her tricycle." "Alex fall" or "Fall bike" may be the nearest it can manage. By three to four years of age children use three and four word sentences ("don't want hot milk" and questions like "where daddy gone?"). These are examples of "telegraphic speech" (the small "connecting words" are left out).

	First words		First sentence	
	Age (in months)		Age (in months)	
	Mean	Median	Mean	Median
First society	13	14	22	23
Second society	9	9	18	19
Third society	11	10	20	22

1 What is a mean and a median?

2 What was the total sample size?

3 How was the sample drawn, and what were the dangers in using this method?

4 Which society has children who are quickest to start learning language?

5 What is a cross cultural study?

6 What are the major drawbacks of cross cultural research?

7 Write one or two sentences about whether you think the results obtained from this survey would support the original hypothesis, giving your reasons.

Roger Brown's study

An American researcher, Roger Brown, has conducted a very detailed ten year, longitudinal, naturalistic observation study (published 1973) of the speech of three children he called "Adam", "Eve", and "Sarah". One of the things he was interested to find was the way in which children acquire 14 of the most commonly used morphemes, since these would give an indication of the kinds of grammar they are capable of using and understanding as they grew. He tape recorded each of the children talking, for an average of one hour per week, until each was five years old. Here is an extract from Adam's first session (when he was 27 months old.)

Adam	Mother
See truck Mommy	Did you see the truck?
See truck	
No I see truck	No, you didn't see it?
	There goes one.
There go one	Yes, there goes one.
See a truck,	Put the truck where?
See a truck Mommy	
See truck	
Put truck Mommy	
Put truck window	I think that one's too large to go in the window.

This example points out some features that are common to conversations between children and their parents at this age. For example the subject is immediate, that is, they are talking about real things that are happening now. The mother's sentences are short and contain simple words. She uses grammatically correct replies, and Adam repeats a shortened version of what he has heard.

Adam says "See truck" after his mother said "Did you see the truck?" Later he says "There go one", in response to his mother's "There goes one". Children leave out the least important words. Brown calls this shortened version "telegraphic speech" (since it's what people did when they sent telegrams). Here are some examples from Roger Brown and Colin Fraser's study. The responses of three children of different ages are shown here. Each child is repeating a "model" sentence.

Sentence	Child's age (in months)		
	25.5	30	35.5
I showed you the book	I show book	CORRECT	Show you the book
I will read the book	Read book	I read the book	CORRECT
Do I like to read books?	To read book?	I read books	CORRECT

The third sentence is rather more difficult for a child to understand than the first two. Can you see why?

This table illustrates the rapid progress children make between about two and three years of age. The 25.5 month old child seems to use telegraphic speech for the simpler sentences and misses larger parts of the more difficult sentence. By three years of age even this difficult sentence can be imitated correctly.

Exercise – Telegraphic speech

1 Write these sentences in telegraphic speech: "I've fallen off the swing and hurt my knee." "Shall we go for a walk?" "Let Daddy sit there." "How long is the train?" "Didn't you have some milk yesterday?"

2 How would you describe the main differences between these sentences spoken by Eve:

At 18 months	At 27 months
More grapefruit	I got a pencil 'n' write.
Mommy soup	Don't stand on my ice cubes.
No mommy read	I put them in the refrigerator to freeze.
Write a paper	An' I want to take off my hat.

The explanation for why children repeat certain words and not others might be because the adult puts more stress on the most important words than on the least important ones. Roger Brown calls the less important words "**functor words**". They may not always add much to the basic meaning of a sentence, but are used to make the sentence grammatically correct. The message "No, and you may not go to the swimming baths either" contains the functor words "No, and, you, may, to, the", and "either". The way that adults put stress on certain parts of a word may also explain why children repeat parts of a word when the whole word is too difficult for them to say. For example "Mummy's computer" may become "Mummy's puter", and "Daddy's screwdriver" may become "Daddy's driver".

Brown also noted that parents often imitate their children's speech. They usually expanded the child's statement. For example Adam's mother says "Yes, there goes one" when Adam had said "There go one". The adult's replies provide models for the child to expand its understanding of language. Although the age at which Adam, Eve, and Sarah mastered the rules of grammar varied, each child mastered them in exactly the same sequence. This led Brown to suggest that language develops in five stages.

Roger Brown's five stages of language acquisition

Stage One Simple two or three word sentences which describe actions ("hit ball") or possession ("my ball"). Brown describes these sentences as telegraphic speech. Children miss out the unimportant words, probably because they can't remember every word. Instead they repeat the words which have had more stress put on them.

Stage Two Language becomes more complicated as children learn the names for objects and events ("that a pencil") and they're using word endings ("Adam walking", "Eve sleeped".)

Stage Three They have started asking questions, what?, why?, where?, and questions like "does Eve like juice?"

Stage Four What used to be two short sentences "Who's that?", and "Singing song?" are now joined to become "Who's that singing that song?"

Stage Five Children can now join more complicated sentences together ("I ran and I kicked the ball"), and they can deal with sentences containing two subjects ("Michael and John are eating apples".) They are now ready for school which relies very much on a child's ability to understand and use language.

What Brown is suggesting is that children learn about the rules of grammar by concentrating on one or two ideas at a time. They begin with words about action, then possession etc. When they have expanded their basic ideas (or *sensory motor schemas*, as Piaget called them), for one thing they go on to the next. By the time children reach school they have usually mastered enough rules of grammar (called "**syntax**") to be able to communicate quite well, although they continue to play with language in things like silly jokes which involve a play on words, nursery rhymes, riddles etc.

Exercise – Brown's study

1 What must a child do to solve this riddle?
  "Adam and Eve and pinch me went down to the river to bathe, Adam and Eve were drowned, who was the only one saved?"

2 Describe the method that Roger Brown used to study his sample of children. What is the main advantage of this method in studying children's language development?

3 Divide this sentence into telegraphic speech and functor words. "David will be going to London on Thursday." Does the telegraphic sentence make sense? Do the functor words make sense?

Being able to move around on their own feet, to use their hands to pick things up and explore them, and to use their language to ask questions, make statements etc transform the potential for development. Children's intellects can grow very quickly.
Can you think of an example of such a study? HINT "Czechoslovakia".

A Summary of the development of language

By around three to six months babies start to "babble". They make all the sounds that appear in any language in the world.

By 10 to 12 months they are making their first "words".

By 18 months children probably have a vocabulary of about 50 words although they still spend a large amount of time "babbling".

By 24 months not only has the number of words increased, but children are putting two words together to make simple sentences such as "take cup", "see car" etc. Not only can the child name an increasing number of objects and actions, he can also interact with other people.

By 30 months babbling will have mostly disappeared, and the child spends time extending its vocabulary. Several new words may be learned each day. Two, three, four and even five words are strung together in a "sentence", for example, "no coat, too hot." Whilst the communication may not be grammatically correct, it is a powerful and adequate system of communicating feelings, needs, and opinions. Further, whilst the child's ability to respond may be limited it can understand a great deal of what is said by other people.

By three years old the child may have a vocabulary of about 1,000 words, and about three quarters of his utterances are understood, even by strangers.

It was thought that these first few years are crucially important for learning language. During their first two years of life many human babies make two enormous advances. Firstly they start to communicate through language, and secondly they start to be able to move around their environment on their own, by crawling then walking. Both of these skills occur when the child is mature enough, and they tend to occur together. However, as we saw earlier, the maturation process varies for each skill. It is not uncommon to find a one year old who talks constantly, but makes little effort to walk, or an 18 month old who rushes around everywhere, but who rarely speaks. Further it is wrong to think that these early years are so crucial. A number of studies have shown that children who have learned no language at all during their early years can still learn it perfectly well later.

REVIEW – The first sentences

From around 12 months children are expanding their idea that some sounds that they hear can have some meaning. By 24 months they've learned that these bits of meaning can be strung together in a particular order, and the meaning can be expanded or made more precise.

Exercise – A child's communication

Here is a description of a conversation between a young mother and her 27 month old daughter which a student tape recorded recently. The daughter was helping her mother to fill some small fruit pies that she was making.

Daughter	Mother
Me do Mummy	
Me do.	Do you want to fill a pie?
Me want fill.	Don't drop any off the spoon will you?
(15 second pause)	Be careful, you're tipping the spoon.
(Some of the apple filling must have fallen on the floor.)	
	(Sounding a bit annoyed.) Look what you've done. You've dropped apple all over the floor. Fetch me the cloth, oh never mind, I'll do it.

In English we use the past and present tense, we can make things plural, we can describe the location of something etc. Some of these skills are harder to grasp than others. Roger Brown and others have shown that there is a fixed order in which children acquire these rules of grammar.

(Sounding unhappy)
I clean. I clean Mummy.
The apple don't mind.

1 Give an example of telegraphic speech from the passage.

2 Name some functor words which are used by the mother but not by the child.

3 What is "animism"? Give an example of it from the passage.

---

4 *The main theories of language development*

In 1957 B F Skinner outlined the **operant conditioning** approach. He said that any "speech like" sounds that babies babble will be reinforced and become learned words. Sounds which go unreinforced will extinguish. After these words are learned the parent stops reinforcing them when they are spoken by the child. To be reinforced now the child must produce strings of words. This is a fairly simple "*behaviour shaping*" explanation. Skinner totally rejects any reference to any mental structures (such as inherited aspects of language or *schemas*). Instead he says the child learns to name objects and ask questions. With these two abilities his vocabulary will be expanded by selective reinforcement.

A major criticism is that this may explain how children learn single words, ie how their vocabulary grows, but doesn't begin to explain how children manage to combine all the words they have learned into so many original sentences. If we had to learn everything we communicate by reinforcement it would probably take several lifetimes, and we'd still be very poor communicators. Another criticism stems from research which has shown that parents do not generally reinforce their children's speech. If the child says something which is wrong, or a lie, or something which is hurtful, its parents are likely to correct it. They are less likely to correct simple grammatical faults. If Skinner's explanation was true then children would learn to tell the truth, and not to be hurtful, using bad grammar! This simply is not true.

A few years after Skinner's theory appeared, an American theorist called Noam Chomsky proposed that we are biologically programmed for language. He totally rejects Skinner's view, and is dissatisfied with the vagueness of Piaget's. Chomsky says that we are born with all the things we need to produce language, ie parts of the left hemisphere of the brain, where language centres are located, and the speech producing apparatus in the throat and mouth. We will also be able to control our breathing, which is also necessary for speech. Chomsky calls these things which human beings inherit, a "**Language Acquisition Device**" **(LAD)**. Unlike any other animal we are also born with the potential to understand the structure (grammar) of any language, and the vocabulary and grammar of the particular language we use.

Chomsky's theory does explain why children make some mistakes in the way they join parts of words together. The morpheme "ed" means to make something into the past, as in "walked", "picked", and "painted". The LAD is said to apply such rules of grammar as "how to make a past tense" which it has learned, to new words which it is learning. Hence a child may say "drinked", "goed", "runned", "felled", and "eated". Chomsky claims that LAD contains the skill of being able to distinguish "surface structure" (the actual words and grammar used) from "deep structure" (the knowledge of underlying meaning, of what the child is meaning and trying to communicate).

A problem with this explanation is that if language acquisition is innate, surely it would develop soon after we were mature enough to control our voices, sometime around our first birthday. Why does language need to take even a few years to develop? And why do children make so many mistakes, like over and under extension? And why are there such wide individual variations between children?

For the last 20 years or so it has been recognised that to use "adult speech" as the measure of how good a child's speech is, may be quite wrong. Piaget has shown us that children's thought processes are not the same as an adult's. They don't use the same logic, and aren't able to use the same problem solving behaviour. According to Piaget symbolisation is the process of learning the right words to describe the schemas which the child is developing through his manipulation of objects in his environment. NB schemas develop first, the right words for them appear second. Such schemas as "milk", "walk", "mine", and "cuddle" are well know to a child before it has any idea of what the correct word for them is, or even that there exists any word for them, or even knowing what "words" are at all. Knowing the right word allows the child to communicate better and helps imagination to grow. Thus allowing more schemas and the words to describe them to be learned. So the role of language is to allow the correct word to be used for a schema which will help to clarify and reinforce it in the child's mind, and help to refine it, for example, "hot" and "cold" are useful words, but the schemas hot and cold can be considerably refined by "below freezing", "freezing", "very cold", "bitterly cold", "warmish", "very warm", "boiling" etc.

REVIEW – Theories of language

Piaget explains language development as a factor contributing to cognition. The main explanations of how we acquire language come from learning theory, which says that selective reinforcement of some sounds rather than others is the main reason, whilst Chomsky argues that certain key features such as "deep structure" are innate.

Exercise – The theories of language acquisition

1 Write the title "The origins of language" on a new sheet of paper. Divide the page into two columns. Head one column "NATIVIST VIEW", and the other column "NURTURIST VIEW". Give a brief description (with examples) of each argument.

2 Briefly contrast Skinner and Chomsky's explanations for the origin of language.

3 Piaget used the clinical interview as one of his major methods for investigating children's thinking. In view of what he says about the relationship between language and cognition can you suggest a problem he will have?

5 Can animals be taught to use language?

Until the influence of biologists such as Darwin started to spread, most people in the West were taught that human beings were created by God, in His own image. We were special, and had been given many special gifts by God, such as the ability to think and communicate. Darwin's suggestion that human beings were merely descended from the animal kingdom caused a furious outcry against him from some sections of the church. If we were descended from the apes, then might they share any of our "special gifts"?

Several attempts have been made to teach non human primates to communicate with Man. If Man uses spoken language, and Man descended from the apes, then might there be some apes who are able to speak? The few attempts to teach monkeys and chimps to speak which have been made were complete failures. During the 1930s the Kelloggs tried to teach a chimp to speak. They raised Gua from when he was about ten months old with their own son, Donald. They tried to teach Gua everything they taught Donald. By the time Donald was 16 months Gua "knew" the meaning of 95 words, but couldn't speak any of them. (A chimp's larynx is quite different from a human's. Chimps can eat, drink, and breathe all at the same time. They probably could not produce speech sounds.) The Kellogg's experiment was abandoned because of the possible dangers to Donald from the rapidly maturing and playful chimp. During the 1960s and 70s attention turned to see if some animals can learn to communicate in other ways. Several attempts have been made to teach chimpanzees to communicate.

One of the best known was a study by Allen and Beatrice Gardner. They tried to teach a female chimpanzee called Washoe to use **American Sign Language** (ASL or sometimes called AmeSLan). To avoid confusing the animal they never spoke in front of her. They helped her by showing her how to shape her hands, and they rewarded her with tickles when she made the sign correctly. She was 10 months old when they started teaching her. By 18 months she knew four signs, by 30 months she used 30 signs, and by 60 months she used 160 signs. Here are the first signs that she learned, in the order in which she learned them: "come–gimme", "more", "up", "sweet", "go", "hear–listen", "tickle", etc. She used signs in the same way that children produce words, always knowing more signs than she could use, using one sign, then, later, combining two or three signs. The order in which Washoe learned and used signs was rather similar to the way children learn language, from holophrases to telegraphic speech.

The Gardners claimed that Washoe wasn't simply conditioned to give responses when stimulated. It was possible to hold a simple "conversation" with her. One exchange went:

Human: "What's that?"
Washoe: "Bed."
Human: "Whose?"

Washoe: "Mine."
Human: "What colour is it?"
Washoe: "Red."

Washoe sometimes began a "conversation" too. She asked for things, and could describe them. She seemed to understand some of the basics of language. However she never learned very much grammar and couldn't use different tenses. She made very few original statements, although when she saw an aeroplane (she knew the sign "plane"), she pointed to it and said "You me ride plane". And the first time she saw a duck (which she didn't know the sign for) she combined the two signs "water" and "bird". However most of her utterances were rather simple responses to rather simple questions, and some of her signs didn't make much sense at all. Washoe's language never progressed beyond what might be expected of a two to three year old human.

When Washoe was physically mature the Gardner's gave her to a zoo where one of her trainers worked with a group of chimps. She mated and gave birth to several infants. She was seen trying to teach them ASL. Washoe often "talked to herself" in ASL too.

Washoe learns ASL

Exercise – Washoe the chimp

1 What increase had taken place in Washoe's vocabulary between 10 and 60 months?

2 What is the name of the method used in this study?

3 Name two limitations of this method as used by psychologists.

4 Why didn't the Gardner's let Washoe hear them talk?

Ann and David Premack used operant conditioning to teach a six year old chimp called Sarah that red plastic shapes could stand for particular objects or descriptions, for example, there were shapes that stood for "Sarah", "apple", "chocolate", "is", "?", "give", "take", "no", "yellow", "brown" etc. She also had shapes for the names of her trainers. By arranging them in order on a board she could construct "sentences". Sarah lived in a laboratory and was trained for an hour each day, using operant conditioning techniques.

Over a 30 month period Sarah learned meanings for hundreds of shapes, and did learn to construct fairly complicated answers to specific questions. Her training did not allow her to "play" with the symbols she was learning, nor to communicate freely with her trainers. However what Sarah has learned are some specific skills for a particular form of communication. This isn't really the same as learning or using language. "Real" language involves asking questions, making statements, giving instructions, making requests etc. Sarah couldn't do any of these things.

Duane Rumbaugh taught a two year old chimp called Lana to press various symbols which were put onto keys on a computer assisted machine. Pressing the keys would cause lighted symbols corresponding to them to appear on the machine. If she could construct the symbols to make a reasonable "sentence" the machine would provide what she requested. For example if she wanted some apple she would have to press "Please", "give", "Lana", "some", "apple". She learned that particular symbols "stood for" things such as "open a window", and "give Lana some banana". Lana learned over 100 symbols, and could press them in appropriate ways to communicate. She certainly appeared to know the difference between "Tim groom Lana", and "Lana groom Tim"!

Again this isn't really language as we know it. Lana has simply learned to associate some specific symbols with some particular reinforcers, although she has also learned something about the order in which the symbols have to be arranged.

Exercise – Methods of studying chimps communication

Outline the methods which have been used to teach animals to communicate.

Conclusion – Chatty chimps? Or conditioned chimps?

These studies show that chimps can communicate, to some extent, but not that they can use language. Twenty years ago no one imagined that a chimp could learn any ASL, and if they learned the signs they wouldn't be able to use them appropriately, but Washoe did. She made lots of mistakes, she never learned about past and future, and she could understand more signs than she could use herself. But some psychologists are more sceptical of the claims that such chimps are

REVIEW – Animal language

Whilst it might be a pleasant thought that one day we could talk to the animals it's extremely unlikely ever to come about. Most do not have the ability to produce the kind of phonemes that humans would understand, even if they had anything which they wanted to say. Attempts to teach animals to communicate have been made. How successful they have been seems to depend on who is interpreting their findings. Nativists say that only Man can use language, nurturists say that other primates may be able to, although few possess very much intelligence or learning capacity.

using language. Herbert Terrace started as a believer in the idea that chimps did have some idea about communicating in ideas which are similar to those used by humans. He taught a chimp (called Nim Chimpsky – a play on the name of Noam Chomsky) to use sign language, but later realised that the animal wasn't using its signs in an inventive or original way at all. It seemed that the chimp was simply making some signs as a response to the signs he had made. This is simple operant conditioning. He reviewed the reports and films of the other studies like these or Washoe, Lana, and Sarah, and concluded that none of these chimps used "language" at all. What they did was to give some operantly learned response to a stimulus from their trainers, presumably expecting some reward.

Nativists (like Chomsky) argue that humans are alone in having a capacity to use language, since we alone have the biological structures (The Language Acquisition Device) which are needed. David Premack argues that animals can use language, and the only reason why they don't learn very much is because they don't have the intelligence, not because they lack any LAD. Francine Patterson and some deaf assistants taught a gorilla named Koko to use ASL, using a similar approach to the Gardners. Gorillas are much bigger than chimps, and were not thought to be as intelligent as chimps. Within 29 months Koko learned to use over 200 signs, and she combined them in original and creative ways. Patterson claims that Terrace is quite wrong in his interpretation of animal's communication. She said that Koko "talks to herself" a great deal, using her signs, and has even scored around normal on a non verbal intelligence test for four to five year old humans!

Exercise – Teaching animals to use language

1 Why didn't these researchers try to teach the animals to speak?

2 What are the main criticisms of the claims that animals can be taught to use language?

14 Acquiring Gender Roles

Once children start using language the amount they can take in increases greatly. They can ask questions and understand the answers. Piaget has shown how important **symbolisation** is to cognitive development. One of the many important things children must learn during their first few years is what sex they are. This knowledge is called "sex identity". At first they aren't sure whether the sex they are is permanent or will change, and they judge what sex other people are largely by their appearance. It takes time for children to learn their "sex identity". During the first few years children also learn that boys and girls are expected to behave in different ways. Boys are often encouraged to be active and independent. Girls may be encouraged to be quieter and more caring. Learning to behave in the way which is "appropriate" for their sex involves learning their "gender identity". Sex identity and gender identity are both aspects of cognition, they are bits of knowledge that children have acquired. "**Gender role**" refers to the actual behaviour that each person has. A male may perform his gender role in a very "macho" way, or may be something of a "wimp". A female may behave in a very feminine way, or may be quite tomboyish.

For the last couple of centuries gender roles in Western societies have been fairly clear. Boys were supposed to be strong, brave and "masculine", girls were supposed to be weak, passive, and "feminine". The subjects children took at school reflected this too. Boys did the more technical subjects, whilst girls often did the more domestic subjects. These gender roles were seen in the media too.

Male and Female Socialisation

Background reading – Some questions developmental psychologists ask

Around what age do children acquire their sex identity? When do they realise that they are going to stay that sex all their lives? When do they become aware of the "appropriate" behaviour for "boys" and "girls"? When do they acquire their gender identity and when do their gender roles start developing? Are the differences in the way the two sexes behave genetically transmitted or socially learned? Do children in all societies show the same pattern of development?

The results of their studies indicate that most children begin to acquire their sex identity from around 18 months. By about two years they begin to identify what sex other children are, although they're not too sure of their own gender identity until somewhere between two and a half and three years. Piaget, and others,

have shown that children's ideas about objects are dominated by what the objects look like. The same principle applies to deciding what sex someone is. If you show a two and a half year old child a picture of another child, and ask it whether the picture is of a boy or a girl, it will look at the hair, and what the child in the picture is wearing. Although a three year old may know that she is "a little girl", she doesn't really know what that means. For example a five year old girl may still think that "she can become a daddy" if she changes her appearance to look like a "daddy". Children begin to conserve their sex from around seven. This is about the same time that Piaget thought that they were beginning to conserve other things too.

We inherit our sex, we learn our gender. What kind of toys would you give a) your son, b) your daughter?

How do we acquire our gender roles?

Our sex is determined by the chromosomes we inherit from our parents. Those who support the "nature" side of the "nature nurture" debate will argue that the behaviour that goes with being male or female is also explained by biological forces. Those who support the "nurture" side will say that each society expects males and females to behave in certain ways. They claim that we acquire our gender roles by observation, modelling, and being reinforced for behaving accordingly.

Gender Roles?

Name some of the things that Piaget says we learn to conserve from around seven years of age. What are the major changes in the way children think, that Piaget claimed occurred from around seven years? Does the way children learn that their sex does not change, confirm or contradict Piaget's claims?

Theories emphasising biological forces look for experimental evidence, mainly from animal studies, that links certain kinds of male hormones with certain kinds of behaviour. For example research has shown that some adolescent boys who are highly aggressive also have higher levels of **androgens**, the male sex hormones. Girls with large amounts of male hormones also tend to be aggressive and "tomboyish".

Contrasting with this view are the social learning theorists who have shown that genetic forces can be overcome by social ones. Aggression in children, for example, can be reduced by using a combination of reinforcements and punishments. Freud's Psychoanalytic theory attempts to combine both biological and social forces whilst Lawrence Kohlberg suggests a cognitive explanation for learning gender identity.

So, in this chapter we will study:

1 Biological explanations.

2 Social learning theory.

3 Freud's psychoanalytic approach.

4 Kohlberg's Cognitive theory.

REVIEW – Sex and gender

Those biologists and psychologists who emphasise the role of instincts and genetic inheritance explain gender role behaviour in terms of chromosomes and hormones. Social learning theorists maintain that whatever our genetic inheritance, it can be overcome by social pressures. Traditional Freudian psychoanalysis sees gender roles emerging as a result of identification. Cognitive theorists emphasise the process by which children acquire their ideas about their sex.

Exercise – Sex and gender identity

1 What is meant by "sex identity"?

2 What is meant by "gender identity"?

3 What are "gender roles"?

1 Biological theories of gender roles

John Bowlby argued that some differences in the attitudes and behaviour of males and females are genetically transmitted instincts. Since babies need to form attachment bonds with their mothers (or mother substitutes) then, Bowlby argued, mothers must have maternal instincts to form bonds with their babies. According to Bowlby, these "maternal instincts" will show themselves some time after puberty. A girl child will spend time with, and become like, her mother because she has certain "maternal instincts". This explanation is not widely believed now. Males and females may well have different levels of hormones in their bodies, and these hormones may be linked to certain kinds of behaviour, but that does not mean that socialisation cannot overcome biological urges. For example many women nowadays are deliberately choosing not to have children, for various reasons.

There are obviously biological differences between males and females. For example each sex is the result of different combinations of chromosomes, (males having XY and females XX combinations). As a result of this their hormonal balance is different, and their sexual and reproductive organs are different. These biological differences explain someone's sex, that is not the same as explaining their gender role. If

Bowlby claims that the role of caregiver is simply something which girls are born with.

Background reading – The major hormones in physical and sexual development

Hormone	Gland	Effects
Many growth hormones	Pituitary	This "master" gland affects the rate of maturation, controls the activity of some other glands, stimulates sexual development such as ovulation and milk production in females, and sperm production in males.
Thyroxin	Thyroid	Metabolism, brain development, and aspects of physical growth are stimulated by thyroxin.
Adrenalin	Adrenal	Adrenalin has many uses in the body, including changes at puberty, some sexual effects, and general levels of "arousal".
Testosterone (boys)	Testes	Testosterone is one of the main hormones in the male. It influences general male characteristics, for example, body shape, muscle growth, voice change at puberty, body hair, levels of aggression, body fat etc.
Oestrogen (girls)	Ovaries	The oestrogens affect female sexual characteristics such as body fat, breast development and menstruation.

gender role differences were genetically transmitted then we would expect that any differences in the behaviour of males and females would begin to appear soon after birth. Also each person's "sex related" behaviour would be determined by their levels of sex hormones. This should also be true of the higher non human primates such as gorillas, chimps, and monkeys. And people in all societies would have similar "sex related" behaviour. We will examine each of these three points in turn.

Early differences in male and female behaviour

Male babies are generally bigger and heavier than female babies. They often sleep less, cry more, and they are generally more active. They are usually more irritable, and are harder to comfort than females too. Female babies usually tend to be rather "hardier" than boys. They are often talking before the average males, and they usually reach physical maturity more quickly too. Reading these differences might make us think that boy and girl babies are genetically programmed to follow the roles that will be expected of them later.

Comment Social learning theorists do not dispute that there are these early differences between males and females. They do say that social factors will also be important. Perhaps parents are more likely to play more "rough and tumble" games with their boys, and be more quiet and cuddling with their daughters. It might be that daughters are spoken to more often, and so pick up language sooner than boys. We will return to these ideas shortly.

The effects of hormones

Many of the body's glands and organs need to send "messages" to other glands and organs. They do this by making chemical substances called hormones. These hormones are carried around our bodies by our blood. Males and females have different amounts of various hormones.

Certain glands in our body produce hormones which change the state of some other organs. The main female hormones are called **oestrogens**, the male hormones are called **androgens**.

Experiments with animals

Some research on lower order animals such as rhesus monkeys has shown that their behaviour is greatly influenced by their levels of sex hormones. For example W C Young injected a pregnant monkey, whose foetus was genetically female, with a course of testosterone. Every day from the 42nd to 122nd day of her pregnancy she received the male hormone injection. When the infant monkey was born, it was genetically female, and had female sex organs. It also had a well developed set of male sex organs. It behaved in the same assertive ways that male rhesus monkeys behave, joining in rough and tumble games, and challenging other males to "fight" for a higher status in the group. When sexually mature it even tried to "mount" a female monkey for mating. Other experiments have shown that monkeys injected with testosterone between birth and puberty developed similar assertive behaviour. Other lower order animals will behave as though they were of the opposite sex when their hormone levels are altered. When females have male hormones they become more assertive and behave more "like a male". When male hamsters were prevented from producing testosterone they behaved as though they were females.

Comment Numerous experiments have shown that altering the balance of various hormones will change the "gender role behaviour" of various animals. We must be careful not to generalise these findings to human beings, who are much more aware of the effects of their behaviour, and much better able to control it.

Research with humans

Some of the main research in the areas of hormonal effects on human gender roles has been collected by **John Money** and his colleagues. They noted the cases of a number of mothers who had been given a drug during pregnancy which would help prevent miscarriage. The drug contained androgens which affected the development of the sex organs of some of their foetuses. At birth the female babies looked as though they had male sex organs. They were diagnosed as suffering from "**Androgenital syndrome**" **(AGS)**, and they needed surgery to restore their sex organs to normal. Money followed some of these cases, and found that many of the girls became much more "tomboyish" than normal girls. They dressed and played like boys, and weren't at all interested in hairstyles, cosmetics, jewellery etc. They wanted a career, and any "family" would have to wait. Those who eventually did have children were quite satisfactory mothers, so their early experiences didn't affect their maternal behaviour.

Comment It seems from this evidence that having a male sex hormone during pregnancy affects girls' behaviour, attitudes and interests. This supports the idea that hormone balances and gender role behaviour are related. However it still doesn't prove that all gender role behaviour is caused by hormone levels.

Do children everywhere acquire the same kind of behaviour?

If such male characteristics as aggression were biologically determined, then they would appear when children reached about the same age, in all cultures. Some research has shown that aggression in males does begin at around two years of age in many cultures. Males continue to be more aggressive. This has been explained by the fact that they have higher testosterone levels than females.

Comment Hormone levels not only cause changes to occur, but can themselves be changed by the experiences we have. It is possible that boys are reinforced for behaving aggressively, and this makes them produce more testosterone. Apart from aggression, there is no other behaviour which occurs consistently between the sexes in many cultures. Margaret Mead's studies will show this most clearly later in this chapter.

Exercise – Biological explanations for gender role differences

1 Mention some of the physical differences between male and female infants.

2 What are some of the main functions of oestrogen and testosterone?

REVIEW – Biological theories of sex typing
Those who emphasise the biological influences on gender role behaviour show how the levels of various hormones correlate with "typically male", or "typically female" behaviour. There is some evidence that males are more likely to be aggressive than females. There are few, if any, other aspects of behaviour which exist in the majority of cultures which are exclusively male or female.

2 Social learning theories of gender roles

Social learning theorists do not accept that chromosomes and hormones determine very much of our behaviour, and even offer an alternative explanation for aggression being largely a male characteristic. They see the environment, the socialisation process, modelling, reinforcement and punishment, and social customs, as being just as important. Attitudes and customs change, and the behaviour that we expect from males and females will also change. In our own society, for example, there has been a dramatic change in the roles of men and women during this century. Women were regarded by most men as being inferior in just about every important way. Today women are being accepted as men's equals increasingly.

A baby's sex is determined at the moment that its father's sperm fertilises its mother's egg. By six weeks of age babies with male chromosomes will start to develop the tissue which will become testes. Parents aren't usually aware of the sex of their child until moments after it is born. From that time onwards just about every aspect of the way the child is treated will be influenced by its sex. Parents have usually already decided on its name "if it is a girl" or "if it's a boy". It will be spoken to differently, dressed differently, handled differently, have different things expected of it, will be encouraged to do different things and act in different ways, and be expected to regard members of the opposite sex in certain ways too. Unfortunately the tradition was to see males and male things and interests as superior, and to see females and female things as inferior.

Cross sex behaviour?

Social learning theorists argue that children learn the behaviour which their society expects of people of their sex in two ways. Children are either deliberately taught what is appropriate, or they see it for themselves and imitate it. Either way many parents encourage their children to behave appropriately and reinforce them when they do. Here we will review some of the evidence for social learning theorists' claims.

Goldberg and **Lewis** sampled 32 girls and 32 boys. When the children were six months old they were observed with their mothers, and the mothers were asked various questions about how they treated their children. The researchers built up a picture of what each mother thought were "normal" or appropriate ways to treat their sons or daughters. When the babies were 13 months old they were brought to a special playroom, one at a time, with their mother. The room contained nine toys, some of the toys could be used in an active way, others were more likely to be used passively, by sitting quietly and loving the toy. More active toys include balls and drums, and such things which involve movement or noise. Goldberg and Lewis also provided some "non toys" which could be explored and investigated,

Making boys and girls

for example a door knob and latch. At 13 months children will usually become distressed if separated from their mother (NB "separation distress" was discussed in Chapter Four), so the mother started by sitting with her child on her lap, in one corner of the room. When the child settled she would put it down on the floor. By this age children

Exercise – Western society and a child's sex

1 Sort this list into "girls toys", "boys toys", or "toys for both sexes".
   doll, ball, drum, chemistry set, pram, nurses outfit, toy shop, gun, skates, skipping rope, sports equipment, cuddly toys, bicycle, construction sets.

2 Here is a list of nicknames that parents have called their children. Which sex would each apply to?
   "darling", "tiger", "boxer", "beauty", "pretty little thing", "tough guy", "matey", "angel", "daddy's favourite", "cowboy".
Add any nicknames which you know of to your lists. Do the lists suggest any differences between what parents will expect of their boy and girl children?

3 Mention one way in which boy and girl babies are dressed differently.

4 What sort of thing do you suppose a parent might say to comfort their daughter who has hurt herself? Might they say anything different to their son when he hurts himself?

5 In view of your answers to the above questions, describe any differences between the ways the two sexes are being treated.

6 If a girl behaves like a boy she may be described as "a tomboy". What would you call a boy who behaves like a girl? Which of the two is more of an insult?

What kind of things are boys between two and four years rewarded for? What kind of behaviour are girls of this age rewarded for?

are usually fairly mobile toddlers, and, so long as they know mother is nearby, they are usually happy to explore. For fifteen minutes the child and mother were observed. The mother received no instructions, but acted in a way she usually acted with her child. Again Goldberg and Lewis observed their behaviour, and compared it to their earlier observations, and the answers the mothers had given to their questions about how they treated their babies. At the end of this series of 15 minute observations of the mothers and babies the researchers noted some distinct differences in the way the boy children and girl children were acting. Here is a summary:

	Reaction to play	Reaction to mother
Girls	Tended to prefer the "passive" toys such as those which could be explored from a position near to mother. Girls generally played with the cuddly toys, using fine movements of their limbs including stroking and caressing.	They usually explored quite briefly, returning to be near mother quite quickly, bringing their toy with them. They seemed more dependent on their mothers, wanting their help, or to share their experiences with the mother. They talked to their mothers and touched them quite a lot too.
Boys	Preferred bigger and noisier toys, or those which could be investigated further, such as the door latch. Their movements were generally less fine than the girls. For example they enjoyed banging things.	They were more likely to play away from their mothers, and didn't seek their help or comfort, or sharing their experiences with their mothers very much. They seemed generally more independent, active, and energetic.

We have a picture of the girls being fairly dependent on their mothers, and the boys being fairly independent. Remember these children aren't much over one year old. Goldberg and Lewis decided to intervene in these observations. In another play session they waited until each child was separated from its mother, and arranged for a mesh fence to form a barrier between the child and its mother. The mothers weren't to go to retrieve their infant immediately. The infant's behaviour was observed. Here is a summary:

Girls   The usual reaction was to look at the mother and try to approach her by going to the centre of the barrier. After a few moments looking through the barrier the girls lowered their heads and started to cry. If they weren't retrieved very soon their cries would increase in intensity.

Boys   Most attempted to explore the barrier. Having failed to find a way through the barrier where they were when they first noticed it, they would move along it until they reached the point where it joined the wall, and continue to try to find a way through.

Taking the evidence from the interviews at six months, and observation and experiment at 13 months, Goldberg and Lewis were able to draw some conclusions to explain the differences in the two sexes dependency on their mothers. At six months (and presumably before and after it) girls and boys were being treated quite differently, and different expectations were being made of them. They were reinforced for different sorts of behaviours too. Girls were more likely to be breast fed than boys. They were handled more than boys too, that is, they were more likely to be picked up and cuddled, and the length of time when they were being held was longer than for boys too. When the parents spoke to their girls they used a softer tone of voice. The boys were treated and spoken to more robustly. Goldberg and Lewis suggest that some of the differences in the children's behaviour at 13 months would have resulted from the differences in the ways they had been treated during their first year of life. By the age of one year or so, gender roles are already being learned.

Exercise – An example of gender role socialisation

Beverly Fagot sampled 24 families, each with a child between 20 and 24 months old. Fagot visited each family's home five times, observing the parents and child playing together for an hour each time. She recorded the kind of behaviour which the parents encouraged, and discouraged. She found that the parents were very deliberately "shaping" the child's behaviour, according to its sex. Here is a summary of some of the behaviour she saw.

Girl children were encouraged to:
ask for help when it was needed, follow and stay near to, a parent, dance, take an interest in girls' clothes for dressing up, play with dolls.

Girls were discouraged from:
running around, jumping, climbing and generally being too active, being aggressive, playing "rough" games, manipulating and exploring objects.

Boys were encouraged to:
play and explore toys such as trucks, building blocks, and things which encouraged strength and muscle building.

Boys were discouraged from:
playing with dolls, asking for assistance, and anything the parents thought was "feminine".

Parents didn't encourage and discourage their children equally though. Boys were more actively discouraged from playing "feminine roles" than girls were for playing "masculine roles".

1 What sample size was taken in this study?

2 What name is given to this method of investigation?

3 Define the term "socialisation".

4 Can you think of any reasons why the parents would discourage their boy children from playing "feminine roles" more than they discouraged their girls from playing "masculine roles"?

5 Summarise Goldberg and Lewis' conclusions about gender roles.

Margaret Mead's studies of "Sex and Temperament"

As we said earlier, if gender roles were controlled by our genetic inheritance, then boys and girls all over the world would behave in very similar ways.

Some of the earliest studies of child rearing styles in other cultures were conducted by anthropologists such as Margaret Mead. During the 1920s and 1930s Mead studied several tribes in some Pacific islands such as Samoa and New Guinea. She claimed to have found considerable differences in gender role behaviour in each culture. Mead's work suggests that sex and gender roles are the result of how people are brought up in their culture, not a result of their genetic inheritance. Here is a brief description of three tribes she studied.

The Arapesh Indians (between 8000 and 9000 of them). Those who lived in the mountains were poor, gentle, humble, caring and co-operative. Both men and women were unaggressive and "maternal". Husbands and wives shared everything, including pregnancy! The man lay next to his wife as she went through labour, and they both "had the baby". They both shared child care, and they raised their children to be like themselves. Acts of aggression were extremely rare, for example rape was unknown, and sexual matters were treated with gentleness and consideration. The Arapesh lived mild, happy, and respectful lives. Gold was discovered in a part of their land, and Western influences changed much of their lives.

The Mundugumor tribe (about 1000 of them), were quite the opposite. Until their lands were taken under the protection of New Guinea "children of 10 and 11 had been cannibals". Both adults and children were aggressive, quarrelsome and arrogant. The adults were suspicious of people in the other villages, and when they weren't actually fighting or making alliances and truces, they were spying on each other. Children were not regarded as being very important to the Mundugumor. The father and his daughters tended to form one group who seemed to compete with the mother and her sons. Consequently pregnancy was not greatly welcomed by either parent in case the child was of its own sex, and would therefore join forces with the other parent. Wives were just as aggressive as their husbands, and were not thought to be inferior to them, just not quite as strong. Parents tended to ignore their children, and the children learned that they had to fight to obtain anything they wanted.

The Tchambuli tribe (of about 500 people) had quite distinct ways of rearing boy and girl children. Their gender roles were the opposite of what used to be the Western pattern. In Mead's words "The women are industrious makers of mats, baskets, rain capes, and mosquito baskets; the men spent most of their time carving, painting, and preparing elaborate theatrical displays." They socialised their boys to be artistic and sentimental whilst the girls were taught to be competitive. Both sexes were reared by the women, and the boys weren't allowed to join male adult company until they were teenagers.

They were spoilt by the women and never learned to be competitive. Women took care of all the tribe's trade and commerce. They were

Margaret Mead's Study

284

efficient. They worked together in an easy, friendly way. They supported the community, and took the lead in sexual matters. The men concerned themselves with gossip, art, looking pretty, and arranging ceremonies. Their lives revolved largely around the women.

Exercise – Margaret Mead's studies

1 According to John Bowlby, children need a close, loving relationship with their mother if "affectionless psychopathy" was to be avoided. What evidence can you find in Mead's work to support or contradict his view?
2 What evidence is there in Margaret Mead's studies that gender roles are socially learned, not biologically acquired?

Exercise – A table of the differences in gender roles

	boys	girls
Traditional view of the West	active, competitive, independent	passive, co-operative caring
Arapesh tribe	unaggressive, caring and co-operative	unaggressive, caring and co-operative
Mundugumor tribe	aggressive, impatient and irritable	aggressive, impatient and irritable
Tchambuli	artistic and gentle	competitive and assertive

1 In which of the tribes are there differences in the ways boys and girls are raised?
2 What is a "cross cultural study"?
3 Describe one problem that people doing cross cultural research face, which wouldn't be encountered when studying a single culture.
4 Does the evidence in this table support or contradict the view that gender roles are genetically inherited? Explain your answer.

Comment If such strong differences as these exist between tribes, social learning must play an important part in learning gender roles, even if there are genetic or hormonal differences between the sexes. However Mead's work has been criticised quite extensively for some shortcomings there may have been in some of the research, so we cannot be certain that all of the differences she noted did actually exist.

Peer group pressure on gender role behaviour

Teachers and parents are important models for children's behaviour since children see a great deal of them, and because they have the power to reinforce some behaviour and punish other behaviour. But can peers affect a child's behaviour since they have the same status as the child? The evidence from many studies suggests that peer group pressure can affect children's behaviour, including their "gender role" behaviour. Michael Lamb studied a number of three to five year olds,

Peer groups are groups of equals. A nursery school child's peer group will be other children in the nursery. The children will usually all have the same status and influence.

Cross Sex Sanctions

285

Imagine you were going to have a debate about what sort of behaviour should be encouraged and discouraged in your local playgroup. What do you see as the arguments for and against allowing peer groups to influence their members to hold these "sexual stereotypes" of what boys and girls "should" be like? ("Stereotypes" are fairly rigid and very simple over generalisations about certain groups of people. They are usually far from the truth. We may categorise the Scots as "mean", and the Welsh as "always singing". A "stereotype" that some Americans might have of a "typical" Englishman is someone who is quiet, reserved, and goes to work in a pin striped suit, bowler hat, and carrying an umbrella and a brief case. How many people do you know who are like this?)

of both sexes, playing with various toys. There were toys that are usually played with more by one sex than by the other, and toys that both sexes could play with. When they played with the toys in a "sex appropriate" way the games were quite inventive and involved everyone. For example a group of boys who were all playing "climbing", or "building" type games were deeply involved in what they were doing. This involvement in the game seemed to reinforce the children's wish to play it again. But if one child started to play in a way usually associated with the opposite sex, then they would be interrupted and criticised. If one of the boys picked up a doll the other boys were very critical.

When a child's peers turned on it, it soon stopped playing in the "wrong" sort of way, and rejoined the group of its own sex. Lamb noticed that the child was usually back with its same sex peers within one minute of picking up the wrong sex's toy! Clearly children as young as three have a good idea about what is "correct behaviour" for their sex and what is "wrong behaviour". They are also keen to make sure than none of the members of the group behave "incorrectly".

Comment Piaget claimed that children under seven years old believe that rules must be obeyed at all costs. They make each other conform because they fear the punishment that they'll receive if one of their group is behaving "wrongly". Beverly Fagot's study shows that some parents do teach their children the rules about how they should behave. Social learning theorists say that children have learned the correct behaviour and reinforce each other for maintaining it.

Apart from being taught what they "should" do, social learning theorists also say that children learn by modelling. If this is so then the ideas they learn from the media will be important.

The effects of the media on gender roles

In Britain and many other countries, children's books, stories, films, and television all used to present a very similar picture of the roles of boys and girls. They were "stereotypes".

Exercise – Early media – Nursery rhymes

Complete the following nursery rhymes
Polly put the kettle on . . .
Mary had a little lamb . . .
Mary, Mary, quite contrary . . .
Little Miss Muffet . . .

1 Each of these nursery rhymes could give children some ideas about what girls are like. What are these ideas?

Complete these rhymes
Little Jack Horner . . .
The Queen of Hearts she baked some tarts . . .

2 What impressions might little boys learn about what boys are like from these rhymes?

In children's media, boys were often shown as the central characters. They were brave and inquisitive and had "adventures". Or they

286

were sneaky and cunning little horrors! Adult males were always brave and took care of people who were weaker than themselves (usually women!). Males usually took the lead in emergencies. They made the important decisions. Any suggestions from females were usually overruled. Girls were often seen as either "helping" the boys, or being a nuisance. They were usually seen as being impractical, indecisive, and dependent on the males. Stories in girls' comics showed them being interested in looking after animals, or in pony clubs or ballet classes. Not many of them had "adventures" which involved being active and brave.

Comment If young children are constantly exposed to these sorts of stereotypes, they will draw some impressions of the sort of behaviour expected of males and females. These effects are found amongst some adults too (particularly those who haven't reached the higher levels of cognitive development and moral reasoning outlined by people like Piaget and Kohlberg). No doubt the success of films and TV programmes starring the strong, decisive male can be explained by males identifying with the characters portrayed. (We will examine the relationship between the media and aggression later.)

Changing socialisation

Earlier we mentioned **John Money's** work on children whose sexual development was disturbed in some way. He studied some children whose **Androgenital Syndrome** was not identified until some months or years after birth. Money found that if the mistake was realised and corrected (with surgery, and teaching the child to have a new gender) before it was about 18 months old, the child could adapt its behaviour and gender identity without serious consequences. If the mistake wasn't discovered until the child was three years or more, then it would be extremely difficult to "re-educate" the child. Social learning theorists argue that children have learned their gender identity by then and that it will be difficult to change.

Money and his colleagues reported the case of a girl who had been identified as a boy at birth. "He" was three and a half years old when the mistake was realised. The decision had to be made whether the child was to continue as a "boy", or should its parents try to change its gender identity to that of a girl. It was decided to continue as a boy, and the child had some surgery and hormone treatment. The child continued to behave like a boy. He preferred male company until adolescence, and then took an active interest in girls. Money suggests that there is a "critical period" of between 18 months and three years for developing a gender identity.

Perhaps the most convincing case which supports the social learning theory was also reported by John Money. It concerned a seven month old identical twin who had his penis badly damaged when a faulty device was used for circumcision. It was decided that the injured twin would have treatment to make him into a female, and at 17 months the child had surgery. Meanwhile the child's parents worked hard on giving "her" a new gender. The child accepted the new roles without any great problems, and by five years old she clearly preferred "feminine" things. Unlike her brother she enjoyed having her face

Think of some popular children's TV drama series. What sort of things do the males do? What sort of roles do females play?

This illustrates that someone whose genotype is female can behave like a male if they have medical treatment and are treated like a male.

287

REVIEW – Social learning theories of sex typing

Social learning theorists believe children learn their gender roles through a combination of being taught by their parents, and observing important models around them. Mead's studies of some Indian tribes shows the influence of socialisation and observation, with each tribe expecting quite different behaviour from their males and females. The media are also influential in providing "role models". John Money's research has shown that social factors and hormone treatments can help children to "change sex".

REVIEW – Freud's psychoanalytic approach

A central feature of Freud's theory is the relationship that exists between a child and its parents between about three and six years of age. The child will learn its gender roles by identifying with its same sex parent. There is very little evidence to support some of the concepts that Freud uses in this explanation.

wiped by her mother since she disliked being dirty. She liked pretty clothes. She moved gently and carefully, and spoke softly. She was neat and tidy, and enjoyed having her hair set into new styles.

Comment This evidence confirms the idea that children acquire their gender roles. Remember, these were identical twins, and therefore had identical genotypes. They both had the same biological forces acting upon them, until the hormone treatment started at 17 months anyway, but they soon had very different gender roles. These differences resulted from the combination of hormones and socialisation.

3 Psychoanalytic theory of gender roles

Freud's theory argues for both genetic and social forces in acquiring knowledge about gender. According to Freud the libido is an instinctive drive which will determine the amount of energy we put into being the sex we are. Our libido is supposed to be genetically inherited from our parents. However we also take on their attitudes to gender roles when we identify with them during the phallic stage of development. A boy will identify with his father in order to reduce his fear that his father might castrate him because of his feelings for his mother. If his father is a good model of what a male should be like, the boy will develop confidence in his own masculinity. If his father is weak, or is frequently absent, the child will be unsure about what his masculinity should be.

There is no equivalent of castration complex in girls. They identify with their mothers, and so develop their ideas about "femininity", because they want to be like their mothers so that their fathers will love them. Their fathers also pay them more attention when they are being "feminine".

Comment As we have said before, there is no evidence for the existence of any Oedipal or Electra Complexes. Castration complex and penis envy assume that children from three years of age know much about the sex organs of their parents, and each other. Recent research shows that even five year olds don't really know the anatomical differences between male and female sex organs.

4 Kohlberg's cognitive development theory of gender roles

As we have seen, social learning and psychoanalytic theories assume that children acquire their gender roles from observing the behaviour and attitudes of both sexes, imitating members of their own sex, and being selectively reinforced and punished for appropriate and inappropriate behaviour. Kohlberg disagrees. He says that children acquire their gender role in the same way as they acquire other cognitive skills. Acquiring gender roles occurs in three stages. Children have some **basic gender identity** from around three years of age. They know what sex they are, although they do not know that this will be fixed for life, nor do they have much idea what it means to be a girl or a boy. Their knowledge of gender at this stage is confined to the name of the sex they are, some of the main features of what members of each sex look like, and some of the differences in their expected behaviour. A child will know that "she" is a "girl", and therefore has something in common with other girls. Knowing this will encourage her to play with other girls. Playing with other girls helps the development of the "schema for girls".

After a time (and the development of further ideas about sex linked behaviour), children realise that gender is fixed, and will not change with age. This is called **gender stability**. For example the child now knows that she will grow up to be a woman, like mummy. The gradual movement to this stage was probably helped by observing other boys and girls and men and women, and asking questions about the roles of the two sexes. Gender stability is also being achieved through mixing with other members of the same sex. However children sometimes make mistakes since they are still judging things by their appearance. For example a long haired male may easily be mistaken for a female, whilst short haired women wearing trousers may sometimes be described as men. Children may also think that a member of one sex might actually become a member of the other.

According to Kohlberg the need to develop the schemas for what "being a girl", or "being a boy" means will *cause* each child to mix with, imitate, and identify with other members of their sex. By the time children reach six or seven years of age they will be realising that gender is fixed, and cannot change, regardless of how people appear or behave. They have now achieved **gender consistency**, that is, they have learned to **conserve** gender identity.

These are the three stages in Kohlberg's cognitive theory of gender. The major difference between Kohlberg's cognitive theory and the others is that where social learning and psychoanalytic theories see learning about one's gender being the *result* of imitation and identification, Kohlberg sees it being the *cause* of imitation and identification.

Comment Other studies have also found that children's gender concept develops gradually, through the stages that Kohlberg identified. However Kohlberg's idea that children start developing their gender concepts from about three is not supported by other studies. Even younger children appear to prefer same sex toys and activities, long before they take notice of same sex peers.

Exercise – Psychoanalytic and cognitive theories of gender

Answer the following questions for   Freud   Kohlberg

1 At what age do children start to acquire their gender concepts?

2 Where do children's gender concepts originate?

REVIEW – Kohlberg's cognitive theory

Kohlberg claims that conservation of gender can only occur when the child is mature enough. Just as it will need to manipulate various objects in order to learn their properties, so the child will learn the properties of being its sex by mixing with other members of it.

3 What "stages of development" are involved in acquiring gender concepts?

Comments on theories of gender roles

Main Points	Comments
Biological theory There are sex differences which are the result of conception, and of hormone balances during maturation. Biological forces do act on us since we are "human animals".	Gender roles vary between people, between cultures, and between members of the same sex in any one culture. If biological factors explained gender behaviour such wide variations would not exist.
Social learning theory Even very young children act according to how they are expected to act. Their behaviour can be conditioned in quite informal ways, by other children, as well as by adults.	Although the behaviour which is generally associated with boys and girls may vary according to their socialisation, the extent or depth of it may be explained by hormone levels.
Psychoanalytic theory Freud saw a child's knowledge of its gender roles being acquired through the process of identification with its same sex parent as a part of resolving the Oedipus Complex. This was a radically different way of looking at gender role acquisition.	There is no evidence to support the existence of the Oedipus Complex, and gender socialisation and gender roles are learned by children who do not have a same sex parent with whom to identify.
Kohlberg's cognitive view Kohlberg sees gender socialisation occurring in stages, as cognitive development occurs. If cognition does develop in ways like those suggested by Piaget and Kohlberg then it seems logical that other aspects of knowledge, like gender, would too.	Not everyone agrees that a) any aspects of development, including cognition, occurs in stages, and b) that the distinctions between the stages that Kohlberg identifies are too vague to be of much value in understanding gender role socialisation.

15 Aggression in Children

Another important issue in child psychology concerns aggression in childhood. Children's sex is *biologically determined*, as we saw in Chapter Fourteen, but they *learn* the roles which society expects of them as boys or girls. Will the level of aggressive behaviour children use also reflect their learning? All children are occasionally aggressive, and some are more aggressive than others. Watch any group of children in a park or playground and you'll easily spot the aggressive ones. For a start, they're usually boys!

Aggression is another of those words that we use, and know more or less what we mean by it. Yet defining it isn't nearly as easy as you might think.

Exercise – Aggression

1 Define "aggression".

2 Name three ways in which three and four year olds might be aggressive.

3 Name three reasons which might make teenagers behave aggressively.

4 Do things MAKE us behave aggressively? Explain your answer.

There are a number of definitions of aggression, most include some idea of harming someone or something. The least harmful kind of aggression may be simply calling someone a name. This is usually intended to be psychologically upsetting. Physical aggression may be more serious. Either way it is generally antisocial and undesirable. However if you are being attacked you may use aggression to defend yourself. Defensive behaviour isn't generally seen as anti-social or undesirable. Aggression clearly isn't a straightforward term to define!

Psychologists tend to use a number of distinctions. There is **hostile aggression**, which is simply intended to hurt someone or something else. It can be verbal, or physical, or both. **Instrumental aggression** covers behaviour which uses aggression in order to achieve a particular end, including self defence. This kind of aggression isn't necessarily a bad thing. Many parents and teachers teach their children to "stand up for themselves" to some extent. A related term which is much easier to define is **violence**. This involves the deliberate use of physical force against someone or something. Violence is the most extreme type of aggression in humans, and has been most widely studied.

A useful distinction is to separate hostile aggression, which is deliberate behaviour intended to harm someone else, from instrumental aggression, where the aggression is incidental.

Background reading – The pattern of aggressive behaviour

Usually children start being physically aggressive, towards things rather than people, from around two to four years of age. After four many children are more likely to use verbal rather than physical aggression. This is intended to "hurt" someone's feelings. From about six or seven many children channel their energies more into competition and sport. Outbursts of aggression are increasingly likely to be controlled as the child grows.

Think of some actual examples of violence, hostile aggression and instrumental aggression which you might see in a playground of six to eight year olds. What sort of thing might have set this behaviour off? Which sex is most likely to be involved in being aggressive, and being violent?

Very young children use instrumental aggression as they try to organise their world. Piaget says that they are totally egocentric, so wouldn't necessarily see their behaviour as intentional aggression. By three or four they may be learning to be hostile.

In this chapter we will be looking at:

1 The evidence for a biological basis for aggression.
2 Studies showing the social influences on aggression.
3 The sense in combining biological and social learning explanations.
4 Does the media affect children's behaviour?

Even very small children sometimes show instrumental aggression, usually towards things or people that are stopping them from doing or having something they want. Their aggression may not be intended to hurt anyone else. Piaget would say that they are thinking egocentrically. Two year old toddlers sometimes hit or kick another child. Perhaps the other child won't "take turns" with the toys, and the aggressive child may be using aggression to try to make the other child play properly. Some children soon learn hostile aggression. They start to tease and call names, and they learn that hostility can be used deliberately to harm others. Social and developmental psychologists have studied the origins of aggression and have found links with both biology and the environment. Those supporting the view that aggression is caused by biological forces show how changing hormone and metabolic levels will alter aggressive behaviour, and have conducted animal experiments to discover which hormones are involved. Social learning theorists have shown that genetic forces can be overcome by social ones. Aggression in children, for example, can be reduced by using a combination of reinforcements and punishments.

Background reading – violent times

Newspaper headlines sometimes refer to "Mindless Hooliganism", "Animal Gangs", "Thugs", "Vandals", "Rioters", "Murderers" etc. We've seen photographs of pensioners who have been beaten for their pension money, football fans who found themselves in the path of those who wanted to fight, the victims of terrorist bombs, and injured pickets and policemen. The stereotype of the male in many Western countries is of a tough, aggressive individual who intends to have his own way.

The number of reported crimes has risen steadily during the last 30 years, but have gone up quite dramatically since 1980. The Home Office suggests that we should not exaggerate the amount of violence in Britain. It claims that "The average person" is likely to be mugged "only once in 500 years", assaulted only "once every 100 years", and burgled "only once in 40 years". They say that violent crime still only accounts for about five per cent of all crime in Britain. Other people claim that we live in

violent times, and that we are so used to violence that we accept it as part of our normal lives.

Aggression isn't all that new however. It has been estimated that a war between some group or other broke out in Europe on average every two years between 275 AD and 1025 AD. Since then there have been wars involving nearly every country in the world. Britain was at war with France from 1337 to 1453, followed by the Wars of the Roses, the war with Spain and its Armada, the Civil War, another war against Spain, and another war against France, yet another with Spain, another against France (over America and Canada), Spain again, France under Napoleon, Russia in the Crimean War, Afghanistan, the Boers, and in the Sudan under General Gordon. All these wars occurred before the start of the twentieth century. During this century there have been two "World Wars" and dozens of small wars.

We shall look at each of these explanations for aggressive behaviour in children.

Exercise – Types of aggression

1 Give two examples of hostile aggression, showing clearly that you know what the term means.
2 Give two examples of instrumental aggression, showing what the term means.

Hostile and

1 Biological explanations of aggression

People have used aggression of one kind or another since humans first appeared on the Earth. This has encouraged some people to think that aggression must be part of our biological make up. There is considerable evidence that aggression is, at least partly, genetically transmitted. It can be seen in animals and humans, at quite young ages, and it has been shown to be affected by hormone levels. (Look in Chapter Fourteen for a discussion of hormones.)

Evidence to support the biological explanation come from those theories which see instinctive forces governing aspects of behaviour, and from experiments using animal subjects. The main theories which concentrate on biological factors are Freud's psychoanalytic theory, and Lorenz's ethological theory.

Instrumental Aggression

Biological theories of aggression

Sigmund Freud's psychoanalytic theory argues that people are born with aggressive impulses (including the death instinct). These urges are thought to be a part of the id. They are irrational and demanding. They try to make the child expose itself to danger, and this conflicts with the life preservation instincts within the libido. From when the child is about three years old, these aggressive instincts must be kept under control by the superego. If the child has not been socialised to think that aggression is wrong, its superego may not be strong enough to resist the aggressive instincts, and they might break through into consciousness as aggression. Unpleasant feelings which have been repressed into the unconscious mind may also be released through aggression. Freud called this release of repressed feelings "**catharsis**". According to Freud Mankind will always be aggressive. Wars will always break out since we have instinctive urges which will occasionally break through into consciousness. Freud did think that aggressive urges could be channelled into aggressive sports, work, other aspects of one's own life, or even to watching others behave aggressively. As we shall see, numerous studies have shown that the opposite of Freud's claim is true!

Comment This early psychodynamic theory seemed to provide answers which appeared to "fit the facts". For example some studies have shown that some people who commit acts of excessive violence

"Catharsis" refers to releasing our repressed anxieties, memories, feelings etc from the unconscious into the conscious. Here they can be dealt with. Freud thought that watching someone behave aggressively will reduce our aggressive feelings. Do you think this is true?

The superego is a major factor in controlling human aggression, according to Freud. Where does the superego come from, and what are its two parts?

were very strictly brought up, and never allowed to express themselves freely. Their repressed feelings may break through into an act of violence. Freud's work also claimed to be scientific. However there's little scientific evidence to support concepts like catharsis and superego.

Konrad Lorenz's ethological theory suggested that we have evolved an instinct or "innate drive" to be violent. His definition of aggression is "the fighting instinct in beast and man which is directed against members of the same species". We would have needed to be "aggressive" in order to catch and kill our food, to defend ourselves against attackers etc. The urge is usually stronger in the male than in the female because the male in most (but by no means all) animal species does most of the hunting of prey, defending himself and his property, and challenging other males. Even today the urge to be aggressive will build up until it has to be released. Sometimes something will simply set the aggression off (we may call it "the final straw"), although sometimes aggression occurs for no apparent reason. According to Lorenz our instinctive energy "boils over" and we behave aggressively.

Have you ever had "one of those weeks" where everything seems to go wrong? You become more angry with each disappointment until, in the end, you do something that we might call "aggressive"? Lorenz thought we have an instinctive urge to be aggressive when tensions mount up.

Comment Instinctive behaviour may well be the result of evolution and adaptation, and aggression may be an instinctive response in some circumstances. However most animals rarely use aggression against their own species, and most only really use it for catching food or in some mating rituals. Humans are not "slaves to their biology". We can control our urges. People in different cultures do not show the same levels of aggression. Mead reported that many of the Arapesh Indians had virtually none, while the Mundugumor were constantly aggressive.

Exercise – Biological theories of aggression

1 Briefly describe Freud's explanation for the origin of aggression in humans.

2 What does Freud mean by "catharsis"?

3 Summarise Lorenz's explanation for aggression.

4 Why may it not help us to understand aggression in humans?

1 Experimental evidence which supports biological explanations

Apart from these theories we do have experimental evidence that biological factors influence aggressive behaviour. We will mention two areas of study, hormone influences, and brain centres.

The Effect of Hormones In the last chapter we mentioned an experiment by W C Young who gave a pregnant monkey a large amount of the male hormone, testosterone whilst its baby was developing in its womb. When it was born the female infant monkey behaved in a much more assertive way. It joined in rough and tumble games, and challenged the males for a higher status in the group. Other experiments have shown that monkeys injected with testosterone between birth and puberty developed similar assertive behaviour.

The Aggression centre in the Brain There is a part of the brain (called the limbic system) which is closely concerned with aggression. Laboratory experiments with numerous animals show that aggressive responses can be deliberately triggered by electrical or chemical stimulation of this part of the brain. Animals as large as bulls have been stopped from charging by certain kinds of electrical stimulation of the "aggression centre" in their brains. By selectively breeding rats and cats who were very docile, laboratory researchers have produced animals who were extremely placid.

Even they will strike out at, and pounce on, things around them when their "aggression centres" were stimulated electrically. It has also been found that those people with brain disorders involving the part of the human brain which controls aggression, are more likely to be aggressive than others.

Comment These experiments and observations support the idea that biological forces are involved in aggression. However much of the research used rats and cats, and other manageable animals. Their brain structures and functions aren't the same as those of a human. The equivalent part of the human brain (the limbic system) is closely connected with cognitive centres, so we are aware of many more factors in the situation than laboratory animals are. There are other brain centres which can overrule any "aggression centre". If aggression was biologically determined in humans, then it would appear at about the same age in all cultures. Research has shown that aggression in males does begin at around two years of age in the cultures studied. Males continue to be more aggressive. This has been explained by the fact that they have higher testosterone levels than do females. But not all males within one society are equally aggressive, and some males are aggressive sometimes and not at other times. It seems unlikely that biological factors alone could explain such variations.

Experiments on various animals have shown there to be some particular brain centres which are involved in aggression.

The organisation of the human brain is rather different from that of animals. We can take many more features of a situation into account before deciding whether and how to respond.

Exercise – Biological explanations for differences in aggression

1 Name the three parts of personality in Freudian psychoanalysis.

2 What is the major criticism of Freud's explanation of the origins of aggression?

3 Why would humans have evolved aggressive drives, according to Lorenz?

4 Briefly state what hormones are.

REVIEW – Biological theories of aggression

Freudian references to the death wish breaking through into consciousness can't easily be checked. Lorenz suggests that some kind of aggression is an "innate drive" which we have acquired through evolution. There is some experimental support for the biological explanation from animal studies, but we must not generalise laboratory research on the behaviour of lower order animals to humans.

2 Social learning explanations for aggression

Animal behaviour generally relies more on instincts than human behaviour does. Therefore animals may not need to learn about aggression. Humans do not have the same instincts, or, if we do, we can control them. The rules we apply in deciding whether to be aggressive are mostly socially learned. We learn "how" to be aggressive, "who" to be aggressive against (and who not to!), "when" to show aggression etc. People from some cultures show less aggression than others. The most aggressive Arapesh child may have been less aggressive than the average American or British child. Arapesh children must either have learned to control their urges, or to control the behaviour that the urges give rise to.

There are hypotheses, and studies of children in families, which show that at least some aspects of aggression can be explained by social influences.

Social learning theorists such as Bandura, Walters, Ross and Mischel say we learn about aggression through a mixture of tuition, observation, imitation, modelling, reinforcement and punishment. Bandura and his colleagues have conducted many experiments to show the effect of observation and modelling on many aspects of behaviour, including aggression. When a sample of pre-school children saw an adult behaving aggressively towards the "Bobo" doll, they were more aggressive towards it. Bandura and Walters also asked a group of nursery school children to call their dolls "bad", and "wicked". They gave them small presents as reinforcements. A control group was reinforced for not verbally abusing their dolls. The two groups were then observed playing with various toys. Not only were the children who were reinforced for verbally abusing their dolls more verbally abusive towards other toys, they were more aggressive in other ways too. They were more likely to hit, kick, or throw their toys down. It seems that reinforcing aggressive behaviour increases the likelihood of a child being aggressive again, and it increases the chances of the child being more aggressive in the future. Observation, imitation, and reward are apparentlly powerful influences on the likelihood of children behaving agressively.

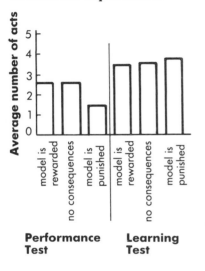

Bandura's experiment

Average number of acts

Performance Test — model is rewarded, no consequences, model is punished

Learning Test — model is rewarded, no consequences, model is punished

Frustration and aggression

One early attempt to explain aggression in learning theory terms saw aggression always being caused by frustration, and frustration always leading to aggression. This is known as the "**frustration/aggression hypothesis**". One psychologist deliberately frustrated some pre-school children by giving them difficult tasks to do before a play session with their dolls. They were observed to be much more aggressive than a control group who hadn't been frustrated. However not all aggression is the result of frustration. People who deliberately go looking for fights do not behave aggressively because they've been frustrated. A modification of this hypothesis says that frustration can lead to anger, and anger can lead to aggression. This is true, but not all aggression is the result of anger either, nor does everyone behave aggressively when they are angry.

Comment No doubt each of these explanations has something to offer. As children we've probably all observed and imitated some behaviour. If our parents approved we were probably rewarded, if they didn't we were probably punished. No doubt we've all turned to aggression because we've been frustrated in some way when we were young. However these theories do not explain "the causes of aggres-

Since humans have great powers of cognition it seems likely that we may learn that we can use aggression quite deliberately, or we may learn that we can choose not to respond aggressively.

sion", only "the factors which contribute to some aggression in some people at some time".

Studies of aggression and the family

The family is usually the first, most important, and most long term influence on the child. It is usually an intimate grouping, and parents usually provide love, security, models for children to imitate, and a range of discipline. Its influences on most aspects of the development of the child are likely to be great.

All over the world, parents bring up their children in different ways. Some are very firm and strict. (They may be called "**authoritarian**".) They make firm rules and only reward their children when they think it appropriate. Other parents are easy-going. (They may be called "**permissive**".) They let their children do very much as they like. Yet others are fair and just, and yet are firm. (They may be called "**authoritative**, or **democratic**" parents). These different ways of bringing up children are called "**child rearing styles**".

Here are some studies which have shown the effect of various aspects of "child rearing style" on children's aggression.

Mother's consistency John and Elizabeth Newson studied levels of aggression and mothers' attitudes to it in 700 four year old children (1968) in Nottingham. They found that 61% of the mothers told their children to "hit back" if someone showed aggression towards them. At the same time the children were discouraged from showing aggression towards their parents! These mothers tended to come from the lowest social classes and tended to be less well educated, and poorer. Telling four year old children to behave in one way in one situation and another way in another situation will make it difficult for them to understand what they should and should not do. Young children need a more consistent message if they are to learn appropriate behaviour.

Sex differences Most people accept, almost without a second thought, that boys are more aggressive than girls. Mary Rothart and Eleanor Maccoby analysed tape recordings of parents and children interacting normally. They found that daughters were told off far more for acts of aggression than were sons. The mothers seemed to expect their sons to be aggressive, but not their daughters. Numerous such studies suggest that the reason for the differences in levels of aggression between the sexes is much more to do with how the two sexes are treated than it is to do with biology.

Exercise – Female offenders

Here is an extract from an article by F Heidensohn. Read it and answer the questions at the end.

"If we were to try to show a portrait of the 'typical' female offender . . . she would be a young girl, a first offender charged with shoplifting, and her likely destiny would be a caution or a non custodial sentence (that is, not being sent to prison or remand centre etc). There are, of course, small groups of women who deviate from this: the regular drunk with a string of convictions, or the prostitute regularly fined for soliciting, as well as a

The frustration/aggression hypothesis was the result of an early attempt to apply the principles of learning theory to biological claims about the origins of aggression. Under what sorts of circumstances are you less likely to be aggressive? HINT Think of practical things like "who", "when", "where" first! Then try "mood".

sprinkling of women convicted of serious crimes such as murder, and offences associated with terrorism."

1 What is being suggested is the "typical" first offence for "young girls"?
2 What is likely to happen to the "typical" female offender if she is caught?
3 Does the "typical" female offence involve any "aggression"?
4 What evidence is there in the passage that females are less likely to be involved in aggression?

Parental discipline One of the most famous studies of aggressive behaviour in children was conducted in the 1950s by **Robert Sears**, **Eleanor Maccoby**, and **Harry Levin**. They interviewed 379 American mothers of five year olds to study the relationship between the two variables, **child rearing style**, and **parents' reports** of their children's aggressive behaviour (ie the researchers asked parents what kind of things they punished their children for). They found the following relationships. "Permissive" parents use very little discipline, and were very inconsistent in the way they used punishment. They allowed their children to do almost anything they want to. They say things like "anything for a quiet life", and "boys will be boys" as simple excuses for their own failure to discipline their children. Occasionally they used quite severe punishments. The children of these parents were highly aggressive. Since their parents "give in" to the children's demands, so the children learn that being aggressive and making demands is the way to obtain what they want.

Sears *et al* identified a group of parents who seemed just the opposite. They used excessive discipline, and punished their children for relatively minor faults. Their children were almost as aggressive as those of the permissive parents. These children would feel frustrated at their treatment, and since their parents modelled aggressive behaviour towards their children, the children learned that aggression was an appropriate way to achieve what they wanted.

A third group of parents seemed to take a more reasonable attitude towards discipline and punishment. They used measured discipline and punished their children's occasional bouts of aggression (without punishing them unduly). They explained to their children what was expected of them, and explained why they expected their children's co-operation. Their children were more in control, and were least aggressive.

Six years later Sears re-visited the children (now 12 years old). The children of permissive parents continued to be aggressive whilst the children whose parents punished them excessively had become less aggressive than they had been, but they had also become more anxious and nervous. The children of the disciplined group still showed the least aggression.

Parental conditioning **Diana Baumrind** has also studied the relationship between parental child rearing styles and children's behaviour. Her sample comprised 134 preschoolers and their parents. Each child's behaviour at home, and in nursery school, was observed and rated for sociability, independence, self reliance, self control, achievement etc. Their parents' behaviour towards the children was found to fall into one of three broad categories. There were authoritarian parents who make rules which children are expected to obey. If the children obey they are sometimes rewarded. If they do not obey they are punished. Authoritarian parents are very strict.

A second group which Baumrind identified were "authoritative". Authoritative parents are firm, but fair. The children are encouraged to be independent, but the parents make it clear to the child what standards of behaviour they accept, and what they do not. They will be consistent in the way they impose discipline on the child if its behaviour falls below the standards set.

The third group of permissive parents do not use sensible discipline at all, or they use discipline inconsistently.

Baumrind found that permissive parents have children with very low social skills and poor cognition. Children of authoritarian parents were almost as poorly socially and cognitively developed. The children of the authoritative parents were most highly socially and cognitively developed.

In the last 50 years there has been a movement away from "punishment centred" childcare in Britain and America (although there are signs that it may re-emerge, as some parents are being encouraged to believe that they should be more strict with their children.)

The studies on child rearing styles reflect the importance of parental models. What do these studies suggest is the most sensible way to use punishment?

Exercise – Learning from our parents

1 What three groups of parental child rearing style did Sears *et al* identify?

2 How would social learning theorists explain the effects of child rearing styles?

3 Here is an extract from Diana Baumrind's description of the authoritative parent.
"The authoritative parent . . . attempts to direct the child's activities, but in a rational . . . manner. She encourages verbal "give and take", and shares with the child, the reasoning behind her policy. . . . She balances her own special rights as an adult [against] the child's individual interest."
Rewrite the extract in your own words.

4 Here is an extract from Diana Baumrind's description of the permissive parent.
"The permissive parents attempt to behave in a nonpunitive, acceptant, and affirmative manner towards the child's impulses, desires, and actions. She consults with him about policy decisions, and gives explanations for family rules. She makes few demands . . . [and] presents herself as a resource for him to use as he wishes, not as an active agent responsible for altering . . . his behaviour."
Rewrite this extract in your own words.

5 Describe the major differences which Baumrind found between authoritative and permissive parents.

REVIEW – Parental influences

Children learn many of their attitudes and behaviour from their parents. Parents who are over strict, or too easy going, may have children who are less able to control themselves and their demands, less self reliant and independent, and generally less mature.

A study of the role of the peer group in aggression

Gerald Patterson and his colleagues found that one child's behaviour can act as a model and reinforcer for another child's behaviour. If four year old Christopher hits four year old Susan, who then "gives in" and cries, her submissive behaviour will give some satisfaction to Christopher. Satisfaction is a reinforcer which will increase the likelihood of Christopher hitting a third child. Also, by showing other children that she "gives in", Susan is likely to be attacked even more. If, on the other hand, Susan fought back when Christopher hit her, then Christopher is more likely to back off and find someone else to hit. The problem is that "victims" who find that fighting back can be rewarding may well become aggressors themselves who then go on to attack other children.

To summarise Gerald Patterson's conclusions:

If Child A (aggressor) attacks Child B (victim) and Child B "gives in", Child A may be reinforced by Child B's response and attack another child.

If Child A (aggressor) attacks Child B (victim) and Child B retaliates, Child B may be reinforced by Child A's response and may attack another child.

Patterson also noticed that no one child was always the attacker, but that the "attacker" one week tended to be the "victim" the next, and vice versa. It seems that children do influence each other's aggression.

Exercise – Social learning

1 Why do humans rely less on instinct than other animals?

2 How does the "frustration aggression" hypothesis explain aggression?

3 What did Bandura and Walters conclude about aggression in pre-school children from their study?

4 Why will it be difficult for some children to learn about aggression according to the Newsons?

5 Summarise the conclusions of Sears, Maccoby, and Levin's study.

6 Outline the findings of one psychological study of the role of the peer group on aggression in children.

3 Putting the theories together

Both biological and social learning theories are correct as far as they go. They both explain aspects of aggression. Neither can fully explain "why some people are aggressive". Rather than seeing them as separate, opposing explanations we might understand more about aggression if we combine them.

Psychoanalysis, and Lorenz's ethological theories see the urge for aggression building up slowly until it finally "breaks out". Something might finally trigger the aggression, or someone might just start being aggressive for no apparent reason. The "frustration/aggression hypothesis" sees some frustrations causing the aggressive drive to build up,

Patterson's study emphasises the importance of conditioning in explaining how children use aggression. It doesn't explain why they use it.

REVIEW – Social learning theory of aggression

Social learning theorists stress that children observe and imitate behaviour that they see around them. If adequate reinforcements or punishments are applied, children's aggression can be controlled. Bandura and Walters have shown that children may generalise and increase their aggressive responses after reinforcement. Other studies have shown the importance of both parents and peers as models for their children's behaviour.

until it is finally released. It isn't always possible to release the aggression when and where it is being caused.

Exercise – Releasing aggression

Stacey is seven years old and lives with her mother, father, and their cat. Stacey's father comes home from work one Thursday evening, and doesn't give her the sweets he normally brings on a Thursday. Stacey had been looking forward to her sweets all day. Her father just dropped his tool bag in the hall and went straight into the kitchen. Stacey heard him complaining to her mother about a customer for whom he'd done some electrical work. They phoned his boss and complained about the mess that had been left. He'd tried to explain that he'd left the apprentice to clear up when he went off to the next job, but his boss wouldn't listen and blamed him. He'd moaned about his boss several times before. Stacey's mother hadn't had a very good day either. Several clients of the advertising agency where she worked had cancelled their contracts that day, and she was worried about how she could find new ones. When she tried to tell her husband he kept on moaning about his own problems.

Meanwhile Stacey was becoming rather annoyed and bored playing with her ball. She had been patient long enough. She wanted her sweets, so she opened the kitchen door and went into the kitchen. Her father was sitting at the table and her mother was trying to struggle past him to the fridge. Stacey was right in the way. Her mother shouted at her to get out of the way and pushed her back through the door. Stacey was furious. She saw the cat sitting in the hall, and threw her ball at it.

1 Why had his boss made Stacey's father angry?

2 Why didn't he do something about these feelings in front of his boss?

3 What did he do instead?

4 How might some social learning theorists explain the unfortunate cat's involvement in the drama?

Unlike some animals, humans have the ability to control their anger and frustration. Many people can reason, even when they are angry, that it would not be wise to be aggressive in some situations, for example, when talking to one's boss, teacher, or a policeman. They can release their anger in more socially acceptable ways. Knowing what makes us aggressive, and when and what to do about it, is a result of social learning. We are probably all born with different amounts of the things which will produce aggression, and we each learn whether, when, how, and where to release aggression.

4 The relationship between aggression and the media

During the last 30 years or so there has been an increase in the amount of violence in our society. There has also been an increase in the number of people who watch television, an increase in the number of hours of television to watch, and an increase in the amount of violence shown on it. Put simply, a correlation could be found between the

REVIEW – Biological and learning theories of aggression

Rather than trying to explain aggression as being the result of either biological or social forces it might be more useful to see how they act together to produce levels of aggression in children. Each child may be born with the potential to behave in aggressive ways, but the levels of aggression they actually show are largely explained by social influences.

amount of violence shown on television, and the amount of violence in society. This alone does not prove that one variable causes the other, but it has led a large number of people to assume that it does, and to blame television for the violence.

There are essentially two arguments here. One says that the media is a powerful influence on young minds, and should be regulated in some way. The other says that there are many influences on young minds, television may be one, but restricting it will not make a great difference to general standards of behaviour. Psychologists are in-

---

Comments on the main theories of aggression

Claim

Biological explanations

Humans are animals and some of our moods, attitudes, and behaviour will be affected by hormone levels and other internal biological forces.

Aggression has been shown to be linked to instincts and to other biological events in numerous animal experiments.

Aggressive behaviour may sometimes have "survival value", and the basis of "survival value" may be partly instinctive.

Comment

Humans also have higher brain centres which can control our behaviour according to our perceptions, previous experiences etc.

Human behaviour is not so governed by instincts as is other animals'. We have consciousness which other animals do not.

Many consciously worked out strategies which avoid aggression may have even better "survival value". Aggression only has survival value if the aggressor "wins"!

Watching TV

Social learning theories

Because human beings have consciousness they develop an awareness of themselves. Part of what we know about ourselves comes from seeing how others treat us. Our behaviour is constantly changing to adapt to changing circumstances around us. If others behave aggressively towards us, we may learn that aggressive behaviour is an appropriate response.

Some groups of people, and even some entire cultures, are more aggressive than others. It is unlikely that they all have aggressive genotypes or instincts. It is more likely that they have learned their aggression as they grew up.

Some people are more likely to resort to aggression than others in certain circumstances. If they are generally more aggressive it may be because they have higher aggression related hormone levels.

People in different cultures have different diets, different climates, different experiences etc. Over a period of time these differences could well affect their genotypes. Some research has suggested that people who eat meat may be generally more aggressive than those who do not. (This assertion is far from proven!)

---

volved in this debate.

An outline of the first case Albert Bandura, and other social learning theorists, have shown that children imitate some models more than others. Those who appear to be powerful and have higher status are more likely to be imitated. Children may find models in their comics, story books, and particularly, television. Many television programmes contain acts of violence performed by powerful or attractive models. We've probably all seen children playing at being "Superman", "Batman", or "He-Man". In America children between about three or four years of age until about puberty watch between three and four hours of television a day. In Britain we watch slightly less television, although the figures are still very high. After puberty, television watching may decline, as children become interested in other things like hobbies, sport, and games. If social learning theorists are correct then TV can have a very powerful influence on young minds.

An outline of the second case However television isn't the only, or even the major influence. What children see in their everyday lives is likely to have more effect than what they view during a few hours of television. Michael Rutter has pointed to the influence of home conditions on children's behaviour. In homes where there is generally contentment, children are more likely to become well adjusted. In homes where there is parental conflict the child is more likely to feel anxious, and this anxiety may contribute to children's anti-social behaviour. If children are exposed to many hours of television, because other people aren't with them, then its influence may well be stronger, but we must not blame television for the way some families "look after" their children. Add to this the poor living conditions and shortage of money, boredom, and lack of hope, which some children and young people endure, and we have a recipe for potential anti-social behaviour. Several crimes have been committed by teenagers who admitted that their general poverty and lack of prospects led them to break the law. They claimed rarely to have watched television, and couldn't afford to go to the cinema.

There is a third possibility Supporters of the biological explanation might say that children whose hormones and chemicals make them more aggressive are more likely to want to watch programmes containing aggression. This case cannot be proved since it is impossible to measure exactly how much of these chemicals and hormones individuals have.

Exercise – Psychological theory and the influence of the media

1 Summarise social learning theory's explanation for some learning during childhood.
2 Outline one piece of experimental research conducted in social learning theory.
3 Outline how social learning theorists would explain the influence of television.
4 List some other explanations for why some children behave aggressively.

If you believe that the media are corrupting young minds, and making society less stable, then you will want to see some regulation. Applied psychologists suggest that older children and adults are not so easily influenced, and that regulating the media will have little benefit to general standards of behaviour.

Children do not spend all their time watching television. Popular indoors pursuits amongst seven to 10 year olds apart from TV are drawing and painting, model making, sewing and knitting, making scrapbooks, looking at books and comics, and collecting things. Can you think of any games that children play which might involve aggression? Do both sexes play these games equally?

Human behaviour is the result of the interaction of many complex influences, including association, reinforcement, punishment, modelling, cognition, moral development, motivation, and others. Television is only one influence on these.

Make a list of television programmes that children might watch, which contain acts of violence.

Children do appear to enjoy exciting, colourful, and even "scary" images, and they do watch many hours of programmes containing such scenes throughout childhood. These programmes also often contain acts of violence.

REVIEW – Aggression and the media

Many children watch a lot of television. Some children's programmes contain aggressive acts. Social learning theorists say that children may learn to be aggressive by watching these programmes, and the British government is pressuring the broadcasters to reduce the amount of violence they show. Others believe that there are many important influences on children's behaviour, and television needn't be a major one.

A large part of the rest of this chapter is devoted to examining the first two claims. Calls are being made to the government and broadcasting authorities to reduce the amount of violence that we see on our screens. There are groups of viewers and listeners who complain about the content of certain programmes, whilst making recommendations about others. The British government has agreed to set up a new committee to monitor the content of broadcasts. Many programmes, including those for children, show acts of violence and aggression. There must be a market for it judging by the popularity of such American imported programmes as "Miami Vice" and "The A Team".

What do children watch on television?

Tom and Jerry is a popular cartoon programme which was originally made for children. It relies on aggression for much of its humour. The Daleks and other enemies of "Doctor Who" often threatened to exterminate anyone who stood in their way too. "Batman" and "Robin" had to "sock", "pow", and "zap" their way out of many difficult situations. Children have been seen behaving quite aggressively after watching such programmes. Children do not only watch children's television. Many eight and nine year olds also watch quite a few adult programmes. When asked what programmes they prefer, children say they like situation comedies such as "Dif'rent Strokes" and "Happy Days". Even some situation comedies include verbal abuse and sarcasm. The other kind of programmes they enjoy contain excitement. Fast action sequences, like car chases in "Knightrider", and special effects, like those in "Starwars" and "Battlestar Galactica", are also popular. Programmes including these features also often include scenes of aggression.

A 1981 report found that American families watched, on average, six and a half hours of television each day. Not all of this will be "active", that is, paying attention to the programme. Adults often have "passive" TV viewing, ie it's on, but they are not taking very much notice of it. Younger children's viewing is usually more "active", and so more restricted to early evening "prime time" television. It is estimated that about 80% of all "prime time" television programmes in America contain at least one scene of violence. On average there are 7.5 acts of violence an hour during prime time. There are about seven acts of violence during the same time on British TV. (This is hardly surprising since one third of all programmes broadcast in Britain are American imports!) Two American psychologists estimated that average 16 year old American children will have spent more hours watching TV than they have in school, and they will have witnessed over 13 000 killings on TV. The question has to be asked, does seeing all this violence on TV encourage children to become more aggressive? We would like to think that parents and teachers try to teach children self control, and not to behave aggressively without good reason. There are two points here. Does watching aggression and violence on television reduce any inhibitions children might feel about being aggressive, and does watching violence make children less sensitive to its effects on the victim?

The effects of television aggression and children

There are two main ways in which we can find out whether watching violence makes children more aggressive. These are "before and after" experiments (laboratory or field experiments), and correlational studies.

a) Experimental data

One method of discovering the effects of TV on levels of aggression in children is to measure their general levels of aggression, then show them some violent TV programmes for a few weeks, then measure their behaviour again. (This is what we mean by "before" and "after".) Many hundreds of experiments along these lines have been conducted (mostly in America). The majority of them show that watching violence on TV does increase the number of aggressive acts amongst children. Even if they are given an opportunity to "help" or "hinder" another child, those who'd seen violent TV preferred to "hinder" or "hurt" the other child. Some experiments have shown children models who were being helpful and caring. Helpful, co-operative, and caring behaviour is called "**prosocial behaviour**". This "prosocial" behaviour has also been modelled. However several of these experiments can be criticised for being rather "artificial", and other research has given contradictory results.

One notable experiment was conducted by Aletha Stein and Lynette Friedrich in 1972.

Stein and Friedrich's experiment

Stein and Friedrich chose to study the effects of anti-social and "prosocial" models on very young children. This immediately poses a problem. What programme could they show to the children which would be sufficiently interesting for the children to want to watch, and sufficiently aggressive for the researchers to know that the children were behaving more aggressively after seeing it? At the same time the programme must not be so unpleasant as to offend any of the parents of the children. Stein and Friedrich settled for "Superman" and "Batman" cartoons.

In the first part of the experiment Stein and Friedrich observed 92 preschool children over a three week period to discover exactly how often each of them behaved aggressively. By taking an average of the number of aggressive acts which each child performed during one hour, they established a "baseline" of aggression which could be used for comparison purposes later.

In the second part of the experiment the children were randomly assigned to three experimental conditions. Each experimental group would inevitably contain some children who had been observed to be generally quite aggressive, some who appeared moderately aggressive, and some who hadn't seemed aggressive at all. For the next month these three groups of nursery school children were shown one television programme each day, as a part of their day's activities.

Children in one group were shown one Superman or one Batman cartoon, which contained a number of "aggressive" acts. Children in

The British Home Office has collected evidence about the influence of some aspects of the media, for example pornography. The American government have commissioned many experiments to test the relationship between the media and people's behaviour.

Modelling TV?

another group saw one prosocial programme (an American show called "Mr. Rogers' Neighbourhood"). Children in the third group watched neutral programmes about circuses and farm animals.

After a month of watching their television programmes the third part of the experiment began. This was the "postviewing period". The children's play was observed for two weeks to see if their behaviour had changed in any way.

Stein and Friedrich found that those children who had seen the programmes containing aggression did behave more aggressively than either of the other two groups. Those children in this group who had appeared to be the most aggressive before the start of the month's viewing had the largest increase in their aggressive behaviour. Even those who were fairly timid at the beginning behaved more aggressively having watched Batman and Superman programmes for a month. This finding suggests that television can have a bad effect on the behaviour of very young children. However the group who watched the prosocial programmes increased their co-operation. They were even more caring and co-operative than before. The third, control group showed no change.

As with all research on young children's play, we have to be careful about what we define as aggression, and what the child might think of as aggression. Adults can distinguish **hostile** from **instrumental** aggression, and we might observe a child behaving in a way which we would define as hostile. The child may not see it as aggression at all. When we watch Batman "sock" and "pow" his way through the criminals, we would describe that as aggressive. Can we be sure that three to five year olds would also see it as aggression? The children who behaved "aggressively" towards the Bobo doll after seeing an adult be rewarded for such behaviour may not have been modelling aggression, but rather "appropriate behaviour". When children "play out" what it feels like to be "Batman" they may not be modelling aggression at all.

Stein and Friedrich found that these preschool children did behave more "aggressively" when they saw "aggression". Look at the models the children in this group actually saw. Do you think copying these characters necessarily means behaving "aggressively"? Explain your answer.

Exercise – Stein and Friedrich's study

1 What is a "before and after" study?

2 Why did Aletha Stein and Lynette Friedrich establish "a baseline of aggression" for each child before starting their experiment?

3 What sample size was used in Stein and Friedrich's experiment?

4 What does "the children were then randomly assigned to three experimental conditions" mean?

5 What independent and dependent measures are being taken here?

6 Do Stein and Friedrich's conclusions support or reject Bandura's explanation for children's learning? Explain your answer.

7 "TV viewing is bad for young children." Does the evidence so far support or reject this claim?

Feshbach and Singer's study

Stein and Friedrich claimed that "These [aggressive or prosocial] effects occurred . . . in a naturalistic setting . . . that was removed in both time and place from the viewing experience. They occurred with a small amount of exposure ... and they endured during the postviewing period." Not everyone agrees that the setting was so "natural".

Feshbach and Singer conducted what they claimed was a naturalistic study of two groups of boys living either in private homes for underprivileged children, or in boarding schools. The boys ranged in age between nine and 15 years, and their television viewing was controlled by the staff. One group was allowed to watch comedy shows, variety shows, and almost any show which didn't contain acts of violence. The other boys were allowed to watch quite a number of shows containing scenes of violence. The behaviour of both groups was easily observed. It soon became clear that the opposite of what you might have predicted was happening. The boys who weren't allowed to watch any violent television were more likely to become angry and lose their temper, and became involved in more arguments and fights, than the other boys. The boys who watched the violent programmes actually became less aggressive and those boys who had previously been quite aggressive became very much less so.

These findings seem to contradict other research, such as Stein and Friedrich's. Feshbach and Singer are not suggesting that the way to reduce aggressive behaviour is to make children watch violence. They suggest that one possible reason for their findings is that theirs was a "real life" study, that is, the boys in the two groups were allowed to talk to each other, just as in "real life". Each would have known that the other group were seeing different things on the television. Those who weren't allowed to watch any violence may have felt cheated, or that they were being treated unfairly. These feelings may have led to increased frustration, anger, and aggression. The boys who watched the aggressive programmes may have felt that they were being given a privilege, and this might have reduced their aggressive behaviour.

One of the differences between this study and others like Stein and Friedrich's, is that whilst Stein and Friedrich studied young children who were very impressionable, Feshbach and Singer studied adolescents, who were much more in control of their behaviour. They know whether they are acting aggressively or not. Older children won't simply "observe and imitate" in the way that young ones might. Their "cognitive centres" in their brains are sufficiently well developed to know what they are doing, and what it means.

b) Correlational Research

Evidence exists that those children who watch a great amount of violence on television behave most aggressively themselves. For example L D Eron and some colleagues drew a sample of over 800 male and female eight and nine year olds. They needed to establish a baseline of aggression for each child, so they observed each child, and they asked other people about whether the child was aggressive. They then found out when he or she watched TV, and what kind of programmes they enjoyed. They found a positive correlation between the amount of violence watched on television, and the amount of violence that children used in their everyday behaviour.

Feshbach and Singer's study claims to be more "natural" than many others. They found that older children will resort to aggression for social reasons which have nothing to do with the amount of violence seen on television. However no one is claiming that all violence is caused by violent television, only that some might be.

REVIEW – Experimental data on aggression

Many experiments, such as Stein and Friedrich's, have found that deliberately exposing young children to aggression leads them to behave more aggressively. Perhaps they think that this is the appropriate way to behave. However Feshbach and Singer say that the case isn't proven since most of the experiments are artificial. Their study was conducted "in real life" and found that adolescent boys are less influenced by what they watch on television than by other things which they know are happening to them.

Eron found a positive correlation between the amount of violence watched on television, and the level of aggression in a large sample of children's behaviour.

There are actually four correlations in Eron's study. One is between watching violence on television and violent behaviour in eight and nine year olds. Another is between watching violence on television and violent behaviour in adolescents. A third one is between watching violence as a child, and watching it as an adolescent. And the fourth is between behaving aggressively as a child, and behaving aggressively as an adolescent.

Social learning theorists would say that girls are not usually reinforced for being aggressive, and so are less likely to behave aggressively, regardless of television viewing. Also there are fewer female aggression models to imitate. Supporters of the biological explanation would say that males are genetically more likely to behave aggressively and would watch programmes containing aggression.

REVIEW – Correlational data on aggression

Eron's study found positive correlations between the amount of television violence watched by young boys, and how aggressive they were as young adults. There are other factors involved in why certain boys tend to watch certain TV shows, so we may not say that watching aggression on television causes aggressive behaviour.

Exercise – Frustration and aggression

1 How old were the boys in Feshbach and Singer's study?
2 What was the main difference in the viewing between the two groups in the study?
3 Summarise Feshbach and Singer's suggestion why one group was less aggressive than the other.
4 How would supporters of the "frustration/aggression" hypothesis explain Feshbach and Singer's findings?
5 How might Freud explain why the boys who watched the violent programmes became less violent? (HINT "catharsis")
6 How would supporters of the biological explanation for aggression explain that those who watch violent television programmes tend to behave more aggressively?
7 If each of the groups in Stein and Friedrich's experiment contained children with equal amounts of "biological aggression", would their findings support or contradict the biological explanation?

Ten years later Eron followed up half the sample. (The rest weren't available for various reasons.) Again how aggressively each individual behaved was measured. They were given a test which measured their tendencies towards delinquency, and their friends and people who knew them were asked questions about how aggressive the adolescents were. The adolescents' favourite television programmes were also noted. Again there was a positive correlation between watching scenes of violence on TV, and behaving aggressively, that is, those who watched the most violent television programmes behaved most aggressively. Eron also found a high positive correlation between the amount of television violence watched at around eight or nine years of age and the amount of aggression shown by the child 10 years later at 18 or 19. Those who didn't watch many programmes containing violence at eight or nine weren't very aggressive when they were adolescents.

All of these findings were only true for boys though. Girls did not behave particularly aggressively, whatever programmes they watched.

Television as a prosocial informer

So far we've stressed the potentially harmful effects of TV programmes. But TV can have good effects too. Some TV programmes are prosocial, for example, "Sesame Street", "Lassie", "The Waltons", "Magpie", "Blue Peter" etc. They try to encourage children to be constructive, imaginative, and co-operative. Some, such as the annual "Blue Peter" appeal, encourage sharing and helping too. Experiments show that after watching these programmes children do behave more caringly. Stein and Friedrich's prosocial experimental group did behave more co-operatively. This seems to confirm the social learning theory explanation. However adults also often encourage prosocial attitudes and behaviour, so the child's cognitive awareness is increased. Knowing that what it is doing is approved of may explain some of its "good" behaviour, rather than simply learning by modelling on someone else.

Biological theorists do not claim that there are hormones which promote prosocial behaviour, nor is there likely to be a "prosocial area" in our brain.

Exercise – The uses of television

1 Give three examples of "anti-social" behaviour, and three examples of "prosocial" behaviour.

2 What was Feshbach and Singer's sample size?

3 What is a "positive correlation"?

4 What correlations did Feshbach and Singer's study provide?

Television can be used to inform, to educate, and to model desirable behaviour. These will be the kind of programmes that the government's committee will probably be looking for. Some argue that television should be used to teach "desirable" behaviour, others believe television should not be used to model either kind of behaviour. What do you think?

Conclusion

In conclusion we can say that a great deal of evidence supports the view that television can influence our behaviour. However the evidence often appears contradictory or inconclusive. A number of other variables are involved, which aren't always taken into account. For example;

What exactly is the operational definition of "violence" as used in research? Would an incident lasting five seconds of a cowboy punching a card playing cheat in a Western Bar be classed as an act of violence, in the same way as a five minute massacre of dozens of the enemy in a war film?

Must the violence be actual, or will imagined violence have the same effect? ("Imagined" violence isn't actually shown, the audience is led to believe that it has happened.)

Can children discriminate "real" from "fantasy" violence? Does watching news stories from war zones showing the effects of shelling and bombing on people have the same effect as watching the Daleks destroy their enemies?

Background reading – Should TV be used to socialise children at all?

Some argue that TV is a very powerful conditioner and that it should never be used deliberately to change a child's behaviour, even if it was trying to make the child more co-operative and caring. The reply to this is perfectly simple. Television is being used (unintentionally of course) to a very considerable extent already, to give children the idea that the world is a violent place, and to be aggressive is normal. For example a housemaid in California was just in time to see a seven year old child emptying some ground glass into his family's food after seeing someone do it on television!

The level of violence in general TV programmes is said to have increased and seems to cater for those people who enjoy watching others being ill treated. The British Government is likely to impose some new rules to limit the growing trend in "video nasties". In California a number of "copy cat" murders and bank robberies have taken place, soon after films showing similar situations have appeared on television. Already some defence lawyers have claimed that their clients had murdered, raped, tortured, or mutilated some innocent victim only after watching such films. Concern is being expressed that young children are also seeing such programmes. If the television is already being used in this conditioning way, then many people claim that it should be used to encourage prosocial, rather than antisocial, behaviour.

REVIEW – Television and socialisation

Television can have "pro-social" as well as "anti-social" consequences. It can be a major influence on those young and impressionable minds who see a lot of it. Whether the influence is for good or bad depends on what is watched. Television mustn't be blamed for all aggression in children. The real life models they have, and the expectations these models have of them could be far more influential.

Are children more likely to model on "real people" than on "fantasy" models? Children are much less likely to "pretend" to be either Tom or Jerry than they are to be "Superman".

Will a young person become bored, and therefore less likely to be influenced by violence in the media if they watch many hours of televised violence? In the early 1970s each tragic killing in Northern Ireland made "front page" news. Violence in Northern Ireland doesn't have the same impact in the rest of Britain now.

The age of the child is important. Very young children may not be sufficiently aware of the impact of their behaviour, and may not be "learning to be aggressive" when they imitate various models.

There are many variables which will need to be examined before we can say for certain exactly what effect being exposed to all sorts of images in the media will have on children and young people. For the time being it would be wrong to blame television alone for influencing children to be aggressive. When parents physically punish a child they are modelling the use of aggression to get their own way. Research suggests that children who are given aggressive toys like guns and knives are also likely to behave more aggressively than children who have neutral toys. Television is just one source of information, both pro- and anti-social.

Exercise – A "knowledge test" on aggression

1 What is aggression?

2 What do Freud and Lorenz's explanations have in common?

3 Summarise Bandura and Walters' conclusion from their experiment involving reinforcing preschool children for being verbally abusive to their dolls.

4 Outline any sex differences which psychologists have found in aggressive behaviour.

5 How do supporters of the biological theory explain sex differences in aggression?

6 How do social learning theorists explain sex differences in aggression?

7 Outline Stein and Friedrich's conclusions?

8 Outline Feshbach and Singer's conclusions.

9 Outline Eron's conclusions.

10 Why can't we blame violence on television for violence in children?

Index